Windows® 98 Registry For Dummies®

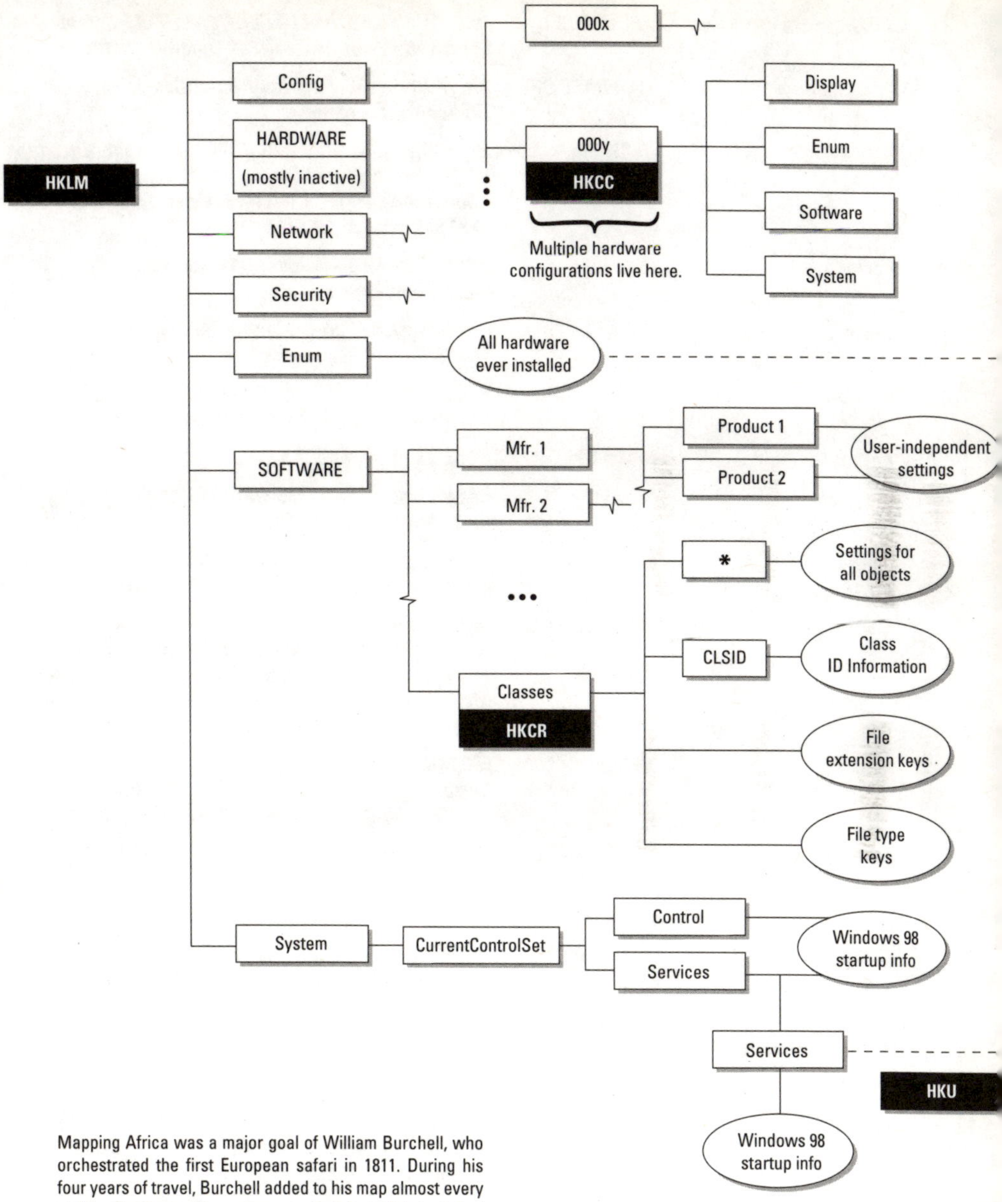

COMPUTER BOOK SERIES FROM IDG

```
                                    000x ──────────/
            Config ──────────┐
                             │
HARDWARE                     │              Display
(mostly inactive)            │
HKLM ──┬──                   ├─── 000y ──┬── Enum
       │    Network ──/      │   HKCC    │
       │                     │           ├── Software
       │    Security ──/     └──┬──      │
       │                        │        └── System
       │    Enum ──── All hardware
       │              ever installed ──────────────
       │
       │                    Mfr. 1 ──┬── Product 1 ── User-independent
       │    SOFTWARE ──┬──           │                settings
       │               │             └── Product 2
       │               │    Mfr. 2 ──/
       │               │
       │               │    •••              *  ── Settings for
       │               │                         all objects
       │               │
       │               │                   CLSID ── Class
       │               │                            ID Information
       │               └── Classes ──┬──
       │                    HKCR     │        File
       │                             │        extension keys
       │                             │
       │                             └──── File type
       │                                   keys
       │
       └── System ── CurrentControlSet ──┬── Control
                                         │              Windows 98
                                         │              startup info
                                         └── Services
                                                    │
                                              Services ────────
                                                    │          HKU
                                              Windows 98
                                              startup info
```

Multiple hardware configurations live here.

Mapping Africa was a major goal of William Burchell, who orchestrated the first European safari in 1811. During his four years of travel, Burchell added to his map almost every night – finally creating a map nearly 8 feet high by 9 feet wide. Our map is smaller, but we hope, handier.

Effects of Control Panels on the Registry

Control Panel	Filename	Registry Keys Affected
Add New Hardware	SYSDM.CPL	*HKLM\Enum, HKLM\hardware, HKLM\System\ CurrentControl Set\Services\Class*
Add/Remove Programs	APPWIZ.CPL	*HKLM\Software, HKCU\ Software, HKLM\Software\ Microsoft\Windows\CurrentVersion\Uninstall*
Date/Time	TIMEDATE.CPL	*HKLM\System\CurrentControlSet\Control\ TimeZoneInformation*
Display	DESK.CPL	*HKCC\Display\Settings,HKCU\ Control Panel\Desktop, HKCU\Control Panel\Colors, HKCU\Control Panel\ Appearance, HKU* for each user, can also modify SYSTEM.INI and WIN.INI
Fonts	*n/a*	*HKLM\Software\Microsoft\Windows\ CurrentVersion\Fonts*
Game Controllers	JOY.CPL	*HKLM\System\CurrentControlSet\control\ MediaResources\joystick*
Internet	INETCPL.CPL	*HKCU\Software\Microsoft\Internet Explorer, HKLM\Software\Microsoft\Internet Explorer*
Keyboard	MAIN.CPL	*HKCU\Control Panel\Keyboard*
Modems	MODEM.CPL	*HKLM\System\CurrentControlSet\Services\ Class\Modem, HKLM\Enum*
Mouse	MAIN.CPL	*HKCU\Control Panel\Cursors, HKCC\Display\Settings,* and (typically) *HKCU\Control Panel\Mouse, HKU* for each user
Multimedia	MMSYS.CPL	*HKCU\Software\Microsoft\Multimedia, HKCU\ Software\Microsoft\Windows\CurrentVersion\ Multimedia, HKLM\System\CurrentControlSet\Control\ MediaResources, HKLM\System\CurrentControlSet\ Services\Class\CDROM, HKU* for each user
Network	NETCPL.CPL	*HKLM\Enum\Network, HKLM\Network, HKLM\System\ CurrentControlSet\ Services\Class\Net* (and *. . .~\NetClient, . . .~\NetService,* and *. . .~\NetTrans*)
Password	PASSWORD.CPL	*HKLM\System\CurrentControlSet\Control\ PwdProvider, HKU* for each user
Power Management	POWERCFG.CPL	*HKCU\Control Panel\PowerCfg, HKU* for each user
Printers	*n/a*	*HKLM\System\CurrentControlSet\control\Print\ Printers, HKCC\System\CurrentControlSet\ Control\Print\Printers*
Regional Settings	INTL.CPL	*HKCU\Control Panel\International*
Sounds	MMSYS.CPL	*HKCU\AppEvents, HKU* for each user
System	SYSDM.CPL	*HKLM\System\CurrentControlSet\Control\FileSystem, HKCC\Config\Display, HKLM\Enum,* and *HKLM\Config.* Can also modify SYSTEM.INI
Users	INETCPL.CPL	*HKCU\Software\Microsoft\Windows\CurrentVersion, HKU* for each user

Windows® 98 Registry For Dummies®

Cheat Sheet

The REGEDIT window

Menu bar   Key   Active key   Value name   Value data

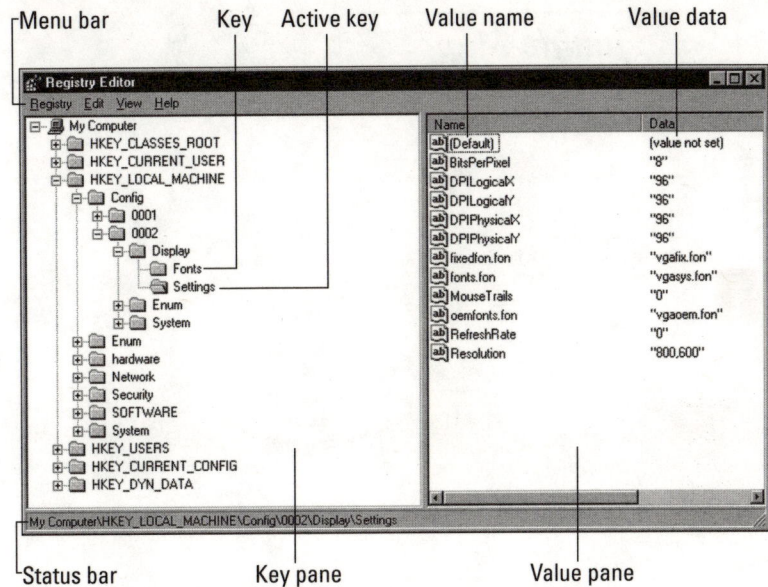

Status bar   Key pane   Value pane

Registry Checker Command Options

Option	Description	Mode
/AUTOSCAN	Scans every time, backs up once/day, no user prompt	Protected only
/BACKUP	Doesn't scan, backs up each time, no user prompt	Protected (compression) and Real (no compression)
/COMMENT= "comment"	With /BACKUP, saves comment that appears with /RESTORE	Protected and Real
/FIX	Repairs Registry	Real only
/OPT	Optimizes (compresses) the Registry	Real only
/RESTORE	Lists backups, lets user select and restore	Real only
/SCANONLY	Scans Registry, doesn't repair, doesn't back up	Protected only
/?	Displays options	Real only

Note: Run protected-mode program with Start⇨Run⇨SCANREGW, and real-mode
SCANREG.EXE from "Safe mode, command prompt only" or from MS-DOS mode.

...For Dummies: #1 Computer Book Series for Beginners

Cheat Sheet

Windows 98 Registry Jungle Map

N
W
E
S

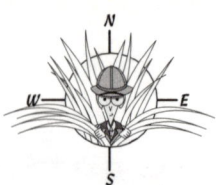

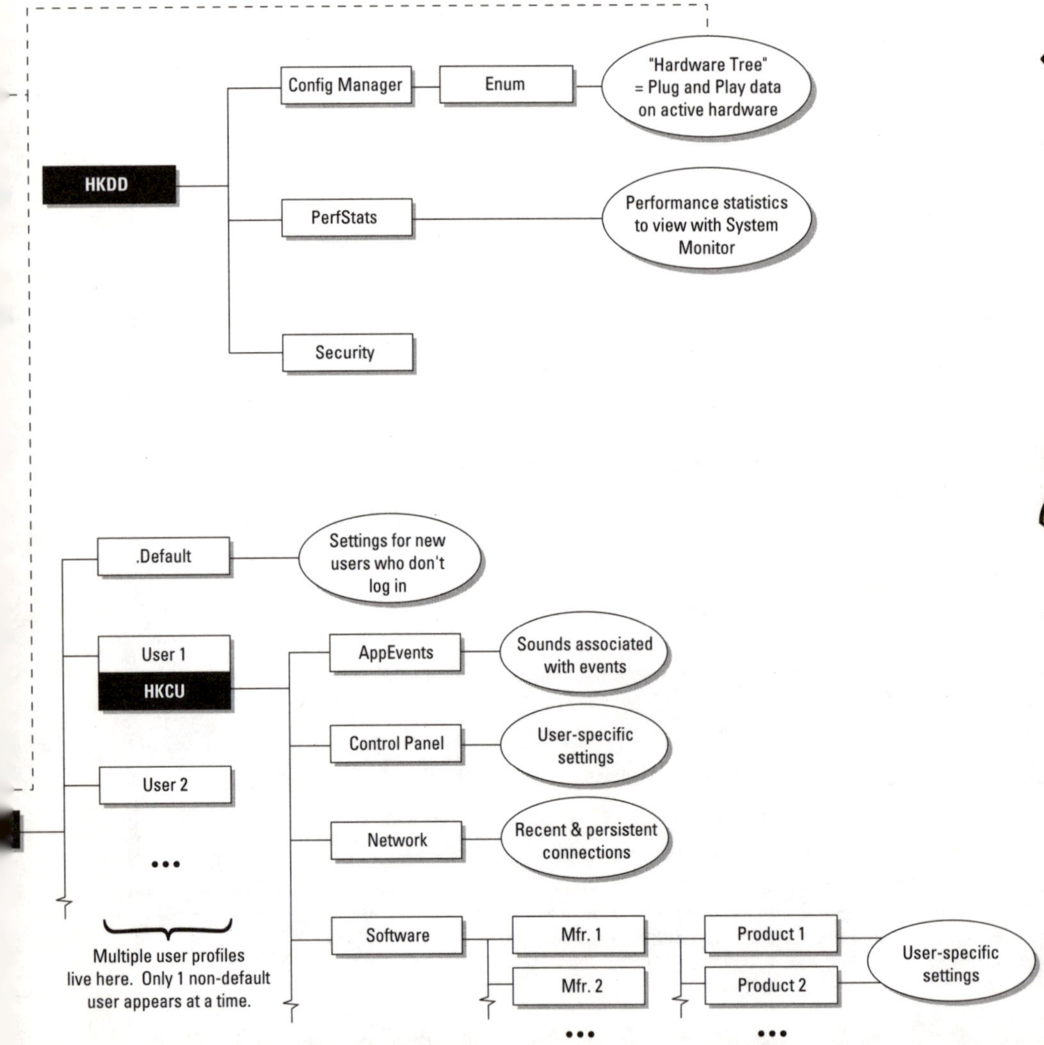

HKDD
Config Manager
Enum
"Hardware Tree" = Plug and Play data on active hardware
PerfStats
Performance statistics to view with System Monitor
Security
.Default
Settings for new users who don't log in
User 1
HKCU
User 2
...
Multiple user profiles live here. Only 1 non-default user appears at a time.
AppEvents
Sounds associated with events
Control Panel
User-specific settings
Network
Recent & persistent connections
Software
Mfr. 1
Mfr. 2
...
Product 1
Product 2
...
User-specific settings

...For Dummies: #1 Computer Book Series for Beginners

WINDOWS® 98 REGISTRY FOR DUMMIES®

by Glenn E. Weadock
and Mark B. Wilkins

Illustrated by Emily Sherrill Weadock

IDG
BOOKS
WORLDWIDE
™

IDG Books Worldwide, Inc.
An International Data Group Company

Foster City, CA ♦ Chicago, IL ♦ Indianapolis, IN ♦ New York, NY

Windows® 98 Registry For Dummies®

Published by
IDG Books Worldwide, Inc.
An International Data Group Company
919 E. Hillsdale Blvd.
Suite 400
Foster City, CA 94404
www.idgbooks.com (IDG Books Worldwide Web site)
www.dummies.com (Dummies Press Web site)

Library of Congress Catalog Card No.: 98-87130

ISBN: 0-7645-0437-1

Printed in the United States of America

10 9 8 7 6 5 4 3 2 1

1B/QR/QZ/ZY/IN

Distributed in the United States by IDG Books Worldwide, Inc.

Distributed by Macmillan Canada for Canada; by Transworld Publishers Limited in the United Kingdom; by IDG Norge Books for Norway; by IDG Sweden Books for Sweden; by Woodslane Pty. Ltd. for Australia; by Woodslane (NZ) Ltd. for New Zealand; by Addison Wesley Longman Singapore Pte Ltd. for Singapore, Malaysia, Thailand, Indonesia and Korea; by Norma Comunicaciones S.A. for Colombia; by Intersoft for South Africa; by International Thomson Publishing for Germany, Austria and Switzerland; by Toppan Company Ltd. for Japan; by Distribuidora Cuspide for Argentina; by Livraria Cultura for Brazil; by Ediciencia S.A. for Ecuador; by Ediciones ZETA S.C.R. Ltda. for Peru; by WS Computer Publishing Corporation, Inc., for the Philippines; by Unalis Corporation for Taiwan; by Contemporanea de Ediciones for Venezuela; by Computer Book & Magazine Store for Puerto Rico; by Express Computer Distributors for the Caribbean and West Indies. Authorized Sales Agent: Anthony Rudkin Associates for the Middle East and North Africa.

For general information on IDG Books Worldwide's books in the U.S., please call our Consumer Customer Service department at 800-762-2974. For reseller information, including discounts and premium sales, please call our Reseller Customer Service department at 800-434-3422.

For information on where to purchase IDG Books Worldwide's books outside the U.S., please contact our International Sales department at 650-655-3200 or fax 650-655-3297.

For information on foreign language translations, please contact our Foreign & Subsidiary Rights department at 650-655-3021 or fax 650-655-3281.

For sales inquiries and special prices for bulk quantities, please contact our Sales department at 650-655-3200 or write to the address above.

For information on using IDG Books Worldwide's books in the classroom or for ordering examination copies, please contact our Educational Sales department at 800-434-2086 or fax 317-596-5499.

For press review copies, author interviews, or other publicity information, please contact our Public Relations department at 650-655-3000 or fax 650-655-3299.

For authorization to photocopy items for corporate, personal, or educational use, please contact Copyright Clearance Center, 222 Rosewood Drive, Danvers, MA 01923, or fax 978-750-4470.

is a trademark under exclusive license to IDG Books Worldwide, Inc., from International Data Group, Inc.

About the Authors

Glenn E. Weadock is president of Independent Software, Inc., a Colorado-based consulting firm he founded in 1982 after graduating from Stanford University's engineering school. One of the country's most popular technical trainers, Glenn has taught Windows topics to thousands of students in the United States, United Kingdom, and Canada in more than 180 seminars since 1988. He has written six intensive two-day seminars for Data-Tech Institute, including *Supporting and Troubleshooting Windows 95.*

Glenn is the author of *Intranet Publishing For Dummies, Small Business Networking For Dummies,* and coauthor of *Windows 95 Registry For Dummies* and *Creating Cool PowerPoint 97 Presentations* (all by IDG Books Worldwide, Inc.). He has also written *Bulletproofing NetWare, Bulletproofing Windows 95, Bulletproofing Client/Server Systems,* and *Bulletproof Your PC Network* (all by McGraw-Hill, Inc.). His first book, *Exploding the Computer Myth,* deals with computers and business productivity. Glenn is a Microsoft Certified Professional and member of the Association for Computing Machinery and American Society for Training and Development.

Mark B. Wilkins is a professor at St. Lawrence College in Kingston, Ontario, where he teaches courses in computer networks and electronics. Mark is also a Microsoft Certified Professional and a member of the Association of Professional Computer Consultants of Canada. He is also a popular lecturer and presenter on Windows 95 and the Registry for Data-Tech Institute, and developed the seminar *Supporting and Troubleshooting the Windows Registry.* Mark is the coauthor of *Windows 95 Registry For Dummies* and *Bulletproofing Netware.*

Glenn and Mark want to share with you their Registry knowledge so that you don't have to spend the thousands of hours they have in studying the Registry, reading about it, experimenting with it, and (occasionally) kicking their computers and spouting decidedly unprofessional language while trying to understand its vagaries.

About the Illustrator

Emily Sherrill Weadock is the Director of Independent Software's Digital Art Studio. An award-winning computer artist whose work has been featured in international magazines, Emily's talent ranges from technical illustration to broadcast-quality 3D animation and multimedia development. She has illustrated nine books to date, and is the co-author of *Creating Cool PowerPoint 97 Presentations* (IDG Books Worldwide, Inc.). Before trading brushes for mice, Emily enjoyed success as a mixed-media construction artist, and studied art at SMU and Baylor University.

ABOUT IDG BOOKS WORLDWIDE

Welcome to the world of IDG Books Worldwide.

IDG Books Worldwide, Inc., is a subsidiary of International Data Group, the world's largest publisher of computer-related information and the leading global provider of information services on information technology. IDG was founded more than 25 years ago and now employs more than 8,500 people worldwide. IDG publishes more than 275 computer publications in over 75 countries (see listing below). More than 90 million people read one or more IDG publications each month.

Launched in 1990, IDG Books Worldwide is today the #1 publisher of best-selling computer books in the United States. We are proud to have received eight awards from the Computer Press Association in recognition of editorial excellence and three from *Computer Currents'* First Annual Readers' Choice Awards. Our best-selling *...For Dummies*® series has more than 50 million copies in print with translations in 38 languages. IDG Books Worldwide, through a joint venture with IDG's Hi-Tech Beijing, became the first U.S. publisher to publish a computer book in the People's Republic of China. In record time, IDG Books Worldwide has become the first choice for millions of readers around the world who want to learn how to better manage their businesses.

Our mission is simple: Every one of our books is designed to bring extra value and skill-building instructions to the reader. Our books are written by experts who understand and care about our readers. The knowledge base of our editorial staff comes from years of experience in publishing, education, and journalism — experience we use to produce books for the '90s. In short, we care about books, so we attract the best people. We devote special attention to details such as audience, interior design, use of icons, and illustrations. And because we use an efficient process of authoring, editing, and desktop publishing our books electronically, we can spend more time ensuring superior content and spend less time on the technicalities of making books.

You can count on our commitment to deliver high-quality books at competitive prices on topics you want to read about. At IDG Books Worldwide, we continue in the IDG tradition of delivering quality for more than 25 years. You'll find no better book on a subject than one from IDG Books Worldwide.

**IDG
BOOKS**
WORLDWIDE

John Kilcullen
CEO
IDG Books Worldwide, Inc.

Steven Berkowitz
President and Publisher
IDG Books Worldwide, Inc.

*Eighth Annual
Computer Press
Awards ≥1992*

*Ninth Annual
Computer Press
Awards ≥1993*

*Tenth Annual
Computer Press
Awards ≥1994*

*Eleventh Annual
Computer Press
Awards ≥1995*

IDG Books Worldwide, Inc., is a subsidiary of International Data Group, the world's largest publisher of computer-related information and the leading global provider of information services on information technology. International Data Group publishes over 275 computer publications in over 75 countries. More than 90 million people read one or more International Data Group publications each month. International Data Group's publications include: **ARGENTINA:** Buyer's Guide, Computerworld Argentina, PC World Argentina; **AUSTRALIA:** Australian Macworld, Australian PC World, Australian Reseller News, Computerworld, IT Casebook, Network World, Publish, Webmaster; **AUSTRIA:** Computerwelt Osterreich, Networks Austria, PC Tip Austria; **BANGLADESH:** PC World Bangladesh; **BELARUS:** PC World Belarus; **BELGIUM:** Data News; **BRAZIL:** Annuário de Informática, Computerworld, Connections, Macworld, PC Player, PC World, Publish, Reseller News, Supergamepower; **BULGARIA:** Computerworld Bulgaria, Network World Bulgaria, PC & MacWorld Bulgaria; **CANADA:** CIO Canada, Client/Server World, ComputerWorld Canada, InfoWorld Canada, NetworkWorld Canada, WebWorld; **CHILE:** Computerworld Chile, PC World Chile; **COLOMBIA:** Computerworld Colombia, PC World Colombia; **COSTA RICA:** PC World Centro America; **THE CZECH AND SLOVAK REPUBLICS:** Computerworld Czechoslovakia, Macworld Czech Republic, PC World Czechoslovakia; **DENMARK:** Communications World Danmark, Computerworld Danmark, Macworld Danmark, PC World Danmark, Techworld Denmark; **DOMINICAN REPUBLIC:** PC World Republica Dominicana; **ECUADOR:** PC World Ecuador; **EGYPT:** Computerworld Middle East, PC World Middle East; **EL SALVADOR:** PC World Centro America; **FINLAND:** MikroPC, Tietoverkko, Tietoviikko; **FRANCE:** Distributique, Hebdo, Info PC, Le Monde Informatique, Macworld, Reseaux & Telecoms, WebMaster France; **GERMANY:** Computer Partner, Computerwoche, Computerwoche Extra, Computerwoche FOCUS, Global Online, Macwelt, PC Welt; **GREECE:** Amiga Computing, GamePro Greece, Multimedia World; **GUATEMALA:** PC World Centro America; **HONDURAS:** PC World Centro America; **HONG KONG:** Computerworld Hong Kong, PC World Hong Kong, Publish in Asia; **HUNGARY:** ABCD CD-ROM, Computerworld Szamitastechnika, Internetto online Magazine, PC World Hungary, PC-X Magazin Hungary; **ICELAND:** Tolvuheimur PC World Island; **INDIA:** Information Communications World, Information Systems Computerworld, PC World India, Publish in Asia; **INDONESIA:** InfoKomputer PC World, Komputek Computerworld, Publish in Asia; **IRELAND:** ComputerScope, PC Live!; **ISRAEL:** Macworld Israel, People & Computers/Computerworld; **ITALY:** Computerworld Italia, Macworld Italia, Networking Italia, PC World Italia; **JAPAN:** DTP World, Macworld Japan, Nikkei Personal Computing, OS/2 World Japan, SunWorld Japan, Windows NT World, Windows World Japan; **KENYA:** PC World East African; **KOREA:** Hi-Tech Information, Macworld Korea, PC World Korea; **MACEDONIA:** PC World Macedonia; **MALAYSIA:** Computerworld Malaysia, PC World Malaysia, Publish in Asia; **MALTA:** PC World Malta; **MEXICO:** Computerworld Mexico, PC World Mexico; **MYANMAR:** PC World Myanmar; **NETHERLANDS:** Computer! Totaal, LAN Internetworking Magazine, LAN World Buyers Guide, Macworld Netherlands, Net, WebWereld; **NEW ZEALAND:** Absolute Beginners Guide and Plain & Simple Series, Computer Buyer, Computer Industry Directory, Computerworld New Zealand, MTB, Network World, PC World New Zealand; **NICARAGUA:** PC World Centro America; **NORWAY:** Computerworld Norge, CW Rapport, Datamagasinet, Financial Rapport, Kursguide Norge, Macworld Norge, Multimediaworld Norge, PC World Ekspress Norge, PC World Nettverk, PC World Norge, PC World ProduktGuide Norge; **PAKISTAN:** Computerworld Pakistan; **PANAMA:** PC World Panama; **PEOPLE'S REPUBLIC OF CHINA:** China Computer Users, China Computerworld, China InfoWorld, China Telecom World Weekly, Computer & Communication, Electronic Design China, Electronics Today, Electronics Weekly, Game Software, PC World China, Popular Computer Week, Software Weekly, Software World, Telecom World; **PERU:** Computerworld Peru, PC World Profesional Peru, PC World SoHo Peru; **PHILIPPINES:** Click!, Computerworld Philippines, PC World Philippines, Publish in Asia; **POLAND:** Computerworld Poland, Computerworld Special Report Poland, Cyber, Macworld Poland, Networld Poland, PC World Komputer; **PORTUGAL:** Cerebro/PC World, Computerworld/Correio Informático, Dealer World Portugal, Mac*In/PC*In Portugal, Multimedia World; **PUERTO RICO:** PC World Puerto Rico; **ROMANIA:** Computerworld Romania, PC World Romania, Telecom Romania; **RUSSIA:** Computerworld Russia, Mir PK, Publish, Seti; **SINGAPORE:** Computerworld Singapore, PC World Singapore, Publish in Asia; **SLOVENIA:** Monitor; **SOUTH AFRICA:** Computing SA, Network World SA, Software World SA; **SPAIN:** Communicaciones World España, Computerworld España, Dealer World España, Macworld España, PC World España; **SRI LANKA:** Infolink PC World; **SWEDEN:** CAP&Design, Computer Sweden, Corporate Computing Sweden, Internetworld Sweden, it.branschen, Macworld Sweden, MaxiData Sweden, MikroDatorn, Nätverk & Kommunikation, PC World Sweden, PCaktiv, Windows World Sweden; **SWITZERLAND:** Computerworld Schweiz, Macworld Schweiz, PCtip; **TAIWAN:** Computerworld Taiwan, Macworld Taiwan, NEW ViSiON/Publish, PC World Taiwan, Windows World Taiwan; **THAILAND:** Publish in Asia, Thai Computerworld; **TURKEY:** Computerworld Turkiye, Macworld Turkiye, Network World Turkiye, PC World Turkiye; **UKRAINE:** Computerworld Kiev, Multimedia World Ukraine, PC World Ukraine; **UNITED KINGDOM:** Acorn User UK, Amiga Action UK, Amiga Computing UK, Apple Talk UK, Computing, Macworld, Parents and Computers UK, PC Advisor, PC Home, PSX Pro, The WEB; **UNITED STATES:** Cable in the Classroom, CIO Magazine, Computerworld, DOS World, Federal Computer Week, GamePro Magazine, InfoWorld, I-Way, Macworld, Network World, PC Games, PC World, Publish, Video Event, THE WEB Magazine, and WebMaster; online webzines: JavaWorld, NetscapeWorld, and SunWorld Online; **URUGUAY:** InfoWorld Uruguay; **VENEZUELA:** Computerworld Venezuela, PC World Venezuela; and **VIETNAM:** PC World Vietnam.   5/7/98

Dedication

To our families, for sticking with us in yet another book project.

Authors' Acknowledgments

We would like to "register" our thanks to many people at IDG Books Worldwide, including (in alphabetical order) Mary Bednarek, Heather Dismore, Kathleen Dobie, Angie Hunckler, Brian Kramer, Carmen Krikorian, Kyle Looper, Patricia Pan, Joyce Pepple, Jill Pisoni, and Joell Smith, as well as to the other IDG employees whom we don't know but who helped with the project. Special thanks go to Emily Weadock for her great illustrations and to Gerry Routledge for the eagle-eyed technical review. To the software and hardware vendors who helped us learn more about their latest products, our thanks (again alphabetically) to Jim Barrett of ISES; Tiffany Brown of Network Associates; Diane Carlini of Symantec; Brian Chatterton of ATI; Bryce Cogswell and Kristin Gabriel of Symantec; Steven Hoek, Derek Hurtle, and Christina Karpowitz of PowerQuest; Jan Olsen of Imagine LAN; Mark Russinovich; Mike Sutherland; and Anna Thorn of Quarterdeck. As always, we thank our fine literary agent, Mike Snell. Finally, to all the other writers and researchers who have added to the public store of knowledge about the Registry and therefore made our job easier, our sincere thanks as well.

Publisher's Acknowledgments

We're proud of this book; please register your comments through our IDG Books Worldwide Online Registration Form located at http://my2cents.dummies.com.

Some of the people who helped bring this book to market include the following:

Acquisitions, Editorial, and Media Development

Project Editors: Brian Kramer, Kyle Looper

Senior Acquisitions Editor: Jill Pisoni

Copy Editors: Kathleen Dobie, Patricia Yuu Pan

Technical Editor: Gerald Routledge

Media Development Technical Editor: Joell Smith

Associate Permissions Editor: Carmen Krikorian

Editorial Manager: Leah P. Cameron

Media Development Manager: Heather Heath Dismore

Editorial Assistant: Donna Love

Production

Associate Project Coordinator: Tom Missler

Layout and Graphics: Lou Boudreau, Valery Bourke, Linda M. Boyer, J. Tyler Connor, Maridee V. Ennis, Angela F. Hunckler, Todd Klemme, Heather N. Pearson, Brent Savage, Janet Seib, Kate Snell

Proofreaders: Christine Berman, Rebecca Senninger, Kathleen Sparrow, Janet M. Withers

Indexer: Richard Shrout

Special Help

Publications Services, Inc.

General and Administrative

IDG Books Worldwide, Inc.: John Kilcullen, CEO; Steven Berkowitz, President and Publisher

IDG Books Technology Publishing: Brenda McLaughlin, Senior Vice President and Group Publisher

Dummies Technology Press and Dummies Editorial: Diane Graves Steele, Vice President and Associate Publisher; Mary Bednarek, Director of Acquisitions and Product Development; Kristin A. Cocks, Editorial Director

Dummies Trade Press: Kathleen A. Welton, Vice President and Publisher; Kevin Thornton, Acquisitions Manager

IDG Books Production for Dummies Press: Michael R. Britton, Vice President of Production and Creative Services; Beth Jenkins Roberts, Production Director; Cindy L. Phipps, Manager of Project Coordination, Production Proofreading, and Indexing; Kathie S. Schutte, Supervisor of Page Layout; Shelley Lea, Supervisor of Graphics and Design; Debbie J. Gates, Production Systems Specialist; Robert Springer, Supervisor of Proofreading; Debbie Stailey, Special Projects Coordinator; Tony Augsburger, Supervisor of Reprints and Bluelines

Dummies Packaging and Book Design: Robin Seaman, Creative Director; Jocelyn Kelaita, Product Packaging Coordinator; Kavish + Kavish, Cover Design

♦

The publisher would like to give special thanks to Patrick J. McGovern, without whom this book would not have been possible.

♦

Contents at a Glance

Cartoons at a Glance

By Rich Tennant

page 349

"I wish someone would explain to Professor Jones that you don't need a whip and a leather jacket to edit the Registry."

page 259

"OKAY— ANTIDOTE, ANTIDOTE, WHAT WOULD AN ANTIDOTE ICON LOOK LIKE? YOU KNOW, I STILL HAVEN'T GOT THIS DESKTOP THE WAY I WANT IT."

page 165

page 327

page 111

"SOFTWARE SUPPORT SAYS WHATEVER WE DO, DON'T ANYONE START TO RUN."

page 293

page 11

Fax: 978-546-7747 • *E-mail:* the5wave@tiac.net

Table of Contents

Introduction

· ·

*T*he Windows 98 Registry is a vitally important part of Windows 98. Every document we've seen that discusses the Registry invariably refers to it as "the heart of Windows 98." That's true; the Registry contains just about every bit of information that matters about the hardware and software in a Windows 98 PC. You probably aren't aware of it, but Windows 98 and the programs you run with it use the Registry *tens of thousands of times* in a typical work session. Windows 98 can't blow its virtual nose without accessing the Registry a few hundred times.

For something so important, getting information about the Registry sure hasn't been easy. The documentation that you receive with Windows 98 doesn't tell you anything about it. (Okay, that documentation doesn't tell you much of anything about anything.) The Windows 98 software package contains practically no online help about the Registry. Even the seemingly encyclopedic, 1,600-page *Windows 98 Resource Kit* covers the Registry very lightly. This, despite the fact that the Registry gets 62 pages of coverage versus 18 pages in the *Windows 95 Resource Kit* and includes some TCP/IP and modem settings.

So, we thought that Windows 98 users could use a book like *Windows 98 Registry For Dummies,* which provides the information you need to use the Registry safely and to protect the Registry from problems that can range from inconvenient to disastrous. We give you many down-and-dirty details on how to change the Registry so that it bends to your will, rather than bending you to its. We explain cool Registry features that many Windows 98 users don't know exist, such as user profiles, hardware profiles, and system policies. We even tell you about a few Windows 98 bugs that you can fix by editing the Registry.

Windows 98 Registry For Dummies is very likely the only book you need to read or own on the subject, unless you're a professional programmer, in which case you may need to buy five or six books (but read ours first!). Certainly, our goal as authors is to include everything that the vast majority of our readers would need to know about the Registry.

About This Book

In this book, we present the essentials of the Windows 98 Registry concisely, conversationally, and (we hope!) clearly. We quickly bring you up to speed on the absolute minimum you must know about the Registry in order to use Windows 98 safely. We then take you further and show how you can use the Registry to do cool and useful things with your computer.

Windows 98 Registry For Dummies is not a tutorial. You don't have to do everything in Chapter 1 before going on to Chapter 2. You can jump here and there, finding out cool Registry tips and tricks along the way. The one caveat to this general theme is that before getting into the more heady aspects of the Registry Editor, you should read Chapter 2 on backing up your Registry and make a good backup for safekeeping. Then you can relax and explore.

Windows 98 Registry For Dummies is a reference. You don't have to commit all the various facts about the Registry, Plug and Play, and user profiles to memory (lucky for you!). Use the Table of Contents to find the topic you're interested in. Or, use the Index to zero in on the specific term you're looking for. If you come across a word that's unfamiliar, you can look it up in the Glossary (see Appendix A). Find the information you need, put it into action, and then set this book back on the shelf (preferably where you can get to it easily!) and get on with your life.

If you bought this book but you're actually running Windows 95 rather than Windows 98, hike on back to the store and swap this book for our earlier effort, *Windows 95 Registry For Dummies*. Although much of the material in the two books is the same, the earlier volume contains a lot of information that doesn't apply to Windows 98, and this book contains information that doesn't apply to Windows 95.

You should know right up front that this book deals with a potentially risky subject. Viewing the Registry and modifying it through the various Windows 98 control panels isn't especially dangerous, but modifying the Registry directly, using the Registry Editor or other similar utility, can be. *You can accidentally render a Windows 98 PC unbootable, trash software settings, and lose data files as a result of using the Registry Editor.* Don't get us wrong, we encourage you to experiment with the Registry, we just want you to know that you should **always** create a fallback position for yourself in case something goes wrong. For example, back up your hard disk regularly and back up the Registry files before you make any changes to them. Chapter 2 goes into detail on how to perform these backup tasks. We'll remind you of this caution periodically throughout the book where appropriate. If you don't heed our advice and you get yourself into trouble, Chapter 16 may help you avert total disaster, but we can't guarantee it.

Finally, this book is as scrupulously accurate as we could make it. Everything you read here is something we've tested personally, using the commercial release of Windows 98 (not just beta releases), usually on more than one computer. Also, every word has been scrutinized and authorized by our eagle-eyed technical editor, Gerry Routledge. Nevertheless, if you find what looks like a mistake, please let the publisher know via the online registration site described in the back of this book so we can research it and correct it if necessary. We'll thank you in the acknowledgments section of this book's next edition.

Conventions Used in This Book

Let's see: the Sacred Order of the Scarlet Elk convention, the Democratic National Convention, the Geneva Convention. . . .

Actually, we've made every effort to standardize how we tell you to do things and how we refer to things, because we know that you don't want to guess at what to do. Check out the following conventions:

- ✔ We tend to say "double-click" to mean selecting a desktop icon, even though you can single-click icons to activate them in the Windows 98 Active Desktop's so-called "Web view." We mention the ambiguity in each chapter, but only the first time it crops up.

- ✔ When we show you a keyboard shortcut, we put a + sign between the two keys that you press simultaneously. For example: Ctrl+C.

- ✔ When we show you a series of commands that you use your mouse and menus to accomplish, we put an arrow between the commands. For example: File➪Save As.

- ✔ When we show you a message that you get from the computer, we print that message in a monospace font, similar to what you would see on a manual typewriter. For example: `It is now safe to turn off your computer.`

- ✔ When we show you something that you type into Windows 98 or another Windows 98 application, the information to enter is presented in a bold font. For example: **REGEDIT**.

- ✔ When we show you stuff to enter at the DOS prompt or code to enter, it appears in monospaced font and capitalized. For example:

```
XCOPY C:\WINDOWS\USER.DAT E:\REG\ /H /K /Y /R
```

- ✔ When we refer to both Windows 98 and Windows 95 in the same breath, we economize by using the term "Windows 9x." If you couldn't care less about Windows 95, just read "Windows 9x" as "Windows 98."

> ✔ When we refer to the Windows 3-point-whatever series of products (Windows 3.0 and 3.1, Windows for Workgroups 3.1 and 3.11), we use the term "Windows 3.*x*."
>
> ✔ When we refer to a Registry key, we put that key in an italic font. (In cases where we must break a key because it's too long for a line, we do so at a backslash.) For example: *HKey_Local_Machine\Software\Classes*.

This is a hands-on book, so we give you lots of steps to follow to accomplish your Registry magic. The bolded portion of these steps are things for you to do; unbolded stuff is explanatory, as in the following example:

1. **Save any data files in open programs and close the programs.**

   This step isn't strictly necessary, but we like to walk on the safe side of the street.

2. **Give your PC the three-finger salute (Ctrl+Alt+Del) to display the Close Program dialog box.**

3. **Click Explorer and End Task.**

What You're Not to Read

Here and there, you'll see information marked with the Technical Stuff icon. This is information that isn't necessary for you to get the job done. Don't feel bad about skipping right over this stuff. If you're interested, however, go ahead and read it. Nothing ventured, nothing gained.

Foolish Assumptions

We've written this book for the broad audience of people who work with Windows 98, whether for business or pleasure. You may be a home PC user who wants to protect that machine from common problems and tune it up in useful ways. You may use Windows 98 at work, where you can't afford the downtime that Registry problems can create. You may be a part-time or full-time network administrator who's responsible for managing several Windows 98 PCs and wants to know how to set them up for minimum on-going maintenance and maximum reliability. You may also be a consultant of one stripe or another who needs to advise others about using Windows 98. You may even be a programmer who wants a quick and friendly introduction to the Registry.

The few assumptions we do make about you as a reader are as follows:

✔ **You use Windows 98 and know enough about it to get around the desktop.** If we refer to the taskbar, the My Computer icon, or the Windows Explorer, you know what we're talking about. If not, read *Windows 98 For Dummies* by Andy Rathbone (IDG Books Worldwide, Inc.) or take an introductory class, and then come back to this book.

✔ **You don't necessarily want to become a computer expert, but you want to understand Windows 98 more thoroughly so you can take maximum advantage of its capabilities.** If this book alone doesn't slake your thirst for Registry knowledge, we include references to a variety of additional resources on the Registry in Appendix B at the back of this book.

✔ **You're conscientious enough to actually make Registry backups before trying the various changes we suggest in this book.** (If you're not, and you prefer to live dangerously, please return this book for a refund, with which you can buy a ticket for a high-altitude bungee jump.)

✔ **You have a bona fide copy of Windows 98 and all the files that it comes with, either on hard disk, CD-ROM, or network drive.** (Some of the utilities this book discusses aren't installed as part of a typical Windows 98 installation, so you need to install them as a separate step — a procedure that requires access to the original Windows 98 files.)

✔ **You don't expect to write Windows 98 programs as a result of reading this book.** If you're a programmer, you can get a lot of great information from this book, and you certainly need to know about the Registry in order to write good Windows 98 software. But writing programs isn't our main focus here.

✔ **You don't expect to configure a network as a result of reading this book.** Some of the topics in this book pertain to a network environment, but we don't tell you how to build a network of Windows 98 computers here. For this sort of information, check out *Small Business Networking For Dummies* by Weadock (IDG Books, Worldwide, Inc.) if you work in a company with under 100 employees, or *Networking For Dummies,* 3rd Edition by Doug Lowe (IDG Books, Worldwide, Inc.) for a more general treatment.

✔ **You're no "dummy;" you just need the basics on the subject in a hurry.**

If this sounds like you, read on!

How This Book Is Organized

As with most *...For Dummies* books, you can dip in and out of specific chapters according to what your interests are and what level of knowledge you already have about particular subjects. You can certainly read this book cover to cover, and we do our best to keep it interesting if you do. However, each chapter is designed to give you all the information you need on a specific topic and not leave you hanging if you haven't read the entire book up to that point.

We've settled on a safari metaphor to help explain the purpose of the book's six main parts. Think of this book as a guided trek through the wild terrain of the Windows 98 Registry. So put on your pith helmet and sunscreen, grab the .375 Magnum and Nikon, and take a look at the following aerial map before you hop in the Jeep.

Part I: Hitting the Trail: Introducing the Registry

This part starts out by answering the question "Why do I need to know about the Registry, anyway?" We tell you what the Registry is, what it does, and how it makes Windows 98 different from Windows 3.*x*. The first chapter also gives you a taste of the sorts of things you can do with the Registry once you gain some familiarity with it. Chapter 2, hands down the single-most important chapter in the book, lays out the detailed procedures for backing up the Registry. Follow these guidelines and you can experiment with the Registry in the secure knowledge that if you damage something, you can always get back to where you were before you started experimenting. Chapter 3 presents the various ways you can change the Registry settings without actually directly editing Registry contents, for example with Windows 98 control panels. (Whenever you have a choice between using the Registry Editor and a control panel, use the control panel; it's safer.) Finally, Chapter 4 introduces the Windows 98 Registry Editor, as well as a nifty enhanced version that comes with the Symantec Norton Utilities for Windows 98.

Part II: It's a Jungle Out There: The Registry Structure

Part II takes a closer look at how the Registry is put together. Chapter 5 explains what actual files constitute the Registry (yes, there's more than one), where you can find them on your PC, how to see them (they're normally hidden from view, and for good reason), and what they contain.

Understanding where these files are and what they do is essential to being able to back up the Registry so you don't get into trouble that you can't get out of easily. Chapter 6 takes a look at the Registry structure from a different angle, namely, the "logical" structure. The Registry may consist of several separate files, but it appears as a single, multilevel database when you view it with the Registry Editor, and you need to understand how Microsoft has organized that database in order to use the Registry Editor effectively. Chapter 7 zeroes in on how the Registry stores information about your PC's hardware in order to work with the Plug and Play standard, which Windows 98 supports so that adding and removing devices from your system is as automatic and painless as possible.

Part III: Blazing Your Own Trail: Registry Customizing

In Part III, you discover how to use the Registry to customize Windows 98 to your liking. Chapter 8 explains how you can customize the Windows 98 set-up program so that after you install Windows 98, the Registry looks the way you want it to look. (If you only use one PC and it already has Windows 98 on it, you can skip this chapter, but if you get involved with installing multiple PCs — for example, if you're a network administrator — this stuff is great.)

Chapter 9 goes into detail on how you can customize the Registry to control what a user can do on any given Windows 98 machine. The System Policy Editor is the Registry-modifying tool that this chapter explores, and this Editor is useful whether you're implementing a company network or just trying to figure out how to prevent little Johnny from inadvertently trashing your home Windows 98 PC. Chapter 10 investigates user profiles, a cool technique for making the Registry look and act differently depending on who logs on to the PC (also very handy for both company networks and home computers). Chapter 11 explains ways you can tune the Registry to squeeze more speed out of Windows 98, change how the operating system looks to the user, and do things you didn't know Windows 98 could do — such as provide a multiple-choice list for choosing the program you want to use when right-clicking a data file. The last chapter in this part, Chapter 12, looks at using the Registry to customize the Active Desktop and Internet Explorer.

Part IV: Expert Hunting: Registry Mastery

Part IV is for more advanced users. Chapter 13 explains how you can know exactly what happens to the Registry when you install or remove software or hardware. The knowledge you gain in this chapter lets you troubleshoot

Registry problems faster later on. It also explains how you can easily share the Registry tricks that you discover with others. Chapter 14 offers tips on clearing out Registry debris — the junk that accumulates like bugs on your Land Rover's windshield — so your Registry stays lean, mean, fast, and efficient.

Part V: Escaping from Quicksand: Registry Troubleshooting

Windows 98 is a good operating system, but not a perfect one. It can break in a thousand different ways, most of which relate in one fashion or another to the Registry. Part V helps you deal with the occasional problems that may crop up. Chapter 15 presents the top 20 Registry-related Windows 98 problems, plus suggestions for correcting them (or at least, recovering from them). Chapter 16 gives you step-by-step instructions for recovering from Registry disasters when troubleshooting doesn't work and you must restore the Registry using an earlier version.

Part VI: Trekking Onward: The Part of Tens

The "Part of Tens" is a standard feature of ...*For Dummies* books. Ours has two useful chapters and one frivolous one. Chapter 17 presents ten Internet sites on the World Wide Web that contain useful information or software pertaining to the Registry. If you have an Internet connection, you'll definitely want to check out these Web sites. Chapter 18 presents ten Registry tricks that we think you'll enjoy discovering. Finally, Chapter 19 lists ten Registries that have nothing to do with Windows 98. You know, all work and no play. . . .

Part VII: Appendixes

This book has three appendixes:

- ✔ Appendix A is a glossary with concise definitions of terms used in the book.

- ✔ Appendix B is a reference and resource section that provides details on companies and products mentioned in the book, as well as lists of books and magazines that can help you get more information and stay up-to-date on networking trends and technology.

- ✔ Appendix C is a description of the software goodies on the enclosed CD-ROM.

Icons Used in This Book

Several graphical icons highlight certain kinds of material throughout this book:

This icon guides you to other sections of the book where you can find more information relative to the topic at hand.

You get a CD-ROM with this book, and this icon alerts you that the accompanying text refers to software on that disc.

When you see this icon, you know we've succumbed to the temptation to editorialize a little bit. Other knowledgeable people may disagree with these opinionated comments, but they *are* based on experience.

This icon points out a bit of knowledge or comment that's worth committing to your long-term memory.

This icon clues you in to a precautionary step that, taken now, may save you a world of hurt later.

Here's material you can skip if you don't care about the nitty-gritty details, but may want to read if you like to know a bit more than the average bear.

Short suggestions, hints, and bits of useful information appear next to this icon.

Use this icon to avoid a *gotcha* — a common trap or pitfall. Most of these little warnings come from our own experience fiddling around with the Registry. Benefit from our mistakes!

And there you have it! We hope that this book provides a bounty of useful information that makes your Windows 98 experience more rewarding, fun, and trouble-free. If you can think of ways we could make it even better, please visit the Web site at the back of the book and let us know.

Where to Go from Here

If you don't know much about the Registry, you can find out the background stuff in Chapter 1; otherwise, proceed directly to Chapter 2 to find out how to safeguard your Registry. After that, it's happy hunting in whichever chapters interest you most.

Part I
Hitting the Trail: Introducing the Registry

The 5th Wave   By Rich Tennant

Of the many Registry editing procedures, the most difficult is using REGEDIT on a Windows 98 machine in a herd of restless cape buffalo.

RICHTENNANT

In this part . . .

When we last left our hero George, he was bailing out his storm-ravaged craft, having survived the power and the fury of the Windows 95 Registry. Needing a break, yet not wanting to miss "the adventure of the century," George decided to take a working safari in Africa to solve the curse and mystery of the Windows 98 Registry. Armed with his trusty elephant gun, his 4x4, and his Registry map, George soon would find himself in a brave new world — with no way to turn back!

Okay, so we're not fiction writers. In fact, we may not even be computer writers, according to some people we've met. When we told our acquaintances the title of our *Windows 95 Registry For Dummies* book, their eyes would glaze over. "What's the Registry?" they'd ask. "It's at the center of everything that Windows does," we'd reply helpfully and watch their eyes narrow in suspicion. "Oh, really? I've never heard of it. Are you *sure* you write computer books?" At this point, we're tempted to crack wise. "Actually — now we feel silly — we're movie directors, but we don't want people to think we're boring, so we pretend to write books about the Windows Registry."

Anyway, Part I of this book is where you get ready for your safari across the parched plains and twisted jungles of the Windows 98 Registry, learning the background you need and the tools you'll use to fine-tune your Registry in the safest possible way. You also find out how to create all-important Registry backups, so that if you accidentally drive your Jeep into a swamp, you can hop into your alternate Jeep without missing a beat. (That would be a fun stunt; maybe we *should* be movie directors. George Clooney as Bill Gates in: "Rear Windows." Excuse us, we're off to get financing. Enjoy Part I!)

Chapter 1

Why Do I Need to Know about the Registry?

*I*n spite of the fact that the Microsoft-supplied product documentation all but ignores the Registry, every user needs to know about the heart of Windows 98. In this chapter, we provide you with an aerial view of the Registry from which you can see what the Registry does and why it's fundamental to just about everything you can do in Windows 98. More importantly, we give you some ideas of how you can use the Registry to improve and customize your Windows 98 system.

For those of you who got your feet wet doing stuff with your *INI files* in Windows 3.*x* (by which we mean Windows 3.1, Windows for Workgroups 3.1, and Windows for Workgroups 3.11), we ground you in the differences between the old INI files you're used to and the new Registry paradigm.

So sit back, fire up a Macanudo, and get ready to discover the lay of the land before you pile into the Land Rover and set out on your Registry journey.

What Does the Registry Do?

It's good to start any journey by surveying the landscape from the peak of a mountain or the cockpit of a biplane — looking at the "big picture." In this section, we look at what the Registry is and what it actually does for a Windows 98 PC.

Defining the Registry

If Windows 98 were an office building that you owned, then the Registry would be the wiring. You may never give the wiring much thought until the day you buy a new copier for your office, plug it into a miswired power outlet, and receive an involuntary Don King hairdo. Or, maybe, until the day you decide to improve or customize the building — for example by installing "smart" thermostats, faster elevators, or a security system.

The Registry is much the same. You need to understand it in order to fix certain problems that can crop up, and in order to customize Windows 98 to your liking. Here's our attempt at a one-sentence definition of what the Registry is and all it does:

The Registry is the central store of information that Windows 98, and Windows 98 programs, use to track all the software and hardware on the machine, including details about how that software and hardware are configured.

The following sections expand on key aspects of this definition in more detail.

Central storage location

One of the key features of the Registry is that it brings information that was formerly scattered around the computer's hard drive into a single place. But understanding this depends, of course, on understanding what we mean by the word *place*. The Registry contains more than one file (there may be several, depending on whether the Windows 98 PC is set up for multiple users), but the Registry's actual files don't necessarily all exist in a single directory.

The Registry still *seems* like a single place, however, because you can view all the Registry information from a single window if you use the Registry Editor tool (REGEDIT.EXE) that comes with Windows 98, as shown in Figure 1-1. The Registry Editor is covered in Chapter 4.

Software tracking information

One of the Registry's main functions is to keep track of your PC's software (including Windows 98 itself). The Registry handles this job well with so-called *32-bit programs,* which are written expressly for Windows 98, Windows 95, or Windows NT, but not so well with *16-bit programs,* such as those written for Windows 3.*x.*

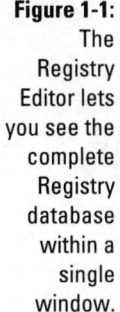

Figure 1-1:
The
Registry
Editor lets
you see the
complete
Registry
database
within a
single
window.

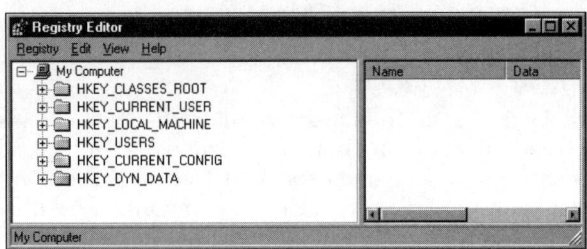

If every program in the world were completely compatible with Windows 98, then the Registry would know all the setup and configuration details for every program on your PC. However, Computerdom is an imperfect kingdom. The Registry's ability to track your software is subject to the following limitations:

- ✔ **Windows 9*x* programs.** Even 32-bit programs don't always store every setting in the Registry. Instead, they may use *private INI files* that the Registry doesn't understand. Some settings for Adobe Acrobat Reader 3.0, a 32-bit application, are stored in ACROREAD.INI. WinZip 6.1, also a 32-bit program, stores some of its own settings in WINZIP32.INI. We could provide dozens more examples, but you get the picture. For more on INI files, check out the sidebar, "History 310: INI files in Windows 3.*x*."

- ✔ **Windows 3.*x* programs.** Because Windows 3.*x* has a Registry of sorts (only one section), Windows 3.*x* programs do update the Windows 98 Registry with some information at install time — such as the *file association* information that tells the program to run whenever you double-click a file with a specific suffix. Windows 3.*x* programs don't make all the entries that Windows 98 and Windows 95 programs typically make, however, such as the information that programs use to "sign in" with Windows and effectively say, "This computer has program ABC installed on it, and here's how to uninstall it later." The Windows 98 Registry also can't capture information that Windows 3.*x* programs typically put into the WIN.INI file or a "private" INI file.

- ✔ **DOS programs.** DOS programs don't make any entries into the Registry, because DOS programs neither know about Windows nor care about it. If you want to know how a DOS program is set up, you must look at the program's own configuration files, and possibly also the DOS startup files, CONFIG.SYS and AUTOEXEC.BAT.

The Windows 98 Registry stores *most* of the details about Windows 98 and 32-bit Windows 9*x* programs; *some* of the details about Windows 3.*x* programs; and *none* of the details about DOS programs.

Hardware tracking information

The Registry tracks *almost* all the hardware on your PC. The Registry contains every bit of information about any hardware that uses a *32-bit device driver* — a program designed especially to enable the Windows 98 operating system and the hardware device to communicate with each other. (Windows 98 comes with hundreds of different 32-bit device drivers, and the Windows 98 setup program installs most of the necessary ones automatically.) Heck, the Registry even keeps details about hardware that you used to use with the PC, but later removed — presumably on the off chance that you may reinstall that stuff later on.

System configuration information

Windows 98 is a highly configurable operating system, meaning that there are zillions of settings that users and administrators can make after installing the base operating system. Similarly, most Windows 98 programs offer a dizzying array of optional settings, so, if you prefer white text on a blue background in your word processor, you can set the program up that way. Finally, the hardware devices in a Windows 98 PC may have a variety of configurable settings, too: for example, whether your network interface card uses the coax cable connector or the twisted-pair cable connector. The Registry tracks all these configuration settings so that users don't need to remake them every time they boot the PC.

The Registry's role

Now that we've cleared up what the Registry is, what's its role in a Windows 98 machine? What does it actually *do?* Go ahead and refill the coffee cup now, because the list is a long one!

Recording installation choices

The Registry fires up and gets working during the Windows 98 installation program. When a user — either an *end user* (the person who purchases a computer) or a *PC vendor* (a computer retailer) — first installs Windows 98, that user can specify information about devices connected to the computer or installed in the computer. The setup program stores that information in the Registry. The user also can choose what pieces of Windows 98 to install: a minimal setup (which leaves off games, wallpaper, and so on), a typical setup, or a custom setup. Again, the setup program records those choices in the Registry.

Real-mode device drivers

Sometimes, Windows 98 PCs communicate with some hardware devices by using software left over from earlier versions of DOS and Windows. These 16-bit programs are called *real-mode device drivers*, and they get activated by the old DOS startup files CONFIG.SYS and AUTOEXEC.BAT, instead of through the Registry.

A typical example is the real-mode device driver for a CD-ROM drive. Many new Windows 98 PCs load 16-bit CD-ROM support software in CONFIG.SYS and AUTOEXEC.BAT. For example, a line in CONFIG.SYS may look like this:

```
device=c:\d011v109.sys /
   D:toscd001
```

and a line in AUTOEXEC.BAT may look like this:

```
c:\windows\command\mscdex /
   d:toscd001 /m:15 /1:e
```

Windows 98 and Windows 98 programs typically don't need these lines in CONFIG.SYS and AUTOEXEC.BAT, because Windows 98 has its own 32-bit device driver for accessing the CD-ROM drive. One reason for activating real-mode device drivers is so that older hardware for which 32-bit device drivers don't exist can still work with Windows 98. Another reason is that users who run DOS programs using the Windows 98 special *MS-DOS Mode*, which removes Windows 98 from memory, need the real-mode device driver in order to run a DOS program from the CD-ROM drive. However, the Registry doesn't store any information about the real-mode, DOS-level CD-ROM device driver. It *does* store information about the 32-bit device driver that Windows 95 programs use. (Windows 98 programs ignore the real-mode device driver in memory.)

Setting up hardware

Your Windows 98 PC is likely different than ours, because Windows 98 supports a great many hardware devices such as graphics accelerator cards, CD-ROM drives, modems, hard disks, and so on. When Windows 98 starts, it must set up all those devices by assigning them the *resources* that they need to function. These resources include *interrupts* that devices use to request the PC's attention, *memory* areas that they use to communicate with the PC, software *drivers* that form the link between the device and Windows 98, and so on.

Windows 98 permits you to define different *hardware configurations,* or *profiles*. For example, you may work with a notebook computer on the road, but you can attach that notebook to a docking station with a different display, keyboard, and network connection when you're in the office. The

Registry stores these hardware profiles so that Windows 98 can configure itself properly depending on the hardware configuration that you need at the time. Chapter 7 discusses hardware profiles in more detail.

Setting up Windows 98

You can change many of Windows 98's operating system settings, so Windows 98 needs to know how to set itself up for operation when it starts. Here are a few examples of startup information contained in the Registry:

- What time zone to use.

- How the Windows 98 PC is to be used: as a typical desktop, as a portable with limited memory, or as a server machine sharing files and printers with other users.

- How quickly Windows 98 can access the PC's CD-ROM drive.

And here are some examples of Registry settings that apply to a Windows 98 PC in a network environment:

- The computer's network name.

- The server that Windows 98 should look for when the user logs on to the network.

- The order in which to load different network components, if the PC connects to more than one kind of network.

Running startup programs

The Registry maintains a list of programs to run when Windows 98 starts, independent of the list that you can create by manually modifying the Start menu. The Registry's run list typically includes programs that absolutely, positively must run every time Windows 98 starts, such as network communication programs and antivirus utilities.

The Registry can also run certain programs one time only. This option typically comes into play when an application needs to restart the computer in the middle of an installation routine, then pick up where it left off. The "Run Once" Registry feature may also be used the first time you turn on a new PC, launching welcome screens and other "first-time" configuration routines that you never see again.

Defining how Windows 98 appears

The Registry tells Windows 98 how to get dressed in the morning. It specifies all the display options the user can set, such as screen resolution, how many colors to display, what wallpaper to use, what fonts and sizes to use for icon titles, and so on. It also tells Windows 98 what icons and folders to put onto the desktop, and what icons to place in the *system tray* (the little box at the opposite end of the taskbar from the Start button).

If you set up the PC for use by multiple individuals, the Registry keeps track of each person's preferences so that when someone logs on, Windows 98 displays the desktop designed by that person. If users roam from machine to machine in a PC network, the Registry maintains desktop preferences on a network server, so that when the user logs on to the network, Windows 98 fetches the user's preferences from the server. Chapter 10 discusses these features, which go by the name of *user profiles*.

Specifying what double-clicking or single clicking does

You can run a program in Windows 98 by double-clicking (or single-clicking if the Active Desktop is actually active) a data file that's associated with that program. Double-click a file with the TXT suffix, and you typically run Notepad. The Registry tells Windows 98 which program to run when a particular type of data file is double-clicked. (Yes, you can change this behavior!)

Specifying what drag-and-drop does

Windows 98 and its programs enable you to do all manner of things by dragging and dropping icons from point A to point B: You can print a file, graft a chunk of data into a different document, compress or decompress a file, and much more. The Registry controls all the drag-and-drop behavior for the various types of data files that it knows about.

Defining right-click behavior

The right mouse button, which in Windows 3.*x* had about as much to do as a gun porter on a photo safari, is a very busy little rodent appendage in Windows 98. When you right-click a file of any kind in Windows 98, a *context menu* appears listing the choices available for that file: open, print, delete, and so on. The context menu can change depending on what type of file you right-click on. The Registry specifies the appearance and function of the context menu for every data type defined on the system.

Keeping track of application settings

Most Windows 98 programs store *user-definable* settings in the Registry. For example, if you're processing words, you can choose to turn the automatic spell-checking feature off (especially if you're writing about computers and your article has lots of weird abbreviations!). Windows 98 programs also store *user-specific* (as opposed to user-definable) settings in the Registry, such as a list of most recently used files. These sorts of application settings should be kept in the Registry, although in reality, many programs (including some written by Microsoft) use other ways to track user settings, too — such as the time-honored INI files (see the "What Does the Registry Replace?" section later in this chapter).

Reporting configuration data to administrators

On a network of PCs, administrators and troubleshooters often need to know the details of a computer's configuration, but they can't always physically go to the user's computer. The Registry can report a user's PC configuration to a remote administrator, as long as both user and administrator are connected to the same network. That network must be a *client/server* type (such as Novell NetWare or Windows NT Server) that uses a centralized database of users and passwords.

The bottom line is that the Registry handles just about every chore on a Windows 98 PC and influences the chores that it doesn't handle. Now you can begin to understand why the Registry is so important, why every Windows 98 user needs to take steps to protect it, and why you can do so many things to improve the functioning of Windows 98 once you understand it.

Conspiracy theories

Why doesn't Microsoft tell you about the Registry if it's so important and you can do so much with it? Here are our theories:

✔ Microsoft's attitude echoes Jack Nicholson's in *A Few Good Men*: "You can't *handle* the Registry!" (We think you can, or we wouldn't have written this book.)

✔ Microsoft intended the Registry to be a behind-the-scenes database with which users should never need to directly interact. (In a perfect world, that might be true, but ours isn't.)

✔ Microsoft knows that their bare-bones Registry editing tool, REGEDIT, is hastily assembled, inelegantly designed, and breaks almost every rule of user-friendly software design, so they don't want to call attention to it. (We wouldn't either.)

✔ They couldn't figure out how to explain the Registry. (Okay, it takes us about 400 pages, so we can sympathize.)

Pick your favorite theory; the truth is probably a combination of all of these. Just remember that Microsoft's scant documentation of the Registry is no indicator of its importance. When you buy a house you don't get a manual describing it, either, but it's probably the most valuable thing you'll ever buy.

What Does the Registry Replace? (For Windows 3.x Veterans)

Many of you reading this book have prior experience with Windows 3.x. You can better understand the Windows 98 Registry by understanding what Windows 3.x files it replaces.

If you've never worked with the combination of Windows 3.x and MS-DOS, feel free to skip this section!

Getting initiated into INI files

Windows 3.x saved the software and hardware settings in various places and forms, but it stored most of these settings in text files having the extension .INI, such as WIN.INI. (For details on other INI files, see the sidebar, "History 310: INI files in Windows 3.x.") The INI stands for initialization, because Windows looks at these files when it starts up. (Windows and Windows programs also look at some of the INI files after startup, too.)

All INI files follow the same simple formatting rules: section headings in square brackets, items underneath section headings can appear in any order, items under the wrong heading don't work, a leading semicolon "comments out" a line so that Windows doesn't process it, and so on. You can (with rare exceptions) edit any INI file with a simple text editor, such as Windows Notepad. Figure 1-2 shows an excerpt from a fairly typical INI file, SYSTEM.INI.

Figure 1-2:
Windows
3.x relies
almost
exclusively
on INI files
to record
software
and
hardware
information.

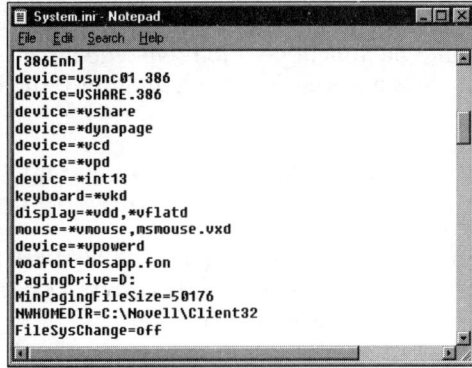

History 310: INI files in Windows 3.*x*

The INI files that Windows 3.*x* uses are as follow:

- ✔ **WIN.INI** includes a variety of desktop appearance information, as well as file type associations — what happens when a user double-clicks a BMP file, for example.

- ✔ **SYSTEM.INI** contains primarily hardware information, including the names of the specific device drivers that Windows must use to speak to the display, mouse, and so on.

- ✔ **CONTROL.INI** contains information pertaining to the Windows control panel, including multimedia device drivers, as well as certain desktop appearance settings.

- ✔ **PROGMAN.INI** contains settings that affect the Program Manager shell, including a few optional restrictions on what users can do within the Program Manager.

- ✔ **Private INI files** contain information that allows individual programs to run, and can appear in various places on the hard drive, such as C:\WINDOWS, C:\WINDOWS\ SYSTEM, or in the application's own directory. EXCEL.INI is an example of a private INI file. These files exist because WIN.INI has a 64K limitation and can't hold every setting for every program without bursting its belt.

Yes, Virginia, there is a Windows 3.x Registry

The first attempt to address some of the INI files shortcomings mentioned in the "What's wrong with INI files?" sidebar was the Windows 3.*x* Registry, although Microsoft actually called it the *Registration Database* (see Figure 1-3). Much narrower in scope than the Windows 98 Registry, the Registration Database limited itself to file type associations (which data files go with which programs), compound document creation (embedding or linking a chunk of spreadsheet data into a word-processing program), and drag-and-drop behavior.

As a practical matter, the Registration Database isn't sufficient to store all the various settings a program may need to keep track of, so it didn't make WIN.INI and private INI files obsolete. However, it represented a good first step toward consolidating at least certain categories of Windows information, and it did a good enough job to encourage Microsoft to extend the concept dramatically in Windows 95 and Windows 98.

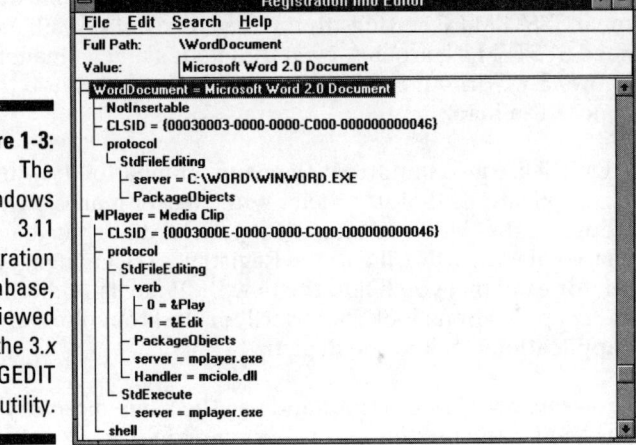

Figure 1-3:
The
Windows
3.11
Registration
Database,
as viewed
by the 3.*x*
REGEDIT
utility.

INI files that Windows 98 needs

So are the INI files now obsolete in Windows 98, given that the new Registry is much more comprehensive than the Windows 3.*x* Registration Database? It's a nice thought, but unfortunately far from reality.

While you can run Windows 98 without the DOS startup files CONFIG.SYS and AUTOEXEC.BAT, you can't run Windows 98 without at least WIN.INI and SYSTEM.INI, yet. In fact, if you try deleting WIN.INI, Windows 98 thumbs its nose at you by rebuilding a minimalist WIN.INI file the next time it starts (see Figure 1-4). If WIN.INI didn't exist, the setup program for most Windows 3.*x* applications would fail.

Figure 1-4:
Windows 98
insists on a
minimalist
WIN.INI
even if you
delete it.

SYSTEM.INI still exists, too, on a standard Windows 98 PC. Microsoft was able to migrate most SYSTEM.INI settings to the Registry, but not all. As a result, you still need SYSTEM.INI around, even though it's much smaller than it was under Windows 3.*x*. Without SYSTEM.INI, the Explorer desktop that we all love would not even load.

WIN.INI and SYSTEM.INI are also important to ensure compatibility with the 16-bit Windows 3.*x* applications that use them. When a user makes a change to the desktop via one of the Windows 98 control panels, that change may very well occur in two places: WIN.INI and the Registry. (Try changing the desktop wallpaper, for example; you'll find the new BMP file listed both places.) Windows 3.*x* applications look to WIN.INI for desktop information and Windows 98 applications look to the Registry.

If you install Windows 98 over Windows 3.1 and use the same directory (usually C:\WINDOWS) for the new operating system, Windows 98 automatically migrates various settings from CONTROL.INI, PROGMAN.INI, SYSTEM.INI, and WIN.INI into the Registry.

INI files that other programs need

Many private INI files still exist on any given Windows 98 machine. You can quickly check the INI files on a given machine using Start➪Find➪Files or Folders and type ***.INI** in the Named field (Glenn counts over 100 separate INI files on a Windows 98 PC with only half a dozen common applications installed!).

While we could understand 16-bit Windows 3.*x* programs using private INI files, Microsoft breaks its own rules by using private INI files for some of its own Windows 98 applications, such as Office 97 and even Internet Explorer 4. Clearly, private INI files are going to be with us for some time. However, the same is not true of the DOS startup files, as the next section explains.

Goodbye to two old friends

Although WIN.INI and SYSTEM.INI still have a place in Windows 98, granted a much less important place than they enjoyed in Windows 3.*x*, two other system files that date back to the original have become dispensable on most Windows 98 PCs. These are the DOS startup files, CONFIG.SYS and AUTOEXEC.BAT.

What's wrong with INI files?

What's the problem with INI files? Why replace the INI file structure with the new Registry system? Well, the INI file system has never been ideal. Here's a short list of its shortcomings:

✔ **Flat structure.** You can't have a subsection underneath a main section; one level of structure is all that's available, limiting the ability of Microsoft and application developers to organize INI file settings more finely.

✔ **Size limit.** Each INI file can be no larger than 64K. (This becomes a big problem for Windows 3.x users who have tons of installed fonts; WIN.INI gets too large, and Windows refuses to start!) The size limitations result in individual applications installing private INI files to keep WIN.INI under 64K.

✔ **Scattered locations.** Although you can say with certainty where the core Windows INI files are (they all have to be together), you never know where programs might put their private INI files.

✔ **Poor separability.** Some INI files contain both machine-specific settings and user-specific settings. As a result, it's difficult to have all the user settings — wallpaper, program groups, and so on — follow a "roaming user" who may work on different networked PCs at different times, or multiple users of the same home PC.

✔ **No remote administration.** Without third-party add-ons to Windows 3.x, no way exists for an administrator to connect to a Windows 3.x PC and access its INI files.

You may need these files (as we mentioned in the "Real-mode device drivers" sidebar toward the beginning of this chapter) if you still use old devices or if you run DOS programs in Windows 98's special MS-DOS Mode. However, most DOS programs run well the usual way (that is, as a separate window executing within the Windows 98 user interface). If you run only Windows programs on a given PC, chances are good that you can simply delete CONFIG.SYS and AUTOEXEC.BAT and never worry about them again. A quick way to find out is to simply rename these files to names such as CONFIG.SAV and AUTOEXEC.SAV, restart the computer, and see if all your programs seem to work normally. If not, renaming the files back to their original names is a simple matter.

What Does the Windows 98 Registry Add?

Okay, so the Windows 98 Registry replaces a lot of information that the DOS and Windows 3.x startup files used to contain. Does the Registry store any new information that DOS and Windows 3.x never needed to track? (You can tell by the fact that we're asking the question that the answer is yes.)

User profiles

Because the Windows 98 Registry divides user specific settings into a separate file, it's now possible for user preferences (desktop color, wallpaper, icons, and so on) to travel with users who roam around a network. It's also possible for a Windows 98 PC to allow multiple individuals to log on to a single machine and see their own preferences. Chapter 10 deals with these *user profiles*.

Plug-and-Play info

The Plug and Play standard helps make installing new hardware easier. It also makes it easier to rip out old hardware you no longer want. Plug and Play maintains a database of hardware settings that helps automate the process of assigning and unassigning computer resources to specific devices. Guess what? That database is in the Registry! Chapter 7 looks at it in depth.

Access restrictions

The Registry adds settings to support the great variety of access restrictions that Windows 98 can impose. It also adds a nifty mechanism for setting up multiple Windows 98 PCs to all use the same set of restrictions: the policy file, which is an optional Registry file that you can create with the System Policy Editor utility (POLEDIT.EXE). Chapter 9 tells you all about policy files.

Improvements since Windows 95

The role that the Registry plays in Windows 98 is greatly expanded from its role in Windows 3.*x*, but there are also some changes to consider when you compare Windows 98 to Windows 95.

If you never worked with Windows 95, you probably don't care about this section!

The hop from Windows 95 to Windows 98 is much shorter than the leap from Windows 3.*x* to Windows 95, and much more like the hop from Windows 3.0 to Windows 3.1. In fact, you can think of Windows 98 as a "dot release," maybe Windows 95.3 (if you consider the OEM Service Release 2 version of Windows 95 to be Windows 95.2). Windows 98 follows in the computer industry's grand tradition of making you pay for new versions to fix the bugs in the version you paid for last year.

Windows 98 seems able to run almost all Windows 95 software without modification (note, though, that the reverse is not true; we've already seen programs written for Windows 98 that don't run under Windows 95). The newer operating system works very much the same under the hood; although, as Microsoft takes a page out of General Motors' book, much of the sheetmetal is new.

As a result, Microsoft hasn't made any earth-shattering changes to how the Registry works between Windows 95 and Windows 98; it's just a bit bigger. We're reminded of the twins, given up for adoption, who were sent to Egypt and Spain and named Amal and Juan respectively. Juan grew up, looked up his birth mother, and sent her a photo. She wished her other son, Amal, would do likewise, but her husband observed that they were identical twins, and if you've seen Juan, you've seen Amal (ba-dum-bum). But seriously, folks, just as with twins, several differences do exist between the two Registries.

New contents

Many new Registry entries exist for the new programs, features, and hardware support files that come with Windows 98. In fact, the Windows 98 Registry starts life at about 1.8MB before you even install any applications — that's nearly twice the typical initial size of the Windows 95 Registry.

Some of the areas that have added to the Windows 98's Registry size include the following:

- Digital video, animation, and other multimedia settings.
- Internet browser capabilities that only appear in Windows 95 if Internet Explorer is installed.
- Settings for the *Active Desktop,* the update to the Windows 95 user interface.
- Security-related settings for e-mail and Java.
- Troubleshooting data to support new Windows 98 utilities.
- New power management features that Windows didn't control in earlier versions.
- More support for voice modems and computer telephony.
- A whole slew of new settings having to do with TV tuners that let you watch hockey in one window while you send e-mail in another.
- Device support for the Universal Serial Bus (USB), Digital Versatile Disc (DVD), and other new hardware types.
- New desktop management capabilities for networked PCs.
- New sections to make the Windows 98 Registry look more like the Windows NT Registry, both for application support and to make future upgrading easier.

New code

Microsoft has improved the Registry-handling code in Windows 98 so the Registry is both faster and more reliable. These improvements are "behind the scenes" — that is, you can't see them if you use the Registry Editor, or even if you're a programmer and you use the Registry API (Application Program Interface) — but they contribute to better overall speed with Windows 98 because Registry accesses are so frequent. For you technically inclined readers, the following two paragraphs provide a bit more detail.

One code improvement has to do with Registry disk writing operations. In Windows 95, before saving a file to disk, the Registry examines the entire file — that is, every memory block — in order to compute a "checksum" that Windows uses to verify the file's accuracy. In Windows 98, the Registry only looks at the part of the file that's changed, saving considerable time (Microsoft claims a factor of ten).

Another code improvement has to do with the *key node table*. This is a database structure that lists every key (a *key* is a data container) in the Registry. Windows 98 stores the key node table more efficiently, using less memory space.

New backups

Windows 95 backs up the Registry automatically at each reboot, but Windows 98 only backs it up on the first reboot of the day, unless you ask to do it more often. Furthermore, the way that Windows 98 makes backups is much different. Instead of creating files with the suffix .DA0, which are actually just backup copies of the key Registry files, Windows 98 creates files with the suffix .CAB, which are compressed files that act as a wrapper containing those same key Registry files, plus WIN.INI and SYSTEM.INI. (The compression helps make up for the fact that the Registry has grown much larger in Windows 98.)

While we're on the subject of backups, we should address a few comments on how to save the Windows 98 Registry before you make any changes to it.

Rule #1: Saving the Registry

If you've been reading this chapter from the start, you've probably begun to realize that Windows 98 depends upon the Registry to much the same extent that novice safari-goers depend on a well-informed guide. If anything happens to the Registry, Windows 98 becomes a panther with no claws. The First Rule of the Registry, therefore, is as follows:

> *Periodically save a "known good" copy of the Registry where it's out of harm's way.*

Chapter 2 gives you details on various ways to save the Registry, but here's what you absolutely must know in a nutshell.

How to save

You have several choices as to how you save the Registry. Here, we just mention one: the Registry Checker. Although you may expect a program with such an important role to be at the top of the Start menu's program list, Windows 98 buries it under a tangle of underbrush. Activate Registry Checker by choosing Start⇨Programs⇨Accessories⇨System Tools⇨System Information, and then choosing Tools⇨Registry Checker (see Figure 1-5). (Chapter 2 gives you the step-by-step procedure for putting the Registry Checker in a more convenient desktop location.)

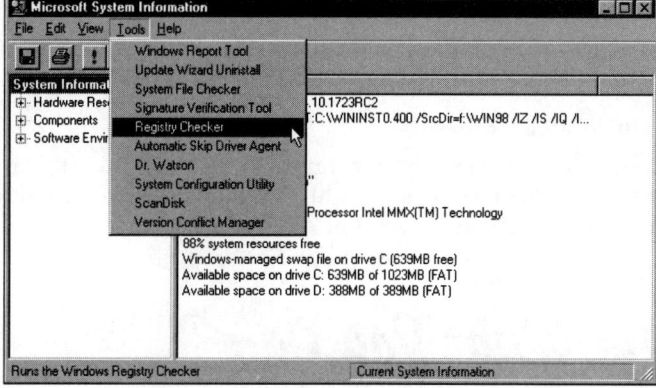

Figure 1-5:
Get to the
Registry
Checker via
the System
Information
utility.

Registry Checker first performs a quick scan of your Registry to make sure it looks halfway intact, then it asks you if you'd like to back up the Registry. All you have to do is click the Yes button, and you're done. Registry Checker puts a copy of the current Registry in a compressed file called RB0*xx*.CAB in the directory C:\WINDOWS\SYSBCKUP, where the "*xx*" is a sequence number that can range from 00 to 99. If you see more than one CAB file, you can see which is the most recent by looking at the time and date stamp. (If you use some other directory name besides WINDOWS to install Windows 98 into, the SYSBCKUP directory will be under that.)

The Registry Checker doesn't give you a graphical dialog box where you can select another destination location (grrr). Because backing up the Registry to the same hard drive as the original files doesn't protect you against hard drive failure, you may want to take one more step. Copy the CAB file that the Registry Checker creates to a diskette (if the diskette has room), a directory on a second hard disk (if the PC has one), a removable magnetic disk (such as ZIP), a writable optical disk (such as CD-R), or a network directory.

When to save

Always save a copy of the Registry at the following times:

- ✔ As soon as you finish a Windows 98 installation and everything seems to work.
- ✔ As soon as you fire up a new PC that came with Windows 98, and (again) everything seems to be working fine.
- ✔ Before you install or remove any program, except perhaps the minor *applets* (such as Calculator and Notepad) that come with Windows 98.
- ✔ After you install or remove any program and everything looks like it's working right.
- ✔ Before you make any significant changes with the Control Panel (for example, installing network software is significant, but changing the time and date is not).
- ✔ Before you make changes with the System Policy Editor, which is a Registry-editing wolf in sheep's clothing.
- ✔ Whenever the moon is full.
- ✔ Before you even think about running REGEDIT or any similar utility (such as the Norton Registry Editor that comes with Symantec Norton Utilities for Windows 95 Version 2.0 or newer).

Finding Out What You Can Do with the Registry

So what can you *do* with the Registry, besides make backup copies of it to ensure against future problems? Quite a lot. Chapters 8, 9, 10, 11, and 12 provide many examples of how you can use the Registry to customize a Windows 98 PC. For now, here's a sampling of five useful things you can do once you understand the Registry's ins and outs.

Fixing Windows 98 bugs

Windows 98 comes with a few bugs that range from the cosmetic to the serious. An example of a serious bug is a problem with modems and power management. When Windows 98 puts a modem to sleep in order to conserve power, it may not give the modem enough time to wake up when the user

needs to use it. The fix is to tell Windows 98 to give the modem more than
the usual three seconds between issuing the wake-up call and trying to
actually use the modem. How do you tell Windows 98 to do this? You modify
the Registry! (See Chapter 7 for the grisly details that we hint at in Figure 1-6.)

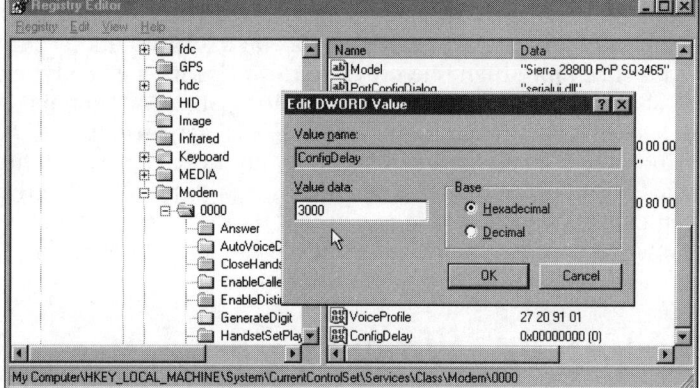

Figure 1-6:
A Registry
fix gives
your modem
more time to
regain con-
sciousness.

Recovering from crashes

Although it's noticeably less crash-prone than Windows 95, Microsoft didn't
write Windows 98 with reliability as the number one design goal. Compatibility was the prime directive: Microsoft wanted Windows 98 to work with as
wide a variety of software and hardware as possible. In many cases,
Microsoft had to sacrifice the goat of reliability on the altar of compatibility.
End result: Windows 98 can crash (even if Bill Gates is at the controls!).
Further end result: Windows 98 can damage the Registry when it crashes.
The situation gets worse when you consider that many (all?) application
software vendors don't write perfectly reliable programs. Third-party
programs can crash Windows 98, too, and they can also damage the Registry.

You can recover gracefully from a Windows 98 system with a damaged
Registry if you heed the previous section on backing up the Registry. For
example, if you use the Registry Checker, you can restart the PC to a DOS
prompt and type **SCANREG /RESTORE** to get the Registry back to where it
was the last time that you ran Registry Checker. SCANREG isn't the only way
to get out of trouble, though. Chapter 17 goes into some depth on various
step-by-step procedures for restoring a damaged Registry, and when to
use them.

Making the desktop easier to use

You can customize the Registry to make the Windows 98 desktop more user-friendly. For example, when you right-click a data file, a *context menu* pops up and gives you the option to "Open" the file. The file type association stored in the Registry determines the program that runs: for example, opening a file having a BMP file type (the three-letter filename suffix) runs the Microsoft Paint program, for example. In many situations, however, users may use more than one program to work with a given type of file. Microsoft Paint may be fine for casual editing of a BMP graphic — changing a couple of pixels here and there — but a user may need to use a more powerful tool, such as Adobe Photoshop, for more serious editing, such as applying color corrections to a scanned photograph. By using the Registry, you can change the context menu so that it offers a convenient list of all the programs the user might need (see Figure 1-7, and Chapter 11).

Speeding up Windows 98

Various user interface settings in Windows 98 tend to slow down how fast the operating system feels in daily use. For example, the hesitation that Windows 98 makes on the Start menu when the user points at an entry that leads to a subsidiary menu is a "feature" that makes the desktop feel more sluggish than it needs to. You can't modify this hesitation with a control panel, but you can use your knowledge of the Registry to reduce the lag time for snappier response. Chapter 11 tells you how to perform this customization as well as several others, and Chapter 12 helps you speed up the Active Desktop and your Internet browser.

Figure 1-7: Changes to the Registry enable a more convenient menu to appear when the user right-clicks a data file.

Increasing security

Windows 3.*x* offered practically no tools for limiting user access to the operating system. By contrast, Windows 98 lets you secure the desktop seven ways to Sunday, and all the security features happen via the Registry. Security is very important in a business environment, but it also can be convenient on a home PC (you don't want your 6-year-old making direct Registry edits!). A great security feature is the ability to run the System Policy Editor, which can disable the REGEDIT program. When you disable REGEDIT, any user (including 6-year-old children) who tries to run it sees the screen in Figure 1-8. Chapter 3 gives you the procedure, and Chapter 9 deals with the System Policy Editor in detail. The gist, though, is that the Registry makes security-related programs like the System Policy Editor possible, and those programs, in turn, can help protect the Registry.

Hiking into the Future with the Registry

Microsoft seems highly committed to the Registry concept. This chapter shows that Windows 3.*x* employed the concept to a limited extent, and that Windows 98 relies heavily on the Registry. Windows NT 4.0 uses the Registry extensively, also, as explained further in Appendix D. And, as it turns out, the Registry is a major part of Windows NT 5.0, too. The Registry is therefore going to be important well past the year 2000, assuming that any of our programs still work after January 1 of that year!

The good news is that after you read this book, the knowledge you gain will continue to be useful and applicable for years to come — not always the case with computer books! Even if you move to NT 4.0 or 5.0, there's enough similarity between the Registries of all these different products so that you'll feel at home — even if you do have to bone up on the aspects of the Registry that are unique to each operating system.

Figure 1-8:
One
Registry
security
feature
prevents
users from
editing the
Registry
with
REGEDIT.

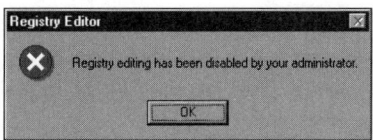

Chapter 2

Before You Embark: Backing Up the Registry

●●

In This Chapter

▶ Discovering why you need to make Registry backups

▶ Understanding how to customize the Registry Checker's backups

▶ Dealing with the backup "Ws" — when, where, and what

▶ Using export files as a backup technique

▶ Creating your own custom Registry backup batch file

●●

*W*hen you embark on a photo safari, your guide will advise you to take two cameras, just in case you drop one where an elephant has lost some unwanted weight. Making a complete and completely usable Registry backup is not quite as simple as packing a second Nikon in a duffel bag (and definitely not as simple as it should be!). However, making a backup isn't difficult at all after you set up your computer to make the process fast and convenient.

In Chapter 1, we introduce the First Rule of the Registry, restated here:

> *Periodically save a "known good" copy of the Registry where it's out of harm's way.*

The most important action that you can perform as a result of reading this book is to back up the Registry. If we can help you get into the habit of backing up your Registry successfully, then this book has paid for itself in one chapter. (Think of the other 18 chapters as a bonus!)

You may have heard something about how Windows 98 makes Registry backups for you automatically, and that's certainly true. However, we show you that those automatic backups are limited in some important ways. Rely on them blindly, and you may find your backup against a wall. (Groan.)

Our job here, then, is to present the why, when, where, what, and how of Registry backups and describe enough alternatives so that you can choose a method — or, more likely, a combination of methods — that works best for you. After you set up a Registry backup plan and adhere to it, you can relax a little whenever you need to modify the Registry. Even if you do make a mistake, and at some point mistakes are inevitable, you can always get back to where you were before. (If only life in general could work that way!)

This chapter focuses on *creating* backups, and Chapter 16 looks more closely at *restoring* from your backups. The later chapter discusses some of the same programs that we discuss here, in the context of disaster recovery.

Why Backups Matter

Here's why you really do need to back up the Registry:

✔ The Registry is at the center of everything that Windows 98 does, as Chapter 1 explains. Problems with your Registry can affect every program on your PC and even prevent Windows 98 from starting properly.

✔ In severe cases, a damaged Registry may require you to completely reinstall Windows 98 and perhaps even all Windows 98 applications, if you don't have a good Registry backup.

✔ The Registry is vulnerable to damage from disk media failure (hard drives, like milk, eventually go bad) and from buggy software install and uninstall programs.

✔ The Registry files have characteristics, or *attributes,* that preclude them from being affected by certain commands, such as COPY, that you may use to back up other key files.

✔ Damaging the Registry during a session with the Registry Editor is easier than overeating at Thanksgiving.

✔ The Registry files aren't text files. Unlike a Windows 3.1 INI file, if something goes wrong with the Registry, you can't fix it by loading it in a simple program like Notepad.

When to Back Up the Registry

A solid Registry backup plan includes both *landmark* and *scheduled* backups.

Landmark backups

A *landmark backup* is a backup that you perform at an unscheduled time, when backing up seems prudent. In this book, we usually display the *Safety First!* icon to point out when a landmark backup makes sense, but here's a general list of situations that call for a Registry backup:

- ✔ As soon as you finish a Windows 98 installation, and everything seems to work

- ✔ As soon as you fire up a new PC that came with Windows 98, and (again) everything seems to be working fine

- ✔ Before you install or remove any program, except perhaps the minor *applets* (such as Calculator and Notepad) that come with Windows 98

- ✔ After you install or remove any program, and everything appears to be working right

- ✔ Before you make any significant changes with the Control Panel (for example, installing network software is significant, but changing the time and date is not)

- ✔ Before you make changes with the System Policy Editor, which is a Registry-editing wolf in sheep's clothing

- ✔ Before you run REGEDIT or any similar Registry-editing utility

If you're reading this book start to finish, the preceding list may seem familiar (that's because we present it in Chapter 1, too). Sorry, but certain points bear repeating, and you may be the kind of reader who always skips a book's first chapter. (We usually do!)

Scheduled backups

A *scheduled backup* (also known as a *recurring backup*) is a backup that occurs on a regular basis. For example, many computer users back up everything on their hard drives to a tape drive once a month; that's called a full backup.

One kind of scheduled backup you must remember to perform, and the other kind the computer remembers for you. The second option is usually better but it takes a bit more planning. You need a scheduling program, such as the Scheduled Tasks utility that comes with Windows 98, or the Norton Scheduler that comes with Norton Antivirus, if you want to run regularly scheduled Registry backups that go beyond Registry Checker's automatic backups (for example, backups that occur via a batch file that you create;

see "Batch file solutions" later in this chapter). The online help for the Scheduled Tasks program lays out the details for specifying the file you want to run (say, REGBAK.BAT) and how often you want to run it (every Friday night at 2:00 a.m.). Access the Scheduled Tasks utility by choosing Start⇨Programs⇨Accessories⇨System Tools⇨Scheduled Tasks.

If you're on a network, you may be able to use a server-based backup program, in combination with a *backup agent* program running on your PC, to set up periodic, unattended Registry backups over the network. Your server-based backup software should document the steps in detail, and you can get backup agents from Seagate, Cheyenne, or whichever backup software vendor you use. This type of backup is a very slick solution!

Scheduled backups that include Registry files can be risky if they overwrite older scheduled backups. Sometimes you don't notice a Registry-related problem right away, and if a scheduled backup wipes out an earlier scheduled backup, it may create a backup with the same problems that your current active Registry files have. If you use scheduled Registry backups, which is a great idea, save the files in a location different from the location that you use for your landmark backups.

Where to Back Up

Here are the places that you can back up your Registry files to, in approximate order of desirability:

- ✔ **A network drive.** You're likely to have plenty of space on a network drive, and you're protected if your hard drive fails totally.

- ✔ **A removable cartridge drive.** The popular Iomega ZIP and Jaz drives are examples. Norton Utilities version 3.0 for Windows 95 includes a diskette-plus-ZIP-disk option for creating a Rescue Disk set that boots Windows 9*x* into graphical mode instead of command-prompt mode. Again, a hard drive crash doesn't trash your backup.

- ✔ **A diskette drive.** This method is slower than network or cartridge drive backups, and you should use it only with software (such as the WinZip program provided on this book's CD-ROM) that can create a multiple-diskette set containing your entire Registry. Note that neither the Windows 98 startup disk program nor the Norton Rescue Disk program back up Registry files that are too large to fit on a single diskette!

- ✔ **A tape drive.** Even slower than a diskette drive, but again, you still protect yourself against a hard drive failure.

> ✔ **A different directory on your local hard drive.** Very fast, but hard
> drive failure wipes out your backup.

If you're fortunate enough to have two hard drives in your PC, backing up
Registry files to the second hard drive is faster and safer than backing up to
a different directory on your first hard drive.

What to Back Up

The files you're mainly concerned with are C:\WINDOWS\USER.DAT and
C:\WINDOWS\SYSTEM.DAT. You may also want to back up some other
important system files, such as WIN.INI and SYSTEM.INI (also in the
C:\WINDOWS directory) and AUTOEXEC.BAT and CONFIG.SYS (in the root
C:\ directory).

If you use multiple user profiles, so that different users can log on to the
same PC and see their own settings, or so that users can log on to any PC on
the network and see their settings, then you need to think about backing up
some additional Registry files. These user-specific versions of USER.DAT,
plus user-specific folders like Favorites, History, and Recent, live under
C:\WINDOWS\PROFILES in subdirectories having the same name as the
users who can log on to that PC. Most Registry backup solutions ignore
these files, so you may find that Microsoft Windows 98 Backup or a custom
batch file is your best bet.

If you back up to a device other than your main hard drive, you may also
want to back up the PC's automatic Registry Checker backup files (see
"Registry Checker's behind-the-scenes backup" later in this chapter).
They're named RB0*.CAB in C:\WINDOWS\SYSBCKUP.

For more details on Registry files and where they live, check out Chapter 5.

Backing Up the Registry
with Freebie Software

You don't have to buy any software in order to make Registry backups. You
just have to know about the tools and techniques available to you already,
and what their advantages and disadvantages are.

Registry Checker's behind-the-scenes backup

When Windows 98 starts successfully for the first time on any given day, its built-in Registry Checker utility makes an automatic Registry backup into an archive file named C:\WINDOWS\SYSBCKUP\RB0xx.CAB (that's a zero and not the letter O as the third character in RB0). The "xx" in the file name is a sequence number that can range from 00 to 99. Note that SYSBCKUP is a hidden folder, so you may not see it unless you turn on Windows 98's ability to view hidden folders and files in My Computer's View⇨Folder Options⇨ View property sheet.

The actual command that Windows 98 runs during an automatic Registry backup is SCANREGW.EXE /AUTORUN, which you can determine by looking at the Registry key *HKLM\Software\Microsoft\Windows\CurrentVersion\Run* (see Figure 2-1). This key lists programs that should run when Windows 98 boots. If it looks like Greek to you, that is, assuming you're not Greek, it won't after you read through Chapter 6.

Although the Registry Checker backs up the Registry for you automatically, remember that it only does so a maximum of *once per day,* the first time you boot Windows 98 on that day. (This is different behavior from Windows 95, which backed up the Registry at every restart.)

You can make Registry Checker perform another backup for you any time you like, by running the program manually. For example, choose Start⇨Run, type **SCANREGW,** and press Enter. (Or, if you prefer, choose Start⇨ Programs⇨Accessories⇨System Tools⇨System Information and then choose Tools⇨Registry Checker.) If you've already booted Windows 98 that day, and if Registry Checker doesn't find any problems with the Registry, you see the message in Figure 2-2 asking if you want to create another backup. Click the Yes button to confirm that you do. (If Registry Checker *does* find a problem with the active Registry files, it gives you the option to restore from the previous backup.)

Figure 2-1:
The
Registry's
Run key
activates
Registry
Checker at
boot time.

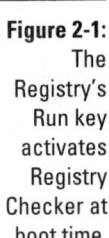
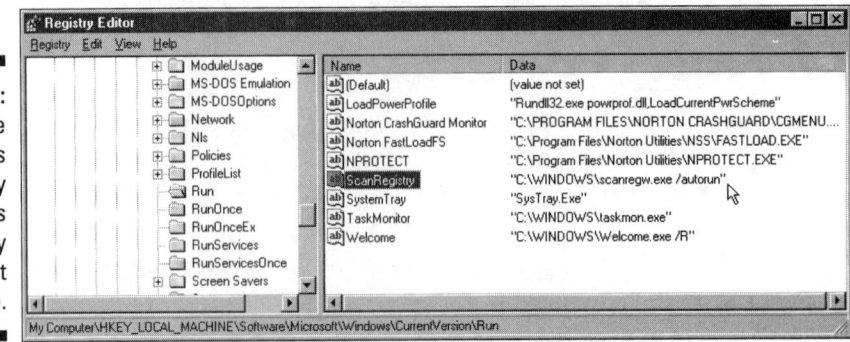

Figure 2-2:
Registry
Checker
offers to
create a
Registry
backup
for you.

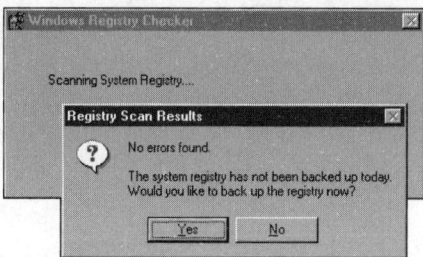

If you happen to be at a DOS prompt, for example because Windows 98 won't boot to its graphical user interface, you can run the real-mode version of Registry Checker, SCANREG.EXE, to back up your Registry by typing the simple command **SCANREG /BACKUP**. (SCANREG.EXE, like SCANREGW.EXE, lives in C:\WINDOWS.) The differences in the real-mode program's behavior are that it doesn't check the Registry for errors first, it doesn't compress your backup (so the created CAB file turns out to be much larger), and it doesn't give you the confirmation message before making the backup. Figure 2-3 shows you the command-line options for SCANREG.EXE.

Figure 2-3:
The
Registry
Checker in
real-mode
garb.

Note that the real-mode SCANREG Registry Checker program is *not* the same program as the SCANREG utility that comes with the Windows NT 4.0 Resource Kit and that we mention in Chapter 4.

Registry Checker is handy, and in the following sections we show you how you can modify its behavior to some degree. However, it's not the intelligent, industrial-strength backup utility we were hoping Microsoft would provide. As it runs "out of the box," Registry Checker has some limitations you should know about:

> ✔ **It doesn't back up the settings for every user, just the current one.** Be aware of this if you're using user profiles to allow multiple people to log on to the same PC with different settings. This statement holds true for manual backups as well as for the automatic ones.

✔ **Microsoft provides no graphical utility for customizing Registry Checker.** Instead, you have to edit a text file with Notepad to change the program's behavior (quelle gauche!).

✔ **Registry Checker normally stores the RB0*.CAB files on the same disk as the primary DAT Registry files.** Lose that disk to hardware failure, and you lose your automatic backups as well as your primary Registry files.

See the sections "Changing the backup location" and "Changing the backup file list," later in this chapter, for advice on working around these limitations to some extent.

Call me a Checker cab

CAB files are a special Microsoft compressed archive format (CAB is short for "cabinet," as in "file cabinet"). You've probably seen them before; for example, most of the actual Windows 98 files live in CAB files on the Windows 98 CD-ROM, and the SETUP program extracts and expands the files to your hard drive. Microsoft Office, and some other Microsoft programs, make heavy use of CAB files, too.

Each RB0xx.CAB file contains a copy of WIN.INI and SYSTEM.INI, as well as the USER.DAT and SYSTEM.DAT files in C:\WINDOWS. You can look inside a CAB file by double-clicking it (single-clicking in the desktop Web view), and you can manually extract a single file by right-clicking the file and choosing Extract. (This method beats the heck out of the old command-line EXTRACT command, which is still present if you need to extract a file manually at a DOS prompt.)

DA0 is DOA

Those of you who have experience with Windows 95 may be puzzled when you look on a Windows 98 system for the USER.DA0 and SYSTEM.DA0 files that Windows 95 creates as Registry backups at every restart. (Windows 95 also backs up individual user profile copies of USER.DAT to C:\WINDOWS\PROFILES\username\USER.DA0 when a user logs in on a system with user profiles enabled.) The new Registry Checker backup mechanism has removed the need for *.DA0 files, so you won't find them on a Windows 98 PC.

Unfortunately, however, the automatic user profile backups of USER.DAT are gone now, too, even though Registry Checker doesn't back them up. Oops — two steps forward but one step back. (Well, that's the history of PC computing in a nutshell!) See the sections "Changing the backup location" and "Changing the backup file list" later in this chapter.

Changing the backup location

Registry Checker normally stores backups in C:\WINDOWS\SYSBCKUP, a hidden directory whose main purpose is to store copies of device drivers in case unruly applications overwrite the ones in C:\WINDOWS\SYSTEM. This is a change from Windows 95, which stored its automatic backups in C:\WINDOWS. Storing Registry backups to the SYSBCKUP directory has a fatal flaw: If your boot hard drive fails, your Registry backups are gone. Fortunately, you can tell Registry Checker to put its backups (both automatic and manual) onto another device.

The vehicle for controlling Registry Checker's behavior is SCANREG.INI, a plain text file that you can edit, Stone-Age style, with Notepad. Here's how SCANREG.INI looks before any modifications (lines beginning with a semicolon are comments provided by Microsoft):

```
;
; Scanreg.ini for making system backups.
;
;Registry backup is skipped altogether if this is set to 0
Backup=1


;Registry automatic optimization is skipped if this is set
            to 0
Optimize=1

ScanregVersion=0.0001
MaxBackupCopies=5


;Backup directory where the cabs are stored is
; <windir>\sysbckup by default. Value below overrides it.
; It must be a full path. ex. c:\tmp\backup
;
BackupDirectory=

; Additional system files to backup into cab as follows:
; Filenames are separated by  ,
; dir code can be:
;       10      : windir (ex. c:\windows)
;       11      : system dir (ex. c:\windows\system)
;       30      : boot dir (ex. c:\)
;       31      : boot host dir (ex. c:\)
;
;Files=[dir code,]file1,file2,file3
```

To change where Registry Checker stores its CAB files, place a full path name (that is, one that begins with a drive letter) of your choosing after the line BackupDirectory= in SCANREG.INI. You can specify a secondary hard drive, ZIP disk, optical disc, network drive, or other storage device here; you can specify a subdirectory too, but leave off the final trailing slash. (Specifying a network drive is okay because Registry Checker doesn't make its backup until after the user logs on to the network, assuming you've set up Windows for a unified logon – see the following warning.) Now, you've protected your Registry backups from catastrophic boot drive failure.

On a network, if a PC uses different passwords for Windows logon and for the network logon, a user can log on to Windows without logging on to the network. The Registry Checker jumps into action after the logon dialog box, but if that dialog box only accomplishes a Windows logon and not a network logon too, then the network isn't available. If Registry Checker can't find the drive that you specify in SCANREG.INI, it does something very strange: Without offering any sort of error message, it saves the backup to C:\WINDOWS, not C:\WINDOWS\SYSBCKUP. Moral of the story: Set up the PC for a *unified logon,* in which the Windows logon name and password is the same as the network logon name and password. (We don't have room to give you the details here, but check out the *Microsoft Windows 98 Resource Kit* if you need them.) Also, make sure your network has very high uptime, because even a unified logon doesn't help if a server is down. Related moral of the story: If you use a ZIP drive or some other device for your backup destination, make sure that the device is powered on all the time.

Changing the backup file list

Out of the box, Registry Checker backs up your USER.DAT, SYSTEM.DAT, WIN.INI, and SYSTEM.INI files. However, you may want to change this file list. For example, on a PC with multiple user profiles enabled, Registry Checker doesn't back up all the possible user profiles (USER.DAT) stored under C:\WINDOWS\PROFILES\username1, C:\WINDOWS\PROFILES\ username2, and so on. Modify SCANREG.INI to tell Registry Checker where those user profiles live, and to include them in its automatic backup, by editing the FILES= line. (Remove the leading semicolon in order to activate the line.)

You have to use one of the precoded directory values (10, 11, 30, or 31) shown in SCANREG.INI (see the file listing in the previous section for an explanation of the codes). For example, use a line like **Files=10,profiles\ bob\user.dat,profiles\ray\user.dat**. (Registry Checker keeps track of the different USER.DAT files by remembering their locations.) If you just type a full path name after the = sign, Registry Checker doesn't process the file. It pretends to, but the file has a zero length when you view the contents of the

CAB file. On top of that, Registry Checker gives you no warning about the problem. (We *told* you it wasn't an industrial strength program.)

Registry Checker doesn't support wildcard characters, such as * and ? in file names.

Changing the number of backups to keep

By default, Windows 98 keeps your five most recent Registry backups, incrementing the sequence number in the CAB file name each time Windows 98 creates a new archive. This is a big improvement over Windows 95, which only kept one Registry backup. That was a problem for users who ran into Registry trouble, rebooted their system, and thereby damaged the automatic backup copy of the Registry as well as the active files. With the new system, as long as you catch a Registry problem before an entire work week goes by (five days), you can restore your Registry from a known-good backup.

You can change how many backups Windows 98 makes before it starts dropping old ones off into oblivion. Just fire up Notepad and change the number that appears after the MaxBackupCopies= line in SCANREG.INI to whatever number you want, up to a limit of 99. Be aware, though, that the more backups you let Registry Checker keep, the more disk space you give up.

Putting Registry Checker on the desktop

If you use Registry Checker to make manual Registry backups, it's a great idea to make the process faster. You can simply create a *shortcut* icon on your desktop that points to SCANREGW.EXE. Just right-click the desktop, choose New➪Shortcut, type **SCANREGW.EXE /BACKUP** for the Command line, click OK, type **Registry Backup** for the shortcut name, and click Finish. You now have a desktop icon you can select to make a quick Registry Checker backup.

If you want to add Registry Checker to your Start menu, Windows 98 now supports drag-and-drop for this purpose. Drag-and-drop the icon you just created onto whatever position you like on the Start menu or any of its submenus. (When dragging and dropping, you have to hover over the Start button a second or two before its menu pops up, and the same is true of subsidiary menus.)

Table 2-1 lists the command-line options for Registry Checker, both the protected-mode version (SCANREGW) and the real-mode version (SCANREG).

Table 2-1:	Registry Checker Command Options	
Option	*Description*	*Mode*
/AUTOSCAN	Scans every time, backs up once/day, no user prompt	Protected only
/BACKUP	Doesn't scan, backs up each time, no user prompt	Protected (compression) and Real (no compression)
/COMMENT= "comment"	With /BACKUP, saves comment that appears with /RESTORE	Protected and Real
/FIX	Repairs Registry	Real only
/RESTORE	Lists backups, lets user select and restore	Real only
/SCANONLY	Scans Registry, doesn't repair, doesn't back up	Protected only
/?	Displays options	Real only

Windows 95 leftovers: Worth reheating?

Those readers who've grown familiar with Windows 95 may know about the two Registry backup programs that come with that product: Configuration Backup and Emergency Recovery Utility. You can still use these programs with Windows 98 if you've grown accustomed to them in Windows 95, or if you must manage a mix of Windows 95 and 98 PCs on the same network, but read this section before you decide to do so.

Configuration Backup

Microsoft Configuration Backup, or CFGBACK for short (that's also the name of the EXE file that you run), is so badly flawed that we don't even waste your time telling you how to install and run it. (If you happen to inherit a Windows 98 PC where someone has installed and used CFGBACK, we do tell you how to attempt a restore operation in Chapter 16.)

CFGBACK doesn't run in Safe Mode, which may be the only way that you can run Windows 98 after severe Registry damage. Also, it uses a special data file format (*.RBK) that no other program can understand, so if you can't run Windows 98, then you can't run CFGBACK, which renders your backups useless. The program doesn't work unless the backup files are in

C:\WINDOWS, which doesn't help you much if your hard disk fails. But the most damning fact is that Microsoft itself suggests you not use this tool, in its published technical note Q142572. (We omit the full text of the tech note because all it says, in essence, is "don't use CFGBACK.") This program is one Windows 95 leftover that is not worth reheating.

Emergency Recovery Utility

Microsoft provides another Registry backup tool with Windows 95 called Emergency Recovery Utility (ERU for short). You can download this program from www.microsoft.com/windows/download/eruzip.exe, but installing it from the Windows 95 CD-ROM is easier. (If you have the *Microsoft Windows 98 Resource Kit*, the program's on that CD-ROM, too.)

Don't install ERU through the Add/Remove Programs control panel wizard. Just copy the files from the CD-ROM's \OTHER\MISC\ERU directory into a directory of your choosing on your hard drive. (We suggest C:\Program Files\ERU.)

To create a Registry backup with ERU, follow these steps:

1. **Run the program by double-clicking the ERU.EXE file in My Computer or Explorer.**

   You see a short message describing the program.

2. **Click Next and select a target location for your backup.**

   We suggest that you choose Other Directory rather than Drive A: because the Registry normally can't fit onto a single diskette, and ERU doesn't make multiple-diskette backups. If you choose Other Directory, click Next again to specify that directory.

3. **Click Next again to see the screen shown in Figure 2-4.**

   If you don't see ten files listed here, ERU won't make a complete system file backup.

Figure 2-4:
The list of files that ERU backs up, if they exist and if the target location has room.

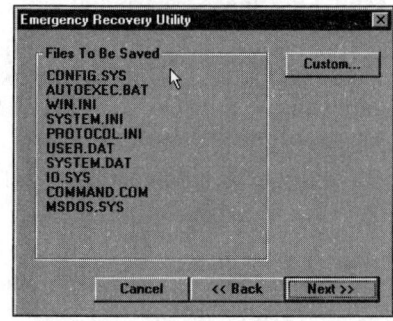

4. **If you want to change the file list, click the Custom button to display the screen shown in Figure 2-5. Make sure that you check the USER.DAT and SYSTEM.DAT check boxes if you intend to back up the Registry. Click OK when done.**

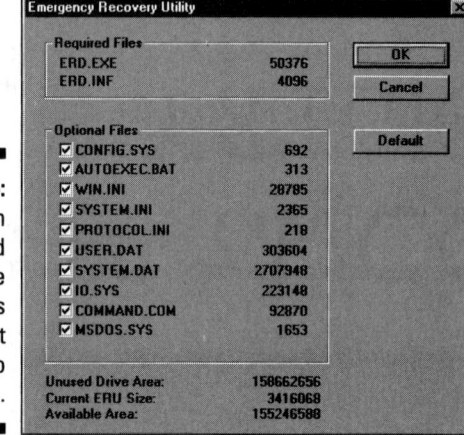

Figure 2-5:
You can
pick and
choose
which files
you want
ERU to
back up.

5. **Click Next to begin the backup process.**

ERU displays a progress window and finishes with a dialog box explaining briefly how to restore the files if you ever need to.

We like ERU for its inclusion of several important system files above and beyond the core Registry files, for its ability to restore backed-up files when Windows 98 can't boot to its graphical mode, and for its ability to save backup files onto any directory, hard drive, or network drive. Nevertheless, although ERU is a much better choice than CFGBACK, it has its flaws:

✔ If any of the files that ERU expects to find on your system are absent, such as AUTOEXEC.BAT or CONFIG.SYS, then ERU may not work. If the Registry backup isn't successful, ERU doesn't warn you, either.

✔ ERU wants to back up your system files to a diskette, but a diskette probably doesn't have room for SYSTEM.DAT — one of the two critical Registry files — so ERU blithely omits it, without so much as a tiny computer beep to let you know anything's amiss.

✔ ERU doesn't compress your backups so they take up less disk space, as Registry Checker does.

✔ ERU's customization options are more restrictive than Registry Checker's. (For example, you can't add just any old file to the backup set; you must select from ERU's predefined list.)

✔ ERU doesn't back up all the individual user settings on a PC that's set up for multiple users. (These settings are the various USER.DAT files in C:\WINDOWS\PROFILES — see Chapter 10 for the details.) To be fair, neither does Registry Checker.

If you have to restore an ERU backup that you or someone else made, you must start Windows 98 in command prompt mode. Chapter 16 provides the details. Just remember not to restore a Windows 95 Registry backup to a Windows 98 computer — you won't even be able to boot Windows 98 if you do this!

When you consider these drawbacks, it's clear that the Windows 98 Registry Checker is a better choice than ERU. Unless you must manage both Windows 95 and 98 PCs, and insist on using a single utility to handle Registry backups, leave ERU behind — as Microsoft did by not including it on the Windows 98 CD-ROM.

Windows 98 startup disk

You can create a Windows 98 startup disk (or, as Microsoft sometimes calls it, an Emergency Boot Disk) by using the Control Panel's Add/Remove Programs wizard. Just click the Startup Disk tab, pop a fresh floppy into drive A:, and click the Create Disk button. However, although you can boot with such a diskette, *it doesn't contain your Registry files!* (Try this method and see whether you can find USER.DAT and SYSTEM.DAT on the diskette.)

Go ahead and make a startup disk; as Martha Stewart might say, it's a good thing. Just don't expect to back up your Registry there.

Export and import

One of the simpler and more frequently recommended ways to back up your Registry is to run REGEDIT (or a similar program, such as Norton Registry Editor) and export the entire Registry to a text file. The procedure with REGEDIT is as follows:

1. **Run the Registry Editor, for example by choosing Start⇨Run⇨REGEDIT and clicking OK.**

2. **Choose Registry⇨Export Registry File to display the dialog box shown in Figure 2-6.**

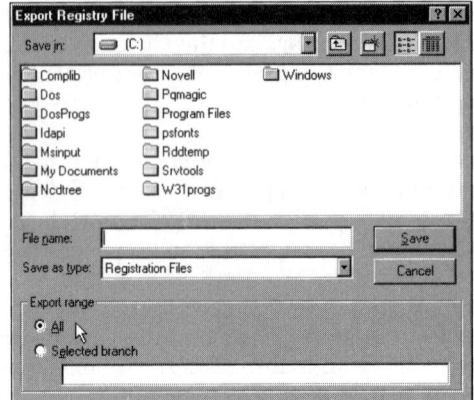

Figure 2-6: Backing up the entire Registry to a text file with REGEDIT.

3. **Specify the target directory in the Save In field and name the file in the File Name field.**

   REGEDIT automatically gives the file the .REG suffix.

4. **Click the All radio button under Export Range and click Save.**

Although very easy, this procedure has a couple of problems.

✔ As Chapter 16 explains in greater detail, you can't restore a full Registry backup when Windows 98 is running in its graphical mode and be completely certain that the resulting Registry is identical to the one you backed up. The reason is that a REG file import can't delete existing Registry entries, it can only modify them or add new entries.

✔ The export procedure doesn't back up user settings for the non-logged-on users of a PC that's set up to handle multiple user profiles. However, the export procedure does back up the settings for the currently logged-on user and the default user.

Because of these problems, the REG file export is more appropriate for quickie, partial Registry backups — for example, when you're about to modify a particular Registry key, and want to save the original — than for full backups.

You can create a REG file export using REGEDIT even if Windows 98 won't start. Hold down the Ctrl key during startup and choose Safe Mode, Command Prompt Only from the numbered list. (If you don't see the text message, just hold down the Ctrl key at boot time until the menu of choices appears.) At the C:\WINDOWS> prompt, you can create a full export of the current Registry by using the following command, where *filename* is the file name that you specify:

```
REGEDIT /E filename.REG
```

Microsoft Backup 98

The general-purpose backup program that comes with Windows 98, *Microsoft Backup 98,* can back up your entire disk drive, including the Registry. It can compress files on the fly, and it has no trouble creating a multiple-diskette backup to deal with files (like SYSTEM.DAT) that are typically too large to fit on one diskette.

This program, based on Seagate Software's industrial-strength Backup Exec product, is a *big* improvement over the limited backup utility Microsoft provides with Windows 95. For one thing, the Windows 98 version does back up your Registry files by default, when you select the WINDOWS directory (the Windows 95 backup program didn't!). The program also works with a wide variety of tape drives and other backup devices.

However, Microsoft Backup 98 has one drawback: It requires Windows 98 to be running in order to restore files. If you experience total hard disk meltdown and you have to replace the drive, you first have to reinstall Windows 98 onto the drive before you can run Microsoft Backup 98 in order to restore the files you backed up earlier. True, you can specify a minimum install and save some time, but doing so is still a pain and adds a half hour to your recovery time.

Creating backup jobs

To make a backup with Microsoft Backup 98, you first have to create a *backup job,* that is, a specification that will live on your hard drive and that tells the backup program exactly what you want to do — which files to back up, where to put them, and various other options.

Creating a backup job is easy. Simply run the program (Start⇨Programs⇨ Accessories⇨System Tools⇨Backup). At the initial screen that says `Welcome to Microsoft Backup,` you can choose the Create a new backup job radio button to use the built-in wizard, or you can click the Close button and design your backup job in the utility's main window (see Figure 2-7).

You choose which directories or files you want to back up in the middle section of the main screen (`What to back up`). Then, choose Job⇨Options to set your preferences for this backup job. We usually recommend that you click the top check box in the Backup Job Options screen's General tab (see Figure 2-8) to make the program perform a comparison check. This check makes the backup job longer, but it ensures that your backup matches the original files exactly.

Figure 2-7:
Create your
backup job
at the
program's
main
screen.

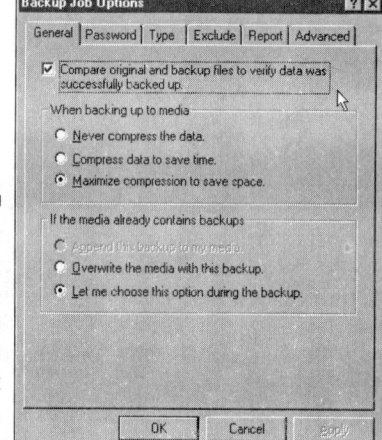

Figure 2-8:
Performing
a com-
parison
check helps
you sleep at
night.

When you finish setting all your options, click OK to close the Backup Job
Options dialog box. Then choose Job⇨Save As and give your backup job a
name. You can now use this job specification without having to set the
individual options each time.

Making sure the Registry is along for the ride

We recommend that you double-check the Microsoft Backup 98 Preferences dialog box (see Figure 2-9) to ensure that the Back up or restore the Registry when backing up or restoring the Windows directory option is checked. (It's checked by default, but make sure someone hasn't changed it.) Access this dialog box by choosing Tools⇨Preferences.

Figure 2-9:
You can
automatically
include the
Registry
any time a
backup job
includes
C:\WINDOWS.

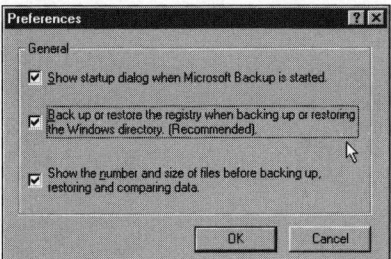

By checking the middle checkbox in Figure 2-9, you instruct Microsoft Backup 98 to automatically back up the Registry whenever a backup job includes the folder C:\WINDOWS. You can verify that this occurs by checking the Backup Job Options dialog box's Advanced tab (get to it by selecting Job⇨Options).

If you want to back up the Registry files only, you can create a special backup job for this purpose. Choose the following files and folders at the program's main screen (refer to Figures 2-7):

- ✔ C:\WINDOWS\USER.DAT
- ✔ C:\WINDOWS\SYSTEM.DAT
- ✔ C:\WINDOWS\PROFILES (if your Windows 98 PC uses multiple user profiles)
- ✔ C:\SYSBCKUP\RB*.CAB (if you want to back up your automatic Registry Checker backups, too, which is a good idea)

Batch file solutions

Another great, free solution for making Registry backups is to write a *batch file* that handles the job for you. A batch file is simply a text file containing a sequence of DOS commands that run one after another. Creating a batch file is the only way we know to avoid all the pitfalls and problems that plague the other backup methods we discuss in this chapter. Writing a batch file involves a little bit of the "P" word — programming — but the programming is easy, and we give you a substantial head start.

If you're not comfortable with writing batch files, consider hiring (or bribing) someone who is and getting him or her to help you set up a batch file that works for you, based on our examples.

Most batch files that we've seen for making the Registry backups use the plain old COPY command and the ATTRIB command to remove the Read-only attribute so that COPY can see the files. However, a simpler approach is to use the XCOPY command, which has a qualifier (/H) that copies hidden files. If you're backing your Registry up to the REG directory on a removable cartridge drive (drive letter E:), you may write a simple batch file that looks like this:

```
XCOPY C:\WINDOWS\USER.DAT E:\REG\ /H /Y /R
XCOPY C:\WINDOWS\SYSTEM.DAT E:\REG\ /H /Y /R
```

In the previous commands,

- ✔ /H instructs XCOPY to copy hidden files.

- ✔ /Y means that XCOPY doesn't ask you if it's overwriting an old file (so the /Y is necessary if you want to run your batch file in unattended mode by using a scheduling utility, such as Scheduled Tasks).

- ✔ /R means that XCOPY can overwrite any read-only files in the target location that are left over from an earlier backup. You don't even have to create the REG directory on the E: drive; XCOPY does that for you if it doesn't already exist.

Now, if you want to get a little fancier, you can make sure that any user-specific parts of the Registry also get backed up if you have a system set up for multiple users (see Chapter 10 for a complete treatment of user profiles). Just add the following line to your batch file:

```
XCOPY C:\WINDOWS\PROFILES E:\REG\PROFILES\ /H /Y /R /S
```

The /S at the end tells XCOPY to include all nonempty subdirectories underneath C:\WINDOWS\PROFILES, ensuring that all user-specific versions of USER.DAT get backed up. You don't even have to know the user names; XCOPY copies every user directory under the PROFILES directory.

As icing on the cake, create a desktop shortcut that points to this batch file, so the batch file is easily accessible. Right-click the desktop, choose New⇨ Shortcut, browse to locate the batch file that you created with Notepad, and name the shortcut something like **Back Up Registry**. Then, right-click the new icon, choose Properties, click the Program tab, select Minimized in the Run field drop-down list, and click the Close on Exit check box.

If you really want to be on the safe side, close all your Windows programs before running your Registry backup batch file. A Windows program may possibly be writing to the Registry files at the same moment that your batch file is backing them up, which can cause USER.DAT and SYSTEM.DAT to get out of synch. You can put a few lines at the start of your batch file to remind you of this caution, like this:

```
@ECHO OFF
ECHO Please close all Windows programs before proceeding.
ECHO If you prefer, press Ctrl+C to cancel this backup.
PAUSE
```

Here's how your batch file looks all put together:

```
@ECHO OFF
ECHO Please close all Windows programs before proceeding.
ECHO If you prefer, press Ctrl-C to cancel this backup.
PAUSE
XCOPY C:\WINDOWS\USER.DAT E:\REG\ /H /Y /R
XCOPY C:\WINDOWS\SYSTEM.DAT E:\REG\ /H /Y /R
XCOPY C:\WINDOWS\PROFILES E:\REG\PROFILES\ /H /Y /R /S
```

About the only drawback of this solution is that it doesn't compress your Registry files as it backs them up. Compression is a nice feature of Registry Checker backups, but you can add this feature to your batch file solutions, too. Just lay your hands on a copy of PKWare's famous PKZIP utility (www.pkware.com) and use it instead of XCOPY in your batch file. The secret is that you have to change the Hidden file attribute for PKZIP to be able to see your files.

As an example, the following batch file fragment compresses and backs up the primary Registry to diskette — something that you can't even do with Registry Checker, once the CAB file size exceeds 1.44MB. PKZIP can handle creating a multiple-diskette backup set (with the -& command) whereas SCANREG cannot. Our example creates the file REGBACK.ZIP:

```
ATTRIB -H C:\WINDOWS\USER.DAT
ATTRIB -H C:\WINDOWS\SYSTEM.DAT
PKZIP -A -& A:\REGBACK C:\WINDOWS\USER.DAT
        C:\WINDOWS\SYSTEM.DAT
ATTRIB +H C:\WINDOWS\USER.DAT
```

Backing Up the Registry with Non-Freebie Software

Okay, if you're willing to fork over a little cash in order to get a great Registry backup utility, what are your options?

Norton Utilities rescue disks

Norton Utilities version 3.0 for Windows 95 has a rescue diskette creation program that's far superior to the built-in Windows 98 startup disk feature. The big differences are that the Norton program creates a multiple-diskette set containing some of the Norton recovery utilities, and that the program creates a Registry backup on the hard drive. You can even back up the Registry to a separate disk, if you have a ZIP drive.

Rescue Disk version 3.0 creates the combined file C:\WINDOWS\ REGISTRY.RSC (see Figure 2-10), which basically contains a backup of the active Registry (USER.DAT and SYSTEM.DAT).

If you have Norton Utilities, use its rescue diskette procedure (Start⇨ Programs⇨Norton Utilities⇨Rescue Disk) rather than the Windows 98 startup disk procedure.

Figure 2-10:
The Norton
Utilities
rescue disk
feature
blows the
Windows 98
startup disk
program out
of the
water.

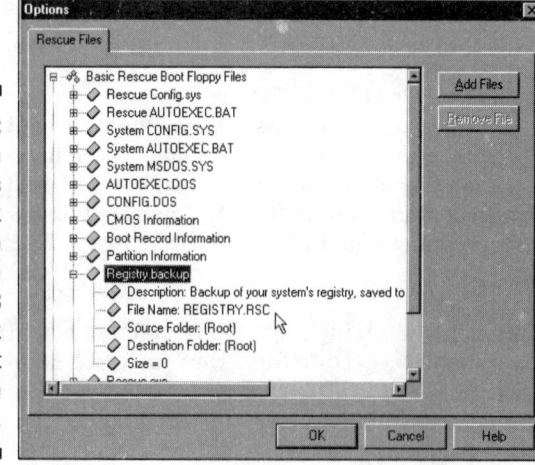

Tell Norton to include the Windows 98 INI files (WIN.INI, SYSTEM.INI, and CONTROL.INI) in your rescue diskette set for a more complete backup. The command for including your Windows 98 INI files is Options⇨Add Files. Use this same command to add C:\WINDOWS\USER.DAT and C:\WINDOWS\ SYSTEM.DAT to the Rescue disk set if you use the ZIP disk option and you want your Registry backed up to a separate device, which we recommend.

Be sure to update Norton Utilities by using Symantec's LiveUpdate feature periodically (we suggest quarterly or monthly).

Norton Registry Editor

We have mixed feelings about the Norton Registry Editor's backup features. (The command for a total backup is File⇨Backup Entire Registry.) This program comes with Norton Utilities 2.0 and subsequent versions, so we're inclined to think highly of it. However, Norton Registry Editor turns out to work just like the REGEDIT export method, except for the fact that it's much slower. In Norton, the export occurs as a background task, so you can continue working while the export occurs; however, the time to complete the backup is much longer. We therefore prefer REGEDIT's export to Norton's.

Norton Registry Editor enables you to back up portions of the Registry by using a nonstandard binary format called *.SRG, or Symantec ReGistry archive. (The command is File⇨Save Symantec Registry Archive.) Why you would want to do this is a little unclear to us. No other program can read these files, and you can easily and accidentally restore the files' contents to the wrong place in the Registry.

Shareware

You can find a variety of shareware Registry backup utilities, including Safety Net, RegBackup, and so on. To be honest, we have yet to find one that works well in all circumstances. For example, Safety Net can back up all DAT files, but if you have multiple copies of USER.DAT beneath your C:\WINDOWS\PROFILES directory, Safety Net doesn't keep them apart for you. It just writes each new USER.DAT over the previous one. That's a problem for systems with multiple user profiles.

General-purpose backup programs

A variety of programs improve on Microsoft Backup for Windows 98. You have to pay for them, but they offer additional features that may sway you into opening your checkbook.

For example, Cheyenne Backup (see Appendix B for contact information) enables you to restore a full backup to a brand-new hard drive by booting to a diskette, so you don't have to reinstall Windows 98 — something that Microsoft Backup 98 can't do.

Also, be sure to check out NovaBACKUP, an up-and-coming backup program that we feature on this book's CD-ROM. NovaBACKUP is a multiplatform, multilanguage program that you can use to back up and restore your files to any disk drive and more than 400 tape drives.

The Bottom Line

Here's a summary of the key points in this important chapter, with our recommendations in italics:

- ✔ Windows 98's Registry Checker makes automatic backups of Registry files, but they only occur at startup once a day, and unless you specify otherwise, they live on the same hard drive as your original files. *Don't rely solely on the automatic behind-the-scenes backup unless you modify it to include user profiles (if used) and to point to a separate device. Make a desktop icon so you can run the backup whenever you want.*

- ✔ There's not much reason to use the Registry backup utilities left over from Windows 95. The Configuration Backup program is fatally flawed, and even its parents have disowned it. *Don't use this method.* The Emergency Recovery Utility is a functional choice as long as: You don't use it to back up to diskette; you have all the files on your PC that ERU thinks you should have; and you don't set up Windows 98 for multiple users. *Use ERU if you must have a single utility that works on both Windows 95 and 98 machines, but look over ERU's shoulder to make sure it works right.*

- ✔ The Windows 98 startup diskette is okay for starting your PC in some situations, but it doesn't contain your entire Registry because it can't make a multiple-diskette set. *Don't use this method to back up your Registry.*

✔ The Registry Editor's export feature is useful for backing up parts of the Registry, and you can restore your backups even if Windows 98 can't start. However, you have no guarantee of being able to restore your Registry exactly as it was before when you use export files. *Use this method for partial Registry backups (selected keys only) but not as your only method for full Registry backups.*

✔ Microsoft Backup 98 can back up your Registry, works with a variety of backup devices (including diskettes), can compress data on the fly, and can perform a post-backup comparison test. *Use this method to save Registry files to a device other than your main hard drive, but make sure the option to save the Registry is checked and include the folder C:\WINDOWS\PROFILES.*

✔ Creating your own batch files works well. This method is convenient, and you can restore your backups even when Windows 98 can't start. Using batch files enables you to back up your complete Registry even if you set up your PC to work with multiple users, and if you combine the PKZIP utility with a batch file, you get compression too. However, creating batch files requires a little up-front work and maybe some expert help. *Use this method if you're familiar with batch file programming or you know someone who is, or if Microsoft Backup 98 doesn't work for you for some reason.*

✔ The rescue diskette method in Norton Utilities 3.0 and newer makes a Registry backup on your hard drive, and can back up the Registry to a ZIP drive if you have one. *Use this method for general system recovery and to protect against total disk failure, but supplement it with another, faster method for daily use.*

✔ Explore shareware Registry backup utilities with caution; most are flawed in one way or another. *Use a shareware or freeware utility only after you research and test it thoroughly.*

✔ Industrial-strength backup programs such as Cheyenne Backup and NovaBACKUP work very well for everything from Registry-only backups to full-disk backups. The big advantage over Microsoft Backup 98 is the ease of restoring an entire C: drive. *Use this method for your regular, full hard drive backups, but consider a simpler method for day-to-day landmark Registry backups.*

We know that this chapter is a little bit complicated, but if you go through it carefully and choose the options that work for your situation, you'll thank us for going into as much detail as we have. Choose a method or a combination of methods that's as easy and convenient as possible, so you'll actually make your Registry backups as often as you should. That, in turn, will let you sleep easier — which is important, considering the journey ahead.

Chapter 3

Editing the Registry without a Registry Editor

* *

In This Chapter

▶ Discovering why the Registry Editor is a risky utility

▶ Getting familiar with the Windows 98 control panels

▶ Using My Computer and Open With to manage file type associations

▶ Uncovering the secret use of the System Policy Editor

* *

Many Windows 98 features allow you to edit the Registry without using the Registry Editor utility, REGEDIT. In this chapter, we introduce you to these features and explain why they're preferable to REGEDIT.

Some books about the Windows Registry focus single-mindedly on the Registry Editor program. We certainly give REGEDIT its due in Chapter 4, and we use it a lot in the chapters that follow (as well as to perform a couple of cool tricks in this chapter). It's the only tool available for making many of the changes you may want to make. However, if the First Rule of the Registry is to save it frequently, the Second Rule is as follows:

> *Never use the Registry Editor unless no safer alternative is available.*

Or, put another way:

> *If you want to hunt butterflies, a butterfly net is better than an elephant gun.*

Whereas every other tool that Windows 98 provides for modifying the Registry has some safeguards (even if they're minimal), the Registry Editor has no safeguards at all. We're all for using the elephant gun when no other tool will do, but fortunately, Windows 98 provides a variety of butterfly nets.

What's So Risky about REGEDIT?

Why is a control panel, for example, safer than REGEDIT? Well, if you take as your starting point that almost nothing is more dangerous than REGEDIT, just about *any* alternative is safer by default. Here's why:

- ✔ **REGEDIT changes occur immediately.** Most programs let you make whatever changes you want without committing them to disk until you choose File⇨Save. But take a look at the REGEDIT menus. No File menu! Changes that you make in REGEDIT head straight for the Registry like a charging rhino as soon as you make them (even though some don't actually take visible effect until Windows 98 restarts). As a result, if you're just horsing around with REGEDIT when the system crashes or experiences a power cut, you may be stuck with a damaged Registry.

- ✔ **REGEDIT offers no undo feature.** Want to reverse yourself and nullify your last change? You'd better have a great memory, because REGEDIT doesn't help you retrace your steps. REGEDIT's lack of an Undo feature can be a major pain. For example, imagine that you accidentally delete the value {25336920-03F9-11cf-8FD0-00AA00686F13}. This is a real Registry value identifying the file MSHTML.DLL, which can display Web graphics within Internet Explorer and in the new Windows 98 HTML Help system. Think you can remember it well enough to correct your mistake? We know *we* can't. There go all those Web page graphics, Windows help screens, and HTML-view folders.

  The Norton Registry Editor that comes with Norton Utilities 2.0 (and newer) for Windows 95 by Symantec *has* an undo feature, and Norton Registry Editor seems to work fine with Windows 98.

- ✔ **REGEDIT offers no warnings.** If you're about to do something that could really damage the Registry, such as delete a whole bunch of essential values, REGEDIT presents the same brief warning message that it presents when you delete a single, trivial value (see Figure 3-1). The program has no built-in warnings to help the user distinguish between minor and major changes.

- ✔ **REGEDIT's help needs some.** The online help for REGEDIT continues to be an embarrassment. For Microsoft to provide such an important utility with practically no information in the help file was surprising in Windows 95, but it's inexcusable when the company has had three years to address the deficiency. (Windows 3.*x* at least shipped with some "read me" files explaining core features of the INI files.) Want to know the purpose of the Registry's six primary branches? The help file doesn't even mention them! In fact, the REGEDIT help file consists of a total of nine little windows' worth of information — equivalent to about two pages of this book.

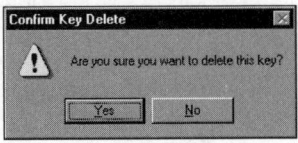

Figure 3-1:
The standard REGEDIT deletion warning.

What's So Safe about Alternatives?

Most of the Windows 98 alternatives to REGEDIT give the user more guidance to warn of certain potentially harmful actions and make complex tasks much easier; these alternatives can often also modify the Windows 98 INI files when necessary.

Extending a helpful hand

As an example, consider the issue of giving a Windows 98 computer a network name. The network name identifies the computer to other computers on a local area network. In the Microsoft naming scheme, a computer name (BarneyFifesPC, DeputyDesk, and so on) may not exceed 15 characters. If you work with the Network control panel, you can receive this advice by clicking the **?** help icon on the control panel's menu bar and pointing-and-clicking on the Computer Name field, as shown in Figure 3-2.

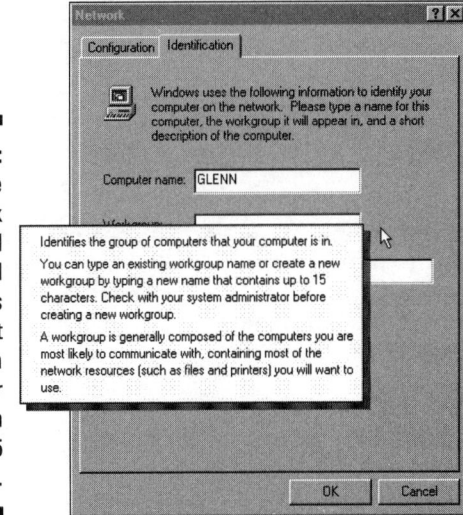

Figure 3-2:
The Network control panel warns against creating a computer name with over 15 characters.

If you use REGEDIT to change a computer name, however, you have no way of finding out that you shouldn't exceed 15 characters. You wouldn't even know there's a problem until someone tries to access the wrongly named computer over the network. The control panel method not only warns you if you use the built-in help feature, it won't even let you key in a name longer than 15 characters. If you're cautious enough to use the control panel, you've got both insecticide and mosquito netting in a jungle full of bugs.

Simplifying complex changes

Some of the chores you need to perform with Windows 98 are mind-numbingly complex if you attempt to perform them by directly editing the Registry. For example, adding new network software to the system can involve dozens of changes to the Registry. Take a look at Figure 3-3, which shows a small subset of all the Registry entries that Windows 98 creates when a user installs the Novell NetWare client software via the Network control panel.

Figure 3-3:
Adding
what
appears to
be a single
software
component
in a control
panel can
add or
change
dozens of
Registry
entries.

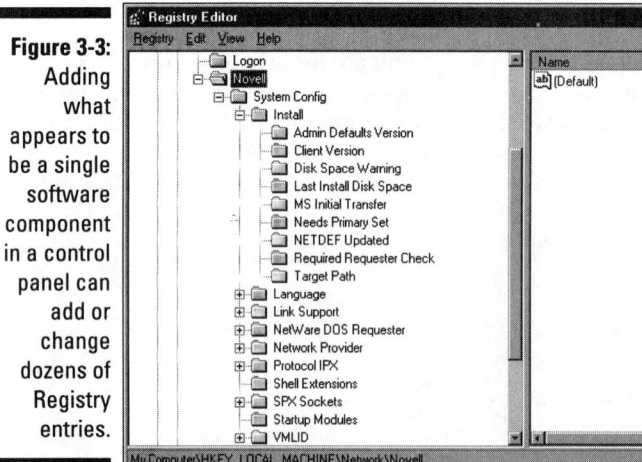

Admittedly, we're giving you an extreme case: Certain control panel settings only change one or two Registry entries. Even in those cases, however, you can make the change using the control panel more easily than you can figure out precisely which Registry entries correspond to the change and precisely what to type into REGEDIT to accomplish it.

Taking care of INI files

Sometimes, Windows 98 settings reside in the Registry and also in one of the INI initialization files, which are holdovers from the Windows 3.*x* world.

Windows 3.*x* programs may look for a given setting in an INI file rather than in the Registry, so keeping the Registry and INI files in synch is necessary for your Windows 3.*x* programs to work happily. If you make a change using REGEDIT, you don't necessarily know whether a corresponding change needs to occur in WIN.INI or SYSTEM.INI. If you make the same change with a control panel, however, Windows 98 knows to update the INI file or files.

See Chapter 1 for more discussion of INI files.

Some Windows 98 settings don't even exist in the Registry. (Heresy!) For example, for some reason that we bet even Bill Gates doesn't understand, the swapfile settings reside in SYSTEM.INI alone. (The *swapfile* is the mechanism that Windows 98 uses to run programs and load data files that don't fit into available Random Access Memory, or RAM.) As long as you use the System control panel to change swapfile settings (see Figure 3-4), you don't have to worry about where Windows 98 stores the data — the control panel knows.

For the curious, the relevant settings are in SYSTEM.INI's [386enh] section. You can view these if you're only able to boot your PC to a command prompt and can't get to the System control panel (which is where you should make any changes under normal circumstances). PagingDrive= specifies the swapfile disk (usually C:), MinPagingFileSize= specifies the minimum swapfile size in kilobytes, and MaxPagingFileSize= specifies the maximum swapfile size, also in kilobytes.

If you have two hard drives and your D: drive is faster than your C: drive, you may want to change the swapfile settings from C: to D:. Also, setting a minimum swapfile size that's at least twice the amount of installed RAM can improve performance. This tip doesn't have anything to do with the Registry, really — we just thought you might like to know.

Figure 3-4:
Some control panel settings don't even modify the Registry, such as these swapfile settings.

In general, we save the nitty-gritty details of Registry settings for situations where you can't change or view a setting more safely or conveniently any other way. For example, we don't tell you exactly which Registry settings get modified when you change the desktop wallpaper, because it's easier and safer to change it in the Display control panel. We figure that you don't want to know the difficult and risky way to do things unless no better option is available.

Having said that, there may be times when you legitimately need to see what effect a control panel (or any other action, for that matter) has on the Registry, or when you're just curious and want to understand more about what the control panels actually do. Chapter 13 presents some tools and techniques for tracking Registry changes (wherever they may come from) and the list of control panels in the next section gives you clues as to which control panels affect which Registry branches.

Control Panels

The Windows 98 control panels are the most common and useful alternatives to the Registry Editor for making changes to the Windows 98 configuration. Most of the control panels modify the Registry; but some also modify various INI files on the disk, too, as with the swapfile settings we discuss in the section, "Taking care of INI files."

Which control panel icons appear depend on which control panel files (they have the suffix .CPL) are present in the C:\WINDOWS\SYSTEM directory. In fact, one way to hide a particular control panel is to remove or rename the associated .CPL file, but take care: Some CPL files, such as MMSYS.CPL, handle more than one control panel icon. A better way to control access to control panels is to use the System Policy Editor, as described in Chapter 9.

We don't go into all the details of every control panel here — that would take a book in itself (and although our editors aren't too keen right now on producing *Windows 98 Control Panels For Dummies*, we suspect it's only a matter of time) — but we do mention the more common control panels. Spend some time, if you haven't already, getting familiar with these control panels, and using their online help features (usually a little **?** on the menu bar that then lets you click on individual settings) so that you get an idea of what the control panels do for you. The goal is to become aware of when you can use a control panel instead of the Registry Editor to make a change to Windows 98.

Primary control panels

The primary control panels are those that appear on just about every Windows 98 PC. You can fire up the control panel main screen by choosing Start⇨Settings⇨Control Panel (see Figure 3-5).

Figure 3-5:
The
Windows 98
main
control
panel
window.

The last column of Table 3-1 tells you the more important part or parts of the Registry that the particular control panel modifies. We explain the structure of the Registry in Chapters 4 and 6, so check those chapters out to figure out what a *Registry key* is and where it lives in the Registry.

Table 3-1	Control Panel Effects on the System and Registry		
Control Panel	*Filename*	*Description*	*Registry Keys Affected*
Add New Hardware	SYSDM.CPL	Activates the Add New Hardware wizard, a series of question-and-answer dialog boxes that guide you through the process of installing a new device (such as a sound card). The wizard modifies the hardware-related Registry settings by reading INF files supplied by the device manufacturer; see Chapter 13 for more on INF files.	*HKLM\Enum, HKLM\hardware, HKLM\System\ CurrentControlSet\ Services\Class*

(continued)

Table 3-1 *(continued)*

Control Panel	Filename	Description	Registry Keys Affected
Add/Remove Programs	APPWIZ.CPL	Enables you to conveniently install and uninstall components of Windows 98 as well as 32-bit Windows 98 applications that supply their own installation and deinstallation programs.	*HKLM\Software* for settings affecting all users, *HKCU\ Software* for settings affecting individual users, *HKLM\Software\ Microsoft\ Windows\ CurrentVersion\ Uninstall* for the deinstallation info
Date/Time	TIMEDATE.CPL	Enables you to set the clock and time zone. Access it quickly by double-clicking the clock on the taskbar.	*HKLM\System\ CurrentControlSet\ Control\ TimeZone Information*
Display	DESK.CPL	Enables you to change screen size, color options, wallpaper, screen saver settings, monitor power saving settings, visual effects, the desktop view (as Web page or not), display acceleration settings, and the desktop color scheme. Varies in appearance on depending the kind of video card the PC has. Easily accessible by right-clicking any empty area of the desktop and choosing Properties.	*HKCC\Display\ Settings, HKCU\ Control Panel\ Desktop, HKCU\ Control Panel\ Colors, HKCU\ Control Panel\ Appearance, HKU* for each user (if user profiles are being used), and several others. Can also modify SYSTEM.INI and WIN.INI

Control Panel	Filename	Description	Registry Keys Affected
Fonts	N/A	Functions a little differently from most other control panels — actually is a shortcut to viewing the directory in Explorer. Opens a window showing all the TrueType fonts installed on the system. You can add or delete TrueType fonts from this window. If you use Adobe Type Manager to provide PostScript fonts, you can't add or delete them from here; you have to use the ATM control panel that Adobe supplies separately.	*HKLM\Software\ Microsoft\ Windows\ CurrentVersion\ Fonts*
Game Controllers	JOY.CPL	Changes joystick settings (usually for computer games).	*HKLM\System\ CurrentControlSet\ control\ MediaResources\ joystick*
Internet	INETCPL.CPL	Sets Internet Explorer options (but not other browser options). A quick way to get to this control panel is to right-click the Internet Explorer icon on the desktop and choose Properties.	*HKCU\Software\ Microsoft\Internet Explorer, HKLM\ Software\ Microsoft\Internet Explorer*
Keyboard	MAIN.CPL	Handles key repeat delay and repeat speed, as well as the text insertion cursor blink rate (don't ask us why that last one is a keyboard setting).	*HKCU\Control Panel\Keyboard*

(continued)

Table 3-1 *(continued)*

Control Panel	Filename	Description	Registry Keys Affected
Modems	MODEM.CPL	Runs the Install New Modem wizard if no modem is set up, or the Modems control panel otherwise. Set modem speeds, dialing properties, and commun- ications options here.	*HKLM\System\ CurrentControlSet\ Services\Class\ Modem, HKLM\ Enum*
Mouse	MAIN.CPL	Enables you to set not only mouse preferences but also cursors (or mouse pointers).	*HKCU\Control Panel\Cursors, HKCC\Display\ Settings,* and (typically) *HKCU\ Control Panel\ Mouse, HKU* for each user (if user profiles are being used)
Multimedia	MMSYS.CPL	Enables you to set audio, video, digitized music, and CD music preferences (for example, whether to play back video clips at original size or full screen).	*HKCU\Software\ Microsoft\ Multimedia, HKCU\ Software\ Microsoft\ Windows\ CurrentVersion\ Multimedia, HKLM\System\ CurrentControlSet\ Control\ MediaResources, HKLM\System\ CurrentControlSet\ Services\Class\ CDROM, HKU* for each user (if user profiles are being used)

Control Panel	Filename	Description	Registry Keys Affected
Network	NETCPL.CPL	Functions as the nerve center for all your network settings, such as which network communications language you want the PC to use. Get here quickly by right-clicking the Network Neighborhood desktop icon and choosing Properties.	*HKLM\Enum\ Network, HKLM\ Network, HKLM\ System\ CurrentControlSet\ Services\Class\Net (and . . .~\NetClient, . . .~\NetService, and . . .~\NetTrans)*
Password	PASSWORD.CPL	Enables you to set up the PC for remote administration (for example with the Remote Registry Editor), set up user profiles so multiple people can use the same PC, and change the Windows logon password.	*HKLM\System\ CurrentControlSet\ Control\ PwdProvider, HKU for each user (if user profiles are being used)*
Power Management	POWERCFG.CPL	This control panel sets the computer's power saving features, such as turning off a hard drive after so many minutes of inactivity.	*HKCU\Control Panel\PowerCfg, HKU for each user (if user profiles are being used)*
Printers	N/A	Opens a special folder called the Printers folder, where you can adjust settings such as resolution, print darkness, and so on. (Functions similarly to the Fonts control panel.)	*HKLM\System\ CurrentControlSet\ Control\Print\ Printers, HKCC\ System\ CurrentControlSet\ Control\Print\ Printers*
Regional Settings	INTL.CPL	Enables you to set location-specific preferences for how Windows 98 displays numbers, currency, and time-and-date information.	*HKCU\ Control Panel\ International*

(continued)

Table 3-1 *(continued)*

Control Panel	Filename	Description	Registry Keys Affected
Sounds	MMSYS.CPL	Enables you to associate sounds (for Windows 98 and certain applications) with particular events, such as minimizing a window or closing a program.	*HKCU\AppEvents, HKU* for each user (if user profiles are being used)
System	SYSDM.CPL	Enables you to tune Windows 98 performance (the Performance tab), run down hardware problems (Device Manager tab), and set up multiple hardware configurations (Hardware Profiles tab).	*HKLM\System\ CurrentControlSet\ Control\FileSystem, HKCC\Config\ Display, HKLM\ Enum,* and *HKLM\Config.* Can also modify SYSTEM.INI
Users	INETCPL.CPL	An alternative user interface for setting up multiple user profiles, duplicating features in the Passwords control panel. See Chapter 10 for more details on this icon.	*HKCU\Software\ Microsoft\ Windows\ CurrentVersion, HKU* for each user

Secondary control panels

We define secondary control panels as those that may or may not appear on a given PC: control panels that pertain to specific applications you may install or that you obtain from other sources (such as the Microsoft Office programs). Here is a list of some common secondary control panels, but many others exist:

- ✔ **32-Bit ODBC** (File: ODBCCP32.CPL): You may see this one if you use Microsoft Access or any other database program that speaks the Structured Query Language (SQL).

- ✔ **Accessibility Options** (File: ACCESS.CPL): Here's a control panel with a variety of helpful desktop modifications for users with disabilities.

- ✔ **Desktop Themes** (File: THEMES.CPL): By installing one or more desktop themes via the Add/Remove Programs wizard (use the Windows Setup tab), you can dress up your desktop with custom setting groups including wallpaper, colors, sounds, screen savers, animated cursors, desktop icons, fonts, and so on.

✔ **Find Fast** (File: FINDFAST.CPL): This control panel comes with Microsoft Office 95 and 97 and is supposed to make opening Office documents faster. It seems to slow down our machines, though, so we usually turn it off.

✔ **Mail and Fax** (File: MLCFG32.CPL): If you have Microsoft Exchange (tucked away on the Windows 98 CD in \TOOLS\OLDWIN95\MESSAGE) or one of its successors, Outlook 97 or Outlook 98, installed on the PC, this control panel lets you set e-mail and related options. You can right-click the Inbox icon on the desktop and choose Properties as a quick way to get to this control panel.

✔ **QuickTime 32** (File: QT32.CPL): Here's where you can set preferences for playing digital movies (*.MOV) that use Apple's QuickTime format.

✔ **Scanners and Cameras** (File: STICPL.CPL): If you have one or more scanners or digital cameras installed, this control panel offers configuration options.

✔ **TweakUI** (File: TWEAKUI.CPL): This control panel is a freebie from Microsoft provided on the Windows 98 CD-ROM, and it also comes with the PowerToys package assembled by Microsoft programmers. TweakUI is so handy that we look at it further in Chapter 10.

Showing your control panel who's bwana

If you're like us, you're always looking for ways to reduce the number of clicks, double-clicks, and keystrokes that common Windows 98 procedures require. One way to save clicks when using the control panels is to put them onto the Start menu in such a way that you can pluck the particular control panel you need from a cascading menu (see Figure 3-6), instead of having to select the icon in the main control panel window and wait for Windows 98 to display the window's pretty (but slow) graphics. Coincidentally, performing this bit of wizardry introduces an important Registry concept: the *Class ID,* which merits further explanation.

You can't just drag-and-drop the Control Panel icon from the My Computer window to the Start menu button and get the cascading effect in Figure 3-6. Instead, you have to create a Start menu item that points to the Windows 98 control panel object with its unique identifier, called a *Class ID* (or `CLSID`, as it appears in the Registry). This identifier needs a word or two of explanation. Every kind of object in a Windows 98 system, including data file types (such as a PowerPoint slide show) and program modules (such as the code that displays and processes dialog box radio buttons), has a special Class ID all to itself. Notice that we say "every *kind* of object" has its own unique identifier, not every *object*. That is, if you create three different PowerPoint slide shows, they don't have three different Class IDs; all three are part of the same "class" and share the same Class ID.

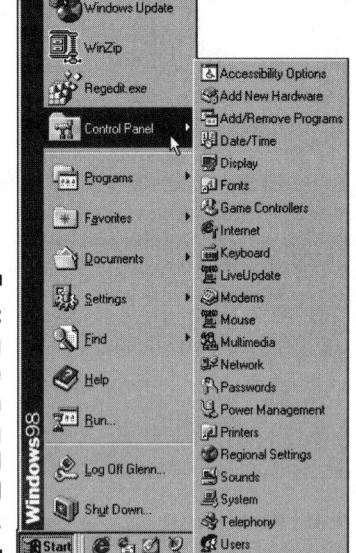

Figure 3-6:
Saving
mouse
clicks with
a cascading
Control
Panel
menu.

First, you have to figure out which Class ID runs the control panel. You won't be modifying the Registry to do this, but it's still a good idea to make a backup before you run REGEDIT (see Chapter 2 for details if you're not sure how to back up the Registry). Once you've made a Registry backup, follow these steps (note that many of them require *right*-clicking):

1. **Choose Start⇨Run, type** REGEDIT **in the Open field, and click OK.**

   The Registry Editor window appears.

2. **Press Ctrl+F to bring up the Find dialog box.**

   Make sure all the checkbox options inside the Look At rectangle are selected. (You don't yet know exactly where you're going to find the control panel Class ID; checking all three boxes tells REGEDIT to look everywhere it can.)

3. **Type** control panel **in the Find what field, and click the Find Next button.**

   In a few seconds, the Registry Editor finds the Class ID for the control panel object. It appears as a long string of seemingly random letters and numbers next to an opened folder in the left window pane (see Figure 3-7). You could jot this long Class ID down on a piece of paper (it's 21EC2020-3AEA-1069-A2DD-08002B30309D), but you might make a mistake, and there's an easier way: copy the Class ID to the invisible Windows Clipboard.

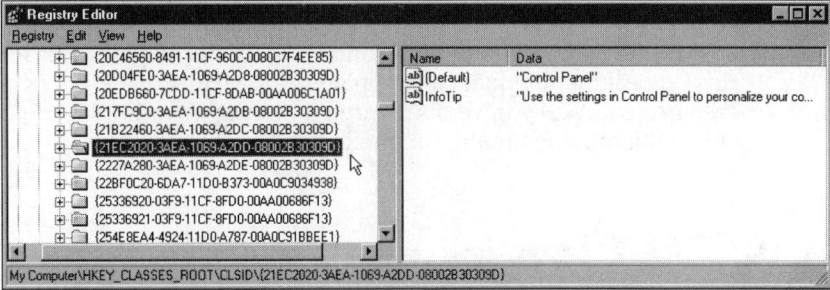

Figure 3-7:
Finding the
control
panel's
class
identifier
using the
Registry
Editor.

4. **Right-click the opened folder in the left window pane.**

5. **Choose Copy Key Name.**

   This action copies the key's name, including the Class ID, to the
   Windows Clipboard. We'll paste it into a folder name in a minute.

6. **Close the Registry Editor by clicking the close box in the upper right
   corner (it looks like an X).**

   Now it's time to create the Control Panel item on the Start menu in
   Steps 7 through 12.

7. **Right-click the Start button and choose Explore.**

   You should see an Explorer window showing the structure of the Start
   menu, and the Start Menu folder should appear highlighted in the left
   window pane.

8. **Choose File⇨New⇨Folder to create the new menu entry for the
   control panel.**

9. **In the highlighted area for the new folder's name, type** Control Panel.
   (including the final period).

10. **With the folder name still highlighted, press Ctrl+V to paste the Class
    ID from the Windows Clipboard into the space right after the period.**

11. **Delete everything to the right of the period, except the Class ID
    number and its enclosing curly braces.**

    Putting the Class ID right after the period in the folder name tells
    Windows 95 to make this new folder work just like the control panel
    object. You can use this little trick with other Class IDs, as we show you
    in other parts of this book.

12. **Close the Explorer window by clicking the close box in the upper-
    right corner.**

You're done! Now, click the Start button to see your new menu, with the Control Panel entry on it. Move the mouse up to highlight Control Panel, hold it there for a second or so, and Windows 98 displays a cascading menu showing each individual control panel. You've just made your control panel easier to use, and you've discovered that every Windows 98 object has a unique identifying number in the Registry.

The SETUP Program

The Windows 98 setup program, SETUP.EXE, is responsible for copying Windows 98 files onto a PC and for building the very first version of the Registry on that PC.

If you're reading this book because you already have a Windows 98 PC and you want to make it work better, what actually happens during setup doesn't concern you a great deal. You probably never plan to run it again, and you shouldn't need to. However, if you're responsible for other Windows 98 PCs, you may be interested to know how you can customize the SETUP program to build a Registry that's more nearly the way you want it from the very start. Chapter 8 provides all the details.

My Computer and Explorer

My Computer, which displays a single-paned window into the computer, is supposedly for "typical" Windows 98 users, while Explorer, which displays a double-paned window, is for "advanced" users. Most Windows 98 users get frustrated with the limitations of My Computer and end up using Explorer. Whichever navigational tool you prefer, you can use it to edit the Registry!

As long as we're discussing Explorer, we should mention a terminology "gotcha" that confuses many Windows 98 uses. The term *Explorer* actually means two entirely different things in Windows 98: the file management program (Start⇨Programs⇨Windows Explorer), and the Windows 98 desktop shell itself. Try this experiment: press Ctrl+Alt+Delete with no programs running. See the entry for Explorer? It's not referring to the file management program, because you're not running it. The Explorer entry refers to the Windows 98 *shell,* or graphical user interface. Now click the entry for Explorer and then click End Task. You should see the "Shut Down Windows" dialog box — exactly what you expect when you shut down the Windows 98 user interface. When you press Ctrl+Alt+Delete with the Windows Explorer file management program running, it typically shows up as "Exploring" rather than "Explorer." Yes, it's confusing, but when you think of how many hundreds of people worked on Windows 98, a little left-hand/right-hand syndrome is probably inevitable.

Deciding not to reinstall Windows 98 to fix your Registry

From the "olden" days of Windows 3.*x* to the present, reinstalling Windows has been a favorite suggestion of technical support staff who can't figure out any other way to fix a given problem. At some point in your experience with Windows 98, you may encounter a technician or Help Desk analyst who tells you to rerun SETUP. Be very cautious before accepting such advice!

When you reinstall Windows 98, depending on the method that you use, SETUP may create a brand new Registry for you from scratch. It's possible that doing so will fix the particular problem you've run into, but the cure may be worse than the disease. If you reformat the hard drive before reinstalling Windows 98 or if you install Windows 98 into a different directory than the one you installed to originally, you zap all the customizations you've made to the Windows 98 desktop. All the Registry entries for application software you've installed also get zapped. You end up having to reinstall all your software and reenter all your software-specific configuration settings.

Yes, you can just reinstall Windows 98 over your existing installation and retain most, if not all, of your application settings. But, because this method leaves some settings

in place, it may not resolve the problem you're facing. For example, if you reinstall Windows 98 because your modem stops working, you could end up with two modems defined in the Control Panel, neither of which work!

We're guessing, based on our extensive experience with Windows 95 and some pretty intensive work with Windows 98, that reinstalling Windows 98 is almost never truly necessary to fix a problem. We've both run Windows 95 computers for more than three years, running an amazing variety of software, without ever having to reinstall the operating system. If a software vendor tech support person (including Microsoft) tells you to rerun SETUP, politely ask to speak to a senior tech support analyst who may be able to give you more specific and less drastic advice. For example, the Registry Checker may be able to conveniently restore your Registry to the last version that worked. For another example, the new System File Checker utility looks for system files and device drivers that show evidence of recent tampering or damage. (Get to this utility by choosing Start⇨Programs⇨ Accessories⇨System Tools⇨System Information, and then choosing System File Checker from the Tools menu.)

Most people don't think of either My Computer or Explorer as making changes to the Registry, but they can, and they're very convenient tools for certain kinds of changes. Open either program and choose View⇨Folder Options, and then click the File Types tab. You should see the screen in Figure 3-8.

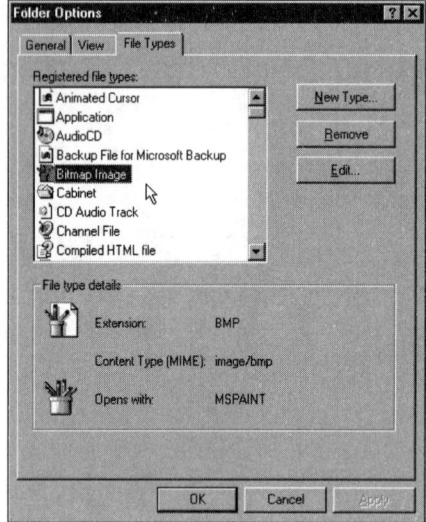

Figure 3-8:
The File
Types tab is
a miniature
Registry
editor for
file type
associations.

Figure 3-8 shows a window into the branch of the Registry that handles file type associations. (See the little line of text that says `Registered file types`, just above the scrolling list? The word *Registered* clues you in to the fact that you're looking into the Registry.) Typically, when you install a new application program, that program registers one or more new file types, and they appear on the list in Figure 3-8 after installation. For example, in Figure 3-8, you can see that the BMP file type associates with the MSPAINT program. When you double-click (or single-click, in the Web view desktop) a file with the suffix .BMP, Windows 98 runs Microsoft Paint — the little graphic editor that comes with Windows 98 as an accessory program.

Don't make any changes to the Registered file types list just yet. Chapter 11 explores (pardon the pun) how you can use this property sheet as a user-friendly Registry editor in order to make the Windows 98 desktop more convenient. For now, we'll just mention that you may want to make a different program run when you double-click on a particular kind of file — or even change the menu that appears when you right-click on that file type. It's much nicer to make such changes here than in REGEDIT.

Opening a Program with Another Application

At some point you may have bumped into the tip that if you hold down the Shift key when right-clicking any highlighted data file in My Computer or Explorer, a new option, Open With, appears on the context menu that pops up. If you select Open With, you see the dialog box in Figure 3-9. You can then scroll through the list of registered program types and choose which one you want to use to open the selected data file.

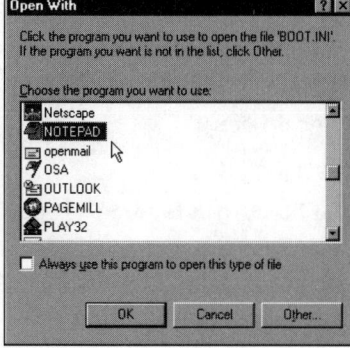

Figure 3-9:
The Open
With dialog
box lets you
open a data
file with any
program.

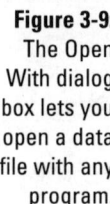

Notice the little check box at the bottom of the scrolling list, with the label `Always use this program to open this type of file`. If you check the box, then from that moment on, any time you double-click a data file with the same suffix as the one you originally right-clicked, the program you've chosen will run the data file.

You've figured it out by now: The Open With dialog box lets you modify the list of file type associations that we looked at in the preceding section. Open With is a miniature Registry editor, too!

System Policy Editor

And now, a bit of information on PC administration, for you network managers and parents with home PCs. The System Policy Editor, POLEDIT.EXE, has two roles in life. Its main job is to create *policy files* that modify the Registry and restrict what users can do on a Windows 98 PC. However, the System Policy Editor can also work as a Registry editor — and a much more user-friendly one than REGEDIT, at that.

Chapter 9 discusses the installation and use of the Policy Editor in detail.

Just to give you a taste for how you can use the System Policy Editor to modify the Registry, here's how you would turn off a user's ability to run REGEDIT on a given Windows 98 PC.

1. **Run the System Policy Editor by choosing Start⇨Programs⇨ Accessories⇨System Tools⇨System Policy Editor.**

   Windows 98 doesn't install the System Policy Editor in a typical installation, so if you don't see it listed, refer to Chapter 9 on how to install it.

2. **Choose File⇨Open Registry.**

   Two icons appear in the System Policy Editor window, corresponding to the two main files of the Registry: USER.DAT and SYSTEM.DAT.

3. **Double-click the icon labeled Local User.**

   The Local User Properties window appears.

4. **Click the + sign to the left of the book icon labeled** Windows 98 System.

   The Windows 98 System book opens, and a new book labeled Restrictions appears underneath it.

5. **Click the + sign to the left of the book icon labeled** Restrictions.

   The screen should now look like Figure 3-10.

6. **Select the Disable Registry Editing Tools check box.**

7. **Click OK in the Local User Properties window.**

8. **Close the System Policy Editor by clicking the close box in the menu bar's upper-right corner.**

9. **Click Yes in the dialog box that asks you if you want to save changes to the Registry.**

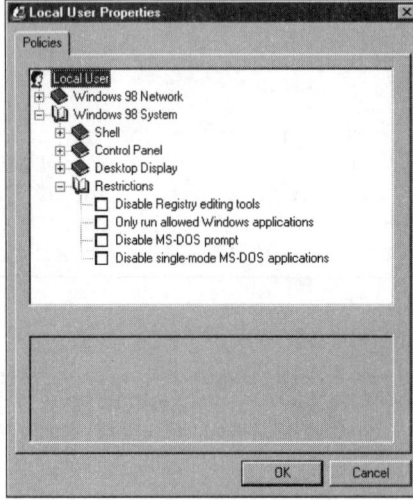

Figure 3-10:
Using the
System
Policy
Editor to
disable
REGEDIT.

Now, try to run the Registry Editor by choosing Start⇨Run and typing **REGEDIT** in the Open field. Access to REGEDIT is now *verboten* for the current user. (Don't forget to change it back if you're experimenting on your own PC and with your own logon name!)

For those of you who are interested, you just changed the Registry entry *HKCU\Software\Microsoft\Windows\CurrentVersion\Policies\System\ DisableRegistryTools*. We explain the structure of the Registry in Chapter 6, if this looks a bit hairy to you right now.

Fortunately, access to the System Policy Editor is not forbidden by the change you just made, so you can run POLEDIT again and change the setting back to its original value. We should also mention in passing that disabling REGEDIT doesn't disable the Norton Registry Editor, if it's present, nor does it prevent users from importing Registry settings indirectly by selecting a REG file. Not exactly ironclad security, but good enough for many situations, and in Chapter 9 we show you how to tighten up policy restrictions so that they're very difficult to sidestep.

Application Software

Last but not least, application software programs modify the Registry, both when installed and when users modify program settings to suit their own preferences. Here are the typical ways users can modify application program settings:

- ✔ **Choosing Tools⇨Options, or View⇨Options from the program's menu bar.**

  Microsoft is not consistent in where it places the Options choice, and other software vendors sometimes choose other locations. You might say the location of the Options command is optional.

- ✔ **Running a wizard.**

  Wizards are little automated programs that lead you step-by-step through a procedure such as setting up an application program's user preferences. Microsoft's Internet Connection Wizard is an example: It runs the first time the user selects the Internet desktop icon.

- ✔ **Modifying an application's private INI file with Notepad.**

  Private INI files are now considered clumsy and passé, but many programs still use them.

- ✔ **Right-clicking the program icon and choosing Properties.**

  This method often produces the same results as selecting Options from within a program menu, as in Microsoft Internet Explorer 4 (where the command is View⇨Internet Options).

An application program doesn't always let you change every setting that you may want to change. For example, Internet Explorer 4 always opens a particular page if a user runs the program without establishing an actual Internet communications link. (The actual page that appears is NAVCANCL.HTM, which you can see in Figure 3-11, but you won't find it in any file listing — Microsoft hid the file away inside the container file SHDOCVW.DLL.) You may prefer a different file to run in this situation — say, a file on a network server that displays helpful information on how the user can create an Internet link. (Or maybe a file that, unlike NAVCANCL.HTM, you can modify without being a C++ programmer!) Changing this setting requires delving into the Registry with REGEDIT. (The precise setting to modify is the value NavigationCanceled in the key *HKLM\Software\ Microsoft\Internet Explorer\AboutURLs*, but if that doesn't mean anything to you, don't worry — we explain it all in Chapters 4 and 6.)

The main point to remember is that if you can make an application setting via a menu option, wizard, INI file, or property sheet, do so. Save your Registry editing for cases that require it, and save your elephant gun for elephants (or, at least, elephant-sized mosquitoes).

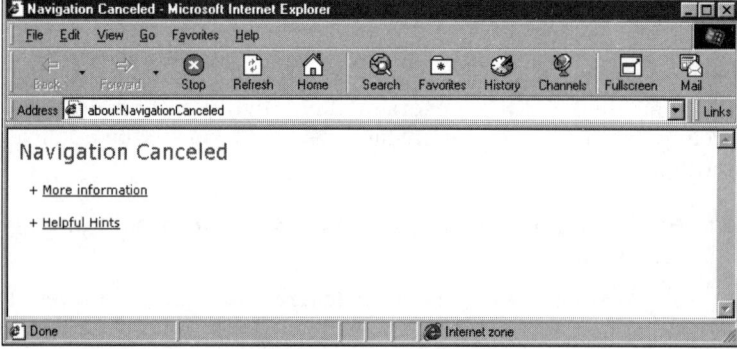

Figure 3-11: You can change the screen that Internet Explorer displays when a link fails.

Chapter 4

Getting Your Gear Together: Registry Editors from Antelope to Zebra

● ●

In This Chapter

▶ Letting REGEDIT know who's boss (you are!)

▶ Editing elegantly with Peter Norton

▶ Adding shareware and freeware to your duffel bag

● ●

Knowing your tools makes working with the Registry safer, easier, faster, and more fun. This chapter lays out the fundamental features of Microsoft REGEDIT, as well as a few other less well-known but valuable tools.

The Windows 98 Registry isn't a simple text file, so you can't use a program like Notepad to view or edit it. Also, the Registry consists of more than one file, so you need a program to bring these files together into a single view. The most common tool for viewing and modifying the Registry is the Registry Editor program that comes with Windows 98: REGEDIT.

Mark Twain once said that Wagner's music isn't as bad as it sounds. In the same vein, REGEDIT isn't as difficult as it looks — the complicated underlying structure of the Registry just makes it *feel* difficult. Think of REGEDIT like a magnifying glass that you use to examine an intricate fingerprint. Understanding the fingerprint's details may take some time, but the magnifying glass itself isn't hard to use.

If you've already learned your way around any modern word processor or spreadsheet program, you'll find, as we did, that REGEDIT is much less complicated and much easier to master than those applications. Getting familiar with the ins and outs of the Registry is worth your while before doing any serious Registry tinkering.

Several safari guide books recommend traveling with at least two cameras, one with a zoom lens and one with a wide-angle lens (and maybe a camcorder, too). Similarly, intrepid Registry-editing readers should probably have more than one tool at their disposal for successful journeys. The software industry has provided a few utilities that make up for REGEDIT's shortcomings, and we've picked out a handful of the better ones. We even include some of these utilities on the CD-ROM that comes with this book, so you can try them on for size.

Cautions and Alerts

Before we get going with REGEDIT, we restate the First and Second Rules of the Registry, which appear in Chapters 1 and 3.

Registry Rule #1

Periodically save a "known good" copy of the Registry where it's out of harm's way.

Before you even think about possibly coming close to running REGEDIT, save your current Registry contents to a cool, dry place. Read Chapter 2, reread it, pick your favorite backup method, and then practice it a couple of times.

Registry Rule #2

Never use the Registry Editor unless no safer alternative is available.

If you haven't read Chapter 3, now is a good time to skim over it at least. To recap briefly here: If you can make a desired system change using a control panel, the Explorer, the System Policy Editor, or a specific application program, do it there — not in the Registry. Reserve REGEDIT for those cases when no other method is available, — because REGEDIT is a risky tool. The Registry Editor makes changes immediately; it doesn't offer an "undo" feature; it doesn't offer much in the way of warnings or cautions; and its built-in help is minimal.

REGEDIT, the Lion

Seeing (or hunting) "The Big Five" is the goal of most safari-goers today. The Big Five are lion, elephant, rhino, buffalo, and leopard. The phrase harks back to earlier hunting safaris; these five animals were considered the most difficult and dangerous to shoot (also the best trophies).

It's hard to say which of the five is the most fearsome, but we can all agree that if you're going to mess around with lions, you'd better either have some experience or an excellent guide. Similarly, if you want to use REGEDIT, take a bit of advice from ol' Glenn and Mark before venturing forth, or this utility will eat you for lunch and use your bones to pick its teeth.

REGEDIT is also lion-like in that it's direct and muscular but (unlike the leopard) somewhat unrefined (ever see a lion eat?). The only way to use REGEDIT successfully is to understand it inside and out. Fortunately, if you spend an hour with REGEDIT and this chapter, you'll get it down cold. Try saying *that* about most computer programs!

We'll just get this point out in the open: REGEDIT has changed in a couple of ways since its introduction with Windows 95. You may be asking, "So what's so different about the Windows 98 version of the Registry Editor?" We're glad you asked.

The Windows 98 version of REGEDIT is darn near identical to the Windows 95 OSR2 version, but it's improved in a couple of ways from the Windows 95 OSR1 version. For all the nitty-gritty on the development of Windows 95, check out the sidebar "A (very) short history."

The song remains the same

The burning question on every new Windows 98 user's mind is: Where's the theme song? Microsoft publicized the Windows 95 Start button with the Rolling Stones song "Start Me Up," which dominated the airwaves. Well, we've been wanting Microsoft to put a Stop button on the Taskbar for years now (it still bothers us that you have to shut down Windows 98 by hitting Start first). If the company had done so in Windows 98, it could have hired Diana Ross to do "Stop, in the Name of Love." This would have been a great public relations move and increased sales of Windows 98 up into Viagra territory. Or, Microsoft could have held the product for six months and hired Prince (or "#$%" or whatever) to sing "1999."

Alas, Windows 98 has no theme song. The computer industry still lags far behind the car and beer industries when it comes to cheesy, fun, self-promotion. Witness Intel deciding that a bunch of workers dancing awkwardly in hermetically sealed semiconductor-plant suits would lead consumers to rush out and buy more Pentium PCs ("Forget the kid's shoes, Mavis, we need another PC with Intel Inside!"). Now, if they'd hired the Riverdance troupe to stomp slide rules in half with their heels and toss the pieces gaily into the air. . . .

A (very) short history

Microsoft released two major versions of Windows 95, the original version (referred to generally as OEM Service Release 1, or OSR1) and a new, improved version called OSR2. (OEM stands for Original Equipment Manufacturer — that is, a PC maker.) You can check to see which Windows 95 version you have by choosing Start⇨Settings⇨Control Panel, double-clicking the System icon, and looking at the line right underneath *Microsoft Windows 95*, toward the upper-right corner of the General property tab (see Figure).

✔ If the version number is 4.00.950 or 4.00.950a, it's OSR1. (The "a" just means that the PC includes a bug-fix service pack from Microsoft.)

✔ If the version number is 4.00.950B or 4.00.950C, it's OSR2. (The "C" version inserts Internet Explorer 4 as part of the installation program.) OSR2 appeared in late 1996 and shipped only with new PCs, never as a retail product. It includes a more efficient file system and about two dozen other new features and enhancements.

The version of REGEDIT that Microsoft ships with Windows 95 OSR2 is different from the version that the company provided with OSR1. Specifically, with the newer version:

✔ The Edit menu has an extra command, Copy Key Name, which also appears when you right-click a Registry key (we define "key" in a minute, but it looks like a folder).

✔ Running REGEDIT from a DOS prompt permits you to delete a key by typing **REGEDIT /D**.

✔ REGEDIT can handle a larger Registry without crashing when run from a DOS prompt, for example when you try to import the Registry with REGEDIT /C.

If you had only one Windows 95 PC running the OSR1 version of Windows 95, you couldn't get the new REGEDIT — unless you're rich and could just go out and buy a new computer. The Windows 98 upgrade is the only way for an OSR1 user who doesn't need a new PC to get the better version of REGEDIT. Granted, the three bullet items in the preceding list don't seem earth-shattering, and the first two certainly aren't. However, the third bullet item can be an extremely important one if you ever get into trouble and have to restore your Registry from the command prompt, as Chapter 16 discusses in detail.

The long answer is that Windows 98 has some appearance changes, particularly with its help system. The help system (Help⇨Help Topics) uses the Windows 98 "HTML Help" engine, which presents help subjects in a window that uses some of the same code that Internet Explorer uses to display World Wide Web documents in a browser window. The actual help topics seem to have stayed the same. Aside from that cosmetic change, the Windows 98 REGEDIT is a lot faster, a little safer, and (unfortunately) still bothered by the warts of its predecessor.

A lot faster

The Windows 98 Registry Editor seems to work much more quickly than its predecessor, once you turn off the annoying smooth scrolling feature (see the section later in this chapter titled "Animation is for cartoons"). We notice it most in Find operations when we're looking for a particular Registry entry. When you consider that the Windows 98 Registry is considerably larger than that of Windows 95, the speed increase is that much more laudable.

A little safer

We've noticed one very welcome improvement in REGEDIT safety. With Windows 95, a user double-clicking on a REG file (which contains Registry changes) automatically merges the changes in the REG file with the current Registry. Many times, this behavior creates problems when users accidentally put stuff into their Registry that they don't really want, such as settings that pertain to an earlier version of a program that's since been updated. You can foul up an application pretty thoroughly that way.

However, you can't fault a user for doing this; 99.9 percent of the time, double-clicking a data file simply opens it in its associated program, and doesn't actually write anything to disk. It's really not fair to the user to make REG files act differently than DOC or TXT or XLS files, and we consider the Windows 95 REG file behavior to be a significant bug.

Happily, Microsoft fixed this problem in Windows 98. Now, when you double-click (or, in the Web view of the desktop, single-click) a REG file, you see the warning message in Figure 4-1. It's not much, but it's enough to suggest to most users that they're about to do more than simply open a data file, and that they should cancel the operation if they're not sure about it.

Figure 4-1:
A new
warning
makes life
in the bush
a tad safer.

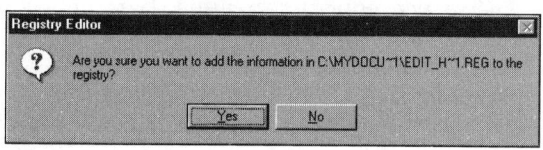

Inherits the warts

Alas, the Windows 98 Registry Editor still has most of the problems we discuss in Chapter 3:

✔ REGEDIT changes occur immediately.

✔ There's no "undo" feature.

✔ You don't get any special warnings when you're about to modify an important part of the Registry.

✔ REGEDIT's built-in help is abysmal.

We wish Microsoft had put more time into improving REGEDIT and less time into user interface window-dressing (that's a pun, son), but the sizzle often sells more than the steak. At least REGEDIT hasn't changed so drastically that we have to learn a whole new set of problems. Better the devil you know than the devil you don't know.

REGEDIT à la mode, part 1: Getting GUI

You can run the Registry Editor program from Windows 98 *(protected mode)* or from DOS *(real mode).* You normally run REGEDIT in protected mode, which is a lot easier because of the graphical user interface (or GUI, pronounced *gooey).*

Adding REGEDIT to your desktop

Windows 98 doesn't put an icon for REGEDIT on your desktop or your Start menu after a typical installation, but it does copy the file REGEDIT.EXE to the C:\WINDOWS directory (or whatever you name your Windows 98 directory). You can start the program by choosing Start⇨Run, typing **REGEDIT**, and clicking OK.

If you plan to spend a fair amount of time with REGEDIT, which we're guessing is true or you wouldn't have dropped a few bucks on this book, you probably don't want to use the Start⇨Run⇨REGEDIT⇨OK method several zillion times. You can create a desktop icon for REGEDIT by right-clicking the desktop, choosing New⇨Shortcut, typing **REGEDIT** on the Command line field, clicking Next, and typing whatever label you like in the Select a Name for the Shortcut field. (The procedure for creating shortcuts actually takes *more* keystrokes and mouse clicks in Windows 98 than it did in Windows 95!)

If you'd rather bury the command a little deeper, so that other people who may use your PC aren't easily tempted to run REGEDIT, you can put the program on your Start menu along with other system tools. Here's the procedure:

1. **Right-click the Start menu button and choose Explore.**

2. **Click the + to the left of the Start Menu Programs folder in the left window pane to expand it.**

3. Click the + to the left of the **Programs** folder in the left window pane to expand it.

4. Click the + to the left of the **Accessories** folder in the left window pane to expand it.

5. Click the **System Tools** folder in the left window pane.

6. Choose **File**⇨**New**⇨**Shortcut** to create the new menu entry for REGEDIT.

7. Type C:\WINDOWS\REGEDIT.EXE in the **Command Line** field of the **Create Shortcut** dialog box. (If Windows 98 resides in a directory other than WINDOWS, substitute the correct directory name.)

8. Click the **Next** button and type Registry Editor in the **Select a Name for the Shortcut** field in the **Select a Title for the Program** dialog box.

9. Click the **Finish** button and close the Explorer window by clicking the close box in the upper-right corner.

   You can now run REGEDIT by clicking Start⇨Programs⇨Accessories⇨ System Tools⇨Registry Editor.

Of course, you can modify the precise placement of the Registry Editor menu listing so that it appears wherever you want. Windows 98 makes doing so very easy: Just navigate through the menus to the Registry Editor item, and click-and-drag the item to whatever menu and position you desire. The ease of reconfiguring the Start menu in this way is one of the best improvements that Windows 98 brings to the user interface.

Hiding REGEDIT from city slickers

If you're in charge of a bunch of Windows 98 PCs, put this book down right away and run from machine to machine deleting REGEDIT.EXE. Leaving this program where novice users can get to it is an invitation to trouble. Carry your copy around on diskette or put it up onto a network directory that only you and your fellow administrators can use. Just know that you may need to reinstate REGEDIT, if only temporarily, during software application installations so that the install routines can process the Registry changes they require.

If you really want to leave REGEDIT on the hard disk, you may also consider relocating it so that it resides in a hidden directory, such as C:\WINDOWS\SYSBCKUP. If you set the computer so that hidden files stay hidden (that's the Windows 98 default setting; you can check it by opening My Computer and choosing **View**⇨Folder **Options**⇨View), it's less likely that anyone will stumble upon the program by accident.

Another choice for hiding REGEDIT is to use system policies to restrict the user's ability to run REGEDIT. Chapter 3 gives you the detailed procedure under the heading "System Policy Editor."

King of pane: Anatomy of the REGEDIT window

Figure 4-2 shows the REGEDIT window, which has many of the usual Windows program features: a *menu bar* at the top, a *status bar* at the bottom (which shows the full Registry path of the currently active selection), and *scroll bars* to help you navigate up, down, and side to side. The REGEDIT window has two panes: the *key pane* to the left presents an Explorer-like hierarchical view of the Registry database, and the *value pane* to the right shows the contents of whatever key you highlight in the key pane. (*Key pane* and *value pane* are our terms, not Microsoft terms. Other writers use different terms; key pane and value pane make the most sense to us.) You can use the Tab key to jump quickly between the key pane and the value pane.

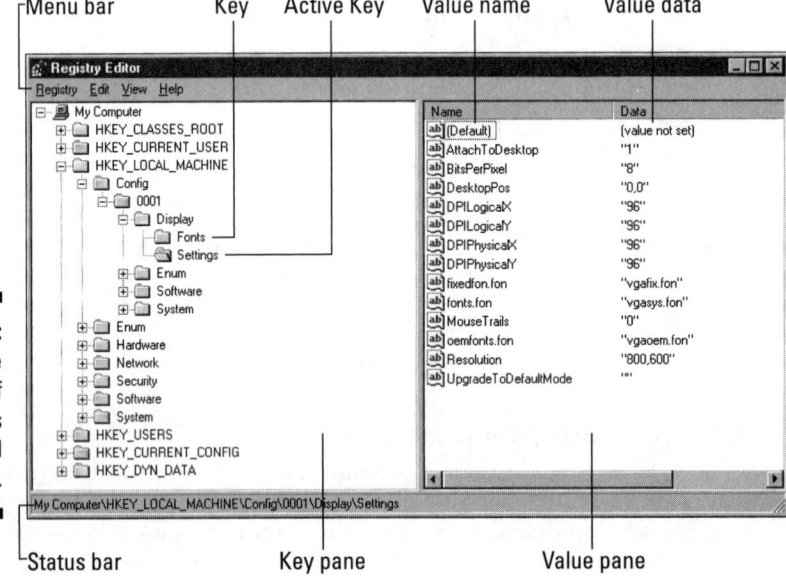

Figure 4-2:
The
anatomy of
REGEDIT's
graphical
mode.

Each folder icon in the key pane represents a Registry *key,* which is a location for storing data. (A key isn't the same as a folder in Explorer, although the icon is the same.) Many keys (the ones with + signs to their left) contain other keys, which can be called *subkeys* — much the same way directories on your hard disk may be called subdirectories if they reside inside another directory. Keys and their contents are limited to 64K in Windows 95, but that restriction no longer applies in Windows 98.

You can expand the tree-like structure of the key pane by clicking the + sign to the left of any key that has one or more subkeys, and you can collapse the structure by clicking the   sign. Or, if you prefer, you can expand and collapse the structure by double-clicking the folder icon itself (it's a bigger target!). You can even right-click the folder icon and choose Expand or

Contract from the context menu. If you have good hand-to-mouse coordination, clicking the + and   symbols is your fastest method.

The active (selected) key in the key pane displays an open-folder icon, while all the other keys display closed-folder icons. The key contents, called *values,* appear in the value pane to the right; every value has both a *name* field (such as "FileLocation"), which identifies the value, and a *data* field, which contains the value's setting (such as "C:\WINDOWS"). Every key contains at least one value, named *Default,* which (if empty) shows the message `value not set` in the data field; but a key can contain a whole bunch of values, and many do. These values have three types: *string, binary,* and *DWORD.* We explain these value types more fully in Chapter 6, but for now just know that the string type (indicated by a tiny icon in the value pane's Name column containing the letters *ab*) is usually for text, and the binary and DWORD types (indicated by a tiny icon containing some 1s and 0s) are usually for numeric information. Demonically, string values can contain numbers, but you can almost always tell a string value because it appears enclosed in double quotes.

Note: Key names aren't unique in the Registry, and the same key name may crop up in several different places. So, when we describe a particular key in this book, we usually give its complete location, such as *HKCR\Drive* or *HKLM\Software\Classes\Drive.* In these examples, we use abbreviations for the *branches,* or top-level keys: for example, *HKCR* is short for *HKey_Classes_Root.* Chapter 6 discusses these primary keys in more detail.

The menu bar in REGEDIT has four menus, but only two of these menus are worth checking out:

- ✔ **The Registry menu** enables you to print, import, and export Registry data from and to text files, and connect to a remote user's Registry (see the "Where's the remote?" section later in this chapter).

- ✔ **The Edit menu** lets you create, delete, rename, and hunt for keys (in the left window pane) or values (in the right pane). You can also copy a key name to the clipboard, which comes in handy from time to time — as when you're searching for complex or long key or value names.

Sometimes you don't want to copy an entire key name, with the full Registry path specification (that is, all the upper-level keys); you want to copy just the name of the currently selected key. Here's an alternative to the Copy Key Name command that lets you do just that. Right-click a key, choose Rename, and use the standard Windows Ctrl+C command to copy the key name. Then, press Esc so you don't actually rename the key, and use Ctrl+V to paste the name somewhere else. (Microsoft chose Ctrl+V because Ctrl+P is already taken: It usually means *print.*) To copy a value's data field, double-click the value name and then hit Ctrl+C to copy the data field.

Two menus in REGEDIT are barely worth a glance:

✔ **The View menu** lets you turn the status bar on or off (why you'd ever want it off is a mystery to us), move the split bar separating the two panes (which you can do much more easily with the mouse), and refresh the display (which just re-sorts the current window contents alphabetically and updates the window to show any changes that Windows 98 or a Windows 98 program may have made since you originally selected the key). You can refresh the display more easily by pressing F5. In other words, if you use a mouse, forget about the View menu.

✔ **The Help menu** provides, alas, very little. Go ahead and take five minutes to read the help screens at least once through; then you can forget about this menu, too.

Sometimes, REGEDIT "grays out" a menu option if it isn't available for the selected item. For example, you can't delete or rename any of the six main Registry keys. (Good thing, too — you'd crash the whole system.)

Changing stuff

Most of the changes you make to the Registry involve modifying a value that already exists. REGEDIT makes this job pretty simple. The basic method is to hunt around in the left window pane (the key pane) until you find the key containing the value you need to change. (If you don't know exactly where that key is, see "Finding" later in this section.) Make a particular key active by clicking it. Then, change the value in the right window pane (the value pane) by using one of the following three methods:

✔ Double-click the value name (fastest method).

✔ Right-click the value name and select Modify (slower method).

✔ Click the value name and choose Edit⇨Modify from the menu bar (slowest method).

Which dialog box appears next depends on the type of value you selected. The Edit String, Edit Binary Value, and Edit DWORD Value dialog boxes you work with are shown in Figure 4-3. Chapter 6 describes the number format for binary and DWORD values. Make whatever change is necessary in the Value Data field and click OK. You may notice that in each case the Value Name field is grayed out, meaning that you can't change the information in this field. (Go ahead, try. We dare you.) The reason you can't change this info is that, while you may have a legitimate reason to change a value's *data,* you're less likely to need to change a value's *name,* and doing so runs the risk that Windows 98 or an application program can't find your renamed value. If you're really certain that you need to rename a value, right-click the value name in REGEDIT's value pane, and choose Rename. Legal characters are A through Z, 0 through 9, space, and underscore.

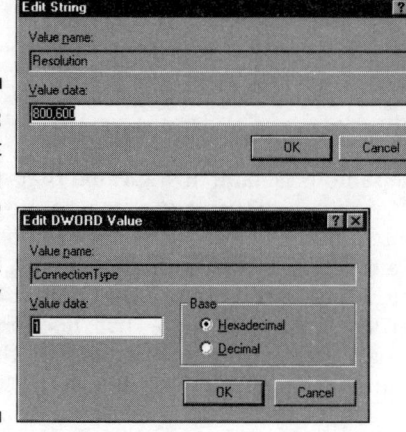

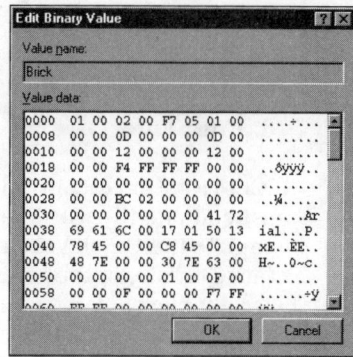

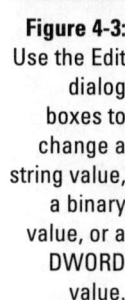

Figure 4-3:
Use the Edit dialog boxes to change a string value, a binary value, or a DWORD value.

If you need to change a value's type, for example from binary to string, REGEDIT doesn't offer a command to do so. You have to delete the existing value and create a new one with the same name. This situation doesn't come up often, but we've occasionally created new values that use the incorrect type. For example, sometimes using a binary value when a DWORD value is required means that the Registry setting just won't work.

When changing a string value, don't put double quotes around it, even though you saw quotes when you looked at the value before you double-clicked it. REGEDIT puts the double quotes around string values automatically.

Sometimes a key appears in more than one place, as we describe in Chapter 6. If you've set up *user profiles,* that is, multiple user accounts on the same Windows 98 PC, changing a setting for the current user doesn't change that setting for all other users. Chapter 10 explains user profiles in detail.

Adding keys and values

You can add two things to the Registry: a key or a value. Adding a key is simpler than adding a value. You can add a new key in a few different ways, but the way that makes the most sense to us is to follow these general steps:

1. In the key pane (on the left), right-click the key that you want the new key to appear beneath, hierarchically.

For example, if you have the Windows 98 Quick View accessory (you can install it from the Add/Remove Programs control panel's Windows Setup tab), here's a tip that adds a Quick View command to the right-click menu of the REG file type (see "Exporting and importing" later in this chapter for more on REG files). Find *HKCR\regfile* and right-click it.

2. **Choose** <u>New</u>⇨<u>K</u>**ey from the context menu and type in the key name over the** New Key #1 **text.**

   In our example, the new key name you type is **Quickview**.

3. **Press Enter.**

REGEDIT automatically adds the famous Default string value that every key must contain; the word Default appears in the value pane, to the right. To complete the Quick View example, double-click the Default value name, type * (an asterisk) in the Value Data field, click OK, and close REGEDIT. Now you can right-click any file with the REG suffix and choose Quick View from the context menu to safely view the file's contents. (Note that the purpose of the Default value for any given Registry key varies depending on the context; sometimes it's not used at all, but the unwritten rules of the Registry state that it must be present.)

(If you want an alternative method to add a new key, you can single-click the key under which you want the new key to appear, and use the menu bar to choose <u>E</u>dit⇨<u>N</u>ew⇨<u>K</u>ey.)

Adding a value to a key is almost as easy as adding a new key; you just have to know a little more information ahead of time. In addition to the value name, you need to be able to specify what type the value should be (string, binary, or DWORD) and what data it should contain. Follow these steps to add a value to a key:

1. **In the key pane, highlight the key in which you want to add the value.**

   For example, if you want to hide a particular file type so that it doesn't show up in My Computer's <u>V</u>iew⇨Folder <u>O</u>ptions⇨File Types list, you can do so by adding a Registry value. Hide the REG file type (Registration entries) by first highlighting the key *HKCR\regfile*.

2. **In the value pane, right-click anywhere within the pane except on an occupied entry in the Name column.**

3. **Choose New⇨<u>S</u>tring Value, New⇨<u>B</u>inary Value, or New⇨<u>D</u>WORD Value from the context menu.**

   Choose Binary Value for this example.

4. **Type in the value name over the** New Value #1 **text and press Enter.**

   For our example, type **Editflags**. This is a special value that controls what actions you can perform from the File Type list.

5. **Press Enter again.**

   The Edit String, Edit Binary Value, or Edit DWORD Value dialog box appears, depending on the value type you're editing.

6. Type the value data in the <u>V</u>alue Data field, and then click OK.

To complete our example, type the hexadecimal values 01 00 00 00. After you close REGEDIT, open the File Types list; `Registration entries` no longer shows up, which is handy if you don't want a user to be able to change how REG files behave. You usually add a Registry value at the direction of a tech support person, a tech note, a book like this one, or some other source, so you can expect some guidance as to what value type and data to enter.

Adding keys and values to the Registry isn't as common as modifying keys and values that already exist, but you will perform these tasks occasionally. Sometimes you add keys and values for your own purposes, without affecting Windows 98 or application programs (see Chapter 18, under "Annotate the Registry"). Other times, as in the examples in this section, you may have to be careful that whatever keys and values you add meet the formatting requirements that Windows 98 or an application expects (see also Chapter 11, "Opening unknown file types"). As always, back up the Registry before you add new entries to it.

Deleting keys and values

Destroying is usually easier than creating, and REGEDIT is no exception. To delete pretty much anything — a key (as long as it's not one of the six main ones), or a value of any type — just display it, right-click it, and choose Delete. (Left-clicking the key or value and hitting the Delete key may be faster, although some people prefer the mouse-only method.) You have to answer Yes in the ensuing dialog box to complete the deletion, so you always have an out if you choose Delete by accident or in haste.

Good thing you have an out, because after you delete something in REGEDIT, you don't have an easy way to get it back. (Chapter 15 gives you a fairly painstaking method that you can use in a pinch.) If you use Norton Registry Editor, you get a nifty Undo command, but REGEDIT doesn't have one. Contrary to what *some* books say, rebooting Windows 98 in Safe Mode does *not* restore the Registry's previous settings.

When you delete a key in the Registry, you also delete every value in that key and every subkey underneath that key. Deleting a key is like sawing a big branch off a tree: In doing so, you also remove every smaller branch that grows from the big branch, and every leaf on all those smaller branches.

Before you delete a Registry key or value, save it by using REGEDIT's Export Registry File command (see the section later in this chapter called "Exporting and importing"). You may even want to designate a special directory on your hard drive (C:\TEMPREG or something similar) for these exports. If everything works fine for a few days after you delete the key or value, you can then delete the export file from your hard disk.

If you want to delete several values in a particular key, you can select a bunch of adjacent keys by clicking the first one, holding down the Shift key, and clicking the last. If you want to delete several nonadjacent values, hold down the Ctrl key and click each value that you want to delete. Then right-click any highlighted value and choose Delete from the context menu that appears.

Finding

Many times, especially when you're just getting familiar with the lay of the Registry land, you may know what a key is called or what a value name is, but you don't know precisely where something lives within the maze-like Registry structure. REGEDIT's Find command, limited though it is, comes in mighty handy in such situations.

Fire up the Find command by choosing Edit⇨Find from the menu or pressing Ctrl+F. However you get there, REGEDIT displays the Find dialog box shown in Figure 4-4.

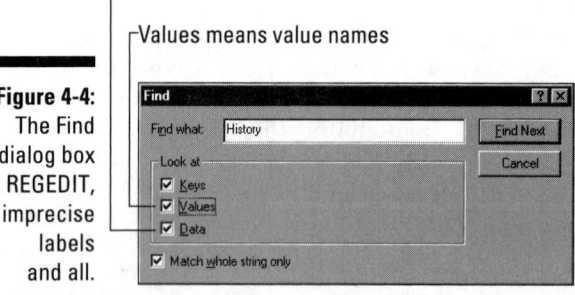

Data means value data

Values means value names

Figure 4-4: The Find dialog box in REGEDIT, imprecise labels and all.

You can type in the value you're looking for in the Find What field and tell REGEDIT where to look by checking the appropriate check boxes in the Look at area. Microsoft isn't precise with its wording here: The Keys check box is self-explanatory and correct, but the Values check box really means *value names* (the left column in the value pane), and the Data check box really means *value data* (the right column in the value pane).

If you know whether the data you're searching for resides in a key name, value name, or value data field, you can uncheck the other two boxes to speed your search a little, but we rarely recommend doing so — the speed difference isn't huge, and there's a chance you'll miss a relevant setting. If you want to find a string fragment and you're not sure you know the entire string, make sure that the check box labeled Match Whole String Only is unchecked.

Click the Find Next button to start your hunt. When REGEDIT locates a match, it highlights the appropriate entry in both the key and value panes. If you suspect that you'll have multiple matches, hit F3 (the "find next" key) to resume the search. When REGEDIT can't find any more matches, or if it didn't find any in the first place, it displays a dialog box saying: Finished searching through the Registry. (Yes, it *would* be nice if REGEDIT said "No matches found" if that's the case, but the program is an uncommunicative sonofagun.)

Neither REGEDIT nor Norton Registry Editor can find data in DWORD or binary values; they can only find data in key or string values. If you want to search for DWORD or binary values, export the key that you think contains the values (see "Exporting and importing" later in this section) and use your favorite word processor's Find command.

The Find command always starts with the currently selected key or value and works downward. So, if you've been bouncing about the Registry and you select something other than the My Computer icon that sits atop the six main Registry branches in the key pane, then you're not going to be searching the entire Registry when you press Ctrl+F. (The search operation never "wraps around" to the top of the document, as the Find command in a decent word-processing program does.) So, always click the My Computer icon before initiating a Registry search. It's a pain, but you get used to it. Or, use a better utility, such as Norton Registry Editor (which we discuss later in this chapter), which searches the entire Registry regardless of which key is highlighted.

Printing

You may think that the best way to print all or part of the Registry is to choose REGEDIT's Registry⇨Print option (or press the shortcut, Ctrl+P). The naked truth is that this command is fine for a quick-and-dirty printing of little chunks of the Registry, but that's about it. Here's the procedure for this quick-and-dirty method:

1. **In the key pane, navigate to the key you want to print and then click it. The folder icon opens.**

2. **Choose Registry⇨Print to bring up the dialog box in Figure 4-5.**

3. **Choose the printer you want in the Name field, and click the Selected branch radio button in the Print Range area.**

4. **Click OK, and fetch your hard copy.**

REGEDIT doesn't go in for niceties of appearance such as margin settings or other output formatting options. If you want to print a serious chunk (a big key or, if you've lost your mind, the whole Registry, which can require several hundred pages), export the desired chunk to a text file, as described in the next section. You can then pull that text file into a bona fide word-processing program, where you can play with the page margins, font style, font size, and so on, before you actually print. You can also delete chunks that you don't want to print, saving the jungle's trees and speeding print time.

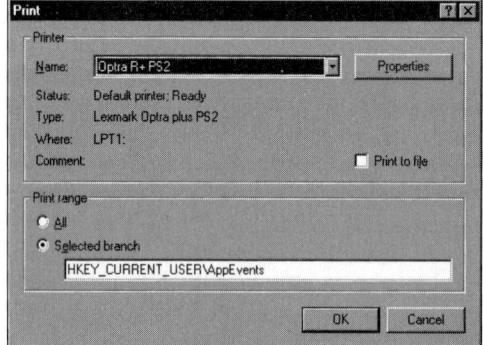

Figure 4-5:
REGEDIT's
Print
dialog box,
suitable
for short
printouts
only.

Exporting and importing

Exporting and importing is the last subject we touch on in this overview of REGEDIT's graphical *modus operandi*. Exporting and importing have very specific meanings in the context of the Registry, and you'll use these commands often if you read very much of this book.

Exporting a Registry key (or the whole Registry, for that matter) creates a text file on disk with the suffix .REG. The text file contains the contents of the specified key, plus any subkeys under that key, plus all the associated values contained in those keys. (The original information stays in the Registry.) You can view an exported REG file in any text editor (Notepad, for example) or word processor. You can also double-click a REG file in order to merge its contents into the current Registry, so exporting is a popular way of backing up a particular key before making changes to it. However, exporting the entire Registry can take a pretty long time, so this method isn't the most convenient way to back up your whole Registry database.

The procedure for exporting a Registry key is simple, although not quite as elegant as we might like:

1. In the key pane, click the key you want to export to make it active, and choose Registry⇨Export Registry File.

It would be slicker if you could just right-click the key and export it from the context menu, but that's an enhancement that you need Norton Registry Editor to enjoy. The Export Registry File dialog box appears, as shown in Figure 4-6.

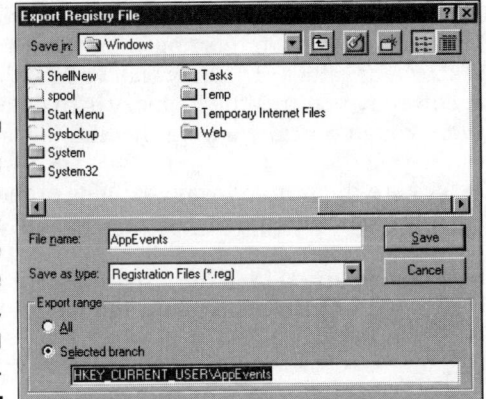

Figure 4-6:
You can export a key, or the entire Registry, using REGEDIT.

2. **Give your export file a destination in the Save In field.**

3. **Give your export file a name in the File Name field.**

   You don't need to specify the REG suffix. If you avoid spaces in both the path and filename and keep the main filename to eight characters or less, you'll have an easier time of it when using REG files at the DOS command prompt.

4. **Check that the Selected Branch radio button is selected in the Export Range area. (Click the All radio button in this box if you want to export the whole Registry.)**

5. **Click the Save button.**

Importing from a REG file is a similar process. Choose Registry➪Import Registry File from the menu bar and specify the REG file that you want to import in the Import Registry File dialog box. Alternatively, you can open Windows Explorer, find the REG file, and double-click it — or right-click the file and choose Merge from the context menu.

Importing a REG file can create new Registry entries and modify existing ones. REGEDIT doesn't warn you if the REG file you're importing is about to overwrite existing values. *Always* back up the Registry before importing a REG file.

Here's a *gotcha* that caught us with our virtual pants down when we were first getting to know Windows 95, and the situation is unchanged in Windows 98. Importing a REG file works flawlessly as long as you're adding values to the current Registry or changing existing values. The problem comes up when you want to import a REG file with *less* information: Importing a REG file doesn't delete existing keys or values. Suppose, for example, that you export your Registry to a REG file because you want to add some keys and values that you think will have a given effect. When you find out that the files don't have the desired effect, importing your old REG file *doesn't* remove the bogus keys and values. The only way you can be sure that the Import operation correctly restores the Registry is to delete the keys from the Registry *before* you import them from the REG file.

After you realize that REG files are the primary way that new programs add keys and values to the Registry, you can appreciate the good sense of this arrangement. You don't want new programs to be able to accidentally trash Registry entries created (and relied upon) by other programs. We take a closer look at REG files and their cousins, the INF files, in Chapter 8.

Animation is for cartoons

You can't customize REGEDIT much at all, but here's one tip for making the program more responsive to the touch. Microsoft has taken the "zooming windows" concept from Windows 95 to an even-more-annoying level in Windows 98. Not only do windows whoosh to and from the Taskbar when you minimize or maximize them, but menus slide into place from one corner to the other, and scrolling lists slink greasily up and down in animated motion. All this pointless movement slows you down when you work with REGEDIT, especially when you have to scroll through a large key such as *HKey_Classes_Root*. (We know Microsoft does usability testing, but are there really any Windows 98 focus group participants who said "Man, that Windows 95 was way too fast, can you slow it down with some sliding menus or something?")

Thankfully, you can turn the animation off. Open the Display control panel by right-clicking the desktop and choosing Properties. Click the Effects tab, and clear the Animate Windows, Menus, and Lists check box. REGEDIT feels much snappier without all that slipping and sliding. Chapter 11 gives much more detail on dealing with Windows 98 animations.

REGEDIT à la mode, part 2: Getting real

You may occasionally need to run REGEDIT in its so-called *real mode,* that is, from a DOS prompt rather than from the graphical Windows 98 environment. For example, you may find yourself in a situation where Windows 98 doesn't boot properly, and you can't even get to the graphical protected-mode environment. This may be the case if your Registry is FUBAR. (FUBAR is a famous computer acronym standing for — at least in polite society — Fouled Up Beyond All Recognition.)

Note: You don't actually run a different program file when you run REGEDIT in real mode. It's the same REGEDIT.EXE; the program just senses whether you're at the DOS prompt or running Windows 98, and starts accordingly.

Running REGEDIT in real mode is riskier than running it in graphical protected mode because you can accidentally and easily type one wrong letter and destroy the entire Registry. Only run REGEDIT in real mode if no other option is available, or if this book advises you to do so in a particular situation.

You can't run REGEDIT in real mode by simply opening a DOS prompt under Windows 98 and typing the command; all this does is open a graphical REGEDIT window. Here's how to get to the real-mode command prompt:

- ✔ If you're already running Windows 98, choose Start➪Shutdown, select the Restart in MS-DOS Mode radio button, and then click OK.

- ✔ If you can't get to Windows 98, try holding down Ctrl at boot time to see the text-mode boot menu; then select the Safe Mode Command Prompt Only menu option.

- ✔ If all else fails, you can boot the PC with the Windows 98 emergency startup disk that you created when you installed Windows 98. (If you didn't make one then, you can make one anytime using the Add/Remove Programs control panel's Startup Disk tab.) The emergency startup disk includes a copy of REGEDIT.EXE.

However you get to the DOS command prompt, change to the C: drive and then the \WINDOWS directory, and you can then type **REGEDIT** and see a fairly cryptic listing of the command line options:

```
REGEDIT [/L:system] [/R:user] filename1
REGEDIT [/L:system] [/R:user] /C filename2
REGEDIT [/L:system] [/R:user] /D [regpath]
REGEDIT [/L:system] [/R:user] /E filename3 [regpath]
```

- ✔ **The /L and /R options** allow you to specify the location of the SYSTEM.DAT and USER.DAT files, respectively, but usually you work with the files in the C:\WINDOWS directory, so you don't need these options. To merge the contents of an existing REG file into the Registry, for example, you just type **REGEDIT filename1.REG** without having to specify /L or /R.

- ✔ **The /C option** is the dangerous one: It creates a brand-new Registry from scratch, importing the contents of filename2 — which must end in the suffix .REG and which should contain a full Registry export. REGEDIT doesn't look at filename2 to verify that it contains a full Registry, and if filename2 doesn't, you can end up worse off than before.

✓ **The /D option** lets you delete a Registry key. This option is potentially dangerous, too, because it lets you wipe out a lot of data with a short command even if it doesn't let you delete an entire primary branch. A sample command to remove a key left over from a program uninstall may be

```
REGEDIT /D HKEY_CURRENT_USER\Software\VendorX\ProgramY
```

✓ **The /E option** exports the Registry to filename3. If you want to export only a portion of the Registry, you can specify the starting key as the *regpath*. (The *regpath* is just the key location, as in the /D example in the previous bullet item. The square brackets around it in the command listing indicate that it's optional; you don't actually type them.)

How can you use REGEDIT in real mode to fix a problem? Chapters 15 and 17 offer some ideas, but the most common technique is to use REGEDIT /E to export the Registry (or a particular key), run a text editor to load the exported REG file, fix what's wrong, save the REG file, and then use REGEDIT again to reimport it. If that sounds like a pain, it is!

You're much better off making Registry backups whenever you make a change, because restoring a backed-up Registry is much easier than troubleshooting with the real-mode REGEDIT program. Chapter 2 lays out the various backup options.

Where's the remote?

Those of you who aren't running Windows 98 on a network or who don't plan to offer technical support to others, feel free to skip this section.

Say you're using Windows 98 on a network and, because of your skills, your job description, or both, other network users look to you for technical support. Now, say a novice Windows user calls you for help, and it becomes clear that some Registry editing is necessary — but you would no more trust that user with REGEDIT than give a 13-year-old the keys to a Corvette. You can always walk over to the user's PC, but if you do a lot of technical support work, you don't want to spend your life walking around the building — and besides, all your handy reference books are in your own office. Plus, you may prefer that the user doesn't see what you're doing, so he won't be tempted to try it himself after you leave! Good news: With the right sort of network and a bit of foresight, you can run REGEDIT on your machine and edit the distressed user's Registry remotely, over the wire.

Getting set up for remote Registry editing
You can use REGEDIT remotely only if all the following conditions are met:

✔ Your network is a *client/server* type, that is, you have a dedicated central server running a network operating system like Novell NetWare or Windows NT Server (or even Windows NT Workstation acting as a small-scale server). In other words, you can't run REGEDIT over a peer-to-peer network like LANtastic or the peer-to-peer network that's built in to Windows 98.

✔ The Windows 98 PCs all use 32-bit protected mode software to communicate over the network (this is the usual setup). In other words, the PCs can't be running real-mode network software that loads via AUTOEXEC.BAT.

✔ The Windows 98 PCs you want to connect over the network share at least one common *protocol* or network language (usually TCP/IP, IPX, or NetBEUI).

✔ The Windows 98 PCs are set up for *user-level security* on the Network control panel's Access Control tab. (This is also the usual setup in a client/server network, where each user has a single ID and password. The alternative, *share-level security,* is common in a peer-to-peer network, where each shared resource has its own password.)

Remote editing also requires a little foresight: You have to install a bit of software on both your machine and the machine you want to access remotely so that REGEDIT can find the remote machine's Registry over the network. This software goes by the name *Microsoft Remote Registry* (some books and magazines call it the *Remote Registry Service*). You may want to go ahead and install this software on every PC on the network. Here's how:

1. **Pop the Windows 98 disc into the PC's CD-ROM drive; or if Windows 98 was installed from a network drive, make sure that you're logged on to the network and that the network server drive containing the Windows 98 setup files is available.**

2. **Click Start⇨Settings⇨Control Panel and double-click the Network icon.**

3. **Click the Add button to display in the Select Network Component Type dialog box.**

4. **Double-click the Service option to display the Select Network Service dialog box.**

5. **Click the Have Disk button to display the Install From Disk dialog box.**

6. **Type X:\TOOLS\RESKIT\NETADMIN\REMOTREG into the Copy Manufacturer's Files From text box (where *X:* is the drive letter of the CD-ROM or network drive containing the Windows 98 files), and click OK.**

   7. **Click Microsoft Remote Registry in the Select Network Service dialog box if it isn't already highlighted, and click OK.**

      You should see `Microsoft Remote Registry` listed as an installed component on the Network control panel's Configuration tab.

   8. **Click OK to close the Network control panel.**

Now that the remote registry software is on the system, a few final steps enable the PC to be administered from afar. You have to tell the computer exactly who is empowered to perform remote administration.

   1. **Click Start⇨Settings⇨Control Panel.**

   2. **Double-click the Passwords icon.**

   3. **Click the Remote Administration tab.**

      If you don't see this tab, your PC isn't set up for user-level security. Make the change from share-level to user-level security on the Network control panel's Access Control tab.

   4. **Select the Enable Remote Administration of This Server check box.**

      In the Administrators list, if you run an NT Server network, `Domain admins` appears automatically; if you run a Novell network, the `Supervisor` (NetWare 3.*x*) or `Admin` (NetWare 4.*x*) account appears. You can add people to the list with (you guessed it) the Add button. For example, if you're not a network administrator but you're the one who may be doing the remote Registry editing, add your logon name to the list. After you finish, click OK.

Running REGEDIT remotely

After you complete setting up a Windows 98 PC for remote editing (see preceding section), using REGEDIT to modify a remote user's Registry is a piece o' cake.

   1. **Run REGEDIT.**

   2. **Click Registry⇨Connect Network Registry.**

   3. **Type in the name of the computer you want to connect to in the Computer Name field of the Connect Network Registry box.**

      You can also select the computer you want from a list by clicking the Browse button.

   4. **Click OK in the Connect Network Registry dialog box.**

      You see a screen like Figure 4-7, showing your local machine's Registry at the top of the left window pane and the remote machine's Registry at the bottom.

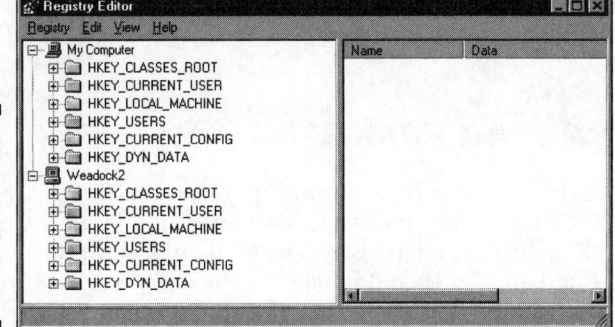

Figure 4-7:
Viewing a
remote
user's
Registry in
REGEDIT.

You can follow a similar procedure to edit a remote Registry with the System
Policy Editor, which Chapter 9 discusses in more detail.

Norton Registry Editor, the Lamb

The Norton Registry Editor (NRE), which comes with Norton Utilities for
Windows 9*x* version 2.0 and above, is a kinder, gentler REGEDIT (see
Figure 4-8). The advantages of NRE include a much better Find command,
bookmarks, safety features, and greatly improved online help. With NRE,
Registry editing isn't quite so baaaaad. (Sorry.)

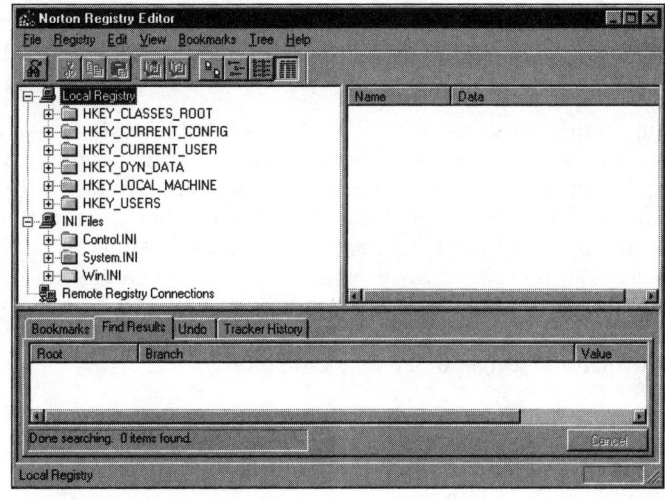

Figure 4-8:
Norton
Registry
Editor adds
a third
window
pane
beneath the
usual two
and also
provides
access to
INI files.

Take an advance look at NRE by installing the Norton Utilities trialware program included on this book's CD-ROM.

Enhanced Find command

Instead of REGEDIT's tedious one-at-a-time find feature, the Edit⇨Find command in NRE lists all the results of a find operation in the lower window's Find Results tab. There, you can scroll up or down to see what your search turned up, and then double-click the entry you want to see. NRE takes you to the selected entry by resetting the two upper window panes to show that entry. The NRE Find method lets you ignore irrelevant find results more easily.

The Find dialog box in NRE Version 2.0 lets you specify orphans instead of particular text strings. (Symantec has moved this feature out of NRE and into the WinDoctor utility in Version 3.0.) *Orphans* are file path names in the Registry that no longer point to files or directories that exist on your computer's hard drive. Usually, orphans occur when a user incompletely uninstalls an application program. Chapter 14 takes a closer look at Registry orphans.

NRE's Edit⇨Replace command lets you perform a global search-and-replace throughout the entire Registry. You may want to use this feature, for example, if you move a program's files to a different directory but don't want to reinstall the program from scratch. You can simply replace all references to the old directory with a reference to the new one.

Bookmarks

One of our favorite additions in NRE is the ability to create *bookmarks*. A bookmark is a Registry location that you create by right-clicking a key and choosing Bookmark from the context menu. NRE then puts a little red dot on the bookmarked key. After you create one or more bookmarks, you can instantly go back to a marked location by double-clicking the bookmark in the Bookmarks tab in NRE's lower window pane. You can save your bookmarks in a file, retrieve a set of bookmarks that you saved previously, and even create multiple bookmark sets that you can use for different purposes: fun tips, security settings, bug fixes, and so on.

Safety features

NRE offers a couple of good safety features that are absent from REGEDIT:

✔ **Undo.** You can choose Edit➪Undo to undo your last action, and the
Undo tab in the lower window pane displays a list of all the actions
you've taken in the current session (that is, since you opened NRE).

✔ **Read only.** You can choose Registry➪Read Only to prohibit any
changes to the Registry. This is a great idea when you're exploring the
Registry structure and want to make sure that you don't inadvertently
change something. Microsoft included this feature in the Windows NT
Registry editor REGEDT32, but left it out of the Windows 98 utility.

Shareware and Freeware Utilities

In addition to Norton Registry Editor, a few other free and shareware
programs deserve consideration for inclusion in your bag of Registry editing
tricks.

We haven't yet seen the perfect Registry editing tool — or the perfect
Registry backup utility, for that matter. (We'd love to see those capabilities
combined into one killer product. Entrepreneurs, take note.) Meanwhile,
throw a few programs into your Registry duffel bag; some are good for some
tasks, others for others.

SCANREG

This little command-line program hails from the Microsoft Windows NT
Resource Kit and enables you to search for a particular string within the
Windows 98, 95, or NT Registry (either local or remote). You can specify
whether you want to search keys, value names, or value data; whether you
want your search to be case-sensitive (that is, match uppercase and lower-
case precisely); and which primary Registry branch you want to search.
Figure 4-9 shows the results of a SCANREG search for the text string
PageMill.

SCANREG isn't as slick as the REGEDIT Find command or the shareware
programs we mention later in this section. However, it's handy if you can't
boot to Windows 98 due to a damaged Registry, and it's free as long as you
or someone in your company has the Windows NT Resource Kit.
SCANREG.EXE resides on the Windows NT Resource Kit CD-ROM under
\I386\REGISTRY. The README file is oddly located in \COMMON\REGISTRY.

Note: SCANREG was written by a Microsoft programmer but isn't supported
by Microsoft, so if you call with a question about it, Microsoft will pretend
they've never heard of the program.

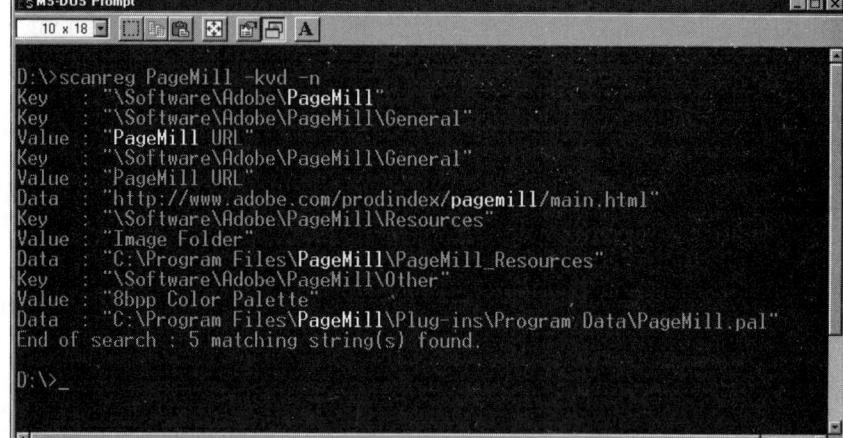

Figure 4-9:
SCANREG
is a Registry
find utility
that works
from a
command
prompt.

Don't confuse this program with the SCANREG utility that comes with
Windows 98 and also goes by the name of *Registry Checker;* these are two
different animals. (Hey, Microsoft is a big company, it's bound to duplicate
program names occasionally.) Be sure you don't overwrite the Windows 98
SCANREG.EXE with the NT version; store it in a separate directory (anywhere other than C:\WINDOWS) and/or rename it to REGSCAN.EXE.

COMPREG

Another program from the Microsoft Windows NT Resource Kit,
COMPREG.EXE, allows you to compare two Registry branches — for example, on two different computers. As with SCANREG, COMPREG works with
local or remote Registries, and it works with Windows 95, 98, or NT. This
little utility can be handy when troubleshooting — you can see what's
different between a machine that works and one that doesn't.

Registry Search and Replace

This $20 shareware utility from Steven J. Hoek Software Development adds
to REGEDIT's Find command by including the ability to replace one chunk of
text with another. If you have Norton Registry Editor, you already have
better and safer search-and-replace capabilities, but if you don't have NRE,
take a look at Registry Search and Replace (RS&R).

RS&R can log your search or search-and-replace session to a file. It works
with remote Registries as long as the usual conditions are met (see the
section "Where's the remote?" earlier in this chapter). You can use RS&R
with Windows NT as well as Windows 98 and 95. RS&R adds a new option to

the Start⇨Find command. The In the Registry option is a quick way to run the program. You don't have to open REGEDIT to run RS&R, and you can save your settings as a *search profile* so you don't have to enter them each time you run the program. Finally, you can choose to look at and approve each replacement separately *(prompted replacement),* which is safer than blindly performing all replacements at once *(specified replacement).*

The program is good but not perfect. Version 2.10 can't search for both value names and value data in the same pass, and it doesn't have an undo feature. (Back up the Registry before you use this program!) Also, like REGEDIT and NRE, RS&R can't find data in DWORD or binary values.

Figure 4-10 shows a screen that's set up to replace every occurrence of C:\PROGRAM FILES\LOCATIONA with C:\PROGRAM FILES\LOCATIONB and to log all results to a file (always a smart idea in case something goes wrong and you need to reverse one or more changes).

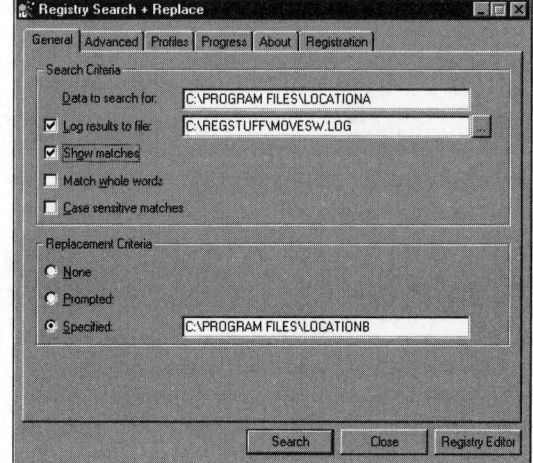

Figure 4-10:
Registry
Search and
Replace is
primed for
action.

Whether you use RS&R or Norton Registry Editor, search-and-replace operations can produce unintended results if you allow partial matches (changing *nut* to *bolt* also changes *doughnut* to *doughbolt*). To be safe, select the Match Whole Words option in RS&R or the Match Whole String Only option in Norton.

RegSurf

RegSurf, a $28 shareware program from ISES, Inc., doesn't do search-and-replace, but it does have the ability to search every Registry key (see Figure 4-11), something that Registry Search and Replace doesn't do. RegSurf also includes a handy option to print the results of your search.

It works with the Windows NT Registry as well as the Windows 98 and 95 Registries, and it's pretty fast (especially if you choose the Minimize While Surfing option).

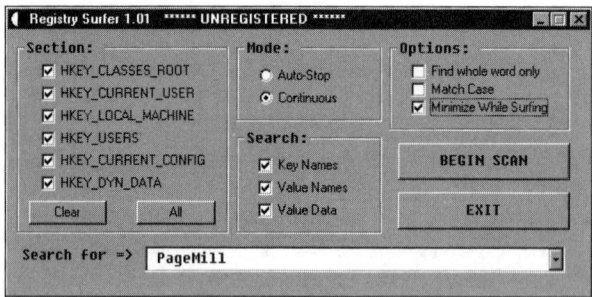

Figure 4-11: RegSurf lets you search every Registry key.

Other stuff we discuss later

Other tools make handy additions to your Registry arsenal, but we save discussion of them for later on in the book. For example, Chapter 9 discusses the System Policy Editor, Chapter 11 explores TweakUI, MTUSpeed, and TweakDUN, and Chapter 13 looks at REGMON and FILEMON. We've covered enough stuff here for one chapter, though!

Part II
It's a Jungle Out There: The Registry Structure

In this part . . .

George awoke to the maniacal hoots of the decidedly
ill-mannered Yanomamo warriors, who had tied him
to the luggage rack of his Land Rover Discovery before
driving him deep into their tribal inner sanctum for untold
dark purposes. George had learned from Harry Houdini the
trick of tensing your muscles while being roped in, and he
knew that he could relax those same muscles now and slip
the ties that bound him. But what then? Which way was his
base camp? Every direction looked the same to him in the
pale moonlight of the stifling summer night.

Knowing your way around the Registry is a goal you'll
achieve through a combination of reading the chapters in
this part of the book and wandering through the structure
yourself with the Registry Editor. Here, you find out about
the two different ways you can view the Registry. You can
look at the actual files that constitute it, or you can use
the Registry Editor to view it as a unified, multilevel
database. We present both views. A special chapter then
explains how the Registry stores information about your
PC's hardware in order to work with the Plug and Play
standard — information that you may need if you plan to
use any of the new hardware devices that Windows 98
supports.

Software or hardware, it's all there in the crazy maze of
the Registry's structure. By the end of this part, you'll
know the lay of the land well enough to get where you
need to go, while avoiding places where you'd rather not
get tied up.

Chapter 5

Where the Files Are

In This Chapter

▶ Finding out where the heck the Registry really is

▶ Discovering why the Registry has multiple files

*W*e refer to "The Registry" approximately nine zillion times in this book, but what actual files on your hard disk are we talking about? This chapter holds the answer.

You can't take proper care of your Registry unless you know what disk files it contains.

Sure, you can run programs such as the Windows 98 Registry Checker without knowing exactly what files the Registry contains. But if you don't at least know the what and where of the Registry files, you may miss some dangerous little quirks of these programs — such as the fact that the Registry Checker doesn't necessarily back up the complete set of Registry data! Windows 98 also automatically backs up your Registry when it starts successfully (but only once a day), and knowing where these backup files are located may just save your bacon one day.

If you set up Windows 98 to provide *user profiles,* which enable multiple users to log on to the same PC, or so that users can log on to any network PC and see their own desktop setup, you need to know where these user-specific Registry files live. (Most Registry backup programs, including Registry Checker, don't back up these user-specific files, so you may need to back them up separately if they're important to you.)

If you ever need to restore your Registry file backups during a troubleshoot-ing session, you need to know where your files are — and which ones to restore. Here again, Registry backup programs don't always give you the flexibility to specify which files need to go where.

Finally, Windows 98 contains a few files that aren't strictly part of the Registry but that relate to it in one way or another: REG, INF, and so on. If you don't know where these files are or what they do, you may inadvertently do some Registry damage that isn't easily undoable.

Convinced? (We hope so.) Now, here's the skinny on the Registry files. After you're comfortable with their names, functions, and locations, you're well on your way to qualifying as a National Expert on Registry Details (NERD). (Now you know where that term comes from! Being a NERD has become cool now that the general public has realized that NERDs make all the money, with the possible exception of NERDs who write computer books for a living.)

Let's Get Physical

You can look at the Registry in two ways: as a logical entity, in which you look at how the Registry's information is organized, or as a physical entity, in which you look at the actual locations of Registry files.

Chapter 6 explores the Registry's *logical structure,* which is the tree-like organization you see when you open the Registry Editor. (Okay, it doesn't always seem all that logical, but that's the term nevertheless.)

The actual files on disk that make up the Registry constitute its *physical structure.* In this chapter, we look at this physical structure. We discuss it first mainly because it's a little simpler than the logical structure. Figure 5-1 shows the physical structure of the Registry, and the rest of this chapter explains the various files and what they do.

Before you drop your jaw looking at the figure, please understand that your Windows 98 PC may not use all these files on a regular basis, or at all. The main files we're concerned with are SYSTEM.DAT and USER.DAT, but you may need to know about the other ones depending on how you've set up your machine and whether your machine is on a network. If you have a simple, single-user, stand-alone PC, you don't have to worry about many of the files this chapter discusses — just SYSTEM.DAT and USER.DAT, and the *.CAB backup files.

SYSTEM.DAT and USER.DAT divide your PC into system-specific and user-specific settings, respectively. Why divide the Registry like this? Doing so enables multiple users to work on the same PC, to roam a network, and to see their own settings when they log on. The SYSTEM.DAT file stays with the PC, but the USER.DAT file can live on a network server or in separate directories on the local PC hard drive for each user. Splitting the Registry into these two main files is a stroke of genius on Microsoft's part.

Before looking at SYSTEM.DAT and USER.DAT in depth, however, you need to be able to view and print Registry files, which the following section discusses.

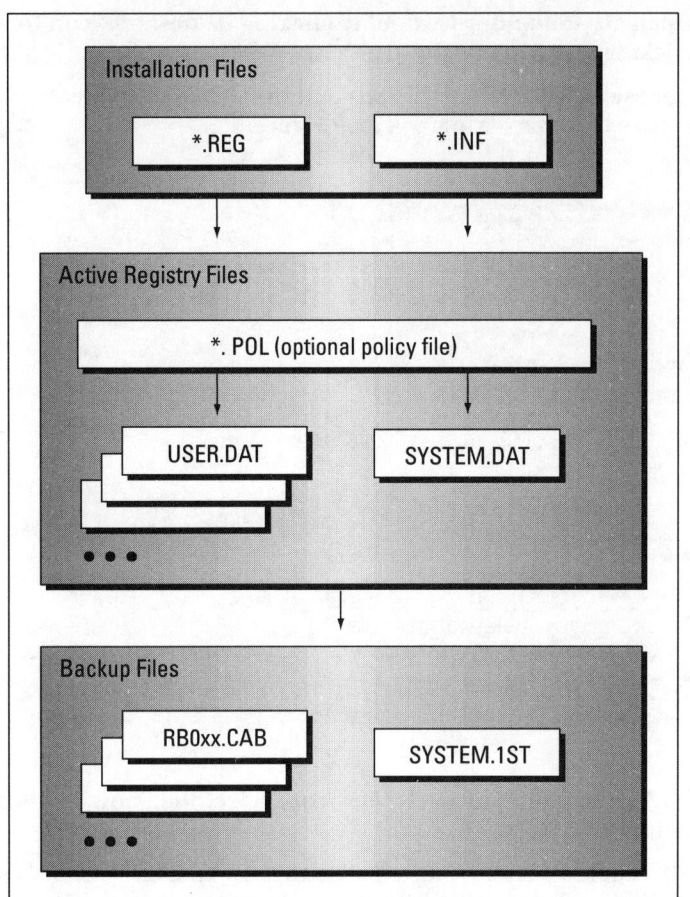

Figure 5-1:
The
Registry's
physical file
structure.

Sharpening your physical skills: Viewing and printing

The first thing to do before wandering around your PC and looking at the Registry's physical structure is to set up Windows 98 so that you can see all the files on your disk with My Computer or Windows Explorer. After a typical Windows 98 installation, many files don't appear in these file management programs because the files have the *Hidden attribute* turned on (see the sidebar entitled, "Windows 98 file attributes"). Here's how to bend Windows 98 to your will and display your hidden files:

1. **Open My Computer by double-clicking its desktop icon (or single-clicking it if you use the Web view desktop).**

2. **Choose View⇨Folder Options and then click the View tab in the Folder Options dialog box (see Figure 5-2).**

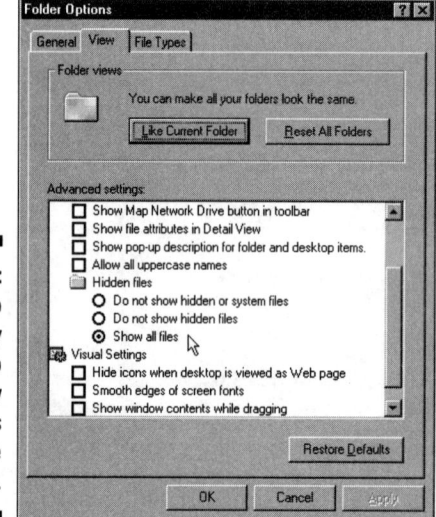

Figure 5-2:
Setting up
My
Computer to
show
hidden files
and file
extensions.

3. **Under the Hidden Files folder icon, select the Show all files radio button.**

   This choice forces Windows 98 to display all files — even files that have the Hidden attribute, which appear in gray in Explorer.

4. **Under the Visual Settings icon, uncheck the Hide File Extensions for Known File Types check box.**

   This choice forces Windows 98 to display the full file names, including suffixes, for all files.

5. **Click OK and close My Computer.**

At some time, you may want to print a list of files in a particular directory. Sorry! Windows 98 Explorer doesn't have a print command! (Someone at Microsoft must have been asleep at the cyberwheel on this one.) See "Printing directory listings" in Chapter 11 for details on how to hack the Registry to add a directory print command.

The soul of your machine: SYSTEM.DAT

One Registry file that appears on every Windows 98 PC is SYSTEM.DAT, and it's one of the two biggies. You can find it in the C:\WINDOWS directory (or whatever you've named your Windows 98 main directory). If you're running a lobotomized PC with no local disk storage so that it boots from diskette or a remote-boot disk image, SYSTEM.DAT resides in the *machine directory* on the server, along with the other Registry files. We don't cover machine directories in this book because few individuals or companies use them, but if you need this kind of information, check out the *Microsoft Windows 98 Resource Kit* from Microsoft Press.

The SYSTEM.DAT file contains information about the computer on which it resides: mainly hardware configuration data and information about installed software (but not user settings). None of the settings in SYSTEM.DAT change from user to user. SYSTEM.DAT is associated with a particular *computer,* not a particular *user.*

SYSTEM.DAT contains the information in the logical Registry branches *HKEY_Local_Machine, HKEY_Current_Config,* and *HKEY_Classes_Root.* We explain these branches in Chapter 6.

SYSTEM.DAT has the file attributes of Hidden and Read-only. (See the sidebar, "Windows 98 file attributes," later in this chapter for details on these attributes). SYSTEM.DAT used to contain the System attribute, too, in Windows 95, but that's changed. These attributes help protect the SYSTEM.DAT file. If this file is hidden, users running a Windows 98 PC that's set up to hide hidden files from My Computer or Explorer can't see it. If SYSTEM.DAT is read-only, even users who can see a file (by changing the view options for My Computer or Explorer as explained earlier in this chapter) can't delete or change the file contents without changing the read-only attribute.

Now hold the phone. If SYSTEM.DAT is read-only, how can we change its contents using the Registry Editor? On top of that, how can a new application program add settings for its own use in this file when you install a new program? The sly answer is that Registry Editor bypasses the read-only attribute, and application install programs bypass it, too, typically using REG and INF files. Just about all the Read-only attribute does is prevent users from doing something silly (and dangerous), like deleting the file in Explorer, or loading the file into a word processor, making a change, and then saving it back.

The "personal" touch: USER.DAT

The other Registry file appearing on every Windows 98 PC is USER.DAT, and it's the second biggie. You can find it in the C:\WINDOWS directory along with SYSTEM.DAT. This file contains information about the users who work with the PC: their desktop preferences, Control Panel options they can set, where to find the list of Start menu programs, application-specific settings (such as recently used file lists), and so on.

Windows 98 file attributes

PC files have had *attributes* since way back in the days of DOS. Attributes are special settings associated with a particular file. These attributes can be either informational, like the Archive attribute in the following list, or restrictive, like the other three attributes. The Windows 98 file attributes include

Read-only (R). You can't change or delete the file.

Hidden (H). You can't see the file unless Windows Explorer is set up to show all files or unless you know the exact file name.

System (S). The operating system uses the file, and you can't see the file unless Windows Explorer is set up to show all files.

Archive (A). The file has been added or changed since the last backup.

You can view these attributes — and change all but the System attribute — by right-clicking a file, choosing Properties, and viewing the General tab. If you need to modify the System attribute, you must use the DOS ATTRIB command.

You can use a couple of grief-saving little tricks while working with the ATTRIB command. If a file, such as C:\MSDOS.SYS, has both the Hidden and System attributes set, you can't remove one at a time — you have to remove both at once, using a command such as

```
ATTRIB —S -H MSDOS.SYS
```

Also, if a file has the Read-only attribute set, and you want to remove that attribute so that you can write over the file (as during a manual Registry restore from a batch file, as mentioned at the end of Chapter 2), you have to

either remove the System and Hidden attributes first, or remove all three attributes at once, as follows:

```
ATTRIB —S —H -R MSDOS.SYS
ATTRIB —H —R SYSTEM.DAT
```

You restore file attributes with the ATTRIB command by using a + instead of a – in the command.

If you want to use the DIR command at a DOS prompt to see files with the System and Hidden attributes, you have to use **DIR /A** because otherwise the DIR command omits such files.

Windows 98 adds some new date and time attributes you need to know about for troubleshooting purposes. Windows 98 not only tracks the date and time of file creation, it also tracks the date and time of last modification and of most recent access. You can sometimes use these new date and time attributes to determine which of two file versions is newer.

Finally, here's a little-known trick: You can use the ATTRIB command to display and print a file listing, like the DIR command does, but ATTRIB includes file attribute information. Open an MS-DOS window and use the ATTRIB command with the /S qualifier, which means "include subdirectories." For example, to display all the files and directories under C:\WINDOWS, type **ATTRIB C:\WINDOWS\ *.* /S**, and if you want the output to go to a printer connected to your first parallel port, for example, type the **ATTRIB C:\WINDOWS\ *.* /S>LPT1:** command. The forward slashes are called *qualifiers* (or *switches*) because they qualify the command and "switch" different features of the command on or off.

None of the settings in USER.DAT are machine-specific. If you set up a Windows 98 network so that users can log on from any machine with their own user ID and password, then their USER.DAT files can follow them from machine to machine. USER.DAT is associated with a particular *user,* not a particular *computer.*

USER.DAT contains the information in the logical Registry branches *HKEY_Users* and *HKEY_Current_User.* We explain these branches in Chapter 6.

USER.DAT has the same file attributes that SYSTEM.DAT does: Hidden and Read-only. (Like SYSTEM.DAT, USER.DAT had the System attribute in Windows 95, but no more.) The same comments we made about these attributes in the preceding section apply here.

If you turn on the Windows 98 user profiles feature (see Chapter 10), Windows 98 creates multiple copies of USER.DAT in subdirectories underneath the C:\WINDOWS\PROFILES directory. The subdirectory names match the names that you define when creating a new user in the Users control panel. So, on some Windows 98 PCs, you may find many copies of USER.DAT on the machine.

If you use user profiles and you work on a client/server network like NT Server or Novell IntranetWare, Windows 98 stores USER.DAT in a user directory on the server (such as the user's mail directory on a Novell 3.*x* server, or the user's home directory on a Novell 4.*x* or Windows NT server). When you log on, if the network copy is newer, Windows 98 copies USER.DAT from the network down to your PC. If your PC copy is newer, Windows 98 copies USER.DAT from your local PC to the network. When you log off, Windows 98 copies USER.DAT back to the network server, just in case you made any changes to your settings.

These multiple copies of USER.DAT are not all the same! Whenever you log on to Windows 98 with a particular name, Windows 98 switches to the USER.DAT file in the C:\WINDOWS\PROFILES\username directory that matches your logon name. If you ever need to restore a USER.DAT file on a PC with user profiles enabled, you must make sure that you use the correct USER.DAT for a particular user. Otherwise, you can create a situation in which Bob logs on and sees Jane's wallpaper (and all Jane's other user-specific settings). Not good — especially if Jane likes a picture of Fabio for wallpaper and Bob prefers Heather Locklear. (The actual problems can be much more significant, of course.)

Many Registry backup utilities, including Microsoft's own Registry Checker, just copy the USER.DAT files in the C:\WINDOWS directory and ignore the ones in C:\WINDOWS\PROFILES. You may want to back up the individual user versions of USER.DAT separately, as Chapter 2 discusses. (If you're wondering what that USER.DAT file in C:\WINDOWS is good for in a multiple-user situation; it's the basis for setting up a new USER.DAT for a new user, and it's also the file that activates if a user skips the Windows 98 logon screen.)

If you run Windows 98 on a client/server network and you enable user profiles, you can create a special version of USER.DAT that users can't change — meaning that they can't modify any Windows 98 or Windows 98 program settings. This version is a *mandatory user profile,* which must have the special name USER.MAN. USER.MAN lives in the user's mail directory on a Novell server or in the user's home directory on a Windows NT Server.

*Waterproofing your tent: *.POL*

A third and optional Registry file may exist, and it's a *policy* file. Policy files have the suffix .POL and, even though they're not DAT files, they still modify the Registry. Policy files act as a sort of security layer, limiting what a user can do with Windows 98. Policy files are not unlike mosquito netting, letting the air in so you can breathe, but keeping out undesirable elements such as tsetse flies. (On a computer network, novice Windows users who like to try out the Registry hacks they pick up in trade magazines are the tsetse flies. At home, your six-year-old assumes the same role. There are certain aspects of Windows 98 you just need to "screen" out from these people.) You can also use policy files to customize your desktop and control certain network settings, including Internet Explorer settings.

Windows 98 reads the settings in a policy file and applies them to the Registry. That is, a policy file effectively modifies USER.DAT, SYSTEM.DAT, or both.Policy files can govern the user settings in USER.DAT, but only if you set up Windows 98 to activate user profiles. Policy files can govern the computer settings in SYSTEM.DAT, whether you activate user profiles or not.

You can't necessarily tell in advance what a policy file's full filename is. We show you in Chapter 9 that this isn't a drawback; it's a handy feature if you want to get fancy with system policies and control precisely how they behave. The main part of the filename may match a user logon name or a computer name, or it may be "CONFIG" in the case of the special network-based master policy file, CONFIG.POL. If you're working with Windows 98 on a network, you can place a master policy file on a network server where the user logs on. Windows 98 looks on the server for the file named CONFIG.POL and uses this file if it exists.

Policy files can reside just about anywhere; however, on a client/server network, the usual locations are the NETLOGON directory of a Windows NT Server, or the PUBLIC directory of a NetWare or IntranetWare server. You can set up Windows 98 to look for policy files on your local PC hard disk, too.

Check out Chapter 9 for the full lowdown on system policies.

Backup for a rainy day: RB0xx.CAB

Every time Windows 98 starts successfully, it makes an automatic backup copy of SYSTEM.DAT and USER.DAT. The backups go into an archive file named RB0*xx*.CAB (the third character is a zero and not the letter O), and they live in the hidden C:\WINDOWS\SYSBCKUP directory (replace "WINDOWS" with a different name if you used one when you installed Windows 98). The "xx" in the file name is a sequence number that can range from 00 to 99; by default, Windows 98 keeps your most recent five Registry backups, incrementing the sequence number each time it creates a new archive. (According to Microsoft, the zero right after "RB" isn't part of the sequence number, which is a bit misleading; looking at a name like RB000.CAB, you'd think the sequence number could go to 999.)

The CAB file backup is quite different from the automatic Registry backups in Windows 95, which went by the names USER.DA0 and SYSTEM.DA0, which Windows 95 created at every restart (not just the first restart of the day), and which lived in C:\WINDOWS. CAB files are a special Microsoft compressed archive format (CAB is short for "cabinet," as in "file cabinet"). Each RB0*xx*.CAB file contains a copy of WIN.INI and SYSTEM.INI, as well as USER.DAT and SYSTEM.DAT. You can look inside a CAB file by double-clicking it, and you can manually extract a single file by right-clicking the file and choosing Extract (see Figure 5-3).

Figure 5-3:
The Windows 98 automatic backups live in CAB files.

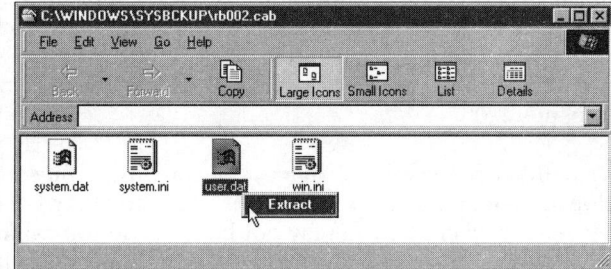

Another difference is that if you turned on user profiles in Windows 95, it would back up the current user's USER.DAT to USER.DA0 in the directory C:\WINDOWS\PROFILES\username every time the user successfully logged on to Windows 95. By contrast, Windows 98 never backs up the USER.DAT files in C:\WINDOWS\PROFILES.If Windows 98 senses at startup that the main DAT files are seriously damaged, it copies the backup files from the most recent RB0*xx*.CAB archive over the DAT files in C:\WINDOWS in an effort to use the "last known good" Registry.

"Now wait a minute," those of you who pored over Chapter 2 may be saying, "Why the heck did we go to all the trouble of understanding how to back up the Registry if Windows 98 does it for us, automatically?" Here's why:

- ✔ You often need to make a Registry backup at times in addition to just when Windows 98 starts. Windows 98 only creates the RB0*.CAB files once per day, when Windows 98 starts up for the first time on that date. Yes, you can run the Registry Checker yourself to make backups on an as-needed basis, but see the next bullet for a caution.

- ✔ Windows 98 doesn't back up the settings for every user, just the default one (C:\WINDOWS\USER.DAT), if you're using user profiles to allow multiple people to log on to the same PC with different settings. This statement holds true for the Registry Checker's manual backups as well as for its automatic backups.

- ✔ Windows 98 puts the RB0*.CAB files on the same disk as the primary DAT Registry files. Lose that disk to hardware failure, and you lose your automatic backups as well as your primary Registry files. (Things are a little better if you're on a client/server network and using user profiles, because a copy of the USER.DAT file resides on a network server.)

- ✔ The Windows 98 definition of a "successful" start is fairly lenient.

This last bulleted item needs some elaboration. As long as your operating system can start and load its primary device drivers, it *thinks* that it has started successfully. An unsuccessful start is one where Windows 98 can't even get out of bed and you never see the graphical desktop at all. Another kind of unsuccessful start is one where you tell Windows 98 not to load the main device drivers and to start itself in so-called *Safe Mode, Command Prompt Only.* (The graphical Safe Mode start, as opposed to the command prompt only start, was considered to be successful by Windows 95 but is not considered to be successful by Windows 98 — a major improvement. That is, booting to Safe Mode doesn't overwrite any of your previous CAB file Registry backups.)

The point to remember here is that a successful start from the standpoint of Windows 98 doesn't mean that your Registry is okay. You may have a serious problem — for example, you may not be able to right-click any icon without getting an error message — but Windows 98 thinks everything is ducky as long as it can load the video and disk drivers properly. So, Windows 98 blithely copies the DAT files to the CAB files — which now have the same Registry problems that your DAT files have. You can go back to an earlier CAB file archive — Windows 98 stores the five most recent ones by default, which is great — but after five days, your insurance policy expires, and your backups catch the same jungle malady that your primary Registry files have.

Backup for a monsoon: SYSTEM.1ST

Take a gander at the root level of your boot hard drive. One of the files you should see is SYSTEM.1ST, which is the SYSTEM.DAT version that Windows 98 first builds when you (or a hardware manufacturer) install the operating system for the first time.

You can delete SYSTEM.1ST without affecting Windows 98's ability to run, but we suggest you leave this file in place. If you ever find your back up against the wall so hard that it hurts, you can use SYSTEM.1ST to replace SYSTEM.DAT. This approach is a major pain because the original SYSTEM.DAT doesn't have any of the settings for software that you installed after installing Windows 98 itself, but restoring SYSTEM.1ST may be better than not being able to boot Windows 98 at all. After restoring SYSTEM.1ST, you have to reinstall all your application programs to get this file back to where it needs to be.

Abandoned campsites: Other backup files

You may run across several other Registry backup files with mysterious suffixes. For example, you may find the following files in the C:\WINDOWS directory (or whatever you named the main Windows 98 directory on your PC):

- **SYSTEM.NU***x* and **USER.NU***x* are Registry backups that Symantec Norton Utilities creates when you install the program (the *x* is a number indicating the version of Norton Utilities that created the files). These files don't change with every successful restart of Windows 98. Symantec documentation advises that you can safely delete these files after you create a set of rescue disks.

- **SYSTEM.NAV** and **USER.NAV** are copies made by the Symantec Norton AntiVirus (NAV) installation program. Again, these files don't change after you install NAV. As long as you're backing up your Registry regularly, you can delete these files.

- **SYSTEM.PCA** and **USER.PCA** get created by (you guessed it) Symantec PCAnywhere. The advice from the previous bullet applies.

Other programs are likely to create their own Registry backups for safety's sake (common suffixes are OLD and BAK). As long as you have a solid plan in place for making Registry backups (see Chapter 2), you probably don't need these files after you make your first "known good" backup. These files can take up a lot of space (10MB on one PC we saw).

Registry-Related Files Not Part of the Registry

You find a certain number of Registry-related files floating around on your hard disk, and we mention them here even though they're not technically part of the Registry.

*.REG

Files with the REG suffix may exist in almost any Windows 98 directory. These special-format text files usually contain partial or full Registry backups created with REGEDIT's export command, or application-specific instructions for modifying the Registry during a program installation. You can also use REG files as a convenient way to copy Registry changes to multiple computers. However, REG files are dangerous! If you double-click one by accident, and blow by the warning screen, you modify the Registry. We show you in Chapter 12 how to prevent such accidents.

*.INF

Files with the INF suffix, most of which reside in the hidden directory C:\WINDOWS\INF, include instructions for installing new hardware devices and programs. These INF files can modify the Registry, and they do so when you install hardware and software. In one sense, INF files aren't quite as dangerous as REG files because the usual behavior after you double-click an INF file is for Windows Notepad to open the file for editing. Right-click an INF file and choose Install, however, and you're likely to modify the Registry as well as move some files around. In another sense, INF files are even more dangerous than REG files, because INF files can delete Registry keys and values while REG files cannot.

Chapter 13 offers more meat on the subject of REG and INF files.

*.INI

Chapter 1 discusses the fact that Windows 98 still uses Windows 3.*x*-style INI files for certain operating system settings, such as the location and size of the swapfile (an overflow file that Windows 98 uses when it's short on RAM). These files, WIN.INI, SYSTEM.INI, and CONTROL.INI, live in the C:\WINDOWS directory and may be modified by control panels. Because Microsoft didn't move every possible system setting from these INI files into the Registry, backing up INI files whenever you back up the Registry is a smart choice.

MSDOS.SYS

MSDOS.SYS isn't technically a part of the Registry, but it does tell Windows 98 where to find the Registry at boot time — and if that information is incorrect, you're likely to see a Registry-related error message. You can also use MSDOS.SYS to force Windows 98 to present the various boot options at each restart. That can be handy while you're troubleshooting Registry problems and need to start in real mode or safe mode occasionally.

MSDOS.SYS is actually nothing more than a plain text file; the SYS suffix indicates that it's an operating system component. However, it does have the Hidden, Read-only, and System attributes (see the sidebar "Windows 98 file attributes" earlier in this chapter), so you must open a DOS window and use the ATTRIB command (again, see the sidebar) to clear these attributes before you can edit the file. You can then just use the DOS EDIT command, which Windows 98 keeps on hand for just such occasions.

Ninety-nine point nine percent of Registry users need to know only three facts about MSDOS.SYS:

- ✔ If the value *WinBootDir* in the [Path] section doesn't actually point to where Windows 98 lives, then Windows 98 won't boot and it may tell you that the Registry is damaged. The actual error message reads `Warning: Windows has detected a registry/configuration error. Choose, Command prompt only, and run SCANREG.` Yes, the first comma in the second sentence is wrong, but you can't expect computer people to know they're grammar.

- ✔ You can disable the automatic ScanDisk-after-an-abnormal-shutdown by changing the value of Autoscan in the [Options] section from 1 to 0 (zero). ScanDisk is pretty reliable these days, but if it sometimes creates problems for you, or if you trust your disks and just find ScanDisk annoying after an application crashes your system, you can turn it off here. We should practice what we preach and tell you that it's better to turn ScanDisk off in the new System Configuration utility; run MSCONFIG.EXE and click the Advanced button.

- ✔ If you want to force Windows 98 to display the startup menu that you'd normally only see by pressing Ctrl during the boot cycle, just add the line `BootMenu=1` under the [Options] section. If you want to get fancy, you can change the default menu choice (`BootMenuDefault=2` for example would start you up in logged mode and create the file BOOTLOG.TXT so you could trace startup activities). You can even change how long Windows 98 waits before accepting the default choice (`BootMenuDelay=x` where *x* is seconds and 30 seconds is the default). You can turn the menu on or off in the new System Configuration utility (see previous bullet), but you can't customize it like you can in MSDOS.SYS.

Okay, that was more than three facts. Sometimes we just say stuff like that so you'll read on — a little like the lawyer who says "I only have one more question." You can bet it'll be a single question with two hundred parts.

REGEDIT

The Registry Editor, REGEDIT.EXE, typically resides in C:\WINDOWS. The help files, REGEDIT.CHM and REGEDIT.CNT, reside in C:\WINDOWS\HELP. (For those readers not familiar with the Windows 98 new help system, the file extension CHM stands for "Compiled HTML" and is the standard file format for Windows 98's browser-like HTML Help engine.) Chapter 4 deals with the Registry Editor from Antelope to Zebra.

POLEDIT

The System Policy Editor, POLEDIT.EXE, makes its usual home in C:\WINDOWS, although (unlike REGEDIT) you have to install it yourself after a typical Windows 98 setup. The help files, POLEDIT.CHM and POLEDIT.CNT, live in C:\WINDOWS\HELP, and the program puts an installation file (POLEDIT.INF) in C:\WINDOWS\INF. You'll need GROUPPOL.DLL too if you use group policies. Chapter 9 deals with the Policy Editor in detail.

Profile files and folders

We deal with user profiles in depth in Chapter 10, but this chapter is supposed to be about where the files are, and it turns out that if you turn on the Registry's user profiles feature, you duplicate more than just USER.DAT. Figure 5-4 shows a PC with two users, Mark and Glenn. Depending on the options you choose when you create a new user with the Users control panel, you may see the Favorites and My Documents folders as well as the ones in the figure. The Registry keeps track of which folders each user gets a unique copy of in the key *HKU\username\Software\Microsoft\Windows\CurrentVersion\Explorer\User Shell Folders*, where *username* corresponds to the user's name (such as Mark or Glenn).

Figure 5-4:
User profiles clone more than just USER.DAT.

Chapter 6

What You Must Know to Use REGEDIT: The Registry's Logical Structure

● ●

In This Chapter

▶ Discovering the Registry's three basic components

▶ Why some Registry branches point to other branches

▶ Using string, DWORD, and binary values

▶ Getting comfortable with the Registry map

● ●

K nowing where the Registry files are is important for backup and recovery purposes. However, if you want to hack through the rain forest with Microsoft's REGEDIT Registry Editor program, you need to spend a little time with the maps describing the Registry's internal structure.

In Chapter 5, we explain that the Registry is contained in two files, SYSTEM.DAT and USER.DAT (and maybe an optional third file called a policy file, like CONFIG.POL). These files represent the Registry's *physical structure* — files that you can back up or copy. However, you can't view or edit these files individually. They're stored in an encrypted binary format, and you need a special viewer to decode their contents.

That viewer, the Registry Editor, integrates the files into a single "logical" structure — much as a typical e-mail program integrates its various data files (MAILBOX.PST and MAILBOX.PAB, for example) and presents them in a logical structure (inbox, outbox, sent items, address book, and so on). You need to understand the e-mail program's logical structure in order to use the program, and you need to understand the physical structure (the files) in order to make backups for safekeeping.

The Basic Components

The Registry's organizational structure is like an upside-down tree (see Figure 6-1). Just like a real tree consists of branches, twigs, and leaves, the Registry consists of *branches, keys,* and *values.* The Registry tree becomes much more comprehensible after you look at the basic components, so that's a great place for us to start. We look at how the branches and twigs actually fan out a little later in the chapter.

If you find only three different basic kinds of components, how many total components exist in a typical Registry? All Windows 98 Registries have six branches. Glenn's Registry has about 18,000 keys and about 33,000 values. For a complete list of each of these keys and values, see Appendix E of this book. (Just kidding!) Seriously, don't let the big numbers concern you. A botanist can understand everything important about a tree without knowing where every single branch and leaf goes.

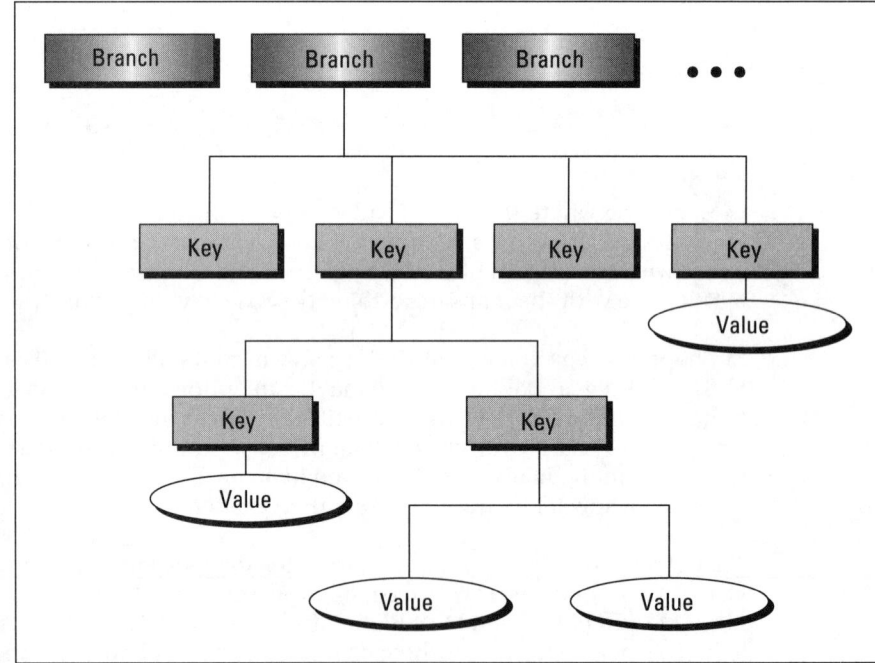

Figure 6-1:
The
Registry is
an inverted
tree.

Branching out

The Windows 98 Registry has six *branches,* listed in Table 6-1, which are the main organizational structures at the top level of the Registry's inverted-tree layout. You can't delete a branch itself, although the Registry Editor typically lets you delete most of a branch's contents.

These branches all start with the quirky notation "HKEY." The "H" stands for *handle,* and so these branch names act as *handles* to particular *keys* (specific Registry entries) that you need to view, change, or delete. People who program in C++ tell us that this notation makes perfect sense; we take their word for it. You can pronounce HKEY different ways; we've heard "high-key" and "aytche-key," but we tend to prefer "hickey," which brings back fond memories of high school.

Table 6-1	Windows 98 Registry Branches	
Branch Name	**Is an Alias for**	**Abbreviation**
HKEY_LOCAL_MACHINE		HKLM
HKEY_CURRENT_CONFIG	HKLM\Config\number	HKCC
HKEY_CLASSES_ROOT	HKLM\Software\Classes	HKCR
HKEY_USERS		HKU
HKEY_CURRENT_USER	HKU\username	HKCU
HKEY_DYN_DATA		HKDD

Unlike a real tree, where each main branch is completely separate and distinct from every other main branch, some of the Registry branches are really nothing more than *aliases,* or pointers, to specific keys located elsewhere. These particular keys are chosen because you use them frequently, so using a shorthand notation to refer to them is handy.

For example, you often spend time in *HKEY_CLASSES_ROOT* (abbreviated *HKCR*) because it contains information about how different file types behave. Saying (and writing) *HKCR* is easier than *HKLM\Software\Classes.* The two locations contain the same exact information, though. Check it out yourself. If you're familiar with the Registry Editor, look at *HKCR\avifile* and compare it to *HKLM\Software\Classes\avifile.*

So, *HKCC, HKCR,* and *HKCU* just point to other places in *HKLM* and *HKU.* The "core" branches *HKLM* and *HKU* actually contain the entire Registry contents, except for *HKDD,* which is a special branch that Windows 98 recreates in memory at each startup. (For the curious, the physical file SYSTEM.DAT contains *HKLM,* and the physical file USER.DAT contains *HKU.*)

The strategy of using aliases is confusing at first, but it's really just for convenience. You'll appreciate aliases as you begin spending some time with the Registry. Unfortunately, no visual clues tell you which branches are aliases and which aren't, and there's no catchy jingle you can use to remember the details, as students of human anatomy use ("the knee bone's connected to the thigh bone"). You just have to get familiar with Table 6-1 (or keep this book near your computer!).

Figure 6-2 provides a more graphical way of looking at the Registry's branch organization.

George, George, George of the jungle — watch out for that key!

A Registry *key* is nothing more complex than a location for storing data. A key is a container. It can contain a *value* (see next section), another key, or any number of both. You can think of a key as similar to a directory or folder in Windows Explorer. In fact, the icon that the Registry Editor uses is the

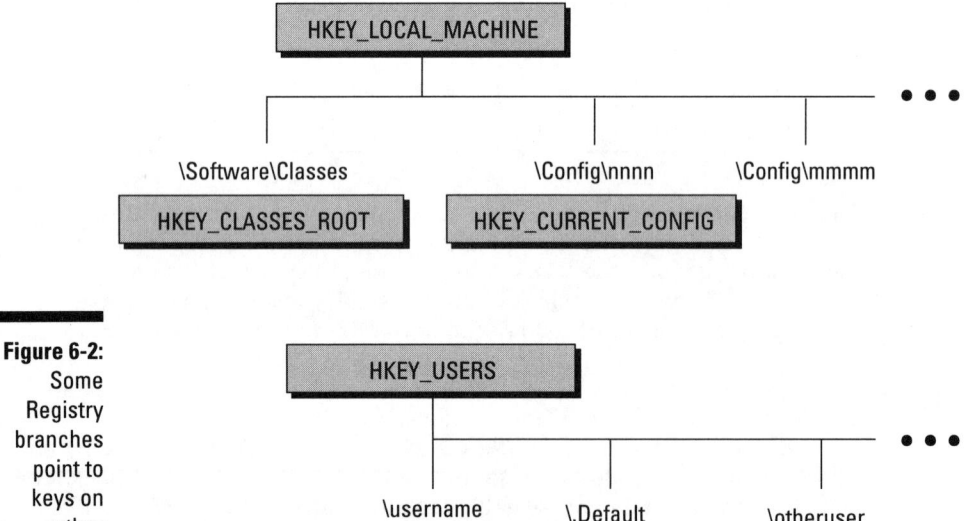

Figure 6-2: Some Registry branches point to keys on other branches.

same for both keys and directories. Or, if you like the upside-down-tree analogy, a key is like a twig or a branch. (A Registry branch is just a key that happens to live at the top organizational layer.)

Many keys (the ones with a + sign to their left in the Registry Editor window) contain other keys, or *subkeys* — in the same way that you can call certain directories on your hard disk *subdirectories* if they reside inside another directory. In this book, *subkey* and *key* really mean the same thing, just in a slightly different context. If we talk about a subkey of Key X, we're just emphasizing the subkey's location in the logical structure.

Complete key names can be fairly long because a key can reside several subkeys deep in the Registry structure. In this book, we separate keys in a complete key name with the backslash character (\), and we usually abbreviate the branch name (refer to Table 6-1). Even so, we sometimes have to break complete key names across lines, in which case we try to make the break at a syllable so you don't have to worry about any invisible spaces at the end of the first line in which the key name appears. Just remember not to include the hyphen.

Adding value

Most of the useful information in the Registry resides in values. A *value* is like a leaf on a tree branch: You can't have anything else hanging off a leaf. It's the end of the line in the organizational chain: "The chlorophyll stops here." Or, if you prefer to think of keys as directories in Windows Explorer, then think of values as individual files.

The Registry uses three types of values: *string, binary,* and *DWORD.* In all cases, Microsoft says that the maximum size of a single value is 16K, which explains why the Registry often points to a file's location on disk, instead of just including all that file's information in a Registry key. (In Windows 95, the sum of the sizes of *all* the values within a single key can't exceed 64K, but Windows 98 removes that restriction.)

Value names can contain letters, numbers, spaces, and underscores.

String

The string value type (indicated by a tiny icon in the value pane's Name column containing the letters *ab*) usually contains text, but may also contain numbers. (As with many aspects of the Registry, the rules are sometimes soft and slow rather than hard and fast.) String values appear enclosed in double quotes. Here are some examples:

```
C:\WINDOWS\SYSTEM
Temporary Internet Files
1024
```

Binary

The binary value type (indicated by a tiny icon containing some 1's and 0's) is usually for numeric information. True binary numbers contain nothing but ones and zeroes, but binary values in the Registry show up as hexadecimal numbers (base sixteen) where each digit ranges from 0 to F. (A is the same as decimal 10, B is the same as 11, and so on.)

It takes a two-digit hexadecimal number to make a *byte*. For example, *ff* represents a byte with the decimal equivalent of 255, and *00* represents a byte with the decimal equivalent of 0. In the Registry, binary values appear as a succession of two-digit, single-byte hexadecimal numbers separated by spaces. Figure 6-3 shows a Registry key containing a single string value (Default) and a bunch of binary values. A binary value can have as few as 4 bytes and as many as 65,536.

Figure 6-3:
The "ab" icon denotes a string value, and the "011110" icon denotes a binary or DWORD value.

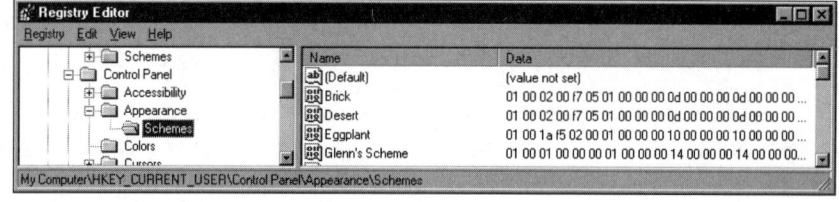

Sometimes you may want to convert quickly between hexadecimal, decimal, and binary values. For example, if you see in the Registry the hexadecimal value *d7 0a,* you probably don't immediately know that this value is the same number as decimal 55,050 or binary 1101011100001010. (If you *do* immediately realize this, then you'll have no trouble finding gainful employment in the computer industry, should you desire it.) Fortunately, you have a nifty conversion tool in the form of the Windows 98 calculator! Open the calculator with Start➪Programs➪Accessories➪Calculator and choose View➪Scientific to unveil the "hidden" calculator in Figure 6-4. You can enter a number in any format you like, and then instantly convert it by clicking the Hex, Dec, or Bin radio buttons (we skip Oct because the Registry doesn't use octal numbers).

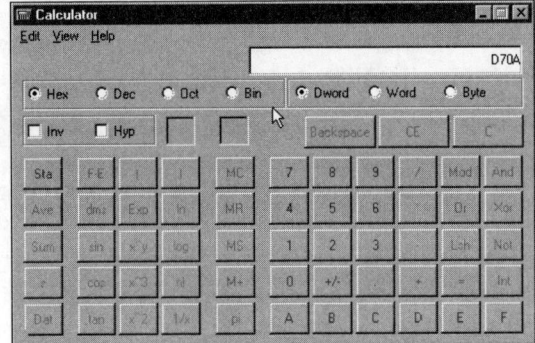

Figure 6-4:
The
Windows 98
calculator,
in its high-
tech mode.

DWORD

The DWORD value type (which uses the same icon as the binary value type) is also almost always for numeric information. You can think of DWORD as a special kind of binary value that's always the same size: four bytes. That translates to eight hexadecimal digits. (*DWORD* is short for *double word*. In computer lingo, two bytes make a word, so a double word is four bytes long.)

The Registry format for a DWORD value is "0x" plus eightnumbersallruntogether plus the decimal equivalent of the number in parentheses — like this:

```
0x00000001(1)
```

Caveat Registry user: Just because a value has four hexadecimal bytes doesn't mean it's a DWORD value. It can be a plain-old binary value that happens to be the same length as a DWORD value. (Hey, we just write about this stuff, we don't invent it.) If a Registry entry is supposed to have the DWORD format, you usually can't get away with putting the same numbers in binary format.

Chapter 4 offers specific information on how to create, change, and delete Registry keys and values with the Registry Editor.

Gross Registry Anatomy

This section presents an overview of the primary branches and the keys near the upper levels of the Registry's inverted-tree organization. We could go several layers deeper in this section, but we won't because doing so would take a hundred pages, no one besides a chronic insomniac would read it, and 99 percent of the material would be info that you'll never need to know about the more obscure keys.

We think giving you a fairly broad view here and then zeroing in on particular keys as necessary in chapters where they're relevant is a more sensible approach. So, we don't cover every subkey in the pages that follow. If you're the kind who really wants or needs to know what *HKLM\Enum\ Root\ *PNP0C05\0000\HardwareID* means, you just have to wait for *Windows 98 Registry For Trivia Buffs* (5,700 pages, publication date indeterminate).

HKEY_LOCAL_MACHINE

The *HKLM* branch stores every bit of configuration information that has to do with the computer, rather than any particular computer user. It corresponds to the physical file SYSTEM.DAT.

Some people assume that because *HKLM* contains the word "machine," it's all about hardware information. Not so, byte breath! *HKLM* contains lots of software information, too. Whatever details about the computer that apply to every user of the computer go into this branch. These details include hardware devices, device drivers, installed programs, and user-independent program settings. You modify *HKLM* every time you install or remove a Plug and Play device, install hardware with the Add New Hardware control panel, install or remove 32-bit Windows programs, or change the settings in the System control panel's Device Manager property sheet.

HKLM also contains the keys that form aliases to *HKCC* and *HKCR* (as you can see from Table 6-1). *HKLM* is definitely one of the two Big Kahunas of Registry branches, *HKEY_USERS* being the other.

HKLM contains at least seven major keys, as described in the following sections.

Config

Here's where the Registry stores the details of one or more hardware configurations. Most Windows 98 PCs don't use multiple configurations. For more on the subject, see "HKEY_CURRENT_CONFIG" later in this chapter.

Enum

This key contains information about every piece of hardware that's ever been installed on your PC since Windows 98 was originally installed. "Enum" is short for *enumerator,* which is software that sniffs around your PC, assigns each installed device a unique identifier, and notes each device's settings.

Chapter 7 goes into more detail about *HKLM\Enum* subkeys.

The organization of the subkeys under *HKLM\Enum* is a little hard to follow, but it roughly parallels the computer's *bus structure* — that is, the layout of slots and device connectors inside the PC. The precise fields the Registry stores for each device varies by device and manufacturer, but Figure 6-5 shows a fairly typical entry. You can expect to see the manufacturer's name, product model number, and certain configuration options. Much of this information feeds *HKDD\Config Manager\Enum* at startup to build the Plug and Play "hardware tree" (see Chapter 7).

Hardware

This key has some minimal serial port information, but the Registry maintains a lot more serial port data elsewhere. Microsoft advises that only the HyperTerminal communications applet uses the serial port information in this key, which is a felony violation of Registry rules. (Keys that pertain to specific programs are supposed to reside under other keys that identify both product and manufacturer, such as *HKLM\Software\Microsoft\Windows.*) Unlike Windows NT, which makes extensive use of *HKLM\Hardware,* Windows 98 doesn't seem to use this key for anything other than HyperTerminal and a few notes on the PC's CPU type.

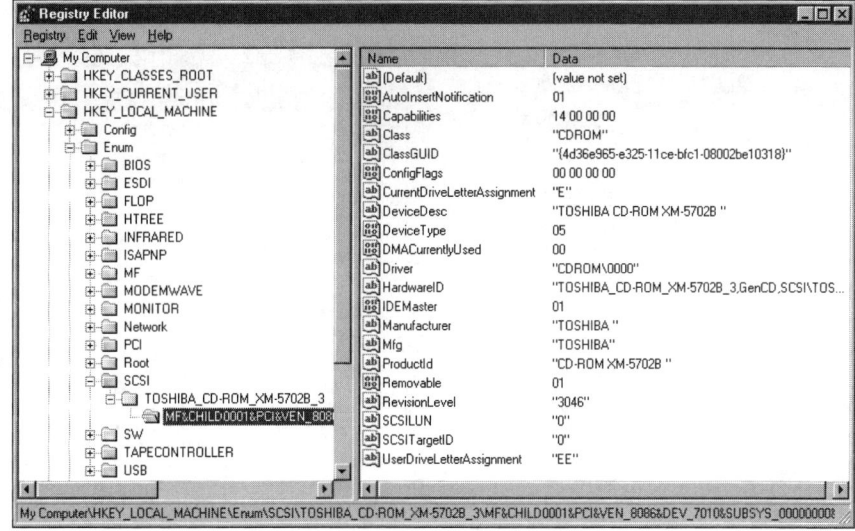

Figure 6-5:
An *HKLM*
entry for an
internal
CD-ROM
drive.

Network

Here the Registry stores various information about your machine's network account: the previous user to log on, the primary network to log onto, whether user profiles are on or off, and (potentially) a whole bunch of other details about your computer's network setup that apply regardless of who logs on. Note that the Novell network client (Client32) leaves all this stuff in the Registry even after you remove the client software. (Who says Novell and Microsoft are all that different when it comes to software practices?)

Security

This key contains details about the security provider for a networked Windows 98 PC — that is, what computer on your network is in charge of authenticating user logons.

Software

This key is *huge,* both in size and in importance. It contains all the user-independent settings for Windows 98 and every application installed on your machine. The Windows 98 settings mostly reside in *HKLM\Software\ Microsoft\Windows\CurrentVersion,* shown in Figure 6-6, a key we visit several times in this book. Various other keys under *HKLM\Software\ Microsoft* relate to bundled applications, such as Internet Explorer, Outlook Express, and so on.

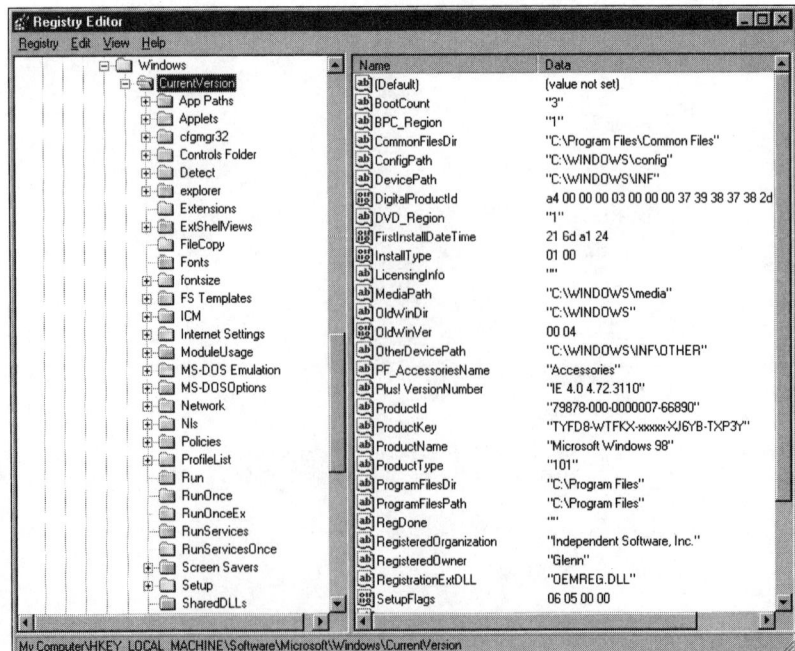

Figure 6-6:
HKLM
stores a
wealth of
Windows 98
settings.

Here are just a few of the subkeys of *HKLM\Software\Microsoft\Windows\ CurrentVersion* that you may be interested in knowing about:

- *Explorer* contains lots and lots of settings for the Windows 98 user interface, or shell.

- *Fonts* lists all the fonts installed on the system.

- *ProfileList* lists all the users set up on PCs with user profiles enabled (see Chapter 10).

- *Run, RunOnce,* and *RunServices* list programs to run when Windows 98 starts up.

- *Setup* contains information that the Windows 98 installation program uses.

- *Uninstall* lists programs that you can activate via the Add/Remove Programs wizard to remove software you no longer want.

Other *HKLM\Software* subkeys you're likely to see after a typical Windows 98 installation include:

- *Clients,* which contains information on Outlook Express and NetMeeting

- *SCC,* for System Compatibility Corporation, the old name for the company (Inso) that licenses the Quick Viewer program to Microsoft

- *Seagate,* whose scaled-down version of Backup Exec goes by the name Microsoft Windows Backup

The general layout is for the software vendor name to appear immediately under *HKLM\Software,* the product keys to appear beneath the vendor keys, and product version keys to appear beneath the product keys. One exception is the key *HKLM\Software\Classes,* which contains all the information about different file types (*.TXT, *.BMP, and so on) and which forms the alias branch *HKEY_CLASSES_ROOT* (see the section by the same name later in this chapter).

When you install a new application program, the installation procedure typically creates new Registry entries in *HKLM\Software* as well as in *HKCU\Software.* The latter location is for user-specific and user-modifiable settings.

System

Here's where Windows 98 stores the machine-specific details it needs in order to get out of its sleeping bag in the morning, that is, to boot. *HKLM\System* typically contains a single subkey, *CurrentControlSet,* which in turn contains *Control* and *Services.*

- ✔ *HKLM\System\CurrentControlSet\Control* contains a wide variety of startup information, including your computer's network name, the order in which to look for types of network connections, what multimedia resources your PC has to offer, printer settings, startup and shutdown information, what time zone to use, which applications have problems running under Windows, and so on ad nauseam.

- ✔ *HKLM\System\CurrentControlSet\Services* also contains a variety of settings, including system resources used (interrupts, memory ranges, and so on), hardware device drivers, file system information, modem initialization settings, agents (such as over-the-network backup agents), network clients, and network communication settings. The *Class* subkey and its contents are especially important.

You should rarely need to modify Registry data in *HKLM\System,* but when you do, be sure you have a current Registry backup. One wrong move when trucking through this key and Windows 98 could refuse to restart.

HKEY_CURRENT_CONFIG

Most people don't use this feature, but Windows 98 offers something called *hardware configurations* or *hardware profiles* (you see both terms in Microsoft documentation). The idea is that you can define multiple sets of devices to use in different circumstances.

The classic example is the notebook user who has a docking station at the office. Such a user would typically define two hardware configurations in the System control panel's Hardware Profiles property sheet: *docked* and *undocked*. The docked configuration can specify a different display adapter, printer, and network connection than the undocked configuration. Using the System control panel's Device Manager tab, you can navigate through the "hardware tree" on a device-by-device basis and specify which hardware configurations any given device should belong to.

So how does Windows 98 choose a hardware configuration at startup? It tries to do so automatically, by sniffing around to see what hardware seems to be connected. If it can't determine which configuration to use, then Windows 98 asks you to pick one from a list that it displays early in the boot process. At that point, Windows 98 copies over the appropriate key from *HKLM\Config* into *HKCC. HKCC* is then an alias that points to *HKLM\Config\ 000n,* where *n* is a number identifying the hardware configuration, as shown in Figure 6-7. You rarely, if ever, need to modify *HKCC* directly.

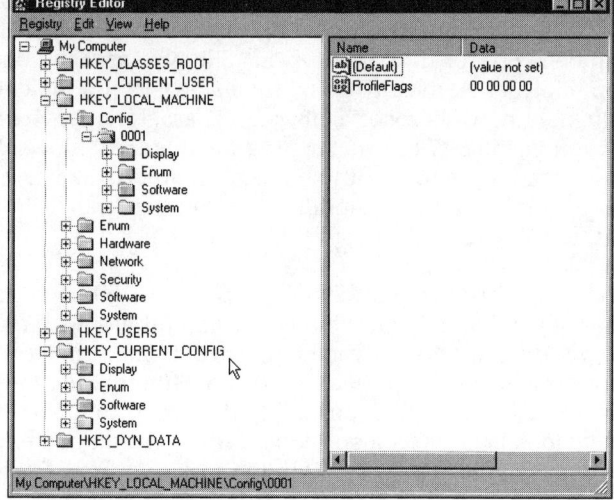

Figure 6-7:
HKCC has
the same
contents as
HKLM\Config
0001 on
this PC.

The *HKCC* subkeys are as follows:

- *Display* contains font information and monitor settings (resolution, colors, and so on).
- *Enum* has Plug and Play BIOS information.
- *Software,* a new key since Windows 95, contains Internet settings having to do with autodialing and proxy servers.
- *System* includes a list of printers available for the current hardware configuration.

In our experience, hardware configurations can be finicky. Sometimes you can just clear a check box in a Device Manager property sheet to disable a device in a given configuration; other times, you have to right-click the device and delete it from the hardware tree. Some hardware settings don't automatically migrate from one configuration to another, so you end up making these settings twice. The list of quirks goes on and on. This technology seems a little half-baked right now, and we suggest that you not use multiple hardware configurations unless you have a compelling reason — such as a notebook that sometimes uses a docking station.

HKEY_CLASSES_ROOT

The existence of *HKEY_CLASSES_ROOT,* which is an alias to *HKLM\ Software\Classes,* testifies to Microsoft's dedication in making Windows 98 work with Windows 3.*x* programs. The Windows 3.*x* version of the Registry, the Registration Database, allows programs to "register" file type associations (TXT with Notepad, BMP with Paintbrush, and so on) as well as the drag-and-drop behavior for those file types. (File type associations and drag-and-drop information used to go by the name OLE, for Object Linking and Embedding, but now Microsoft calls such characteristics *ActiveX properties.*) If you install a Windows 3.*x* program under Windows 98, the Windows 3.*x* program tries to modify the Registration Database; but through a little sleight-of-hand, it actually modifies the Registry branch *HKCR.* Compatibility, at least at the Registry level, is guaranteed.

Windows 98 extends the uses that Windows 3.*x* made of the old Registration Database to go beyond merely guaranteeing compatibility with older Windows programs. *HKCR* not only matches up data file suffixes with the appropriate programs, it defines what icons the different file types use; what commands you can apply to file types by right-clicking; and what the files' property sheets look like. *HKCR* also keeps track of the unique numbers that identify each different file type under Windows 98: the Class IDs.

Class IDs pop up all through the Registry, especially in *HKCR.* A *Class ID,* or CLSID for short, is a unique number, such as {25336920-03f9-11cf-8fd0-00aa00686f13}, that identifies an ActiveX object in Windows 98. *ActiveX objects* include data file types (such as a PowerPoint slide show) and program modules (such as the code that displays and processes dialog box radio buttons). Class IDs take the form of a 16-byte number enclosed in curly braces, each byte expressed by a two-digit hexadecimal number, arranged in a 4-2-2-2-6 byte grouping.

Figure 6-8 shows a big-picture view of *HKCR*'s structure. The following three sections go into more detail on each part.

Ignore the first key? You'd be an asterisk it

The asterisk key *HKCR** contains ActiveX object settings for every sort of Windows 98 file, regardless of type. (You may have guessed this from the common use of the asterisk as a wildcard character in file specifications like *.* and so on.) *HKCR** typically contains the single subkey *shellex,* which stands for *shell extensions.*

The Windows 98 graphical user interface goes by the generic name *shell,* meaning that the user interface presents the operating system to you and defines how Windows 98 looks and acts. A shell *extension* is an add-on that defines how the shell deals with a certain file type. That definition appears in the Registry key *shellex,* through its two subkeys, *ContextMenu-Handlers* and *PropertySheetHandlers. Context menus* are the pop-up menus that appear when you right-click files, and *property sheets* are the tabbed windows that appear when you right-click files and choose Properties.

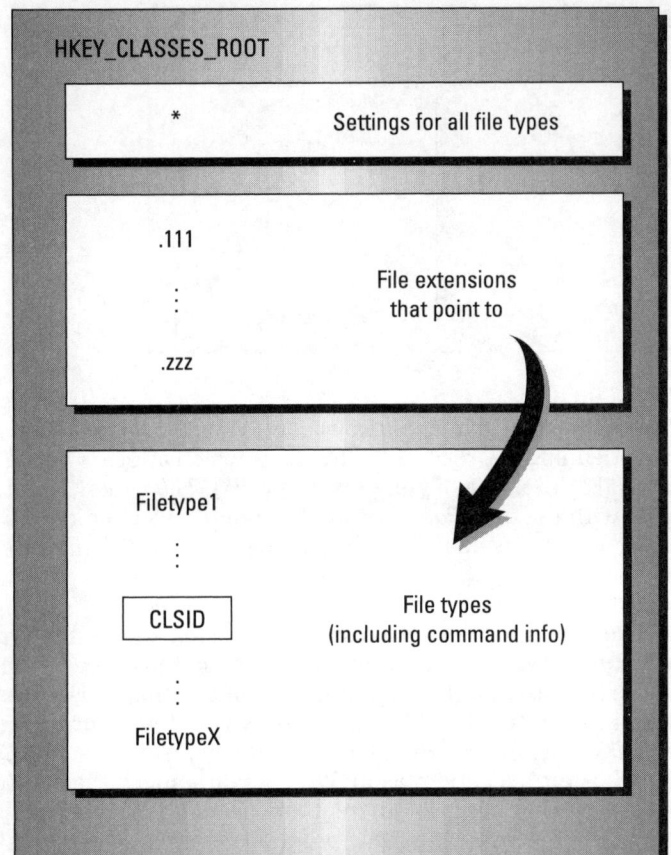

Figure 6-8:
An aerial view of HKCR shows its basic structure.

When you add programs that can work with every file on your computer, such as WinZip, Norton Navigator, or Novell IntranetWare, *HKCR*\shellex* may receive new entries. These new entries are Class IDs that usually point to a chunk of program code. The program code handles the job of providing context menu and property sheet choices.

Top half (filename extensions)

After the *HKCR** key, roughly the top half of all the entries under *HKCR* are *filename extension* keys (see Figure 6-9). An entry appears here for every filename extension (or suffix, like TXT or BMP) that Windows 98 or a Windows 98 program has defined on the PC.

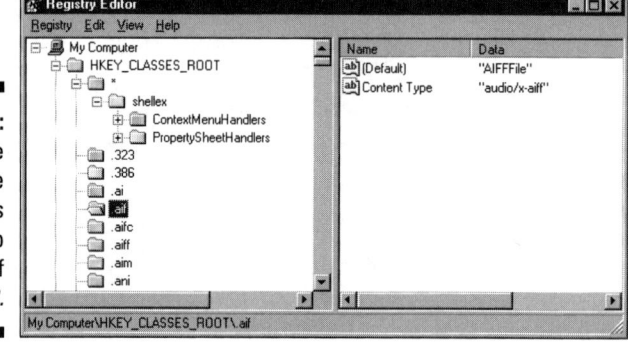

Figure 6-9:
Some filename extensions in the top half of *HKCR.*

Many of these filename extension keys contain nothing more than a single string value defining the related *file type* key, which appears in the bottom half of *HKCR.* For example, if you look at the *HKCR\.bmp* key, it contains a single value with the data *Paint.Picture* that refers to a later key, *HKCR\Paint.Picture,* which has all the details on how Windows 98 handles such a file type.

Why divide up *HKCR* into two halves with extension keys in the top half that point to file type keys in the bottom half — why not just put all the relevant details in the filename extension key instead of creating an additional file type entry in the bottom half? For example, why not just put all the information under *HKCR\.bmp* instead of having that key just point to *HKCR\Paint.Picture?* There's a good reason: What if you want the same program to handle a file type that has two different extensions? For example, you want JPG and JPEG files to open the same program, as well as HTM and HTML files to open another program. Using *HKCR*'s organizational structure, you can have two entries in the filename extension key group (the top half) both point to a single entry in the class definition group (bottom half). For example, *HKCR\.JPG* and *HKCR\.JPEG* both point to *HKCR\jpegfile,* and *HKCR\.HTM* and *HKCR\.HTML* both point to *HKCR\htmlfile.*

Readers familiar with computer database design (or the career of pop singer Madonna) may recognize the relationship between the top and bottom halves of *HKCR* as a *many-to-one* relationship.

One detail about file types must appear in the top half, though, and that's what to do if you right-click the desktop and choose New➪filetype. Windows 98 needs to create the file with the proper filename extension, so you may find a subkey called *ShellNew* under the filename extension key in *HKCR.*

Bottom half (class definitions)

The bottom half or so of *HKCR* contains *class definition* keys, such as *HKCR\Paint.Picture* or *HKCR\jpegfile,* to which the filename extension keys in the top half of *HKCR* point. The class definition keys are where all the action is in terms of defining how different file types behave. Figure 6-10 shows an example of the bottom half of *HKCR*.

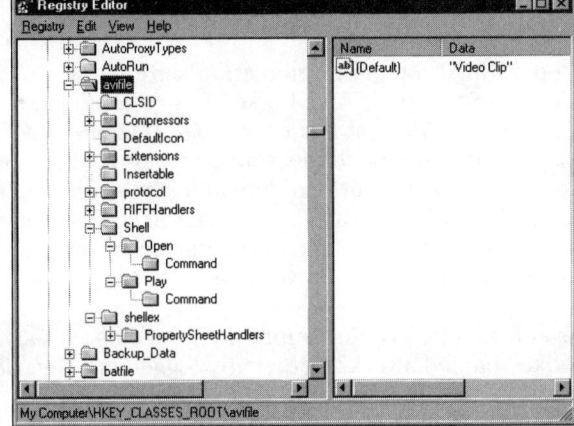

Figure 6-10:
Class
definition
information
in the
bottom half
of *HKCR*.

Some of the subkeys you may find beneath a class definition key include the following:

- ✔ **Shell.** Here's where context menu actions unique to a file type appear. For example, *HKCR\filetype\shell\open\command* contains the actual command to run (usually a program on disk) when you double-click a file of the specified *filetype*. (Or single-click it in the desktop Web view.) In this example, "open" is called the *verb*. Other common verbs are "print" and "edit." Shades of grammar school. . . .

- ✔ **Shellex.** If the file type's property sheet is to display special choices not included on the generic property sheet, here's where the Registry references the Class ID for the program code that provides the property sheet enhancements. The Registry may also include references to a special *ContextMenuHandler* or *DragDropHandler* if special software is required to handle context menus and drag-and-drop desktop behavior.

- ✔ **DefaultIcon.** Here's the location of the icon that Windows 98 displays for files of a specified type.

A special key in *HKCR*'s bottom half, *HKCR\CLSID*, contains a comprehensive list of every CLSID on the system. Each subkey under CLSID is a unique 16-byte identifier and typically contains a default string value describing the object type (such as "Video Clip" or "MS Conference Manager Object"). Beneath each specific CLSID key, you typically find a subkey named *InProcServer32,* which (again typically) contains the path and filename for the chunk of program code that Windows 98 associates with that CLSID.

HKCR\CLSID is important to know about if you're troubleshooting problems with a certain kind of file, because this key can point you to the DLL file on disk that handles that kind of file.

HKEY_USERS

Any Windows 98 operating system or application setting that can conceivably vary from one user to another on a PC set up to support multiple users goes into the *HKU* branch. *HKU* contains user-related Windows settings such as desktop wallpaper and network connections. The application-related settings depend on the software, but could include user preferences such as toolbar placement and data file storage locations. *HKU* corresponds to the file USER.DAT and is one of the two Big Kahuna Registry branches, along with *HKLM*. Its closest relative in Windows 3.*x* is WIN.INI.

This key contains at least one primary subkey, *.Default,* and it may contain one additional subkey named after the currently logged-on user. *HKU* normally never shows more than that, although on a Windows 98 PC with user profiles enabled, the number of different users that can have Registry accounts is practically unlimited. For example, if you set up a PC for users Bob and Ray, when Bob logs on, *HKU* contains the subkeys *.Default* and *Bob*. When Ray logs on, HKU contains the subkeys *.Default* and *Ray.*

The contents of each subkey immediately under *HKU* share the same organization and include the following keys, among others.

AppEvents

Here's where the Registry stores locations and filenames of the sounds that play when specific Windows 98 events occur. (Chapter 18 contains a cool tip to create your own sound events for any program you want.)

Control Panel

Many user-specific control panel settings live here, but watch out. Not all control panel settings can vary from user to user. Remember that modifying control panel settings from a control panel is always better than using the Registry Editor.

InstallLocationsMRU

This key contains directory paths from which the user has recently installed applications, for example, by clicking the Have Disk button in the Add/Remove Programs wizard. (The "MRU" part stands for Most Recently Used.)

Network

Recent and persistent connections to network resources are stored here. (A "persistent" connection is one that Windows 98 tries to reestablish at each logon.)

RemoteAccess

Here's where Windows 98 stores Dial-Up Networking connection details for remote network access sessions.

Software

Here's where all the user-settable and user-specific preferences for installed software applications reside. When you install a new application, it makes entries here and in *HKLM\Software* (where settings exist that don't vary from user to user).

HKEY_CURRENT_USER

On a PC set up to support multiple users, *HKCU* contains the subset of settings in *HKU* that pertain to whoever logged on at the Windows 98 startup prompt. *HKCU* is an alias that points to *HKU\username,* where *username* is the logged-on user's name.

If your PC hasn't been set up to support multiple users, or if the current user bypasses the logon dialog box (for example by pressing Esc), then *HKCU* contains the same information as *HKU\.Default* — the "default" user is the same as the current user. The subkeys for *HKCU* are the same as we defined for *HKU* in the previous section.

If the same desktop or application setting exists in both *HKLM* and *HKCU,* as happens occasionally, the setting in *HKCU* always wins.

HKEY_DYN_DATA

HKDD (the *DYN* is for *dynamic,* or changing) stores information about active hardware, including real-time device status information and performance statistics. It's a unique Registry branch in several ways. *HKDD*'s home isn't USER.DAT or SYSTEM.DAT; *HKDD* lives in main memory, or RAM (Random Access Memory). Windows 98 rebuilds *HKDD* anew at each restart. *HKDD* is also a read-only branch; it's the only Registry branch that neither users nor programs can write information to.

HKDD contains a ton of information, but two keys are of particular interest.

Config Manager

Most of the interesting stuff in *HKDD* resides in the *Config Manager* key. The Configuration Manager is the part of Windows 98 that handles Plug and Play devices — the newer generation of computer components that Windows 98 can set up automatically.

HKDD\Config Manager has a single subkey, *Enum,* under which each active device appears in a key having a unique eight-character identifier. The *HardwareKey* value under a specific device's key in *HKDD\Config Manager\Enum* points back to a key in *HKLM* where the Registry stores static, unchanging details about the device. (No point storing the stuff twice.)

Plug and Play is an important enough subject to get its own chapter. We take a little closer look at the structure of *HKDD\Config Manager\Enum* in Chapter 7.

PerfStats

HKDD\PerfStats contains a huge number of keys and values that point to subprograms that calculate system performance statistics (hence, "PerfStats"). It's kind of fun to highlight one of these keys in REGEDIT — say, *StatData* — and hit the F5 key from time to time in order to update the display. For example, *KERNEL\CPUUsage* varies almost every time you press F5.

Trying to get a good picture of your computer's performance by looking at *HKDD\PerfStats* with REGEDIT is a bit like measuring the acreage of a desert by counting grains of sand. *PerfStats* was never meant for people to look at, just programs — programs like System Monitor, the performance-monitoring accessory that comes with Windows 98.

Some of you may be thinking, "Hey Glenn and Mark, why on earth did Microsoft choose to throw all this stuff into the Registry? Why not just let System Monitor check all the statistics itself, in its own private memory space? And by the way, we're really enjoying your book so far."

First, thanks very much. Second, we asked ourselves the very same question, and the answer appeared to us in a blaze of artificial light when we were writing the part in Chapter 4 about remote Registry editing. Microsoft set up the Registry so that, in the right circumstances (Chapter 4 describes them), an administrator or technician can tinker with another user's Registry over a network link. Now, being able to monitor a remote network PC's performance would probably be equally handy, right? And if all that performance data is in the Registry, then the System Monitor accessory can get to the user's performance data over the network by using the same mechanism that the Registry Editor uses to get to the remote Registry.

After you make a little mental connection like this one, you realize that some pretty clever folks were at work on this stuff, after all. Not that we'll let Microsoft off the hook for some of the boneheaded maneuvers it made in other areas, of course, but we like to give credit where credit is due.

Chapter 7

Making Hardware Work with Plug and Play

· ·

In This Chapter

▶ Discovering where the Registry stores Plug and Play information

▶ Finding out what's so great about Windows 98's new hardware support

▶ Using Device Manager as a hardware-oriented Registry Editor

· ·

*C*ritics of the "Wintel" (Windows plus Intel) PC architecture — and we're referring here mainly to people who mistake the Macintosh computer for the basis of an organized religion — frequently point to the primitive and spastic dance that PC users have had to perform in order to install new hardware. True, the process can involve manually switching jumper settings or switches on hardware devices, changing arcane-sounding settings like IRQs and DMA channels, and (more often than not) waiting long stretches on the phone for help from overworked and undertrained technical support staff. Before Windows 98, if you came up victorious in the battle to install a sound card into a PC that contained a CD-ROM drive, internal modem, and network card, a bearded old shaman would venture out from the veldt to award you your official computer genius nose ring.

Although we tend to focus on its role as a software settings database, the Registry stores all your PC's hardware information, too. Whenever you use the System Control Panel's powerful Device Manager to fine-tune or trouble-shoot hardware settings, you're actually using a Registry Editor. The Registry also makes possible one of Windows 98's key advantages (or frustrations, depending on how well it works for you on any given day): *Plug and Play*. Knowing how the Registry and Plug and Play work together may come in handy when you decide to add or remove a device from a Windows 98 PC.

Incidentally, something else that can come in handy, especially when you're thinking about adding new hardware, is a list of devices that Windows 98 supports. You won't find this list of devices in your user manual, but your Windows 98 CD-ROM contains just such a list. Crank up Windows Explorer and select D:\DRIVERS\DRIVER98.CHM (assuming your CD-ROM is on drive D). The list is in the form a help file using Windows 98's new HTML Help feature (see Figure 7-1).

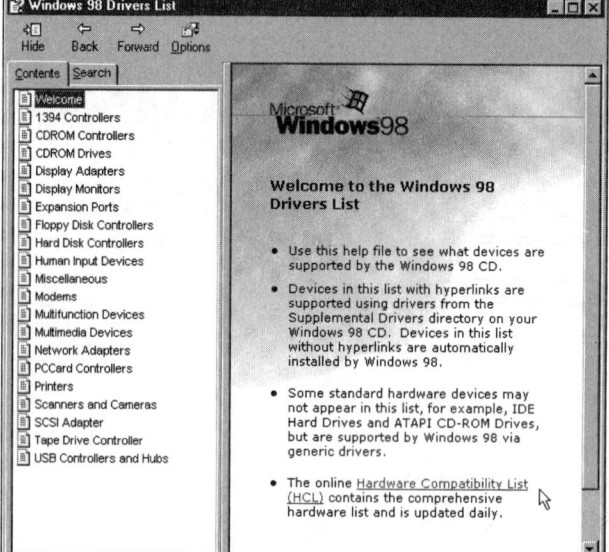

Figure 7-1:
The secret Windows 98 device list includes a link to an even more up-to-date Internet site.

Defining Plug and Play

The ambitious Plug and Play specification tries to set up computer hardware automatically, using the Windows 98 Registry as a central hardware database. The Plug and Play specification was introduced in 1994 by Intel and saw its first commercial application in 1995 when Microsoft released Windows 95.

Plug and Play is a broad hardware and software specification that requires support at all hardware and software levels within a PC — not just the operating system, but also the BIOS (Basic Input/Output System), device driver software, and device hardware. Plug and Play's two main goals are to

✔ Make setting up your PC hardware as painless and automatic as possible

✔ Reduce support costs for company PCs

The specification achieves these goals by automatically managing PC hardware resources — such as IRQs, upper memory addresses, and base I/O addresses. If you want to know more about how these resources work, check out the sidebar titled "The department of PC resources" in this chapter.

The department of PC resources

PC devices, such as network cards, mice, sound cards, and so on, require certain *resources* in order to work. These resources may include one or more of the following:

✔ **Interrupt number.** (Often abbreviated IRQ, for Interrupt ReQuest.) A number from 0 to 15 that specifies a dedicated "hot line" to your PC's central processing unit (CPU). If a device needs the computer's attention, the device sends a message to the CPU on its interrupt line.

✔ **Base I/O address.** A memory range that a device uses to move data between itself and your computer. Four-digit numbers in hexadecimal form express the start and end addresses, for example, 0300 to 030F.

✔ **Upper memory range.** A chunk of memory between 640K and 1024K that devices use for different and unique purposes. Not all devices need upper memory, but many (such as video cards) do. Like base I/O addresses, four-digit hexadecimal numbers list the range boundaries, such as CC00-CDFF.

✔ **DMA (Direct Memory Access) channel.** A number from 0 to 7 assigned to devices that can move data around in memory without bothering your CPU. Sound cards and diskette drives use DMA channels.

The general rule (and we discuss some important exceptions later in this chapter) is that no two devices can use the same resources. So, when you add a new device to your PC without the aid of Plug and Play, you have to figure out what resources the device needs and assign resources to the new device without overlapping with any existing device's resources.

This resource assignment process can be maddeningly difficult, especially considering that many devices are finicky about which resources they can use. For example, a network card may work only with interrupts 5, 10, or 11. If each of these interrupts is already in use, then the installer must change a setting for an existing device in order to free up an interrupt that the network card can use. However, one change may require another, and another. (Ever stand dominoes in a row and tip the first one?)

Taking the drudgery out of hardware installation

Plug and Play tries to shift the responsibility for assigning computer resources from you to your operating system. When you add a new device (and, usually, restart Windows 98), Windows 98 looks at all devices connected to the machine (a process called *enumeration*) and notices the newcomer.

After recognizing new hardware, Windows 98 swings into action to set up the new device. Windows first displays the New Hardware Found dialog box, which asks you whether you want to install software for the device.

Turbocharged Plug and Play buses

How could Plug and Play work better?

Well, it would be nice if you didn't have to restart Windows 98 so often in order to detect a new device (or undetect a device that you unplugged). It would be great if Plug and Play could do more interrupt sharing so you could connect more devices to a PC without a resource conflict. And it would be hands-down wonderful if you could connect one device to its nearest neighbor, instead of having to weave through a rat's nest of cabling to get to the back of the PC's main box. And a little more speed wouldn't hurt, either! Windows 98 introduces support for two new *buses* (PC communications channels) that turn such wishful thinking into reality.

The *Universal Serial Bus*, or *USB*, is gaining market momentum. Windows 95 supported USB to a limited extent in its OSR2.1 and OSR2.5 versions, but Windows 98 does a better job of supporting USB "out of the box." Most new PCs come with at least one USB connector on the back; if yours does, you should see some Registry information under *HKLM\Enum\USB\ROOT_HUB* and *HKLM\System\CurrentControlSet\Services\Class\USB*. Examples of USB devices include monitors, modems, keyboards, mice, speakers, telephones, ISDN adapters, scanners, printers, cameras, joysticks, graphics tablets — you name it.

The speed of data transfer can be one of two rates, depending on device requirements: 1.5MB/second and 12MB/second (*much* faster than a typical PC serial port, and fast enough to handle a whole new generation of peripherals). USB works better than most buses with Plug and Play, permitting hot connect and disconnect operations without requiring a PC restart. (We're tempted to say "Hallelujah," but it's a bit too soon to rejoice.) Windows 98 supports power management with USB peripherals, providing for on, off, and suspend modes. The icing on the cybercake is that you can connect up to 127 devices to a single USB port on the back of a PC. Some of those devices will be *hubs*, which provide device detection and power management support, and usually feature four USB connectors. Some USB peripherals, like monitors, can include a built-in hub as part of their design.

FireWire, known by computer nerds as *IEEE 1394*, is a high-speed serial bus for digital devices that handle a lot of data: cameras, video recorders, videodisc players, and so on. The FireWire connector is the same one used on Nintendo GameBoys. The maximum speed depends on the device, but the three possibilities are 100, 200, and 400MB/second — all much faster than the upper limit for USB devices. You can easily daisy-chain 16 devices on a FireWire bus, but you can extend that number by adding a variety of special-purpose devices. A FireWire extended bus is really a self-contained local area network. You don't even have to have a PC in the picture; you could have a digital camera feeding a still image directly to a color printer, cutting out the middleman.

FireWire supports hot connect/disconnect and Plug and Play. If your PC supports FireWire, you should see detailed Registry information under *HKLM\Enum* and *HKLM\System\CurrentControlSet\Services\Class\1394*. The various standards are still under development, however, and FireWire isn't designed to work with analog consumer electronics products like your VHS camcorder. Get more info at www.adaptec.com/firewire/.

Normally, you click Yes and insert the diskette or CD-ROM that contains the manufacturer-supplied device driver software. Windows 98 automatically installs the device driver software onto your hard drive, assigns any necessary resources to the device based on what the Registry says is available, and updates the Registry's *HKLM* key to contain essential device information. Everything happens behind the scenes, and you don't have to know an interrupt from a hole in the ground.

Windows 98 supports two new PC communications channels, or *buses,* which promise to take even more of the drudgery out of hardware installation and removal: *USB* and *FireWire*. For more on these technologies, see the sidebar titled "Turbocharged Plug and Play buses."

Rating the Plug and Play standard

Plug and Play hasn't gained acceptance as rapidly as Intel and Microsoft hoped. Part of the problem is that Plug and Play devices must coexist with non-Plug and Play devices (called *legacy* devices). Another difficulty is that the success of Plug and Play requires the participation of so many different players in the PC industry — an industry where consumer convenience traditionally has generated roughly the same level of corporate concern as the eventual burning out of the sun.

Configuration data in the Plug and Play system is shared and communicated among hardware, the BIOS (Basic Input-Output System; see the "Motherboard BIOS" section later in this chapter), and the operating system. For a full Plug and Play system, all three levels must support the Plug and Play standard. Windows 98 provides the operating system support; PC and device manufacturers must provide hardware support; and BIOS vendors must provide BIOS support. Getting all three groups to work in concert hasn't been easy.

Microsoft seems committed to the Plug and Play standard, continuing it into Windows NT 5.0. (That's handy, because almost everything you discover in this chapter about Plug and Play, you can also apply to Windows NT 5.0.) Even though Plug and Play doesn't work perfectly, it does make adding and changing hardware easier than before. If you follow the tips in the next section, Plug and Play works even better.

Optimizing Plug and Play

You may run into some snags while adding or changing hardware components, but you needn't sit idly by like a potted plant if Plug and Play doesn't work smoothly for you. The following three tips address some of Plug and Play's more common quirks.

Motherboard BIOS

The *BIOS* (Basic Input/Output System) is an important part of your computer system; it's a set of software code that lives on a chip plugged into the computer's motherboard. At startup, the BIOS looks around your PC and makes a list of the devices it finds and then hands off that list to Windows 98. If your PC's motherboard BIOS conforms to the Plug and Play standard, then Windows 98 can change the BIOS settings itself to make room for new hardware. For example, if your motherboard has a serial port set up to use a particular interrupt, Windows 98 can instruct the BIOS to use a different interrupt for that serial port to accommodate other devices on the system.

Windows 98 can also run with motherboards that don't have a Plug and Play BIOS. In that case, however, Windows 98 must work around the BIOS settings for motherboard devices, which limits its flexibility. That is, Windows 98 can't change resource assignments for motherboard devices in order to accommodate new devices. Also, without a Plug and Play BIOS, Windows 98 can't reliably and automatically detect new Plug and Play hardware, leaving you with only the old method of assigning resources manually ("Plug and Pray").

Periodically check with your PC's manufacturer for BIOS upgrades. These upgrades usually take the form of a program that you can download from the manufacturer's Web site and run once to update the BIOS code. (BIOS code upgradable in this manner is called *flash BIOS*.) Plug and Play tends to work more reliably with more recent BIOS versions. For example, if the list of devices that the BIOS finds at startup is incorrect, so is the Registry. You can typically see your current BIOS version at the top of the screen when you first power up your PC. Failing that, check out the Registry key *HKLM\Enum\Root*PNP0C01*.

Adapter BIOS

Plug-in circuit boards, or cards, typically come with their own specialized BIOS. If a card's BIOS conforms to Plug and Play, then Windows 98 can change any card setting — interrupt, memory address, and so on — without requiring you to perform PC surgery, flip switches, or juggle jumpers.

When you buy new cards for your PC, by all means get ones that are compatible with Plug and Play — compatibility doesn't cost any more — but also ask whether you have the option to *override* Plug and Play and set up the card manually. You'll be frustrated when Plug and Play doesn't work correctly and you can't get around it. In the worst case, you may face having to change resource assignments for every other device in your PC in order to get the card working. Before doing so, we suggest that you trade in the card for one that permits manual resource assignments.

Department of redundancy department

Many times, Windows 98 automatically detects new hardware the first time you install it — and then keeps on redetecting it every time you boot. This situation occurs most commonly with a parallel printer.

To troubleshoot the problem of redundant detection of the same parallel printer over and over, follow these steps:

1. **Run REGEDIT.**

2. **Export the Registry key** *HKLM\Enum\Lptenum,* **just in case.**

   This key is where Windows 98 stores information about Plug and Play devices connected to parallel ports. (If you're unsure as to how to export a Registry key, please see Chapter 4.)

3. **Delete the** *HKLM\Enum\Lptenum* **key and then restart your machine.**

4. **Install the software (that is, the device driver from the manu-facturer's diskette or CD) when Windows 98 autodetects the printer.**

   You shouldn't see the New Hardware Found message again.

How Does the Registry Store Plug and Playful Data?

What does all this discussion of Plug and Play have to do with the Registry? Everything! The only way a system like Plug and Play can possibly work is if your PC stores all hardware details in one place, so the Plug and Play configuration manager can keep track of all your devices and resources. In Windows 98, that one place is the Registry. In this section, we take a closer look.

HKDD: A special branch

The *HKey_Dyn_Data* branch, *HKDD* for short, is where the list of currently active hardware resides in the Registry. Each device has its own unique eight-character identifier (like C11B3738) in this Registry branch. Windows 98 rebuilds *HKDD* each time it starts, which explains why *HKDD* never appears in any full Registry backups. No need to store *HKDD* if Windows 98 re-creates it at boot time anyway.

HKDD lives entirely in random access memory (RAM), unlike the other disk-based Registry branches. The reasoning behind storing *HKDD* in memory is to enable Windows 98 to respond quickly to what the Plug and Play specification calls *dynamic reconfiguration events:* in English, somebody plugging something in, or somebody unplugging something. If *HKDD* were disk-based, Plug and Play would be much slower in responding to system changes.

Another unique aspect of *HKDD* is that it's a read-only branch. You never use REGEDIT to modify a key in *HKDD.* In fact, you can make changes to *HKDD* only indirectly, by first modifying *HKey_Local_Machine (HKLM).* The changes that you make to *HKLM* via the System control panel or the Add New Hardware wizard show up at the next reboot in *HKDD.* That's why you usually have to reboot Windows 98 after you add a new device for the first time: Windows 98 needs to rebuild *HKDD.*

HKLM's supporting role

Because *HKDD* lives in RAM and is read-only, you can make changes to the hardware configuration only indirectly, through *HKLM.* So why not just leave all the hardware information in *HKLM* and do away with *HKDD?* We already mentioned the first reason: *HKDD* lives in RAM, so it's fast. Putting *HKLM* in RAM would eat up a lot more memory than necessary because much of the information in *HKLM* doesn't pertain to Plug and Play. Heck, much of the stuff in *HKLM\Enum* may pertain to hardware that's not even in your PC anymore. On the other hand, *HKDD\Config Manager\Enum* contains information about the currently active devices only.

Rather than duplicate all the information about each device in both *HKLM* and *HKDD,* the currently active list in *HKDD\Config Manager\Enum* points back to the appropriate key in *HKLM\Enum,* where the Registry stores most of your device details.

The elephant never forgets

Any time that a hardware device or protocol is installed or reinstalled it will be recorded in *HKLM\Enum.* Any time, anywhere, anyhow. So if you install six different monitors, three different mice, and two LAN cards over the life of your Windows 98 PC, *HKLM\Enum* knows about it and remembers it.

The structure of the *Enum* key is not real logical at first glance, but your hardware is in there somewhere. Here are some of the common subkeys under *HKLM\Enum:*

✔ **BIOS** contains Plug and Play information about devices that the Basic Input/Output System detects, stuff like timers, the keyboard and joystick controllers, parallel and serial ports, onboard sound hardware, and so on.

- ✔ **ESDI** is a misnamed key that supposedly contains IDE controller information. (IDE controllers typically manage hard drives and CD-ROM drives.) On many systems we've seen, this key contains disk *drive* information, but not disk controller information. Incidentally, nobody uses ESDI disks anymore.

- ✔ **FLOP** (bet you can guess this one) holds diskette controller info.

- ✔ **HTREE** doesn't do anything yet. Wait for Windows 2001.

- ✔ **INFRARED** is where Windows 98 stores details on your PC's infrared controller. This key may appear even if you don't have such wireless communications hardware, which is more common on notebooks than desktops.

- ✔ **ISAPNP** holds info for Plug and Play devices on your PC's ISA (Industry Standard Architecture) bus — those old AT-compatible slots. Install a Plug and Play network card into an ISA slot, for example, and it shows up here.

- ✔ **MF** (short for *manufacturer*) is where PC makers put info unique to their systems. We often see IDE controller information here, rather than in ESDI, where Microsoft says it should go.

- ✔ **MODEMWAVE** is where voice modem info goes. PCs that can act as telephone answering machines have this subkey.

- ✔ **MONITOR** contains info on, well, you know.

- ✔ **Network** (not capitalized) has a bunch of non-hardware-related information about your network control panel settings. We're not sure why a purely software-related key shows up among a lot of hardware keys, but the mysteries of the Registry are dark and deep.

- ✔ **PCI** has info on Plug and Play devices installed on the PC's PCI (Peripheral Component Interconnect) bus. Between this key and ISAPNP, all your plug-in circuit boards are covered. (Yes, it *should* be named PCIPNP.) If you see the subkey *IRQHOLDER,* then your PC can most likely handle interrupt sharing between PCI devices.

- ✔ **Root** supposedly contains info on non-Plug and Play hardware, but we see subkeys that deal with Plug and Play printers here, too. Of special interest is *Root*PNP0C01,* which contains your PC's BIOS manufacturer and exact version.

- ✔ **SCSI** includes details on any Small Computer Systems Interface controllers (such as for high-performance hard drives) in the PC, but it also has info on IDE CD-ROM controllers.

- ✔ **TAPECONTROLLER** pretty much says it all.

- ✔ **USB** includes details on a Universal Serial Bus root hub, if one is present in the PC. (See the sidebar in this chapter, "Turbocharged Plug and Play buses.")

INFormation, please

Every device that you install under Windows 98 comes with an INF file that contains details on how to set up the Registry to work with the device, as well as which files (called *drivers*) should go where. The INF files themselves live on your hard drive in the hidden folder C:\WINDOWS\INF. The Registry knows where those INF files are, too, and it also knows which INF files go with which devices.

This INFormation lives in *HKLM*, specifically, in *HKLM\System\ CurrentControlSet\Services\Class*. Highlight this key in the Registry Editor's key pane and perform a Find operation for "INF" to see what we mean. This section of the Registry is a master list of all hardware devices that Windows 98 can install and also devices that it has installed.

Chapter 13 offers a different slant on the subject of INF files.

There's something else interesting about this key, as the next section explains.

A touch of Class (ID)

In Chapter 6, you read about *Class IDs,* or *CLSIDs* for short. They're unique, identifying numbers that the Registry uses to refer to every sort of Windows 98 file type and object. The Windows 98 Registry makes more extensive use of CLSIDs than the Windows 95 Registry, and *HKLM\System\ CurrentControlSet\Services\Class* is a perfect example (see Figure 7-2). In Windows 95, this key contains no CLSIDs, but in Windows 98, it's full of 'em.

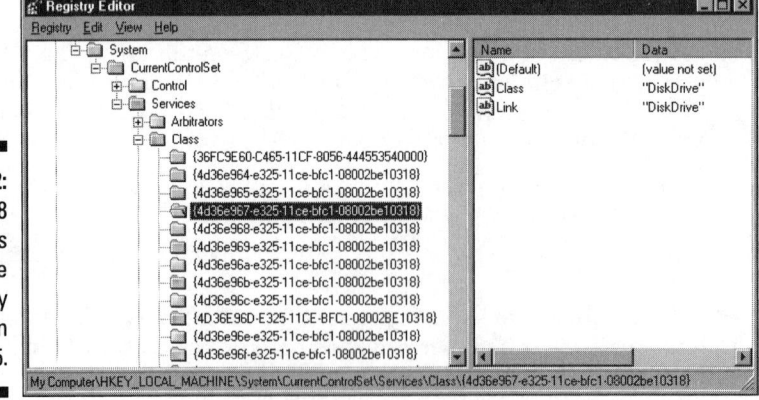

Figure 7-2: Windows 98 uses CLSIDs more extensively than Windows 95.

The CLSIDs point to device types that appear later in the Class subkey (see Figure 7-3), in much the same way that CLSIDs point to file type classifications in *HKCR*. The CLSIDs that you see in Figure 7-3 also refer to CLSIDs in

HKLM\Enum, where the Registry maintains information about every device ever installed in the system (see the earlier section "The elephant never forgets").

Figure 7-3:
Later
entries in
the Class
subkey
refer back
to the
device
CLSIDs.

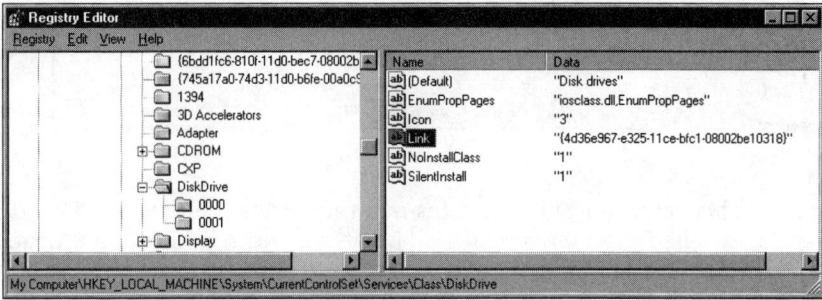

Figure 7-3:
Later entries in the Class subkey refer back to the device CLSIDs.

You can more easily understand this new, expanded use of CLSIDs for hardware as well as software if you pick a CLSID in *HKLM\System\ CurrentControlSet\Services\Class* and then use the Registry Editor's Find command (Ctrl+F) to locate other references to the same CLSID. And don't be confused: Microsoft sometimes uses the acronym *ClassGUID* instead of CLSID, but both terms mean the same thing.

The advantage of assigning CLSIDs to hardware is that it unifies the method that programmers use to locate hardware objects as well as software objects. Joe and Jane End User won't see much direct benefit, but over the long run, software costs tend to drop as programmers' lives become easier.

Stalking the wild circuit board

Here's a quick example that illustrates how the three main Registry hardware areas *HKDD\Config Manager\Enum, HKLM\Enum,* and *HKLM\System\ CurrentControlSet\Services\Class* all relate to each other. You may need to read this section twice (shoot, we had to write it three or four times), but once you do, you have a solid grasp on how the Registry handles hardware information.

We picked a key at random under the key *HKDD\Config Manager\Enum* on Glenn's PC. (The monitor's dart scratches should come off with soap.) It's C29BEF50, and it includes the values shown in Figure 7-4. We know this is a currently active device, because that's the only kind that *HKDD\Config Manager\Enum* contains.

The *Problem* value is all zeroes, which indicates that the device seems to be working okay as far as Windows 98 can tell, and doesn't conflict with any other device. Notice the *HardwareKey* value, *ISAPNP\TCM5095\08532D7E.*

Figure 7-4:
An active
device's
key and
values in
*HKDD\Config
Manager\
Enum.*

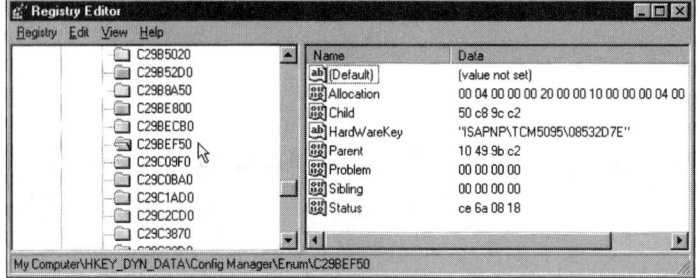

This value not only indicates that the device is a Plug and Play device installed in an ISA slot, it also points us to the subkey underneath *HKLM\Enum* where you can get more details on this active hardware device.

So if you tromp on over through the underbrush to *HKLM\Enum\ISAPNP\ TCM5095\08532D7E,* as shown in Figure 7-5, you see a lot more information about the device, as follows:

✔ The *DeviceDesc* value shows that the device is a 3Com Etherlink III ISA network interface card, running in its Plug and Play mode. (If this card were not running in Plug and Play mode, it would have a *ForcedConfig* value in the Registry key to indicate that the user told Windows 98 which settings the card needs to use, instead of letting Windows 98 figure them out on its own.)

✔ The *Mfg* value confirms that 3Com makes the device.

✔ The *ClassGUID* value is the device's Class ID, which appears as a subkey under *HKLM\System\CurrentControlSet\Services\Class* and confirms that the hardware class is "Net." (See Figure 7-6.)

✔ Finally, the *Driver* value, *Net\0002,* gives us a clue as to where to find the device's INF installation script. The magic secret is that you tack this value's data field to the end of *HKLM\System\CurrentControlSet\ Services\Class* to get *HKLM\System\CurrentControlSet\Services\ Class\Net\0002.* Navigate to this key (see Figure 7-7), and you see the value *InfPath* pointing to the file NETEL5X9.INF. Sure enough, that file exists in C:\WINDOWS\INF. (Whew — we would have been pretty embarrassed if it didn't.)

At this point, we've navigated the Registry to learn just about every relevant fact about this device: its description, manufacturer, Registry class ID, and associated INF file on disk. As you can see, when it comes to hardware as well as software, the Registry knows all, sees all. (Well, almost; it still doesn't contain any information on which device is going to break next.)

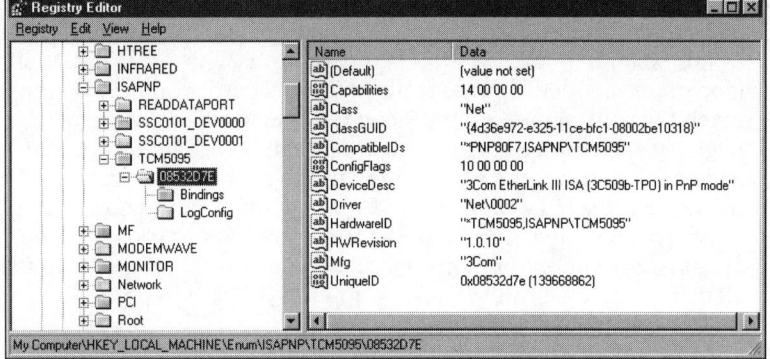

Figure 7-5:
More information about the device resides in *HKLM\Enum.*

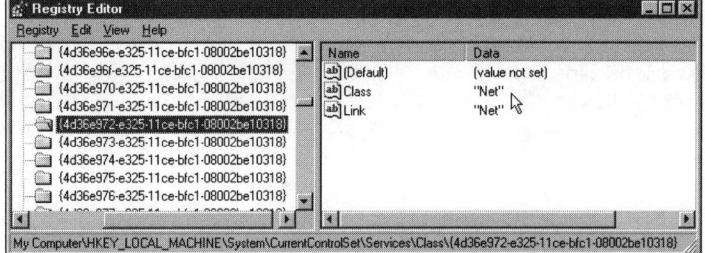

Figure 7-6:
The Class ID for the device is indeed "Net."

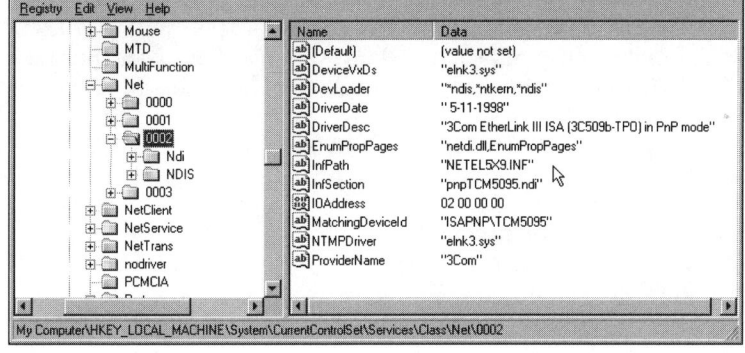

Figure 7-7:
And now you know which INF file controls the device's installation.

Don't waste time looking for hardware information in *HKLM\Hardware*. Yes, finding device information in this key does seem logical, but this key is practically empty. (It actually holds settings for the communications applet HyperTerminal.)

What can you use this sort of knowledge for, besides impressing the khakis off your computer guru friends? When Plug and Play refuses to "play nice," as for example it may when it erroneously assigns COM5 to your new modem or misidentifies your new network card, you may be tempted to reach for your elephant gun. However, using your new knowledge of the Registry's hardware keys, you can outmaneuver Windows 98 with wile and guile. Follow the steps we outlined in the previous paragraphs: Head under the hood to *HKDD\Config Manager\Enum,* then to the corresponding section under *HKLM\Enum,* and finally to the corresponding section in *HKLM\ System\CurrentControlSet\Services\Class\.* Deleting the relevant subkeys in all three locations (after backing up first, of course) obliterates all traces of the offending hardware device.

Of course, if you always had to use REGEDIT to view the details of your PC's hardware configuration — or to change the hardware by adding, removing, or reconfiguring a device — you'd go rapidly bananas. Fortunately, Windows 98 provides two much friendlier programs for accessing the hardware information in the Registry: the Device Manager and the Add New Hardware wizard. The Device Manager, in particular, is worth a closer look before we end this trip into the Registry's "chamber of hardware."

Swinging from the Hardware Tree

The so-called *hardware tree,* which you display by clicking the Device Manager tab in the System Control Panel, is a graphical representation of *HKDD\Config Manager\Enum* and various subkeys under *HKLM\Enum.* You're looking at the Registry's hardware database here, but instead of REGEDIT, you're using a much more comprehensible tool. (See Figure 7-8.)

In theory, on a completely Plug and Play computer, you never need to look at Device Manager. Windows 98 would juggle interrupts and memory addresses for each device in the system, and you've no reason to care what they were. However, not all devices work with Plug and Play. You may have to use Device Manager to assign such devices the PC resources that Windows 98 cannot figure out on its own.

Mousing around Device Manager

The hardware tree in Device Manager expands and contracts just like directories in Windows Explorer: Click + to expand a branch, click – to collapse it. After you've expanded a branch to show its individual entries, you can double-click any entry to see its property sheets.

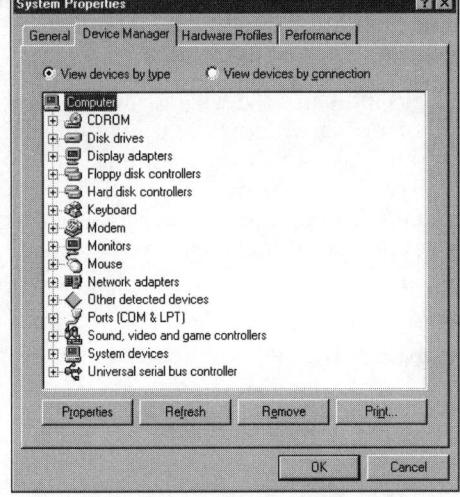

Figure 7-8:
The Device
Manager,
where the
Registry's
hardware
information
becomes
under-
standable.

The radio buttons at the top of the Device Manager display enable you to look at the hardware tree from two perspectives: devices grouped by type, or devices grouped by hardware connection. The second view matches up more closely with how the Registry organizes devices in *HKLM\Enum,* but most people find the first view a little easier to understand.

Double-click the Computer icon at the very top of the hardware tree, and you get a very handy display with two tabs: View Resources and Reserve Resources. The View Resources tab lets you see the current device resource assignments by category, as shown in Figure 7-9. (We explain these categories in the sidebar entitled "The department of PC resources" in this chapter.) The Reserve Resources tab enables you to tell Plug and Play not to assign a particular resource because you intend to add a device in the near future that needs it — or because you use a device (such as a scanner card) that Windows 98 doesn't auto-detect, that doesn't appear in the hardware tree, and that must use a particular hard-wired interrupt number.

Identifying device conflicts

The Device Manager uses three different identifiers to alert you to potential problems:

> ✔ **A black exclamation point on a yellow field** indicates a device in a problem state — for example, a device using a resource that conflicts with another device, or a device that uses different resources than Windows 98 thinks it uses. This identifier doesn't necessarily mean that the device isn't working, just that it *may not* work, and if it does work, some other device probably doesn't.

✔ **A red "X" mark** indicates a device that's physically present in the system but that is disabled and has no protected-mode device driver loaded. The device may still function, but usually does not.

✔ **A blue "i" on a white field** indicates a device for which you've forced manual settings instead of letting Windows 98 use automatic settings. That is, you have cleared the Use Automatic Settings check box on the device's Resource property sheet. The device probably works just fine, but Windows 98 loses some flexibility in configuring other devices because this manually set device is "locked in" to one specific set of resources.

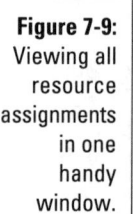

Figure 7-9:
Viewing all
resource
assignments
in one
handy
window.

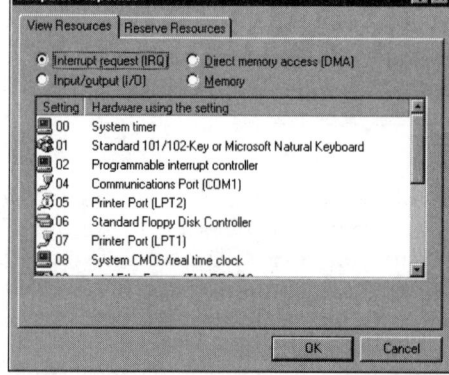

On a 100 percent pure Plug and Play system, you don't see any of these identifiers. However, their presence doesn't mean that you have a conflict — just that you need to take a closer look at the device and its settings, and perhaps change those settings as described in the next section.

Manually assigning resources

You may need to override Windows 98 and its Plug and Play system and manually assign PC resources to a device, in the following situations:

✔ The device doesn't conform to Plug and Play, and Windows 98 doesn't detect the device as one of the thousands it knows about already.

✔ The device is Plug and Play compatible, but for some reason, Windows 98 can't figure out how to set it up correctly. (This problem often happens with internal modems.)

✔ The device's documentation advises you to make different resource settings than Windows 98 makes on its own.

The Device Manager is very helpful when you set about assigning resources to a device by hand, and you should not use the Registry Editor for this purpose. Editing *HKLM\Enum* with REGEDIT is very rarely necessary.

To manually assign resources in Device Manager, follow these steps:

1. **Expand the hardware tree by clicking + beside the desired device.**

2. **Double-click the device in question and then click the Resources tab. (See Figure 7-10.)**

   The Resources tab shows all the resource assignments.

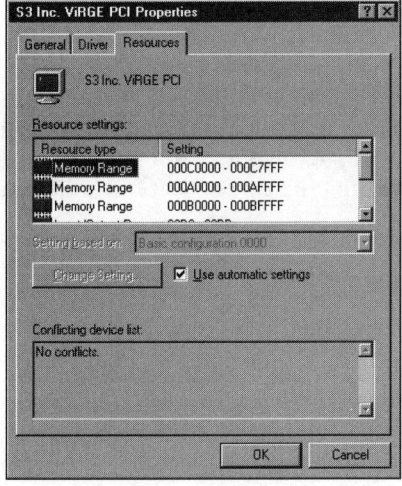

Figure 7-10: The Resources tab for a specific device enables you to edit the device's Registry settings.

3. **Uncheck the Use Automatic Settings check box.**

   Unchecking this check box tells Windows 98 not to try autoconfiguring the selected device.

4. **Try the predefined configurations listed in the Setting Based On field by choosing them from the list and watch the Conflicting Device list for any messages indicating a resource conflict.**

5. **After you find a configuration that works with no conflicts, click OK.**

   If a configuration doesn't work out, click the Change Setting button and specify the resources individually, again watching for conflict information. You can use trial and error here, or take your cue from the device manufacturer's user manual.

The Registry usually contains a value called *ForcedConfig* for each device that you configure manually. Search the Registry for this value and look at the devices that show up. The more devices with forced configurations, the less flexibility Windows 98 has in configuring new devices, because it

can't change the resources assigned to devices with forced configurations —
those assignments are locked down. So, for example, if a new device can
only use interrupt 10, and an existing device has a forced configuration that
specifies interrupt 10, Windows 98 can't change the existing device to a
different number and give 10 to the new device.

Sometimes you don't want to change a device's settings; you just want to
shut the durn thing off. Plug and Play can make shutting off a device difficult
by automatically redetecting the device at each reboot and adding it to the
hardware tree. The trick to forcing Windows 98 not to assign resources to a
device is to double-click the device in the hardware tree, choose the General
property sheet, and check the check box that reads Disable in this hardware
profile.

Device Manager is a handy way of editing the Registry's hardware database,
and it may be the only way of changing certain settings (such as notebook
PC Cards), but it doesn't necessarily show you every device that connects
to your PC. It doesn't show printers, for example; that's the job of the
Printers control panel. Device Manager also may not show devices that
piggyback on other devices, like the tape drives that hook up to a diskette
controller cable.

Part III

Blazing Your Own Trail: Registry Customizing

The 5th Wave   By Rich Tennant

"OKAY—ANTIDOTE, ANTIDOTE, WHAT WOULD AN ANTIDOTE ICON LOOK LIKE? YOU KNOW, I STILL HAVEN'T GOT THIS DESKTOP THE WAY I WANT IT."

In this part . . .

*A*s George lounged lazily by the tranquil watering hole
and looked up from his sandwich, he was jolted by the
sight of a charging rhinoceros who meant business — fatal,
nasal business. Our hero quickly reached into his vest and
removed a tiny remote control. A 3-D laser holograph unit
atop the safari truck whirled into action and projected a
stunningly lifelike image of a female rhino a few feet to
George's side. By the time the sidetracked male beast
realized in fury that the object of his animal lust was a
mere mirage, George was safely in his truck — finishing
lunch instead of becoming it.

There's nothing quite so satisfying to a computer user as
hotrodding a PC to do things that seem remarkable, if not
impossible, even to computer-savvy friends. In Part III, you
apply your Registry knowledge to customize Windows 98
to your liking.

A slick but nearly unknown utility can customize the
Windows 98 install program so that the initial Registry looks
the way you want it to — handy if you manage Windows 98
on a network. But we cover customizing Windows 98
for individual computers as well. You can modify the
Registry's behavior with the System Policy Editor in order
to restrict what a user can do with Windows 98. By using
user profiles, in which multiple users have their own
version of the Registry's user-specific half, USER.DAT, you
can customize a single Windows 98 computer for several
different people. This part also explains ways you can
tune the Registry to squeeze more speed out of Windows
98, change how the operating system looks, and improve
how the Registry handles file types. A final chapter zeros
in on customizing new Windows 98 goodies: Active
Desktop and Internet Explorer.

Chapter 8

Customizing SETUP for Easier, Cleaner Installations

*Y*ou can customize the Registry many ways, but one of the slickest is by creating your own custom Windows 98 installation program. In this way, you can modify the Registry's initial contents when a new user installs Windows 98 over a network, or even from a local hard drive. Getting the Registry to look more like you want it to as part of the Windows 98 setup program sure beats running around to a lot of PCs and making dozens of customizations after the fact.

Many people never actually install Windows 98. It appears like a neatly set table on most new PCs, along with a cornucopia of bundled software. Why, then, do so many network managers ruthlessly reinstall Windows 98 afresh whenever a new PC hits the office? Why toss that cornucopia aside and spill perfectly good fruit all over the floor?

Two words: *consistency* (each machine is set up the same way) and *convenience* (technicians have fewer changes to make on each machine). This chapter summarizes how you can customize the Windows 98 SETUP program to create a Registry that's closer to the way you want it from day one. As it turns out, you can preset every one of the Registry changes that this book discusses! Very cool!

If you don't have to worry about taking care of anyone's PC but your own, you can trek right around this chapter.

A LAN with a Plan

Using a network server to install Windows 98, instead of using an installation CD-ROM, is a great example of how to put your local area network (LAN) to productive use. Anyone who must support or troubleshoot multiple Windows 98 PCs knows that the job becomes far easier when all the PCs are set up the same way (for example, without keyboards) — fewer trouble-shooting variables to consider. And by reinstalling Windows 98 according to a customized script, a technician knows that many necessary options are set correctly in advance.

These advantages are so compelling that many LAN managers don't care that new PCs usually come with Windows 98 preinstalled. These managers get a new PC, connect it to their network, and then install Windows 98 from their network server, wiping out whatever was already on the system. Sort of like basic training.

Installing Windows 98 from a central network server works really well in situations where you have a hodgepodge of PC makes, models, and components. Because you're actually running Windows 98 SETUP on each computer, SETUP can still autodetect PC hardware and make adjustments for the fact (for example) that Stanley has a 3Com network card while Livingstone has a Madge network card. The customized script that you create to guide the SETUP program doesn't mandate that everyone's initial Registry looks identical — that doesn't work, for example, with the two different network cards — only that *certain* settings are identical on each PC, such as the time zone, standard networking language, and so on.

Copying the Files

The first step in creating a network-based setup procedure is to install a complete copy of the Windows 98 source files onto a server, called a *distribution server,* from which a new user can install Windows 98 across the network onto the workstation. (The server "distributes" Windows 98 to the network users, who use the server as the source for their Windows 98 files instead of the Windows 98 CD-ROM.) If you don't have a network available, you can still use a custom installation script by copying the Windows 98 files to a PC's hard drive, along with your script. The following sections provide details on both approaches.

Getting the distribution server ready

Microsoft provided a handy utility with the first release of Windows 95. NETSETUP automatically copies your Windows 95 files to a distribution server via a user-friendly wizard. Going back a bit in time, Windows 3.*x* included a command (SETUP /A) that did essentially the same thing. Alas and alack, in Windows 98, we have no such automated tool for getting a distribution server ready for action. That's not a huge problem, but it is a bit of an inconvenience.

To prepare your distribution server for Windows 98 installations, you need to copy the contents of the Windows 98 CD-ROM to a network directory. Log on to the network as an administrator or supervisor, create a directory that's available to everyone on the network, and use Windows Explorer to copy the CD-ROM files to that network directory. The WIN98 directory on the CD-ROM is the essential one, but we recommend that you upload the TOOLS directory, too, which contains a lot of handy utilities. Don't follow Microsoft's documentation and just copy the CAB files; copy the entire directory contents. (In general, when there's a conflict between this book and Microsoft's documentation, this book is your better bet. We have a lot less money, so we have to be more careful.)

Your server doesn't have to support long file names in order for this procedure to work properly. Microsoft has taken care to use old-style 8.3 filenames for every folder and file in the WIN98 and TOOLS directories. This was smart, as it means you can choose almost any kind of server to use as a distribution server.

You (or your network manager) may want to flag the files read-only after you copy them over to the server, so that network users can't accidentally delete or modify them.

Note that you must have a legal Windows 98 license for each PC onto which you install Windows 98 from a central distribution server. The *Windows 98 Resource Kit* mentions network-based installations without any special legal provisos, suggesting (to our nonlegal brains, at least) that Microsoft is OK with this installation method as long as you have the required licenses.

Getting the hard drive ready

If you don't have a network server, but you have several PCs onto which you'd like to install Windows 98 using a custom script, no problem! The general approach is to copy the Windows 98 files to a special directory on each PC's hard drive (call it anything you like, except WINDOWS — we suggest WINSTALL), instead of to a distribution server as we describe in the previous section. Then, again on each PC, copy your custom script to the same directory where the WIN98 files reside. (The next sections describe how to create the custom script.)

A side benefit of this method is that you cut down the usual 30 minute installation time to about 15 minutes. You do have to have about 200MB of additional hard disk space available, though, on each PC, compared to the network-based setup method. Windows 98 is a *big* sonofagun.

Customizing the Install

After you comfortably nestle the Windows 98 files onto your network server or local PC hard drive, you can exert some control over how future workstation installations from that server behave — specifically, how they create the user's initial Registry.

The really cool part of a custom installation — and the part where we can start tinkering with the prenatal Registry — is creating a special text file known as the *default batch script*. This script kicks in whenever a user runs the Windows 98 SETUP program (SETUP.EXE) from the server or local hard disk directory, and it controls the Windows 98 installation process.

If SETUP.EXE is the Jeep, the default batch script is the driver. The default batch script's name is MSBATCH.INF, and it lives in the same network directory or hard disk directory where you've installed the Windows 98 setup program. (The file is present whether you customize it or not.)

You customize the batch script with a friendly, graphical utility called Microsoft Batch 98, or simply Batch 98 (BATCH.EXE). If you want to get *really* fancy, you can even customize the MSBATCH.INF file that Batch 98 creates so that it installs device drivers and network software that Windows 98 can't ordinarily install. The next two sections deal with both procedures, the easy one first.

Son of a BATCH

Here's an introduction to the Batch 98 utility, which may be all you need to customize your Windows 98 installations. The new version that comes with Windows 98 features better organization and more options than previous versions.

Installing Batch 98

Windows 98 doesn't automatically install Batch 98 in a typical setup, so you have to install it yourself in order to create a custom batch script with this utility. The procedure is as follows:

1. **Pop the Windows 98 CD-ROM into the drive.**

2. **Close all running applications.**

3. **Choose Start➪Run to bring up the Run dialog box.**

4. **Type D:\TOOLS\RESKIT\BATCH\SETUP into the Open field (substitute another drive letter if your CD-ROM drive isn't D:).**

5. **Follow the on-screen instructions.**

Don't use old versions of BATCH.EXE that you may have hanging around your network from Windows 95. If you choose Help➪About and you see anything other than "Batch 98," you have an old version.

After you install Batch 98, running it is simply a matter of choosing Start➪Programs➪Microsoft Batch 98. You then see the main screen as shown in Figure 8-1. (If you want to put the program more nearly where it belongs, you can drag-and-drop the menu entry to the Programs➪ Accessories➪System Tools menu.)

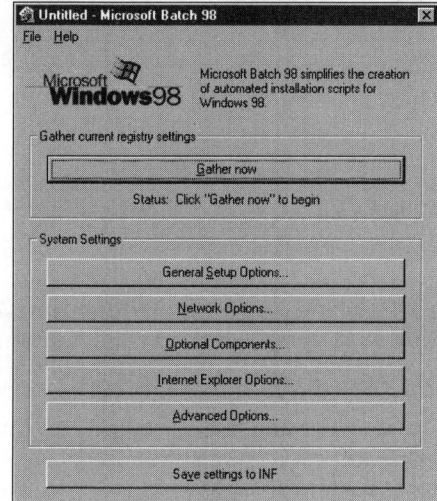

Figure 8-1: Batch Setup's main screen.

Harvesting current Registry settings or "Bringing in the Keys"

The wide button toward the top of Batch 98's main screen that says Gather now (see Figure 8-1) is very handy if you want to set up new PCs similar to the PC on which you're running Batch 98. If you click this button, Batch 98 scans your current Registry for the following settings and adds them to the default batch script:

✔ Network clients, protocols, and services (as long as these networking components come from Microsoft!)

✔ Network card settings

✔ Installed printers

Changes since BATCH Version 2

Those readers familiar with BATCH.EXE version 2 for Windows 95, which Microsoft called "Batch Setup," may appreciate knowing where some of the settings have moved to in Batch 98. Here's a quick rundown:

User and computer name information have moved from the main screen to General Setup Options⇨User Info.

Printer setup information has moved from the Installation Options area to General Setup Options⇨Printers.

Time zone information has moved from the Installation Options area to General Setup Options⇨Regional Settings.

User-level security information has moved from the Network Options area to Network Options⇨Access Control.

Also, the optional component settings list has changed to reflect the current Windows 98 components and applets list.

- ✔ Installed optional Windows components
- ✔ Time zone
- ✔ Security settings
- ✔ Location of the main Windows directory
- ✔ User name, computer name, and description

So, an easy way to use Batch 98 is to set up the PC on which you're running it so that the PC's configuration matches the desired configuration of the PCs onto which you want to install Windows 98.

We levy a certain amount of criticism at Microsoft in this book, but we're the first to admit that this feature of harvesting Registry settings for future installs is very clever and highly practical. Kudos.

Making your own presets

The five buttons in the System Settings area (refer to Figure 8-1) take you to lots of other screens where you can preset Windows 98 Registry settings. Specifically, these are either settings that the setup program asks you for during the installation, or that you must normally set manually, using control panels, after the installation is complete.

Clicking the General Setup Options button takes you to tabbed property sheets (see Figure 8-2) where you can specify the following:

✔ Whether to save uninstall information (from the PC's previous operating system)

✔ User, company, computer, and workgroup names

✔ Whether to skip various usual SETUP prompts

✔ Time zone, keyboard layout, and regional settings

✔ What icons to show on the desktop

✔ Whether to show online services, the Welcome screen, and the Registration wizard

✔ Which printer drivers to install automatically

✔ Whether to set up user profiles (see Chapter 10), although you can't specify what to include in those profiles to the same degree of detail that the Users control panel provides

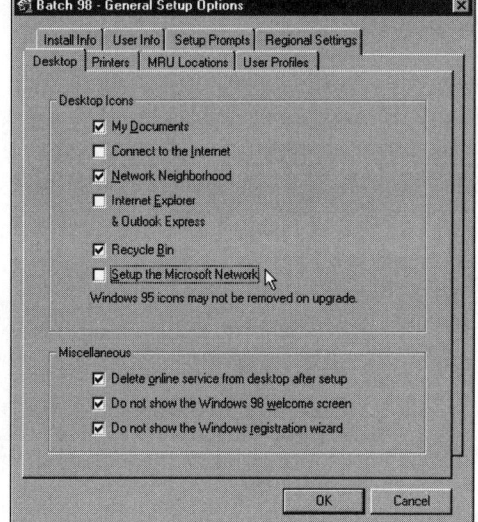

Figure 8-2:
Customize
General
Setup
options with
Batch 98.

Clicking the Network Options button brings up the tabbed dialog box in Figure 8-3, where you can essentially preset the user's Network control panel. The specific settings you can specify include:

✔ Which network protocols to install, including details on IPX/SPX frame type and TCP/IP addresses and services

✔ Whether to include file and printer sharing services for Microsoft or Novell networks, to turn client PCs into mini-servers

✔ Which Microsoft-supplied network clients to install, and which servers provide logon information

✔ Whether you want user-level or share-level security (user-level is more common on client/server networks, share-level on peer-to-peer networks)

✔ Which network clients and services you want to install beyond the usual ones (for example, Remote Registry services to permit you to run REGEDIT over the network)

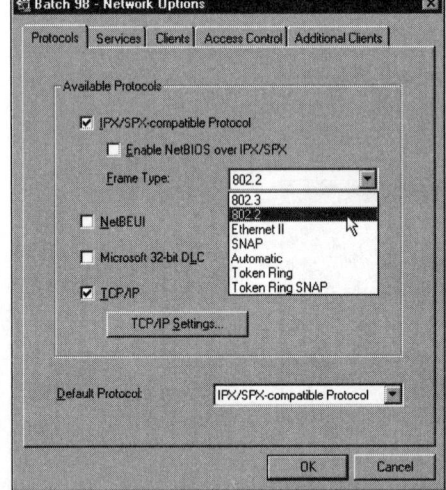

Figure 8-3:
Using Batch 98's Network Options dialog box.

The Optional Components button lets you preselect which Windows 98 utilities and applets the SETUP program will install on user PCs (see Figure 8-4).

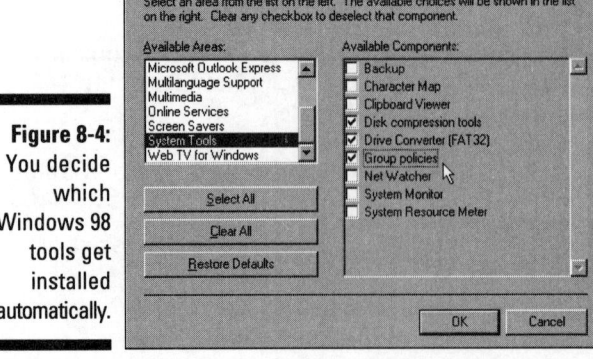

Figure 8-4:
You decide which Windows 98 tools get installed automatically.

The Internet Explorer Options button isn't properly named, because not only does it let you set some browser options, it also lets you define the default desktop behavior (see Figure 8-5). The options here include:

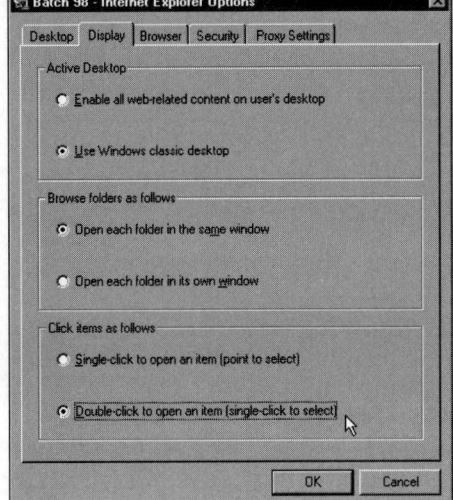

✔ What, if anything, should appear on the Quick Launch toolbar

✔ Whether to display the Active Channel bar

✔ Whether to use the Web view or the classic view of the desktop

✔ Default behavior for opening new folders

✔ Whether single-clicking or double-clicking opens objects

✔ Various pre-set browser Web locations

✔ Security settings for different Internet and intranet zones

✔ Whether to use a proxy server for Internet access and, if so, what its characteristics are

The Advanced Options button lets you set the following features:

✔ What custom Registry files to process (see the section, "Painting on the pinstripes"

✔ Whether to set a special location for system policy files (see Chapter 9)

✔ Whether to enable or disable the Windows Update mechanism (see Figure 8-6), either for drivers, applications, or both

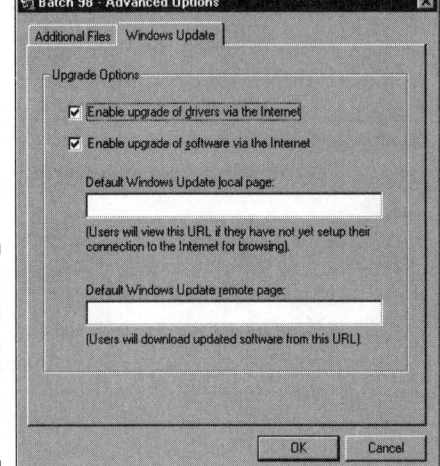

Figure 8-6:
Batch 98
lets you
turn off
Windows
Update.

Painting on the pinstripes

For you Registry-editing hotshots, this is probably the coolest section of this chapter.

After you look over the options that Batch 98 provides in its various property sheets, you may decide that you'd like to go beyond those options and include some Registry settings of your own devising. The best new feature that Microsoft threw into BATCH.EXE since the various Windows 95 versions of the utility is the ability to specify one or more custom REG files to process during the Windows 98 installation. (A REG file contains Registry settings that you'd like to either add or change to the current Registry; see Chapter 13 for tips on creating REG files.)

Batch 98 puts your special REG files into the Registry's RunOnce key so they run when Windows 98 performs its final reboot. The precise location is *HKLM\Software\Microsoft\Windows\CurrentVersion\RunOnce*.

Here's how to incorporate custom Registry settings into the SETUP process:

1. **Create one or more REG files that contain the settings you want.**

2. **Run Batch 98, open any previously-created MSBATCH.INF file that you've customized, and click the Advanced Options button.**

   You see the screen in Figure 8-7.

3. **Click the Browse button and select the first REG file that you want to include.**

4. **Click the Add button to add that REG file to the Batch 98 list.**

5. **Repeat Steps 3 and 4 as necessary until you're done.**

6. **Click OK on the Advanced Options dialog box.**

7. **Click File➪Save to record your changes to disk, and exit Batch 98.**

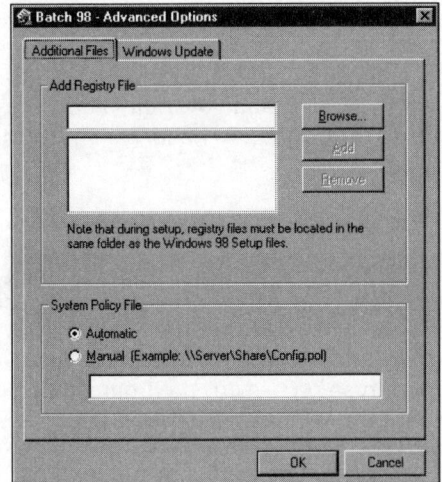

Figure 8-7:
You can tell
Batch 98 to
process
your own
custom REG
file as part
of the
default
Windows 98
installation.

Anything you can put into a REG file, that is, any Registry setting at all, you can now graft into the Windows 98 installation procedure. All of a sudden, Windows 98 SETUP has acquired the flexibility of a double-jointed limbo dancer.

Saving your work

After you finish making your presets, click the Save Settings To INF button on Batch 98's main screen, and save the INF file in the same directory where you've copied the Windows 98 files. Remember to name this file MSBATCH.INF (that's the default) when you place the file on the network server or in the local hard disk's installation directory.

If you want to open your INF file in Notepad to take a look at it, go right ahead; it's just a text file.

Now, test your customized installation script by installing Windows 98 on a test PC. You don't have to do anything special; SETUP.EXE will automatically look for MSBATCH.INF and follow its commands. Just remember, if at first you do succeed, try not to look astonished.

Basic INFstinct

The MSBATCH.INF file is remarkably powerful when it comes to customizing your Windows 98 installation, but you may want to extend its capabilities so that you can install new device drivers and network software that Windows 98 normally can't install. Here, we give you one example: setting up Windows 98 to automatically install the Remote Registry service that lets you run REGEDIT across the wire and modify remote users' Registries.

Skip this optional section if you have no interest in the Remote Registry editing capability, if for example you're running a stand-alone Windows 98 PC, or if your head already hurts from trying to absorb some of the admittedly technical stuff in this chapter.

A bit of background

INF files, which we discuss further in Chapter 13, are an extremely versatile method for creating and distributing Registry modifications. These files also automate the process of installing new hardware devices and new applications. INF files can do a lot of the same things as DOS batch files — copy files, delete files, rename files, and so on — with the bonus that INF files can directly modify the Registry and the Windows INI files. INF files also have their own special grammar rules.

MSBATCH.INF is just one example of an INF file, and it's a great introduction to the subject — partly because the graphical Batch 98 program gives you a head start, and partly because you don't have to do anything special to activate it. Windows 98 SETUP processes MSBATCH.INF automatically when SETUP runs. (You activate other INF files by right-clicking them and selecting the Install option.)

When you start with Batch 98, you create a basic MSBATCH.INF file that contains lots of presets for how Windows 98's installation program should run. (See the earlier section, "Son of a BATCH.") But if you want to add the ability for Windows 98 SETUP to install a network service that it doesn't normally know how to install, you have to add the INF file for that network service to the list of INF files that Windows 98 normally processes. You can do this manually, with a text editor such as Notepad, but it's a pain. Thankfully, Microsoft provides a tool that automates the process: the INF installer.

The INF installer

The handy, dandy INF installer (INFINST.EXE), its related help file (INFINST.CHM), and its text "read me" file (README.TXT) all reside on the Windows 98 CD-ROM in the folder \TOOLS\RESKIT\INFINST. You can choose to run INFINST directly from the CD-ROM, or you can install it on a PC hard drive by manually copying all three files to wherever you want. (We suggest \PROGRAM FILES\INFINST.)

Running the INF installer is amazingly simple. You'd never guess at the complex workings under the hood (read the README.TXT file) by looking at the utility's main screen (see Figure 8-8).

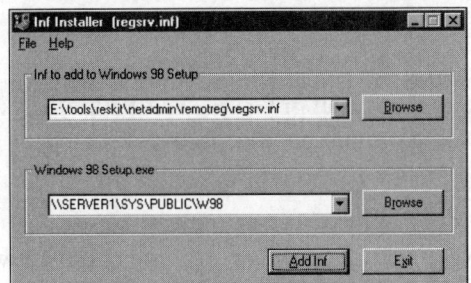

All you have to do in the INF Installer's main screen is specify the location and filename of the INF file you want to add — that is, the one describing the installation specifics for the network service, device driver, or whatever the case may be — and the location from which users will run SETUP.EXE to install Windows 98 (usually, a network server directory). Once that's done, click the Add Inf button, and the INF installer makes all the necessary changes for you automatically. INFINST handles the copying of any required files, so you don't have to lift a finger in Windows Explorer. INFINST also handles a few other housekeeping chores, the details of which we can cheerfully ignore here.

Adding the Remote Registry service

This business about INF and INFINST is all well and good, but how can you put it to practical use? If you read the section in Chapter 4 called "Where's the remote?" then you know about a cool tool called the Remote Registry service. If you have the right sort of network (which Chapter 4 discusses and we won't repeat here), you can use the Remote Registry service to tinker with (excuse us, we meant to say "administer") other network users' Registries, from the comfort of your own cubicle. If that sounds handy, it is, but the unhandy part is that you have to go around installing the Remote Registry service on everybody's PC because the Windows 98 SETUP program can't do it. At least, not until now.

It turns out that Remote Registry is a network service with its very own INF file on the Windows 98 CD-ROM. That means you can add the necessary files to the Windows 98 SETUP directory with the INF installer. The only other thing you must do is use Batch 98 to tell MSBATCH.INF that you want this network service installed automatically.

Batch 98 and INFINST work together. Batch 98 (the brains) sets up MSBATCH.INF to tell SETUP what to do, and INFINST (the muscle) puts the files where SETUP will look for them.

Here's the step-by-step procedure for including Remote Registry service in every Windows 98 installation on your network:

1. **Using Notepad, open the INF file for the Remote Registry service (D:\TOOLS\RESKIT\NETADMIN\REMOTREG\REGSRV.INF on the Windows 98 CD-ROM, assuming it's the D: drive).**

2. **Look for a `DeviceID` in the first few lines of the file.**

   You should find the line `DeviceID=REMOTEREG` about a couple of dozen lines from the top. REMOTEREG is the code name of the network service; you need it to key into Batch 98. (You can also get the code name from the *Microsoft Windows 98 Resource Kit*, if you have it; Appendix D of that book lists the network service codes.)

3. **Close Notepad and open Batch 98.**

   See the section "Son of a BATCH" earlier in this chapter for details on installing and running Batch 98.

4. **Open your previous, customized version of MSBATCH.INF, if it exists, with File⇨Open.**

5. **Click the Network Options button.**

6. **Click the Additional Clients tab.**

7. **In the text entry box labeled Services, type** REMOTEREG **and click OK.**

   Don't use the text entry box labeled Protocols, as the *Windows 98 Resource Kit* directs you to do.

8. **Click the Save Settings to INF button and save your batch script to the directory where Windows 98 will install from (usually a public network directory). Exit Batch 98.**

   Thus endeth the Batch 98 part of the job. Now, you must put the files where Windows 98 SETUP can find them.

9. **Run the INF installer (for example, with Start⇨Run⇨INFINST).**

10. **In the text box in the Inf to Add to Windows 98 SETUP area, type the pathname mentioned in Step 1.**

11. **In the text box in the Windows 98 SETUP.EXE area, type the location from which users will install Windows 98.**

    For example, \\SERVER1\SYS\PUBLIC\W98.

12. **Click the Add Inf button.**

13. **Click Exit.**

This procedure takes longer to read about than it does to carry out. Now, all future installations of Windows 98 will have the Remote Registry service installed and enabled by default. Incidentally, you can use this basic procedure to install *any* networking software that comes with its own INF file.

Adding the Finishing Touches

Whether you just use the graphical Batch 98 program to create MSBATCH.INF, or you take things a step further and use the INF installer to include specific Registry settings for extra devices or network services that you want, you can make upgrading PCs to Windows 98 easier for network users by using your customized INF file. Just include the setup command and batch script name in a network logon script. Here's the procedure:

1. **Set up a special user account (say, UPGRADE) for the user who wants to install Windows 98 to log onto.**

2. **Define appropriate security for the UPGRADE account (no changing passwords, rights to the server with Windows 98 on it, and so on).**

3. **Create a logon script and associate it with the UPGRADE user.**

For a Windows NT Server network, your logon script may include lines like the following, where *server**distshare* specifies the server computer directory containing the Windows 98 source files and *sourcedrive* is a drive letter mapping for that directory:

```
net use sourcedrive \\server\distshare
sourcedrive:setup sourcedrive:msbatch.inf
```

For a Novell NetWare or IntranetWare network, the logon script lines look something like this:

```
attach server/distshare:
map sourcedrive:server/distshare
sourcedrive:setup sourcedrive:msbatch.inf
```

The preceding generic script lines are just a guide. If you create a logon script for the Windows 98 UPGRADE account, you need to be familiar with script creation rules for your particular network type and need to try the script on a test PC before unleashing it to the general network population. A mistake in a logon script can create problems for anyone who logs onto the UPGRADE account.

You can create different INF files for different groups of users. For example, BWANA.INF and TECHIE.INF can be used where we've used MSBATCH.INF in the generic script lines. (Technically, you don't even have to specify MSBATCH.INF as long as you use that filename, because SETUP looks for it specifically, but we include the name for clarity.) You can even set up different network upgrade accounts that call the different INF files.

You can use the general procedure we just described for many other purposes besides installing Windows 98. For example, you can create different network accounts that automatically install other application programs. You can even use a system-wide logon script to distribute Registry modifications via INF and REG files, as we look at more closely in Chapter 13.

If you've created a batch script for non-networked PCs, all you have to do is copy the MSBATCH.INF file to the local hard drive, in the same directory as the Windows 98 SETUP.EXE program. Just as with the network-based setup procedure, you can specify different INF files for different user groups; just copy the one you want (for example, from a diskette) to the user's hard drive and rename it MSBATCH.INF, or don't rename it but specify it on the SETUP.EXE command line (like this: **SETUP.EXE TECHIE.INF**).

Chapter 9

Customizing System Policies for Security and Safety

*W*indows 98 doesn't have its own true security system in the sense that Windows NT does. However, Windows 98 does have a feature to restrict and customize user access to the operating system and programs. This feature is the *system policy file,* and if you use it, it becomes an important aspect of the Windows 98 Registry.

Windows 98 Casual Security

The U.S. Department of Defense assigns security ratings to computer operating systems. However, its ratings are highly complex and highly boring. If we were to assign our own rankings to PC operating systems in terms of how tough they are to break into, we'd come up with a scale like Table 9-1.

Table 9-1	Weadock/Wilkins Security Rankings
Operating System	*Security Equivalence*
Windows NT	Land Rover
Windows 98	Nylon Tent
Windows 3.*x*	Bug Spray
MS-DOS	Loin Cloth

A nylon tent doesn't stop leopards, but it does stop tsetse flies, and that's why we refer to Windows 98 security as *casual security*. You can't prevent a professional cracker from breaking into a Windows 98 system, but you can make messing things up fairly difficult for the average computer user.

This chapter is about securing the tent, which Windows 98 calls the *system policy file*. After you create and deploy it, the system policy file becomes part of the Registry.

If you don't let anyone else use your PC and you don't give a hoot about restricting access to Windows 98, tromp right around this chapter. On the other hand, if this subject interests you but you haven't read Chapters 4 and 6 covering the Registry structure, now is a good time to get out your trusty map and take a look.

Many people believe that system policies only work on a network. While you can usually find system policy files on network servers, you can also use a policy file on a stand-alone PC. You can also use the System Policy Editor program as a Registry editor to impose access restrictions and to customize the desktop, even without creating a policy file.

System policies don't represent the only security mechanism available if you use Windows 98 in a network environment. Industrial-strength client/server networks, including Windows NT Server and Novell IntranetWare, have their own extensive security systems to protect shared programs and data files. We don't consider server-based security in this book except as it applies to system policies, but if you're interested in the subject, check out *Small Business Networking For Dummies* by Glenn E. Weadock, *Networking With NetWare For Dummies*, 3rd Edition, by Ed Tittel, Deni Connor and Earl Follis, or *Windows NT Networking For Dummies* by Tittel, Mary Madden, and Follis (all IDG Books Worldwide, Inc.).

Finally, system policies can get fairly involved. If you're a network administrator who needs to use system policies for sophisticated access control, we suggest you read this chapter through once or twice to get the lay of the land; then hire a Windows 98 consultant with experience on your particular type of network to help you through the process.

"Policies" and Procedures

This section introduces the System Policy Editor, POLEDIT. POLEDIT is strong medicine. Before you start experimenting with it, make sure you have a current backup of your Registry and a current Windows 98 startup diskette (Chapter 2).

Installing the System Policy Editor

The Windows 98 setup program doesn't install the System Policy Editor, so you have to do so separately (but don't install it on every PC in a network; it's a dangerous utility!). You need the Windows 98 CD-ROM to install POLEDIT (or access to a hard drive or network directory that contains all the Windows 98 CD-ROM files and folders). In the following procedure, we assume you're using the CD-ROM and that it's on drive D. Here's how to install POLEDIT:

1. **Pop the Windows 98 CD-ROM into the drive. If a Windows 98 installation or Welcome screen appears, close it by clicking the close box.**

2. **Click Start⇨Settings⇨Control Panel and double-click the Add/Remove Programs icon.**

3. **Click the Windows Setup tab and then click the Have Disk button.**

4. **In the Copy Manufacturer's Files From text box, type:**

   ```
   D:\TOOLS\RESKIT\NETADMIN\POLEDIT\
   ```

   Substitute your CD-ROM drive letter for D: in the above entry if you use something different.

5. **Click OK.**

   The dialog box in Figure 9-1 appears.

6. **Click the check box for the System Policy Editor; then click the Install button.**

   You see a fleeting message about shortcuts being updated, and then the Add/Remove Programs Properties dialog box reappears.

7. **Click OK in the Add/Remove Programs Properties dialog box.**

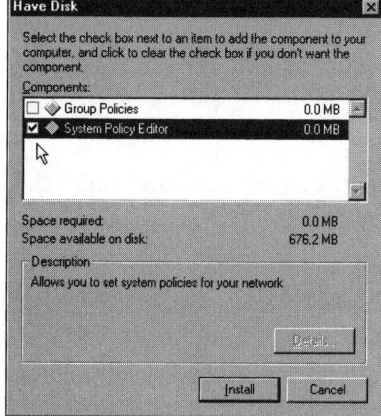

Figure 9-1:
Installing
the System
Policy
Editor.

You're done! Piece o' cake. The System Policy Editor now appears when you click Start⇨Programs⇨Accessories⇨System Tools⇨System Policy Editor.

Because the System Policy Editor is not part of the Windows 98 install, you may just have an old copy of the Windows 95 policy editor on your hard drive. Make sure that you don't open the Windows 95 policy editor by mistake. Although the older version would still work, the Windows 98 version allows you to use multiple templates (which control what settings you can change) at the same time to effectively create a custom "super template" including more settings than a single template does. For more on templates, see "A swarm of templates" later in this chapter.

The two faces of POLEDIT

The System Policy Editor has two modes of operation:

✔ As a *Registry editor,* in which case you're directly editing the Registry of a local or remote computer — just as if you were using REGEDIT, although POLEDIT has a friendlier face. You don't create a policy file, but you do modify the active USER.DAT and SYSTEM.DAT. Your changes take effect after you save and then close the Registry and exit POLEDIT.

✔ As a *policy file editor,* in which case you're creating or modifying a file with the suffix .POL. The POL file becomes part of the Registry after Windows 98 applies the file to USER.DAT and SYSTEM.DAT at the next startup, but nothing changes until then.

In order to use POLEDIT as a Registry editor, simply run the program and choose File⇨Open Registry. You can then double-click the Local User or Local Computer icon, make whatever changes you like to the local (as opposed to remote) Registry. After you save your changes and exit POLEDIT your changes are immediately active.

If you install the extra software necessary for remote Registry editing (as we describe in Chapter 4's section, "Where's the Remote?"), then you can use POLEDIT in Registry-editing mode to edit another user's Registry if that user is on the same network as you. The POLEDIT command to do this is File⇨Connect.

Before you use POLEDIT as a Registry editor, read the rest of this chapter, especially the section titled "Gotchas."

In order to use POLEDIT as a policy file editor, run the program and choose either File⇨New Policy to build a new POL file, or File⇨Open Policy to read a POL file created earlier. You can then double-click the Default User or

Default Computer icon (note the name changes from "Local User" and "Local Computer"), make whatever changes you like, and choose File⇨Save to store the modified POL file.

In policy file mode, the check boxes that appear when you set about making changes are normally grayed out, as shown in Figure 9-2. (They're either clear or checked when you use POLEDIT as a Registry editor.) The grayed-out check box simply means that the user or computer policy you're creating or editing doesn't change that Registry setting from its current status. You want the POL file to contain information only about stuff you want to change, not stuff you want to leave alone (the file is much smaller and faster that way).

Figure 9-2:
Grayed-out
check
boxes
appear
when
you use
POLEDIT in
policy file
mode.

Okay, which POLEDIT mode should you use?

✔ On a network, where you probably want to make a bunch of settings that apply to every user (or at least to every user in a particular network group), you should use POLEDIT as a policy file editor. This way, you can do the work of defining your policy settings one time and then put that POL file up on a server where the file can apply to every user who logs onto the network. You consolidate security settings at a single point.

✔ If you're working with several nonnetworked (stand-alone) PCs, use POLEDIT in its policy file mode. You can create a POL file that you can then copy to other PCs. All you have to do on the other PCs is place the POL file in the C:\WINDOWS directory (or wherever you like) and tell the Registry to look for it there, as described later in this chapter in the section "Single-user policies."

✔ If you're working with a single stand-alone PC, using POLEDIT as a Registry editor is probably more convenient because you're only concerned with one computer and you don't save yourself any effort by creating a POL file. If that single PC is set up for multiple users, however, use POLEDIT in its policy file mode for the ability to specify different policies for each user.

A herd of user policies

As you can tell from the two icons that appear when you use POLEDIT in either Registry editing mode or policy file mode, two kinds of policies exist: user and computer. User policies apply to the USER.DAT file on disk, which is the *HKey_Users* branch in the Registry database. Figure 9-3 shows some of the user policies you can set with POLEDIT.

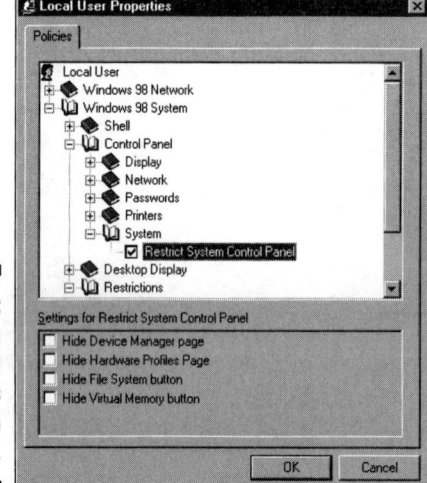

Figure 9-3: Changing user-related policies with POLEDIT.

In order to use system policies to control user settings, whether on a networked or nonnetworked PC, you must activate user profiles. Chapter 10 discusses user profiles in detail, so we won't duplicate the material here.

We don't have space to discuss each of the several dozen policies included in Windows 98. Most are self-explanatory, and the best way to get familiar with these policies is to experiment with them anyway. As you click the check boxes in the upper part of the System Policy Editor window, you may see more detailed settings in the lower part of the window. Here are the user policies that we recommend you look especially closely at:

✔ Restrict Network Control Panel

✔ Restrict Printer Settings

✔ Restrict System Control Panel

✔ Custom Folders

✔ Remove "Run" command

✔ No "Entire Network" in Network Neighborhood

✔ Disable Registry Editing Tools

✔ Only Run Allowed Windows Applications (don't use this one until you read Chapter 15's section, "I Can't Reverse Restrictive Policies")

✔ Disable MS-DOS Prompt

A pride of computer policies

Computer policies apply to the SYSTEM.DAT file on disk, which is the *HKey_Local_Machine* branch in the Registry database. Figure 9-4 shows some of the computer policies you can set with POLEDIT.

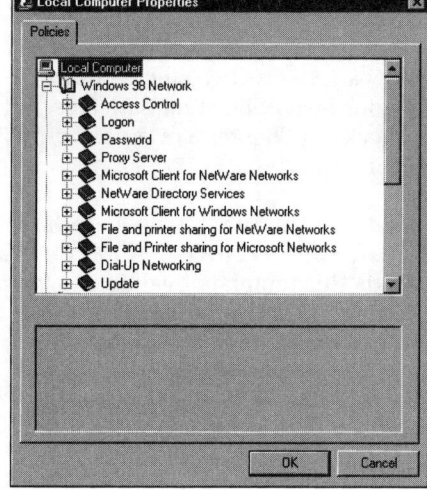

Figure 9-4: Changing computer-related policies with POLEDIT.

Here are some computer policies worth a gander:

✔ Require Validation by Network for Windows Access

✔ Require Alphanumeric Windows Password

✔ Minimum Windows Password Length

✔ Disable File Sharing

✔ Disable Print Sharing

✔ Enable User Profiles

✔ Dial-Up Networking (to disable dialing in)

✔ Programs to Run (every time Windows 98 starts)

A swarm of templates

The user and computer policies in the previous two sections all derive from
the default policy template files, COMMON.ADM and WINDOWS.ADM, which
you can find in the C:\WINDOWS\INF directory. However, you can use other
template files to specify other policies, too. A *template file* is nothing more
than a list of policies that you can set; the template provides the choices
and knows which Registry keys to change as a result. For example, Microsoft
supplies templates for Office 97 programs in its Office 97 Resource Kit
(OFF97W98.ADM, ACCESS97.ADM, and SECURITY.ADM in the Internet
Explorer 4.0 Resource Kit.).

Change the active template file within System Policy Editor by choosing
Options⇨Policy Template (close any POL file or open Registry first). Only
one template can be active for editing at a time; however, you can use as
many different templates as you want to create a single policy file (see
Figure 9-5). You can even write your own policy template files, but that's
beyond the scope of this book; check out Chapter 8 of the *Microsoft Windows 98
Resource Kit* (Microsoft Press) for details.

Windows 95 only had one template file, ADMIN.ADM. Windows 98 has
ten, which all reside in C:\WINDOWS\INF. WINDOWS.ADM is the largest,
and the System Policy Editor loads this template by default, along with
COMMON.ADM, which is just a framework into which you can add your own
policies. We think you should be aware of some new settings for both users
and computers.

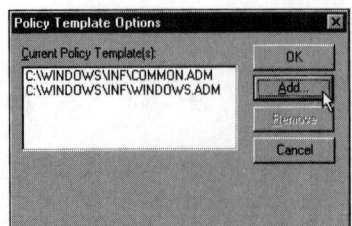

Figure 9-5:
Click the
Add button
to use a
new
template's
settings.

The template SHELLM.ADM allows you to control many user policy settings having to do with the Windows 98 user interface, or "shell." Here's a sample:

- ✔ Remove Start menu options (Documents, Favorites, Find, Run, Settings⇨Active Desktop, Settings⇨Folder Options, Settings⇨Taskbar & Start Menu, and so on).

- ✔ Hide desktop elements (such as HTML wallpaper and the Internet Explorer icon).

- ✔ Keep the desktop pure (by, for example, enforcing the "classic" shell, prohibiting toolbar drag-and-drop, permitting only registered shell extensions, and so on).

- ✔ Prohibit any Start menu changes.

- ✔ Prohibit changes to the Active Desktop (adding, deleting, editing, closing, or any combination of these).

- ✔ Turn off the Active Desktop entirely.

The template WINDOWS.ADM, which contains all of the Windows 95 ADMIN.ADM settings and then some, allows you to control the following new computer policy settings:

- ✔ Restrict the device drivers users can install to those that have a Microsoft "digital signature."

- ✔ Disable the new Web-based "Windows Update" feature.

- ✔ Control the users' NDS (NetWare Directory Services) environment (for users running the Microsoft client software for Novell networks).

Microsoft also supplies template files for its Internet-related software. INETSET.ADM and INETRESM.ADM contain many policies pertaining to the Internet Explorer browser and the Internet control panel. Policies having to do with Internet channels and subscriptions live in the template SUBSM.ADM. If you use NetMeeting, you may want to load the policies in CONF.ADM, and if you use Chat, check out CHAT.ADM.

Applying Policies to Networks, Groups, and Individuals

System policies can apply to everyone on a network, members of particular network groups, or individual users on networked or nonnetworked PCs.

System-wide policies

If you want a single policy file to apply to all users on a client/server network, Windows 98 makes life easy for you. Use the System Policy Editor to create a POL file with the settings you want for the Default User and Default Computer and then save the file with the name CONFIG.POL. (This special name is mandatory.) Where you copy the CONFIG.POL file depends on what sort of network you have:

- ✔ On a Novell network, place CONFIG.POL on the server in the SYS:PUBLIC directory.
- ✔ On a Windows NT Server network, place CONFIG.POL on the server in the NETLOGON share (\WINNT\SYSTEM32\REPL\IMPORT\SCRIPTS).

When any user logs onto the network, Windows 98 looks for the CONFIG.POL file in the predetermined standard location on the server. If Windows 98 finds the file, it automatically downloads a copy and applies the predefined Registry settings in the policy file to the user's Registry. Slick!

Group policies

If your network supports groups of users, you can assign policies on a group basis. To do so, you must install extra software on each user machine. The file needed is GROUPPOL.DLL; it must be copied to each user's \WINDOWS\ SYSTEM directory in order for group policies to work. Add the Group Policies program from the Add/Remove Programs wizard in the Control Panel (specifically, the Windows Setup tab, System Tools checkbox). You can now choose Edit⇨Add Group in POLEDIT and specify an existing network group.

If you create policies for multiple groups, prioritize the groups by choosing Options⇨Group Priority. The highest priority group gets processed last by Windows 98 and therefore overrides other, lower-priority group policies. Prioritization tells Windows 98 what to do when certain users belong to multiple groups that have potentially conflicting policy settings.

Single-user policies

How about assigning system policies to individual users? No problem. If a user or two on the network needs a set of policies different than those contained in the simple CONFIG.POL, you can use POLEDIT to create special user policies just for them. For example, you may want to create a less restrictive set of policies for people who perform administrative duties on the network. Here's the procedure:

1. **Start the System Policy Editor and open the CONFIG.POL file.**

2. **Choose Edit⇨Add User.**

3. **Type the user's network logon name into the Add User dialog box and click OK.**

   A new user icon appears in the Policy Editor window.

4. **Double-click the new user icon and make whatever settings you want for that user by checking the relevant boxes.**

5. **Save the CONFIG.POL file and exit System Policy Editor.**

6. **Copy CONFIG.POL to the network server.**

You can use the same basic trick to set up different SYSTEM.DAT restrictions. Just change Step 2 in the preceding list to Edit⇨Add Computer. The name you give the new computer policy must match the computer name that appears on the Identification tab of the user's Network control panel. Figure 9-6 shows a sample CONFIG.POL as viewed by the System Policy Editor.

Figure 9-6:
The
CONFIG.POL
file can
contain
exceptions
for specific
users and
computers.

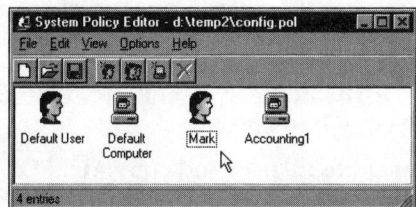

Watch out for the snakes in the grass!

Using system policies can prove hazardous to your health unless you are aware of the policy rules of the jungle. Microsoft's technical documentation is contradictory on these rules, so we did some serious testing to get the straight story.

User Policy Rules:

✓ First, Windows 98 applies the Default User Policy.

✓ Next, Windows 98 applies policies for the groups that the user belongs to, in the order of priority.

✓ Finally, Windows 98 applies the defined user's settings (if present).

Computer Policy Rules:

✓ First, Windows 98 applies the default computer policy.

✓ Then, Windows 98 applies the defined computer policy (if available).

When Mark logs onto the network, his user name appears separately in CONFIG.POL, so Windows 98 applies the "Mark" user policy after applying the Default User policy. If any policy settings in the user policy for Mark contradict settings in the Default User policy, the settings for Mark override those for the Default User, so you can grant Mark rights that the Default User doesn't have. Now, if a user logs on from a PC with the *computer* name "Accounting1," Windows 98 first applies the Default Computer policy and then the specific computer policy for Accounting1. We told you it's a jungle out there!

Windows 98 first assigns the Default User and Default Computer policies to all users even if their names or computer names show up separately in CONFIG.POL.

Now, what if you have a bunch of nonnetworked PCs and you still want to create a POL file that you can copy to their hard drives, in order to impose the same restrictions on every user? Here's the little-known technique:

1. **On your PC, create the POL file in the System Policy Editor. Give it a name (say, ALL.POL) and copy it to diskette.**

2. **Go to the computer you want to restrict and copy ALL.POL from diskette to the hard drive (we recommend the C:\WINDOWS directory).**

3. **Run the System Policy Editor.**

   Install the System Policy Editor if it isn't present, using the steps this chapter presents earlier under "Installing the System Policy Editor."

4. **Choose File➪Open Registry and double-click the Local Computer icon.**

5. **Expand the Windows 98 Network branch (by clicking the + next to it) and the Update branch; then click Remote Update.**

6. **Under Settings for Remote Update, select Manual (use specific path) in the Update Mode field and type in the file location (for example, C:\WINDOWS\ALL.POL) of the POL file in the Path for Manual Update field.**

7. **Click OK, close the System Policy Editor, and click Yes to save the changes to the current Registry.**

8. **Deinstall POLEDIT from the PC using the Control Panel's Add/ Remove Programs wizard (so that the user can't override your settings).**

Repeat Steps 2 through 8 for each computer.

Gotchas

System policies have their weaknesses. For example:

✔ Some Windows 98 help files (with *.HLP extensions, usually found in the C:\WINDOWS\HELP directory) include shortcut buttons to run specific programs. Even though you may have used POLEDIT to restrict those programs, users may still be able to run them from the help files. This is because a system policy restricts only the Explorer shell, and once a help file is executed, requests made inside the help file are not executed at the Explorer shell level. So, a user may be able to open a control panel even if you thought you had restricted it through a system policy.

✔ You can use system policies to disable Registry editing tools, but a user with Norton Utilities can run Norton Registry Editor without a problem. Also, if you leave the System Policy Editor on a user's PC, the user can run POLEDIT and reverse the REGEDIT restriction. (The way around this is to set the user policy. Only run allowed Windows applications by clicking the Policy Editor check box of the same name, and make sure that no Registry editing programs are on the list.)

✔ You can hold down Ctrl (or press F8) when rebooting Windows 98 and choose Safe Mode, and Windows 98 bypasses system policies. You can then run REGEDIT to remove policy settings already present, and run the System Policy Editor to change the restrictions that are reset at boot time by the policy file. (One way around this problem is to add the line BootKeys=0 to MSDOS.SYS, which disables the F8 and Ctrl keys.)

✔ Unless you're using network-based POL files that have been restricted using your network's built-in access control features, a user may be able to locate the POL file and delete it, bypassing system policy restrictions if the user also has access to REGEDIT and can disable the policies already set in the Registry.

If you need bulletproof security, you should be using Windows NT Workstation rather than Windows 98. Nevertheless, the policy component of the Windows 98 Registry can provide enough layers of protection so that even the cunning leopard will have a hard time finding any food.

Chapter 10

Customizing User Profiles So That Mowgli Always Sees Mowgli's Icons

● ●

In This Chapter

▶ Finding out when to set up user profiles

▶ Discovering what user profiles do to your Registry and your PC

▶ Setting up user profiles

▶ Customizing profile settings with the Users control panel

▶ Removing user profiles

● ●

*O*ne of the big problems with Windows 3.*x* is that it isn't network-friendly (or really even network-aware). Windows 98 helps correct the problem by providing a built-in mechanism for splitting up the Registry so that some files go with the user, not with the PC. This chapter tells you all you ever need to know about *user profiles,* maybe even more than you ever *want* to know — including some fairly significant *gotchas* that can send you searching for the bug repellent if you don't know about them ahead of time.

The material in this chapter isn't the easiest in the book, despite our best efforts to make it as straightforward as possible, so please don't be worried if it isn't all crystal clear the first time you read through it. You can save some brain cells and skip over the network-related discussion if your PC isn't on a LAN. You can save even more brain cells if you're working on a single PC that you don't need to share with anyone else — skip the entire chapter with our blessing!

When to Use Profiles

"Remember, you're a unique individual, just like everyone else."

One of the great things about the Registry is the way it splits out user-specific settings from machine-specific settings. This need to split is the whole idea behind creating the Registry with two core files, USER.DAT and SYSTEM.DAT. These two files don't have to come from the same location — unlike the situation with Windows 3.*x,* where all your core INI files have to exist in the same directory on your disk. Furthermore, although a Windows 98 PC starts its life with a single USER.DAT file, no rule exists against having a whole bunch of 'em (although you can't have more than one SYSTEM.DAT file per PC).

Roamin' your network

Nowadays, most PCs in business environments connect in networks. One of the benefits of networking is that you can (theoretically, at least) sit down at any PC, wherever you happen to be at the time, and work as efficiently as though you were at your regular PC.

The ability to log on to any PC is handy for technical support people who have to hoof it around the office working on different users' computers. You can also find networking handy when your usual computer is a slacker of a 486, but the woman in the neighboring cubicle has a zippy Pentium II machine and she's off on vacation for a week. (Just don't leave doughnut crumbs all over her workspace.) Finally, if you work in a company that frequently reorganizes people and teams, you'll be happy that you don't have to lug your PC to your new workplace in order to get working again.

Bringing the theory of roaming users into the real world takes a bit of doing, however. For example, Bob may go to some lengths to get his Windows 98 desktop the way he wants it:

- ✔ Bob's vision isn't great, so he likes larger than normal icon titles.
- ✔ Bob digs Alfa Romeos, and he puts a picture of one onto his system as wallpaper.
- ✔ Bob uses five or six programs on a regular basis, so he customizes his Start menu and his desktop shortcut icons so he can get to those programs quickly.
- ✔ Bob works with a dozen or so data files routinely, too, so they get convenient desktop icons, as well.

After all, PCs aren't called *personal* computers for nothing. Now, when Bob moves over to Janet's fast Pentium II machine, he doesn't want to have to live with small icon titles, a sleep-inducing rustic landscape for wallpaper, and a different set of desktop icons and Start menu options that don't pertain to what Bob does for a living. He darned sure doesn't want to muck around with Janet's PC so that it looks the way he wants, only to have her jump down his throat when she comes back from the Serengeti two days early. Bob's situation is a job for . . . *user profiles.*

Thanks for sharing

User profiles make it possible for different users to share the same computer and for each to keep his or her own settings. Perhaps in the ideal world (in the view of some computer industry executives), there's a chicken in every pot and everyone who wants a PC has one. In reality, although PCs are less expensive than ever, a lot of companies still don't buy every employee a computer.

Have you ever seen a residential real estate office that has a single community PC for the agents to use when the need arises? In a situation like this, Broker A doesn't want to log on to the PC and deal with all the rearranging that Broker B did while using the PC previously.

Consider also the home front, where many families share the same PC. Many grown-ups like having free Internet access and may even enjoy occasionally visiting certain dimly lit alleyways off the information superhighway that would make their parents blush in embarrassment, yet they don't want their kids to be able to see that stuff. Or the adults in the house may want access to the household finances but don't want their teenagers copying their credit card numbers and ordering up designer snowboard equipment by mail.

If you use a notebook PC, you may even want to set up different software configurations for when you're using your notebook at work and at home. You can log on as BobWork and see all the serious stuff; log on as BobPlay and see your fun programs and icons.

For both desktop users who must all share the same computer and road warriors who use the same computer in different settings, user profiles can come to the rescue. The Registry can handle the different needs of multiple users — although you need to be careful how you set up user profiles, and you do pay a price for using this feature.

Setting Up User Profiles

Activating user profiles is deceptively easy. Windows 98 provides two methods: the "standard" documented one and the "secret" one using a control panel that Windows 98 has but Windows 95 doesn't (unless you install Internet Explorer 4 on a Windows 95 machine).

By the book

Here's the standard procedure, published in Microsoft's *Windows 98 Resource Kit*, a method that is substantially the same as in Windows 95 and which you can use if you're already familiar with it. If you're new to user profiles, you may want to skip to the next section, "A better way."

1. **Click Start➪Settings➪Control Panel and double-click the Passwords icon.**

   The Passwords Properties dialog box appears.

2. **Click the User Profiles tab. (See Figure 10-1.)**

Figure 10-1:
Setting
up user
profiles
in the
Passwords
control
panel.

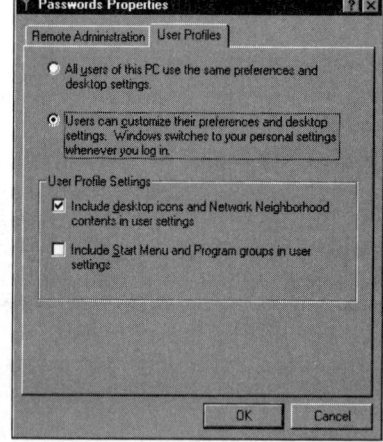

3. **Select the radio button that reads** Users can customize their preferences and desktop settings. Windows switches to your personal settings whenever you log in.

4. **In the User Profile Settings area, select the check box that reads** Include desktop icons and Network Neighborhood contents in user settings.

   You see another check box in this area, which is labeled Include Start Menu and Program groups in user settings. **This option sounds attractive, but watch out!** If you select this option and then want to install a new program on a PC, you may have to run the installation program multiple times to get the new program to appear on each user's Start menu. That is, you have to log on as user A, install the software, log on as user B, install the software, and so forth. (Depending on the software, you may be able to create shortcuts for the other users who are sharing your computer, but reinstallation is the only procedure we know that works for *every* program.)

5. **Click OK and restart Windows 98.**

6. **Log on with a new user name. Click Yes when you see the dialog box in Figure 10-2, and confirm your new password.**

Figure 10-2:
Creating a
new user
profile.

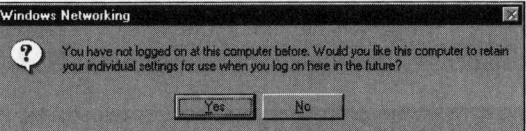

7. **To create more user profiles, choose Start⇨Log Off and repeat Step 6 to create as many users (that is, user profiles) as you need.**

A better way

Windows 98 has added a nifty control panel called Users that enables you to create and maintain custom user profiles more conveniently than you can with the Passwords control panel. If you ever installed Internet Explorer 4 onto a Windows 95 PC, you may have seen a sneak preview of this control panel. Frankly, with the Users control panel on the scene, we're not sure why the User Profiles tab on the Passwords control panel still exists.

The main functions of the Users control panel are:

✔ Add new users without rebooting

✔ Delete existing users without rebooting

✔ Selectively copy an existing user's settings and files to a new user

✔ Automatically install "Microsoft Family Logon" network client

✔ Customize in detail what user profile settings to migrate, reducing both system complexity and disk space requirements

Here's how to set up user profiles with this new control panel:

1. **Choose Start⇨Settings⇨Control Panel and double-click the Users icon.**

   The first time you select the Users control panel, Windows 98 runs the Enable Multi-user Settings wizard, which (although handy) contains no online help.

2. Click <u>N</u>ext and type in the first user's name in the Add User dialog box.

3. Click <u>N</u>ext and type in the first user's password in the Enter New Password dialog box.

   You have to type it twice in order to confirm it, which is a good safe-guard if you type like we do.

4. Click <u>N</u>ext and, in the Personalized Items Settings dialog box (see Figure 10-3), select the categories of settings that you want to be customized for the new user.

   Here's where you start enjoying the benefits of the more detailed Users control panel method versus the Passwords control panel method. In addition to the profile elements that Windows 98 automatically creates, such as USER.DAT, you can specify several other aspects of the user interface that Windows 98 can track separately for this new user: the Favorites folder, the My Documents folder, and so on. This control panel still isn't as detailed as we'd like to see, but it's a step in the right direction.

Figure 10-3:
You have
more
options
creating
profiles with
the Users
control
panel.

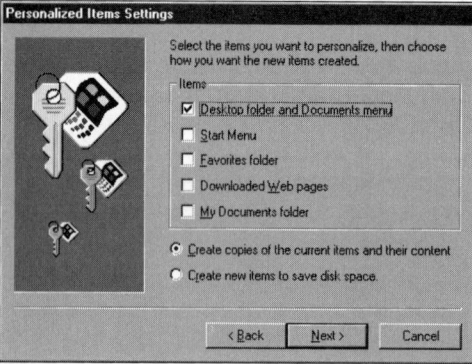

5. While still at the Personalized Items Settings dialog box, click one of the two radio buttons to determine whether Windows 98 makes a copy of the selected features for the new user, or starts with a clean slate.

   Be careful here: If your existing folders contain lots of files — as for example the "Downloaded Web Pages" and "My Documents" folders may — choosing to create copies rather than to create new, blank folders can eat up an elephant-sized chunk of disk space.

6. **Click Next and Finish, and then click Yes at the message asking you to restart the PC.**

7. **Type in your password at the logon dialog box (your user name should already appear).**

8. **Repeat Step 1.**

Now, when you select the Users control panel, you see the User Settings dialog box shown in Figure 10-4. Clicking the New User button takes you through the wizard (Steps 2 through 6). Alternatively, you can change settings for any individual user with the Change Settings button, which brings up the same Personalized Items Settings dialog box in Figure 10-3.

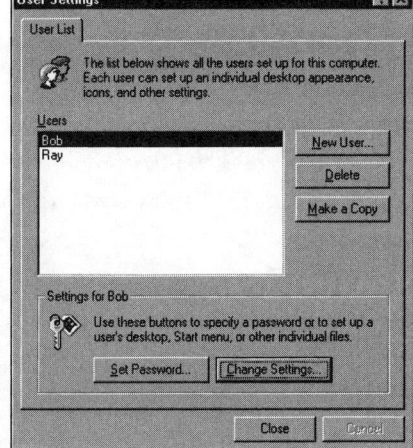

Figure 10-4:
Manage all
user profile
settings
from one
screen.

After you create your user profiles with the Users control panel, if you don't have a network card in your PC, Windows 98 uses the "Microsoft Family Logon" client to present a logon dialog box such as that in Figure 10-5. (FYI, "Microsoft Family Logon" does not refer to the Gates of Seattle, it's referring to *your* family!) As far as we can tell, the only reason this new network client exists is to make it slightly easier for users to log on to PCs that have user profiles enabled. You can click your user name instead of typing it in.

If your PC doesn't have Microsoft Family Logon and you want it, add it via the Network control panel's Add button (Family Logon is a network client and the manufacturer is Microsoft).

Figure 10-5: Logging on gets marginally easier with Microsoft Family Logon.

What Profiles Do to the Registry

Windows 98 user profiles enable different users to make separate settings. Here's a brief list of those settings:

- ✔ User interface settings, such as color schemes, desktop icons, icon spacing and titles, wallpaper, sounds, and so on

- ✔ Most control panel settings, including the display size and color depth

- ✔ Printer settings

- ✔ Application-specific settings (as long as the applications support user profiles, and most 32-bit programs do), such as menu layouts and window customization

- ✔ Network Neighborhood contents and network-related information such as preferred logon server, shared resources, and so on

- ✔ Recent documents list (Start⇨Documents)

- ✔ Start menu settings

- ✔ Temporary Internet files (that is, the Internet Explorer cache)

- ✔ Favorites folder

- ✔ My Documents folder

Naturally, all this information is in the Registry! You can look at the effect of user profiles on the Registry from two angles: the files (physical structure) and the keys (logical structure).

File cloning: The physical changes

User-specific settings live in the USER.DAT Registry file. When you activate user profiles, you tell Windows 98 that it needs to look elsewhere for

USER.DAT than the usual C:\WINDOWS directory. Exactly *where* Windows 98 looks depends on whether you're in a multiple-user-per-PC situation or a roaming-user situation. That is, a stand-alone or networked environment.

Stand-alone PC

In the first case, on a non-networked PC, Windows 98 doesn't bother checking a network server because one doesn't exist. Windows 98 activates the USER.DAT file in C:\WINDOWS, but as soon as you log on with a user name, Windows 98 then proceeds directly to a new, user-specific USER.DAT file in a special location. That location is under the master profile directory C:\WINDOWS\PROFILES, in a subdirectory that's the same as your user name (see Figure 10-6). The USER.DAT in C:\WINDOWS\PROFILES*username* overrides the settings for the USER.DAT in C:\WINDOWS, which Windows 98 loaded just moments earlier.

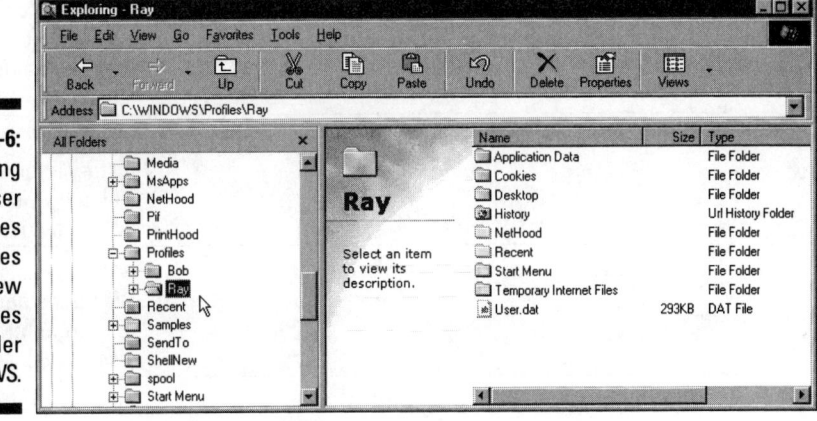

Figure 10-6: Activating user profiles creates new directories under C:\WINDOWS.

Every time you add a user to Windows 98 (for example, with the Users control panel), Windows 98 creates a new subdirectory under C:\WINDOWS\PROFILES and puts a new USER.DAT in that subdirectory, based on the default user information in C:\WINDOWS\USER.DAT.

Windows 98 also creates subdirectories underneath C:\WINDOWS\ PROFILES*username,* depending on the choices you make in the Users control panel's Personalized Items Settings dialog box. The options can be a little confusing, especially when you consider that Microsoft's online help for the Users control panel isn't accurate. Table 10-1 lists these choices, their associated files or folders, and what the files or folders contain.

Table 10-1	User Profile Options	
Option in Users control panel	*Folder or file created in C:\WINDOWS\PROFILES\ username*	*Description of contents*
(none — created always)	USER.DAT	The user-specific Registry component
(none — created always)	Application Data	Outlook Express address book and indexes, QuickLaunch toolbar, and Windows Welcome program
(none — created always)	Cookies	Internet Explorer cookies, files that contain user information used by some Web sites
(none — created always)	History	Internet Explorer history information (recently-visited Web site addresses)
Downloaded Web pages	Temporary Internet Files	Internet Explorer's Web page cache area (recently visited Web sites)
Favorites folder	Favorites	Internet Explorer favorite places, including Active Channels, links, and software update sites
Desktop folder and Documents menu	Desktop	Desktop icons and folders
Desktop folder and Documents menu	Recent	Recently opened documents list
Desktop folder and Documents menu	NetHood	Shortcuts added to Network Neighborhood folder, if any

Option in Users control panel	Folder or file created in C:\WINDOWS\PROFILES\ username	Description of contents
My Documents folder	My Documents	General-purpose document storage folder
Start Menu	Start Menu	Shortcuts added to the default Start menu

The online help for the Users control panel contains an error. Even if you create a new user and you clear the check box marked Downloaded Web Pages in the Personalized Items Settings dialog box, Windows 98 still creates the Cookies folder, which the help system states that Windows 98 creates only if you check the box. Oops.

As you can tell from Table 10-1, you can't inhibit the creation of the folders Application Data, Cookies, and History. If you don't want these, you have to manually delete them (although Internet Explorer then just puts cookies in the Temporary Internet Files folder). This stuff is customizable, but only up to a point. In particular, the fact that Windows 98 insists on putting its Welcome program into every user's profile drives us bananas.

If PCs have a limit to the number of user profiles that you can define on a single machine, we haven't bumped into it yet.

Networked PC

On a networked PC, Windows 98 also maintains a user-specific copy of USER.DAT under C:\WINDOWS\PROFILES\username, but Windows 98 keeps a copy on the network, too. That is, as long as your network is of the client/server variety, and you use a 32-bit network client that Windows 98 supports — such as the built-in network software for Windows NT Server or Novell IntranetWare.

Here's what happens on the network. When you log on, Windows 98 checks for a USER.DAT on your local hard drive in C:\WINDOWS\PROFILES, *and* for a USER.DAT in the user's directory on the server. (The user's server directory where USER.DAT resides is the *mail directory* in NetWare 3.*x* and the *home directory* in NetWare 4.*x* and Windows NT Server.) If either copy of USER.DAT is newer than the other, Windows 98 updates the older version, and then starts up.

If you've enabled some of the user profile options shown in Table 10-1, those can reside on a network server, too, but only the shortcuts — not the actual files.

How USER.DAT is like a Ping-Pong ball

Windows 98 compares the versions of USER.DAT on the server and on your local hard drive. Stop and think for a minute about why this is necessary. You may have logged onto Windows 98 at your last work session without also logging on to the network, in which case the USER.DAT in C:\WINDOWS\ PROFILES*username* is newer than the USER.DAT in your network directory. On the other hand, if you're roaming, then Windows 98 must use the USER.DAT in your network directory because your USER.DAT file may not exist under C:\WINDOWS\PROFILES on a particular PC's hard drive. Even if you've used a PC before, your USER.DAT file on that PC is bound to be stale.

Okay, say you put in some hours on the machine and, before long, it's five o'clock, time to turn off the boss and tell the lights goodnight.

If you change settings during a work session, Windows 98 copies your local USER.DAT up to the network at shutdown to keep everything in sync (that's one reason why shutting down a networked PC can take longer than a stand-alone PC). Remember, you may log on to a different PC later, in which case Windows 98 needs your updated USER.DAT from your directory on the network.

We realize that all this information is a little confusing, so read this sidebar again a couple of times until you get the idea. If you think about it, this system is the only way network-based user profiles *could* work. And the design feature that makes this system possible is the ability to sling USER.DAT files around the network and onto different directories on the PC's hard drive, while leaving SYSTEM.DAT serenely nestled in C:\WINDOWS.

If you use NetWare or IntranetWare file servers and you want to activate user profiles, you must install support for long filenames on the server. If you don't, then only the USER.DAT file can follow a user around the network, because shortcuts (such as those that appear in the Start menu and other selectable user profile components) use long file names. See your network documentation for details, under the subject "OS/2 name space" or "Windows 98 long name space."

Backups

What about backups? Here's an area where Windows 98 takes a step backwards from Windows 95.

When you started Windows 95 initially, after a successful load, Windows copied the default user profile in C:\WINDOWS\USER.DAT to C:\WINDOWS\ USER.DA0, and any custom user profile to C:\WINDOWS \PROFILES\ *username*\USER.DA0. Windows 98 does not back up any custom USER.DAT file (that is, one living under C:\WINDOWS\PROFILES) anytime, anywhere, anyhow — it doesn't even back up your custom USER.DAT file when you're logged on as a profiled user and you manually run the Registry Checker (SCANREGW.EXE).

Why not, Glenn and Mark, you ask? We're scratching our heads too, and it's not because of the tsetse flies out here on safari. No one has been able to tell us, and we think this is a major bungle in the jungle on Microsoft's part.

Chapter 2 gives you some ideas for creating your own custom Registry backup solutions that can include user profile files.

A spare set of keys: The logical changes

The view from REGEDIT changes when you activate user profiles, but things are a bit simpler from the standpoint of the Registry's logical structure. Without user profiles, the *HKU* branch contains only one subkey, *.Default*. With user profiles, *HKU* contains two subkeys: *.Default,* plus a new subkey named after the current user (see Figure 10-7).

When you create a new user profile, Windows 98 uses the contents of *HKU\.Default* (corresponding to the default USER.DAT file in C:\WINDOWS) to create a new subkey with the user's name (corresponding to the new USER.DAT file under C:\WINDOWS\PROFILES*username*). As the new user makes changes to the system, the new subkey (that is, the active profile) changes, but *HKU\.Default* (that is, C:\WINDOWS\USER.DAT) doesn't change.

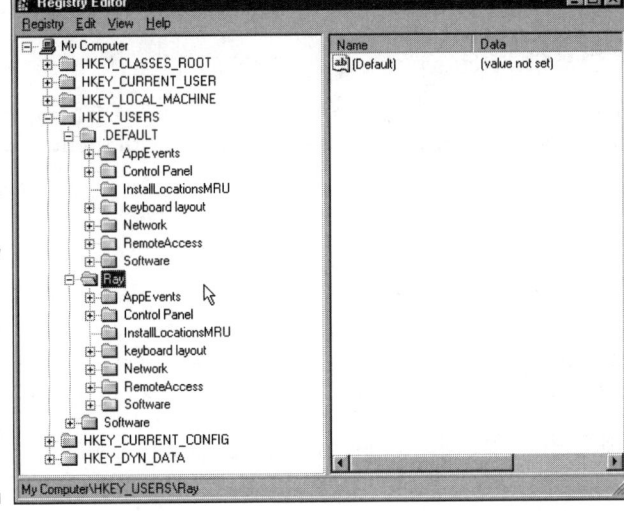

Figure 10-7:
The *HKU*
branch
grows a
new subkey
when you
activate
user
profiles.

Even if you've created many different user profiles on a given Windows 98 PC, only two users show up in *HKU* at any one time: .Default and the currently logged-on user. (You may see some rare exceptions to this rule if you do a lot of profile creations and deletions, but these exceptions appear to be bugs, so put on your bug hat and ignore them.) Any Control Panel changes that affect user settings get logged to the subkey for the current user and don't affect the *.Default* subkey.

What if you've enabled user profiles, but you *want* to modify *HKU\.Default?* For example, you may want to modify the default user profile before creating other user profiles that base themselves on that default profile. You may have activated a screen saver before turning on user profiles, and you don't want that screen saver to become part of every new user's profile. Making changes to the default user is easy: Just don't log on. You can click Cancel or press Esc at the logon dialog box. Now, any changes you make to user settings will apply in the future to anyone else who starts Windows 98 on that PC without logging on. (Note that this tip doesn't work if you use system policies [see Chapter 9] to require a user to log on to the network in order to see the Windows 98 desktop.)

If you want to see where the Registry stores the location of user profile folders for all the different users defined on the PC, peek at *HKLM\ Software\Microsoft\Windows\CurrentVersion\ProfileList.*

If you want to see the new location of the currently-logged-on user's profile files and folders, look at the two locations *HKU\Software\Microsoft\ Windows\CurrentVersion\Shell Folders* and *HKU\Software\Microsoft\ Windows\CurrentVersion\User Shell Folders.*

Profile Downsides

We mention early on in this chapter that you pay a price for the convenience of user profiles. Well, actually, *three* prices. Just think of them as luxury taxes.

Luxury tax 1: Performance

We've never seen this information published in Microsoft or non-Microsoft publications, but we know it to be true from experience: User profiles slow your system down. In fact, user profiles slow your system down a lot more than we think they should. After Windows 98 locates the proper USER.DAT file, things shouldn't take any longer than if you use the default USER.DAT in

C:\WINDOWS, but they do. We freely admit that we're not expert enough to know why user profiles slow down a PC's performance, and if anyone else does, they're not talking so far.

The amount of this "performance tax" varies, but we've run benchmark tests on a few PCs to try and quantify the answer. Based on our tests, you can plan on about a 10 percent performance hit for disk activity with profiles turned on. (Graphics activity doesn't seem to be affected in the least.) That may not seem like a huge tax, but think of it as a dime out of every dollar, and you begin to feel it.

Luxury tax 2: Convenience

The second tax is on convenience. Managing your PC gets more complicated when user profiles are on. For one thing, backing up the Registry gets more involved because you have to worry about those individual USER.DAT profiles under C:\WINDOWS\PROFILES, not just the one in C:\WINDOWS. If you don't back 'em all up when you back up your Registry and if you're unlucky enough to encounter a hard drive problem bad enough to affect several files, you may be up the creek. Even if you do back up the individual USER.DAT profiles, you have to make sure you restore them to the right places.

None of the Microsoft-supplied tools for backing up the Registry — not the Registry Checker, nor the Windows 95 utilities Configuration Backup and Emergency Recovery Utility — can back up user profile information stored in C:\WINDOWS\PROFILES.

The complexity of user profiles also carries a convenience cost when you perform nifty user-oriented Registry edits such as some of the ones that we discuss in this book. If you make a Registry modification that affects USER.DAT (or, in the logical structure, the *HKCU* branch), that modification doesn't apply to all users on the PC — just the one currently logged on. So you find yourself logging on as different users and making your Registry modifications multiple times. You can ease the inconvenience by using a REG file, as Chapter 13 explores, but the process is still drudgery.

Finally, in a company setting, employee turnover is a fact of life. More than one administrator has cursed the user profiles feature while cleaning out hard drives filled with ex-employees' files.

Luxury tax 3: Size

The third tax is on the size of the files on your hard drive. If you choose all the possible options when creating new users, the size of the profile and associated folders easily can be in the megabytes.

Mandatory User Profiles

On a client/server network, you can replace the USER.DAT file that resides in the user's network directory with a USER.DAT file that you want to make mandatory and unchangeable. Name the file USER.MAN, and you've created a mandatory user profile. (You have to make this change for every user individually.)

In the case of USER.MAN, Windows 98 never copies a USER.DAT on the user's PC hard drive back to the network location, as it may do with regular user profiles. Instead, Windows 98 always uses the USER.MAN file.

Not too many companies in our experience use mandatory user profiles, because mandatory user profiles don't provide any control over the settings in SYSTEM.DAT. Yes, you may be able to use system policies (see Chapter 9) in combination with mandatory user profiles, but doing so creates a security environment that is so complex that not many organizations would want to manage it. (We hear that MIT does this, and they may just be smart enough to carry it off!) Organizations can choose either mandatory user profiles or system policies to impose restrictions on users — probably nine out of ten go with the latter. However, mandatory user profiles do one thing that system policies don't: They can freeze user settings for application programs.

 If you want to restrict what users can do with Internet Explorer and its related programs from the security standpoint, use system policies rather than user profiles. Chapter 9 lists some of the policy templates that relate to Internet Explorer; the separately available Internet Explorer Administration Kit contains policy templates as well.

Exorcising User Profiles

So, you turn user profiles on, and you find that a month or a year later, you don't need them anymore. Perhaps your personal computer becomes more personal when your kids go off to college and you're now the exclusive user, or you find that your network doesn't have any users who need to roam from machine to machine. Mindful of our gentle cautions regarding the performance and convenience penalties that user profiles impose, you decide to exorcise them from your PC. With Windows 98 you have two choices: You can remove one user profile, or you can completely remove all user profiles. Depending on how you set up your profiles, removing them may affect the Start menu and various application settings, so be prepared to do some cleanup work!

Removing a single user's profile

Follow these steps to remove a single user's profile from your system:

1. **Start Windows 98 and log on as the default user by selecting Cancel or pressing Esc.**

   You may have to first disable system policies if they're active. (See Chapter 9 for details.)

2. **Choose Start⇨Settings⇨Control Panel and double-click the User icon.**

   The User settings dialog box appears.

3. **Highlight the user that you want to delete by clicking the name.**

4. **Click the Delete button to remove the selected user.**

5. **Click Yes in response to the message "**`This will also delete all <username> s desktop, favorites, and other personal files. Are you sure that you want to delete <username>?`**"**

6. **Repeat Steps 3 through 6 to remove each user individually.**

This procedure also deletes the user's reference in the Registry key *HKLM\SOFTWARE\Microsoft\Windows\CurrentVersion\ProfileList\Username.*

Turning off all user profiles

If you're not already familiar with the Registry Editor, please read through Chapter 4 before performing the following procedure. We also suggest you make a Registry backup. (See Chapter 2 for all the grisly details.)

Here's how to remove all user profiles from your system:

1. **Restart Windows 98 but don't log on. Click Cancel at the Windows logon dialog box.**

   You may have to first disable system policies if they're active. (See Chapter 9 for details.)

2. **Choose Start⇨Settings⇨Control Panel and double-click the Passwords icon.**

   The Passwords Properties dialog box appears.

3. **Click the User Profiles tab.**

4. **Click the radio button that reads** All users of this PC use the same preferences and desktop settings, **then click OK and restart.**

5. **Run the Registry Editor, for example, by choosing Start⇨Run, typing REGEDIT in the Open field, and clicking OK.**

6. **Delete the key *HKLM\SOFTWARE\Microsoft\Windows\ CurrentVersion\ProfileList*, for example, by selecting the key and pressing Del.**

7. **Close the Registry Editor.**

8. **Run Windows Explorer, highlight the directory C:\WINDOWS\ PROFILES, and press Del to delete it.**

   The user subdirectories go away when you delete the main directory.

When you restart Windows 98, every user setting goes back to the value in the *HKU\.Default* key (that is, C:\WINDOWS\USER.DAT). You may have some customizing to do if you've been using a particular user name to make most of your Windows 98 settings and preferences.

Turning off roaming profiles

Our final user profile tip lets you disable the ability to roam the network when you want multiple users to be able to use the same PC, but you'd like to restrict them from roaming the network and having their profiles follow them to different PCs. Use the Registry Editor to create a new DWORD value, *HKLM\Network\Logon\UseHomeDirectory*, and set its data field to 0 (zero).

Chapter 11

Customizing the Desktop for Speed, Form, and Function

In This Chapter

▶ Using the Registry to wring more speed out of your PC

▶ Changing icons and icon names with REGEDIT

▶ Filling the Windows 98 security holes with a nifty INF file

▶ Taming the beast that is ActiveX

*T*he Windows 98 desktop is highly customizable right out of the box, but you can tailor it to your liking in even more ways than the manuals tell you if you don't mind performing a little Registry surgery with REGEDIT as your trusty scalpel.

For many of you, this is the chapter you've been looking for. You may have no interest in future installations of Windows 98 (see Chapter 8), slapping access restrictions on PC users (see Chapter 9), or setting up a multiuser Windows 98 environment (see Chapter 10). However, almost everyone has an interest in tuning up the Windows desktop so it's faster, prettier, and more useful — the subject of this chapter and the next one. The surgical procedures in these chapters range from cosmetic to structural, so there's something for everyone here.

 Many of the tips in this chapter require the use of the Registry Editor. However, we do spend a little time here telling you how to do things with the Registry Editor that you can do in other, safer ways. We do so mainly so that you can share the customizations you make with others via REG files (see Chapter 13), and to do so, you must know exactly which keys and values to export. The bottom line is: Use the right tool for the job. If you're on a network and you want to customize the desktop in ways that the System Policy Editor makes easier and safer, by all means use the System Policy Editor. If you have a single PC and you want to make settings that a standard control panel can make, use the control panel instead of REGEDIT. And if you do use the Registry Editor, which is the *only* way to make some of the changes we mention in this chapter, always back up the key or value you're about to change.

This chapter assumes that you already know your way around the Registry, the Registry Editor, and the Pseudokinetic HKey Demystifizer. If not, please take a look at Chapters 4 and 6 before venturing into this neck of the Registry woods. (We're kidding about that last one.)

What's the "Classic" Desktop?

Windows 98 lets you decide whether you want to use the "Classic style" desktop, that is, the Windows 95-type desktop without any Internet-related content; or the "Web style" desktop, which lets you tack Internet content onto your computer workspace as an underlying layer. (Actually, you can take a little of one and a little of the other, too, via the "Custom" desktop setting.) Just choose View➪Folder Options➪General and pick your poison. (See Figure 11-1.)

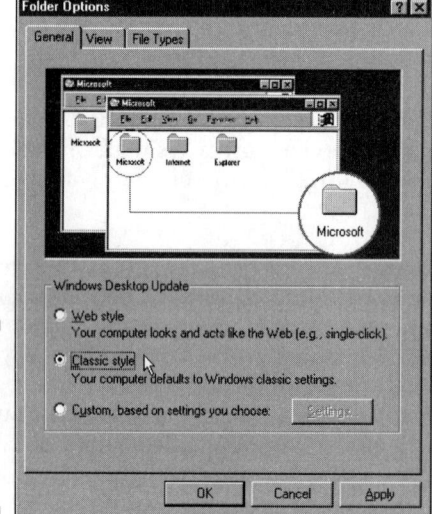

Figure 11-1:
You choose:
Coke, New
Coke, or a
blend?

The terminology is pretty confusing here, so let us clarify a few key points.

✔ Figure 11-1 labels the style choices in a box called Windows Desktop Update, which is what Microsoft called the Active Desktop software that it bundled with Internet Explorer 4 for Windows 95. For all intents and purposes, Windows Desktop Update = Active Desktop.

✔ Lots of the stuff that Microsoft calls Active Desktop, like drag-and-drop for rearranging the Taskbar's Start menu, is still present if you choose the Classic style desktop. Therefore, the Classic style choice doesn't mean that you're turning Active Desktop off, as some people believe.

✔ In fact, there's no easy way to turn off the Active Desktop and make a Windows 98 PC look and work *exactly* like a Windows 95 PC. You don't have an option to uninstall the Active Desktop with the Add/Remove Programs wizard — as you did, for example, with a Windows 95 PC onto which you'd installed Internet Explorer 4.

We like to keep the terminology straight this way: In Windows 98, you're always running the Active Desktop, but you can control whether you *view* that Active Desktop with the Classic style, the Web style, or a hodgepodge of the two.

Anyway, in an attempt to bring a little organization to our look at desktop customization, we segregate the tips that apply *only* to the Web view of the desktop, and to Internet Explorer, into Chapter 12. So, the chapter you're reading now applies regardless of which desktop style you use to view your Active Desktop.

More Power!

You can perform some of the tweaks that we mention here by using freeware or shareware programs in addition to (or, sometimes, in place of) REGEDIT. One program that you can use for customizing your desktop comes on the Windows 98 CD-ROM: the TweakUI control panel, from the Microsoft Powertoys collection. (You can get the rest of the Powertoys free from `www.microsoft.com/windows95/info/powertoys.htm`, although many of the included utilities address deficiencies of Windows 95 rather than Windows 98.) However, Windows 98 doesn't install TweakUI for you. It's unsupported, "swim-at-your-own-risk" software and a little rough around the edges. As a result, you have to install it yourself. Here's how:

1. **Pop your Windows 98 CD-ROM into the drive.**

2. **Right-click the CD-ROM drive and choose Explore.**

3. **Open the \TOOLS\RESKIT\POWERTOY folder.**

4. **Right-click TWEAKUI.INF and choose Install.**

The next time you visit the Control Panel, you'll see the new icon for TweakUI. (Incidentally, the "UI" part stands for "User Interface.") As we go through the rest of this chapter, we'll point out where you can use TweakUI as a Registry editor to achieve specific customizations.

Customizing for Speed

If you've ever gone four-wheeling over rough terrain, you know that it feels faster than if you travel at the same speed on smooth, paved road. The perception of speed can be separate from the objective measurement of speed. And while Windows 98 may be running on a high-speed Pentium II system, it can still "feel" sluggish because of several Registry settings that Microsoft didn't set for speed.

Sluggish performance has two causes: *system settings* that don't let Windows 98 respond as quickly as it's capable of responding, and *common activities* that Windows 98 normally requires you to perform with too many keystrokes and mouse movements. The following tips address both areas.

System settings

Here are a few system settings that you can tweak with the Registry to make Windows 98 more responsive to the gas pedal.

Animated windows and menus and lists, oh my!

Windows 98 uses various forms of animation on the desktop, such as:

- ✔ **Window animation.** When you minimize or maximize a window, Windows 98 displays a zoom effect, or "visual whoosh." Any window shrinks down toward the taskbar when you minimize it and expands up from the taskbar when you maximize or restore it. Microsoft claims this effect helps new users understand where windows go when minimized (the Taskbar); we think Microsoft borrowed too much from the Macintosh in this case.

- ✔ **Menu animation.** When you choose a drop-down menu, it no longer drops down, it slides down from one corner to the opposite one; when you choose a submenu off the Start menu, it also slides into place.

- ✔ **Smooth scrolling.** When you use the scroll bar to click through a long list, say the *HKCR* key in REGEDIT, Windows 98 slides the new items into place instead of snapping directly to them. Also, when you expand or contract a folder in Windows Explorer, you see a sliding effect.

Many of you would prefer that your Active Desktop wasn't quite this active, so this section offers tips for surgically removing the unnecessary and occasionally annoying appendix that is Windows 98 animation. You can turn animation off for windows, menus, and scrolling lists in one fell swoop using the following procedure:

1. **Right-click any empty spot on the desktop and choose Properties.**

   The Display control panel appears.

2. **Choose the Effects tab.**

   You see the screen shown in Figure 11-2.

3. **Clear the check box labeled Animate Windows, Menus, and Lists.**

4. **Click OK.**

   You don't have to restart Windows 98 for the change to take effect.

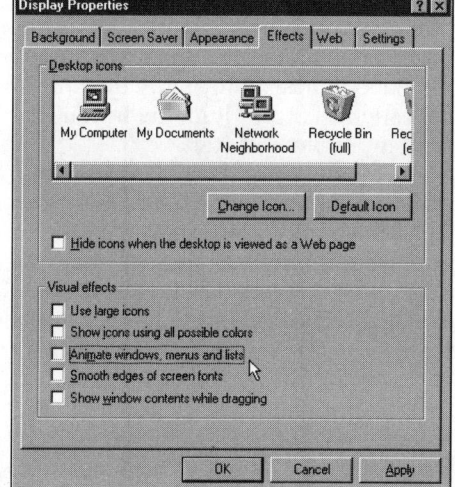

Figure 11-2:
Three
animation
settings
in one
check box.

The problem with the Display control panel method is that it doesn't let you pick and choose which animation effects you want or don't want: it's all or nothing. That limitation doesn't bother your authors much — we don't want *any* animation on our PCs — but you may feel differently. Here's how to set each of the three animation effects separately. The changes take effect on the next restart:

✔ To turn off the window animation effect, run REGEDIT and set the string value *MinAnimate* in the key *HKCU\Control Panel\Desktop\WindowMetrics* to "0." (Add it if it isn't there already.) The change takes effect at the next system restart. The speed with which windows now snap up or down is very satisfying.

✔ Turn off menu animation by subtracting 2 from the leftmost binary number in the value *HKCU\Control Panel\Desktop\UserPreferencemask*. For example, if the value is **AE 00 00 00**, as is probable, change it to **AC 00 00 00**. (AE – 2 = AC in hexadecimal notation; use the Scientific view of the Windows calculator to do math like this.)

> ✔ Turn the smooth scrolling animations off by changing the DWORD value *HKCU\Control Panel\Desktop\SmoothScroll* from "1" to "0."

If you have the TweakUI control panel installed, use the General tab's Effects list to select or deselect these three animation effects individually.

As it turns out, the *UserPreferencemask* value in *HKCU\Control Panel\Desktop* controls more than just menu animation. The value actually controls five other effects, as the next section explores.

Animation, part deux

You may notice (and dislike) the fact that little animated text boxes appear when you point the cursor at one of the small buttons (minimize, restore, maximize, or close) on the far right of an application's title bar (this is called the *hot tracking* effect). Or, perhaps you're annoyed by the following When you open a list in a dialog box, such as Start⇨Run, the list slides into place when you want it to snap to attention immediately.

After a few hours' experimentation, we think that we've figured out exactly how to control all these animated effects — plus one effect that doesn't have anything to do with animation: whether you can see the underlined characters, or "hotkeys," on menu bars and menus (File, Edit, and so on). Every one of these settings resides in the leftmost binary number in the value *HKCU\Control Panel\Desktop\UserPreferencemask*. (The other three numbers are always zeros.)

Here's how it works (and remember, you read it here first — we haven't seen this information published anywhere else):

1. **Start with zero.**

2. **If you want menu animation (see previous section), add 2.**

3. **If you want combo dialog box animation (like Start⇨Run), add 4.**

4. **If you want list box animation, add 8.**

5. **If you want menu underlines, add 20.**

6. **If you want hot tracking, add 80.**

7. **Put the total into the leftmost number of *HKCU\Control Panel\Desktop\UserPreferencemask*, and leave the other three numbers zeroes.**

The trick is that you must perform all this addition with a base 16, or *hexadecimal,* calculator. Fortunately, you have one in the Windows 98 Calculator; choose View⇨Scientific and click the Hex button. A trio of examples can clarify the weird math.

✔ If you're like us and you don't want any animation, but you do want to see underlined menu text, then set *HKCU\Control Panel\Desktop\ UserPreferencemask* to **20 00 00 00**.

✔ If you want underlined menu text and hot tracking, then (20 + 80) = A0 and you'd set the Registry value to **A0 00 00 00**. By the way, this is the setting Windows 98 uses when you *clear* the check box labeled Animate Windows, Menus, and Lists in the Display control panel.

✔ If you want everything animated everywhere, then (2 + 4 + 8 + 20 + 80) = AE and you'd set *UserPreferencemask* to **AE 00 00 00**. This is the setting Windows 98 uses when you select the Animate Windows, Menus, and Lists check box in the Display control panel.

Armed with your new knowledge, you can come up with whatever combination of animated effects you want and transport that combination to any other PC by exporting the contents of *HKCU\Control Panel\Desktop\ UserPrereferencemask*, *HKCU\Control Panel\Desktop\SmoothScroll* (see previous section), and *HKCU\Control Panel\Desktop\WindowMetrics\MinAnimate* (also see previous section).

Why Microsoft chose to make these particular desktop settings so obscure, and to lump six settings into the single value *UserPreferencemask,* is a bit of a mystery. The straightforward approach would have been to use a different Registry value for each individual setting and then give the user the option to control each one independently on the Display control panel. It's this sort of needless complexity that gives the Registry a bad name. Anyway, at least now you're in on the secret handshake.

Taking pop-ups down

Windows 98 includes pop-up *infotips* that appear as if by magic if you allow your cursor to hover over particular icons (My Computer, My Documents, Control Panel, and so on). Some of these text box pop-ups are mildly informative. Others are utterly inane, like the infotip for the desktop icon labeled Set Up The Microsoft Network, which reads "Set Up The Microsoft Network." (We're not kidding: See Figure 11-3).

You can customize these infotips by searching for them in the Registry, and then changing the string values. Each tip has the name "InfoTip," so you can just search for that string if you like.

Figure 11-3:
Infotip,
shminfotip.

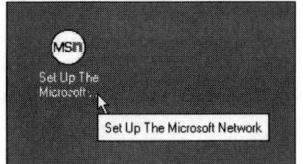

Even better, if you want to save the brain cells that your PC devotes to infotips, turn 'em off. Open My Computer, choose View➪Folder Options➪ View, and clear the checkbox labeled Show Pop-Up Description for Folders and Desktop Items. If you want to put the setting into a REG file, the relevant DWORD value is *HKCU\Software\Microsoft\Windows\CurrentVersion\ Explorer\Advanced\ShowInfoTip*. Zero is off, while one (the default) is on.

Cascading menus: fast or sticky?

You may not be a Type A personality who gets somewhat frustrated at relatively minor delays. However, if you've ever wished in the back of your mind that those cascading menus that branch off the Start button would pop up just a little faster than the default half-second, here's a tip for you.

Run REGEDIT and change *HKCU\Control Panel\Desktop\MenuShowDelay* to the number of milliseconds (thousandths of a second) delay you prefer. The default is 500. (If the value doesn't exist, add it; it's a string type.) We like to change this setting to zero for maximum speed, although you do have to get out of the habit of leisurely moving the mouse diagonally across cascading menus if you eliminate the delay.

If you prefer your menus to be *sticky* rather than fast, set *MenuShowDelay* to the maximum value, which is 65534. With this setting, clicked menus don't follow the mouse cursor any more as you navigate the Start menu. You click it, it stays put. What you give up is the automatic menu-opening feature, but you may be prepared for that trade-off.

Try it both ways and see whether you like your menus better fast or sticky.

Hot-rodding the keyboard

The keyboard control panel's Speed tab enables you to modify the delay period before a key begins repeating, as well as the repeat rate (the speed with which a key repeats after it starts repeating). Experienced typists appreciate the responsiveness that Windows 98 suddenly gains when they set the delay period as short as possible and the repeat rate as fast as possible. For one thing, scrolling around a document with the arrow keys becomes much faster. It's liposuction for the keyboard.

The relevant Registry keys are *HKCU\Control Panel\Keyboard\ KeyboardDelay,* which ranges from 0 (short) to 3 (long), and (in the same key) *KeyboardSpeed,* which ranges from 0 (slow) to 31 (fast). We don't often mention settings that you can change via control panels, but in this case, we find that changing the keyboard settings at Windows 98 installation by modifying the Registry settings in MSBATCH.INF (see Chapter 8), or with a REG file, is handy. Many users, especially Windows 98 novices, don't venture into the control panels for months, if ever.

Common activities

One of the best ways to make Windows 98 faster in your day-to-day work is to put some of the common activities that are usually buried under a series of keystrokes and mouse clicks up onto the Start menu or the desktop, where you can get to them posthaste. Examples may include your dial-up networking connection, various control panels, and even Windows Explorer itself. (Chapter 12 tells you about adding the URL history folder to the Start menu, if you're an Internet user.)

Adding Dial-Up Networking to the Start menu

You may use Dial-Up Networking (DUN) often, either to link to an online Internet Service Provider or to dial up your office network from home or the road. You can get to your Dial-Up Networking connections more easily if you put them on the Start menu. Here's the procedure:

1. **Right-click the Start button and choose Explore.**

   You see an Explorer window that displays the structure of the Start menu.

2. **Right-click any empty space in the right pane and choose New⇨Folder.**

3. **With the new folder name highlighted, type in the following:**

   ```
   Dial Up Net.{992CFFA0-F557-101A-88EC-00DD010CCC48}
   ```

   If you want to make sure that you avoid a typing error, you can use REGEDIT to pluck the Dial Up Networking CLSID out of the Registry by searching for "Dial-Up Networking" in the value data field. After you locate the Dial-Up Networking folder, right-click the CLSID key, choose Rename, and press Ctrl+C to copy the CLSID key to the Clipboard. Press Esc to get out of the Rename operation, and then close REGEDIT. In Explorer, press Ctrl+V to paste the key into the Explorer window, after typing the **Dial Up Net.** Prefix. (Don't forget the period.)

4. **Close the Explorer window and try out your new Start menu option.**

If you haven't defined any DUN connections yet, the menu option shows (empty). After you create one or more DUN connection files, they'll show up on your Start menu.

Making desktop icons for control panels

In Chapter 3, we give you the procedure for adding the Control Panel to the Start menu. That's a cool tip, because you often edit the Registry via the Control Panel. However, you can also make desktop icons for specific control panels that you tend to use more often than others. You can even specify which particular *tab* of a particular control panel you want to open up automatically! Here's the procedure:

1. **Right-click any open area on the desktop and choose** <u>N</u>ew⇨<u>S</u>hortcut.

2. **In the Command Line field, type the following:**

```
C:\WINDOWS\CONTROL.EXE cplfile,iconname,tab
```

You'd replace *cplfile* with the name of the actual control panel file, *iconname* with the control panel's icon name, and *tab* with the number (starting at zero for the leftmost one) of the tab you want to open automatically. For example,

```
C:\WINDOWS\CONTROL.EXE SYSDM.CPL,SYSTEM,3
```

opens the System control panel to the fourth tab, Performance.

3. **Click** <u>N</u>ext **and give your shortcut a suitable name.**

4. **Click the Finish button.**

Okay, so where do you get the control panel file names? You have to guess at them. (Just kidding — we give 'em all to you in Chapter 3, Table 3-1.) Have fun!

Opening My Computer in Explorer view

When managing files, the dual-pane Windows Explorer view is the one most of us actually use because it's more convenient than the single-pane My Computer view. However, right-clicking My Computer and choosing Explore is a two-step process. There's a way to make it a one-step process, so that every time you choose My Computer, you see an Explorer-style dual-pane window. Naturally, you have to edit the Registry to achieve this bit of reconstructive surgery! Here's how:

1. **Fire up REGEDIT and do a Find for "Displays the contents of your computer."**

   That search text is actually the infotip for "My Computer" and looking for it is a quick way to get to the right place in *HKCR\CLSID*. The actual CLSID is {20D04FE0-3AEA-1069-A2D8-08002B30309D} if you prefer to go there directly.

2. **In the key pane, right-click the key named "shell" immediately under the {20D04...} folder and choose** <u>N</u>ew⇨<u>K</u>ey. **Name the new key** open.

3. **Right-click the just-created open key and select** <u>N</u>ew⇨<u>K</u>ey **once more. Name this new key** command.

4. **With the new command key highlighted, double-click the (Default) value in the value pane and type** EXPLORER.EXE **for the value data.**

   Your display should look like Figure 11-4.

5. **Close REGEDIT.**

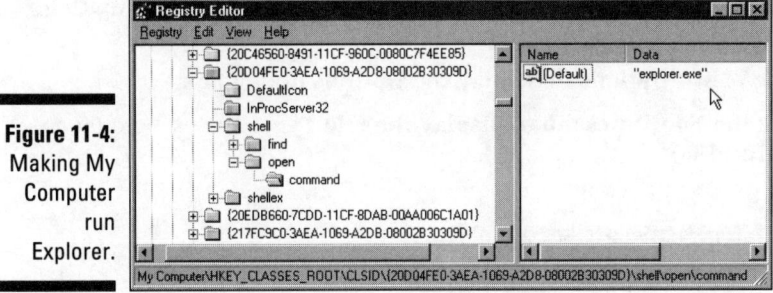

Figure 11-4:
Making My
Computer
run
Explorer.

Customizing for Form

This section is about cosmetic surgery — changing the icons and icon titles that programs and data files and Windows 98 itself use. We throw in a tip for fixing some misleading text in the System control panel, too.

Changing application-related icons

Applications that register a particular file type have the option to define a special icon for that file type, too. The relevant Registry key is *HKCR\filetype\ DefaultIcon,* where *filetype* is a file type entry in the bottom half of the *HKCR* branch. Figure 11-5 shows an example for Adobe Photoshop. The value data "C:\program files\Photoshp\photoshp.exe,1" indicates that the icon is the second one (0 being the first) stored within the main Photoshop program, PHOTOSHP.EXE. (Yep, EXE files can store icons!)

The easiest way to change an icon for a particular file type is not to use the Registry Editor at all because REGEDIT doesn't give you any visual feedback about the alternative icons available. Instead, follow this procedure:

Figure 11-5:
Where the
Registry
stores the
default
Photoshop
icon
information.

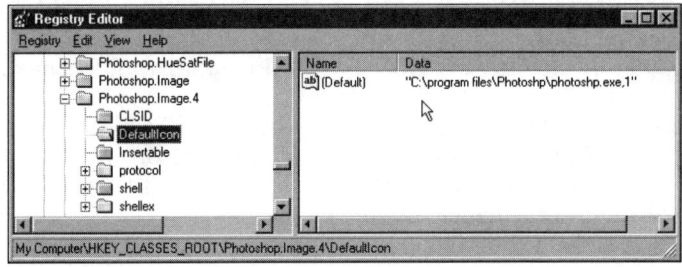

1. **Start Windows Explorer the fast way, by right-clicking the My Computer icon and choosing Explore.**

2. **Click View⇨Options to display the Options dialog box.**

3. **Click the File Types tab to display the File Types dialog box. (See Figure 11-6.)**

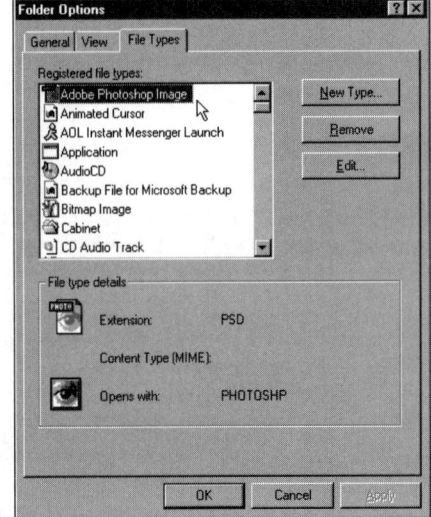

Figure 11-6:
The File
Types
dialog box
is an easy
place to
change
data file
icons.

4. **Choose the file type you want to change and click the Edit button.**

5. **Click Change Icon, type in a File name, and make a selection for the Current icon in the scrolling window.**

    The currently displayed filename may have multiple choices; if you want different ones, specify a filename of C:\WINDOWS\MORICONS.DLL, C:\WINDOWS\SYSTEM\SHELL32.DLL, or C:\WINDOWS\SYSTEM\ COOL.DLL. It turns out that DLL files aren't just for programs, after all!

6. **Click OK, Close, Close, and then close Windows Explorer (for example, by clicking the close box in the upper-right corner).**

The above technique is much safer and easier than using the Registry Editor. You'll find that you still can't change a few icons with this procedure, but not many. If you want to go icon hunting in REGEDIT, look in *HKCR* and *HKCR\CLSID* for keys named *DefaultIcon*.

Changing bitmap image icons

One of the benefits of Windows 98's folder Web view is the ability to see a preview, or *thumbnail,* of a file by simply clicking it in My Computer or Windows Explorer. For BMP files, at least, you can get thumbnail views in the Classic view desktop *or* the Web view desktop, and you don't have to click a file to see them, either. Here's the scoop:

1. **Run the Registry Editor and whip on over to *HKCR\Paint.Picture\ DefaultIcon*.**

2. **Export the key for safekeeping with the Registry⇨Export Registry File command.**

3. **Change the (default) value to %1.**

   This is how you tell Windows 98 to use the file itself as the default icon. Windows 98 scales down the graphic icon size automatically.

4. **Close REGEDIT and restart Windows 98.**

   You should now see BMP files appear in My Computer or Windows Explorer as miniature versions of the actual graphics, instead of as generic paintbucket icons (see Figure 11-7).

If you tire of the bitmap image preview icons, just import the key you exported in Step 2 to restore things to their pre-hacked state.

You can also choose View⇨Thumbnails for any folder within My Computer or Explorer, whether you use the Classic view or the Web view of the desktop, but this is a *lot* slower and typically wastes a lot more screen space than the method just presented (see Figure 11-8). However, the View Thumbnails option is an okay choice if you have non-BMP graphics you'd like to see, such as GIF or JPG files.

Renaming desktop icons

Many Windows 98 desktop icons have names that you seemingly can't change. The usual method for renaming an icon, clicking its name once and then changing it, doesn't work. Here's an example — the Recycle Bin — for how you can change such icon titles. Just remember that if you do so, you may confuse other users who work with your PC.

1. **Run REGEDIT (for example, by choosing Start⇨Run and typing** REGEDIT**).**

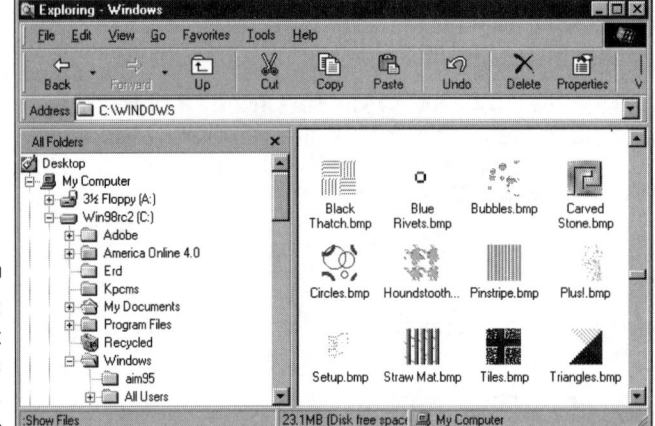

Figure 11-7:
View Paint
files as
miniatures.

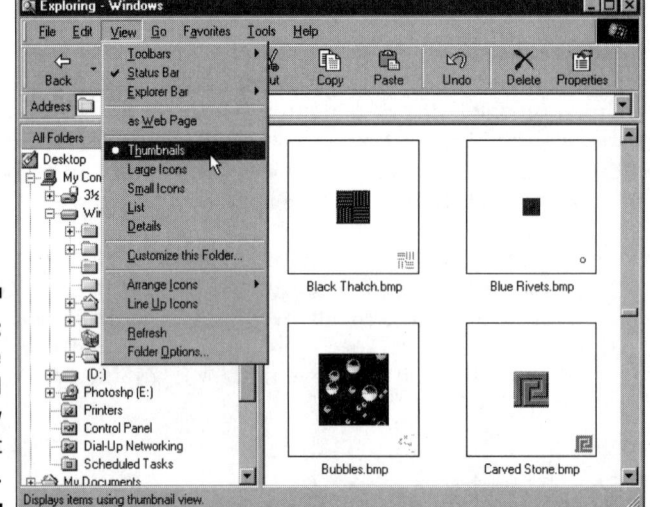

Figure 11-8:
The
thumbnail
view
wastes a lot
of space.

2. **Press Ctrl+F to open the Find dialog box.**

3. **Enter** Recycle Bin **in the Fi̲nd What field and clear all check boxes other than D̲ata.**

   The name *Recycle Bin* appears as the data field in a value under *HKCR\CLSID*, so you can speed up your search by only looking for data field items.

4. **Click F̲ind Next to initiate the search.**

5. **After the key under HKCR\CLSID appears, double-click the (Default) value in the value pane and change the name from Recycle Bin to whatever you prefer.**

6. **Close REGEDIT. Your change takes effect at the next restart (see Figure 11-9).**

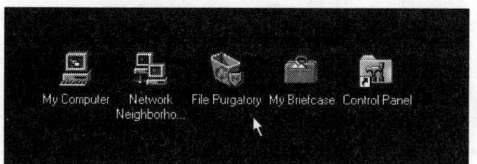

Figure 11-9:
The Recycle Bin gets a nose job.

You can use the preceding steps to rename just about any desktop icon in Windows 98.

Renaming file system profiles

Here's a little tip for making an accuracy correction in the Windows 98 user interface. You can boost performance for PCs with more than 16 megabytes of memory by changing your file system profile to read "Network server" instead of "Desktop computer." Get to the setting via the System control panel's Performance tab; click the File System button to see the File System Properties dialog box (see Figure 11-10).

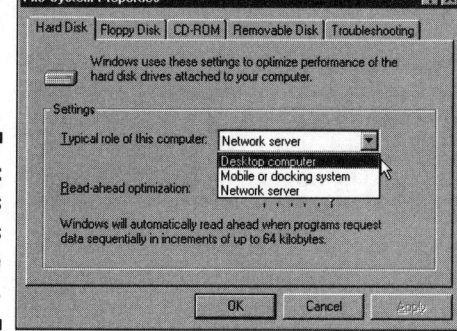

Figure 11-10:
Microsoft's categories are misleading.

You may not be using the PC as a network server, but that doesn't matter. The appropriate setting depends on the amount of installed memory in the PC, not on how you're using the PC.

You can correct Microsoft's inaccurate wording by running the Registry Editor and searching for the text strings *Network server*, *Desktop computer*, and *Mobile or docking system*. (You'll find them in *HKLM\Software\Microsoft\Windows\CurrentVersion\FS Templates*.) Change the text entries to **More than 16MB**, **Exactly 16MB**, and **Less than 16MB**, respectively, in the (Default) values for the three subkeys. Share the change with everyone on your network using a REG file, so that users can make choices based on the right information.

Customizing for Function

Manipulating the Registry can become a powerful tool for enhancing the behavior of Windows 98 in ways that don't pertain to speed or cosmetics. The two areas we look at here are improving Windows 98 security, and making the file association system work the way you want it to.

Filling security holes

Windows 98 maintains several different records of your activities, mainly for your convenience if you want to work later with documents or programs that you recently used. However, these *history lists* do create several security holes. Anyone can easily see what documents you've been working on (say, RESUME.DOC, or perhaps TOP SECRET CLOSELY GUARDED FORMULA FOR DR PEPPER.DOC) by examining the history lists.

Unfortunately, Windows 98 offers no convenient method for turning these history lists off. Fortunately, your Registry knowledge (and a little guidance from us) is all you need.

First, we need to identify the various lists. Here they are:

- **The recent documents list** (Start⇨Documents). Contains the most recent 15 documents that you've opened in a 32-bit Windows program; doesn't list documents that you open in 16-bit Windows programs or DOS sessions.

- **The Run MRU list** (MRU = Most Recently Used). This list appears after you choose Start⇨Run and click the list display arrow; you see a history of program command lines that you've typed via Start⇨Run.

- **The Find MRU list**. When you use the Windows 98 Find facility (Start⇨Find⇨Files or Folders), you can see this list by clicking the arrow next to the Named field.

✔ **The Find Computer MRU list**. You can view this list from
Start⇨Find⇨Computer.

You can completely disable the Recent documents list by adding the
DWORD value *NoRecentDocsMenu* with a data field of 1 to *HKCU/Software/
Microsoft/Windows/CurrentVersion/Policies/Explorer.*

The recent documents list is not stored entirely in the Registry; it's also in
C:\WINDOWS\RECENT. The other three lists exist entirely in the Registry.
You can create an INF file that deletes the Registry entries. (REG files don't
delete existing entries, so the REG technique doesn't work here.)

Chapter 13 covers INF files, if you want to understand the following file
completely. If you don't, trust us, the file works properly.

Here's the text:

```
[version]
signature=$Chicago$
[DefaultInstall]
DelReg=Security
[Security]
HKCU, Software\Microsoft\Windows\CurrentVersion\Explorer\RecentDocs ,
HKCU, Software\Microsoft\Windows\CurrentVersion\Explorer\
   RunMRU ,
HKCU, Software\Microsoft\Windows\CurrentVersion\Explorer\Doc
   Find Spec MRU ,
HKCU, Software\Microsoft\Windows\CurrentVersion\Explorer\
   FindComputerMRU ,
```

Save the INF file as SECURE.INF in C:\WINDOWS\INF. Windows 98 rebuilds
the keys automatically the next time you perform an action that normally
creates an entry in the MRU list. Notice that you *must* put double quotes
around the entry for *Doc Find Spec MRU* because the key name contains
spaces. If you get into the habit of always putting key names in quotation
marks, then you're smarter than the average bear.

Now, create a batch file in Notepad (call it SECURE.BAT if you like) that
activates the INF file and deletes the shortcuts in C:\WINDOWS\RECENT to
clear the Documents list:

```
@ECHO OFF
C:\WINDOWS\RUNDLL.EXE SETUPX.DLL,INSTALLHINFSECTION
   DEFAULTINSTALL 132 C:\WINDOWS\INF\SECURE.INF
ECHO Y | DEL C:\WINDOWS\RECENT\*.*
```

That second line is one long one, although we had to break it to make it fit on this page.

All you have to do now is create a desktop icon to run SECURE.BAT (for example, by dragging and dropping the file to the desktop). Double-click the icon and restart Windows 98 whenever you want to clear all the various history lists. The Documents, Find MRU, and Find Computer MRU lists clear immediately, but the Run MRU list doesn't clear until you restart. If that doesn't bother you, skip the restart in the knowledge that your batch file clears three out of four lists right away.

If you use the TweakUI control panel as described in the earlier section "More Power!" the Paranoia tab lets you do what SECURE.INF and SECURE.BAT do (see Figure 11-11). You still may want to create your own security files if you work for a company that forbids installing unsupported software like TweakUI.

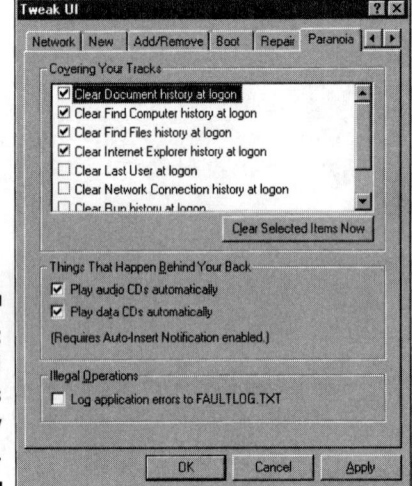

Figure 11-11:
TweakUI
offers
security
settings.

Printing directory listings

We're amazed that after lo these many years, there's still no command in Windows Explorer to print the contents of a highlighted directory. Thankfully, you can add this capability with a simple batch file and a little Registry skin graft.

This tip is a little more advanced than some of the others in this chapter. If you're not familiar with batch files, you may want to skip it, or pass it along to someone who is.

The first step is to fire up Notepad and create a *batch file* that changes to the current directory and then runs the old MS-DOS DIR command with a software switch to send the output to the printer. An example of such a batch file, which we'll call PDIR.BAT, could be as simple as the following, which sends the print job to a printer connected to the first parallel port:

```
CD %1
DIR > LPT1:
```

If you want to get fancier with the various options, type **DIR /?** at an MS-DOS prompt to see what's possible, and modify the DIR command line accordingly. Take a look at **/O**, which forces an alphabetical sort, and **/S**, which forces the inclusion of subdirectories.

In Windows Explorer, right-click the icon for PDIR.BAT and set its Program tab properties to Close on Exit and Run Minimized. These settings make for a tidier, less distracting screen.

Now, run the Registry Editor, and add the keys *HKCR\Directory\shell\print* and *HKCR\Directory\shell\print\command*. Double-click the latter key's (Default) value and edit it to specify the pathname for PDIR.BAT, such as **C:\PDIR.BAT**. Close REGEDIT and you're done! You've just added a "print" capability for the Directory file type classification. When you right-click a folder in Windows Explorer, you see a new command to print the directory listing. Handy!

Two drawbacks though: You may have to touch your printer's "flush buffer" or "print page" button to force any incomplete page to print, and you can't use this trick with PostScript printers that can't handle plain text files.

File associations and ActiveX

One of the more powerful aspects of Windows 98 is something called *Object Linking and Embedding (OLE),* although the trendier term *ActiveX* is becoming more accepted these days. A big part of OLE and ActiveX has to do with file type associations. The little three-letter suffix after the period in a filename unlocks a whole set of OLE instructions that help Windows 98 understand how to deal with that kind of file. Those instructions all live in the Registry — specifically, the *HKCR* branch, and even more specifically, the lower half of that branch. This section presents two ActiveX-related tips, one that involves REGEDIT and one that doesn't.

Opening unknown file types
We've all seen files named READ.ME, README.NOW, README.1ST, DONTLISTENTOTHEMREADME.FIRST, and so on. These files are almost certainly plain old text files that Notepad or Wordpad can open with ease,

but double-clicking such files presents the Open With dialog box — requiring some tedious mousing around and even presenting the risk of inadvertently associating the .ME or .NOW file type with Notepad for evermore.

Here's a better way to open unknown file types that involves a little Registry wizardry. (You can't perform this trick with the File Types dialog box we discuss in the following section.) You can set up the Registry so that if you double-click a file with an unknown file extension, Windows 98 automatically runs Notepad (or Wordpad or whatever other text editor you like). Here's the procedure:

1. **Run REGEDIT (for example, by selecting Start⇨_Run_⇨REGEDIT).**

2. **Scroll to _HKCR\Unknown_ and expand the subkeys.**

   HKCR\Unknown is in the bottom half of the HKCR structure; that is, it's a file type class, not a file extension. (See Chapter 6 for more on the organization of the HKCR branch.) The subkey expands out to _HKCR\Unknown\shell\openas\command,_ where you see the code that displays the usual Open With context menu option.

3. **Add the new key _HKCR\Unknown\shell\open\command_ containing the (Default) string value**

   ```
   C:\WINDOWS\NOTEPAD.EXE  %1
   ```

   You can substitute the path name for any preferred text editor.

   The _%1_ is a stand-in for the actual filename that you want to open. You can often get by without specifying %1 when defining open commands, but we include it here as a matter of good practice. Figure 11-12 shows the old key and the one you just added.

4. **Close REGEDIT and try out your new command.**

Now, when you double-click a file with an undefined extension, Windows 98 automatically opens the file in Notepad. Obviously, if you try this trick with a binary file that isn't a simple text file, nothing productive happens; but no harm's done either.

Figure 11-12:
Adding a
program to
handle
opening
unknown
file types.

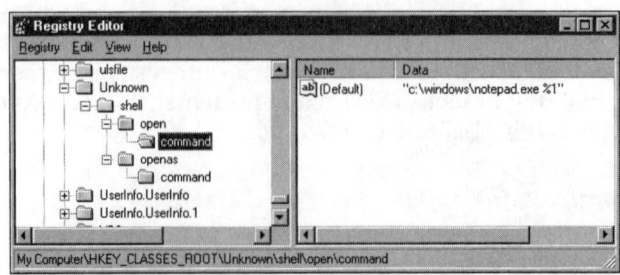

Modifying the context menu

In Chapter 1, we allude to the fact that you can add programs to the right-click menu (that is, the *context menu*) of a data file that you may not always want to open with the same program. Here's a step-by-step example of how you add a context menu option for TXT files to open them in Microsoft Wordpad for Windows.

1. **Start Windows Explorer the fast way, by right-clicking the My Computer icon and choosing <u>E</u>xplore.**

2. **Click <u>V</u>iew⇨Folder <u>O</u>ptions to display the Folder Options dialog box.**

3. **Click the File Types tab to display the File Types dialog box. (Refer to Figure 11-6.)**

4. **Scroll down to Text Document, click it, and click the <u>E</u>dit button to display the Edit File Type dialog box. (See Figure 11-13.)**

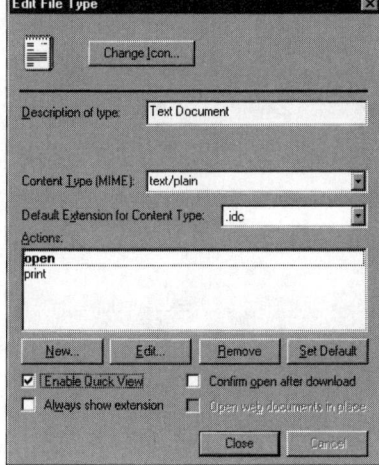

Figure 11-13:
The Actions list in the Edit File Type dialog box defines right-click behavior.

5. **Click the <u>N</u>ew button to display the New Action dialog box.**

6. **In the Action list, type** Open in Wordpad **and in the Application Used to Perform Action, type**

```
C:\Progra~1\Access~1\WORDPAD.EXE  %1
```

(We assume that you installed Wordpad in the usual location.) Notice the use of the DOS-equivalent short filenames here. Also, the *%1* just refers to the data file itself; you may be able to omit it with some programs, but including it is good practice.

7. Click OK, Close, Close, and then close Explorer (for example, by clicking the close box in the upper-right corner).

Now, when you right-click a file with the suffix TXT, you see `Open in Wordpad` as a new option. Having this option may be handy if you know you're opening a large text file that's too big for Notepad.

If you're working with another file type besides a text file, and the Edit button is grayed out in Step 4, you may need to reset a special Registry value called *EditFlags*. See the section in Chapter 18 called "Lock Out File Type Changes" for details.

You can apply the preceding technique to any data file that you may want to use multiple applications with: BMP with Windows Paint and Adobe Photoshop, HTM with Internet Explorer and Netscape Navigator, and so on.

To see the effect that the preceding steps have on the Registry, look up *HKCR\txtfile\shell* and notice the new subkeys, shown in Figure 11-14.

Figure 11-14:
The
Registry
reflects
a new
context
menu
command.

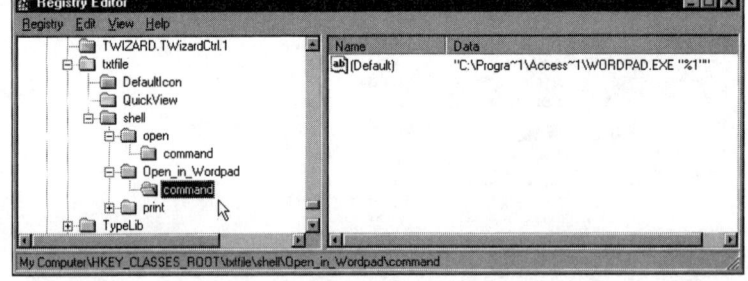

If you want to get a bit fancy, you can change the default action that occurs when you double-click a file. Just click the desired action in the Actions list (refer to Figure 11-13) and click the Set Default button. The double-click action always appears in boldface. For example, it's a smart move to change the default action for REG files from "Merge" to "Edit."

If you want to get even *fancier,* you can specify the letter in your new menu entry that you want Windows 98 to underline as a shortcut key to that option. For example, in Step 6 of the preceding number list, try typing **Open in &Wordpad** instead of **Open in Wordpad**. The ampersand (named after famed German contortionist Helmut Ampers) means that the "W" in "Wordpad" will appear underlined, and "W" becomes the hotkey for that menu option. Note also that the ampersand character will appear in the Registry, so when you're searching the Registry for a context menu label that contains an underline, don't forget to include the ampersand.

Adding an extension to a file type

You may want to activate a particular program when you select data files having one of two or more possible extensions. A good example is the *.LOG file type, which programs such as ScanDisk create to record their activities. LOG files are normally plain text files, so it would be nice to select them and run Notepad automatically.

In the previous section, we explain how you can run several different programs with files having a single suffix, using the File Types dialog box. Here, you have the opposite situation: You want to run the same program when selecting files having multiple suffixes. For example, we want to run Notepad whenever we select either a TXT or LOG file.

There's no way to accomplish this feat using the File Types dialog box. When you click the New Type button, you have to create both a new filetype class *and* the associated file extension; there's no option to merely add an extension to an existing filetype class. So, you have to use the Registry Editor. Here's the technique:

1. **Run REGEDIT and discover the name of the filetype class to which you want to add a file extension.**

   This means locating the "usual" extension in *HKCR* and seeing what filetype class it points to. For example, the usual text file ends in the extension TXT, and the default value under *HKCR\.txt* is txtfile. So, txtfile is the filetype class.

2. **Create a new key, *HKCR\.xxx*, where *xxx* is the new extension you want to activate with the program. (Be sure that you include the period.)**

   In our example, we create a new key, *HKCR\.log*.

3. **Enter the filetype class from Step 1 into the (Default) value for the new key.**

   The end result looks like Figure 11-15.

4. **Close REGEDIT.**

Now, when the user selects either a LOG file or a TXT file, Notepad runs.

You can share your customization by exporting the key you created in Step 2 to a REG file. (See Chapter 13 for more on creating REG files.)

Figure 11-15:
Rigging the
Registry
so LOG
files run
Notepad.

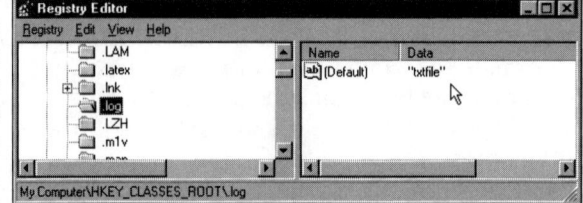

Chapter 12

Customizing the Active Desktop and Internet Explorer

● ●

In This Chapter

▶ Understanding the Active Desktop's Web view

▶ Discovering where the desktop and Internet Explorer live in the Registry

▶ Changing desktop and Internet settings for speed, looks, and fun

● ●

*T*he desktop is active! The desktop is a browser! The desktop can do your laundry! (But only if you use Microsoft soap.)

What exactly *is* Windows 98? Is it a browser, or a desktop? Is Internet Explorer part of the operating system or is it a bundled application? Are changes to the taskbar really part of Internet Explorer? Are there practical advantages to setting up your desktop so that it works like a browser? Is a browser-based help system better than the Windows 95 help system? Do you mind that Microsoft's unremovable Internet Explorer code adds greatly to Windows 98's RAM and disk space demands? And is Microsoft unfairly leveraging its operating system monopoly to take over the Internet?

These are difficult questions, which is why we avoid them completely. We're saving them for our next book, *Software and Federal Antitrust Lawsuits For Dummies*. However, we *do* take a look at how the technologies that Microsoft calls Internet Explorer affect the Registry, and how you can customize the Windows 98 Internet-related features using the Registry. Granted, those two areas could fill a book in themselves, but we at least give you a head start toward unraveling the Registry's role in the Windows Weird Wild Web.

Windows 98 and Internet Stuff

In Chapter 11, we point out that you can view the Active Desktop in the "classic" Windows 95 manner, or in the new "Web view" style (see Figure 12-1, which you reach by opening My Computer and choosing View⇨Folder Options⇨View). The Registry tips in this chapter focus mainly on the Web view style and also on the Internet features that Windows 98 offers.

If you're not already familiar with the Windows 98 Web-view desktop, or with Internet Explorer, this section provides a very brief introduction to both.

If you came here directly without even looking at Chapter 11, do check it out; it has lots of useful tips that work regardless of which desktop style you use.

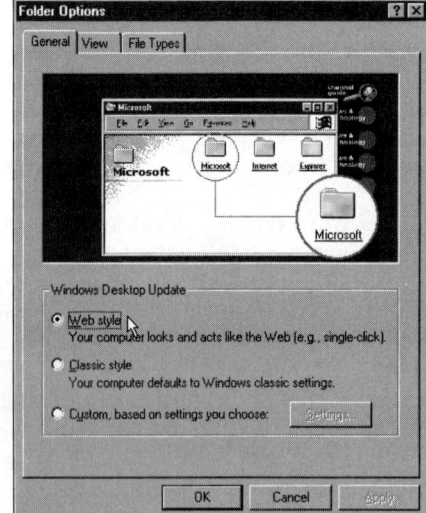

Figure 12-1:
Choosing to
view the
desktop as
a Web
page.

Web desktop, Web folders

The Web view of the desktop lets you browse your local PC in much the same manner you browse the Internet:

✔ Selectable objects appear <u>underlined</u>, as hyperlinks do on a Web page.

✔ Moving the cursor over an object (file, folder, and so on) highlights it and changes the cursor to a pointing hand.

✔ Single-clicking a highlighted object opens or executes it (you may never double-click again!), a feature Microsoft calls *Hover Select*.

Bill G. must have done a mean bounce in the trampoline room out at the "big house" when he thought up this brainstorm. As the story goes, the neighbors heard this loud scream followed by incredible laughter. You'd be happy too if you'd just thought of a way to tie the browser into Windows forever.

You can collect and view a wide variety of Web components: HTML pages, Java applets, and even ActiveX controls, right on your Windows 98 Web-style desktop along with the usual icons. The desktop is now a layered affair; the background is an HTML layer, and the foreground is where the icons reside. The operating system manipulates the desired ActiveX and Java controls from the background layer.

Microsoft maintains a gallery of Web-view goodies online. First, to connect to the Internet, right-click any free area of the Web-view desktop, choose Active Desktop⇨Customize my Desktop, choose the New button, and finally click Yes. You're whisked to Microsoft land for many active components that can pretty up your Active Desktop (see Figure 12-2).

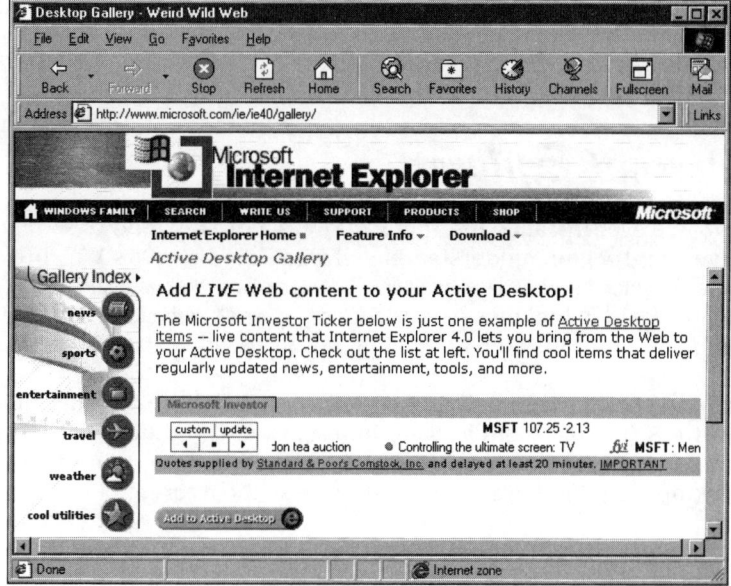

Figure 12-2:
Active Web
content
from
Microsoft.

Even if you don't want to view your desktop as a Web page, you can still tell Windows 98 to display individual folders in Web page view. The My Computer command View⇨Customize this Folder shows you the dialog box in Figure 12-3. You can create an HTML (HyperText Markup Language) page that defines the look of any folder on your PC. Or, less ambitiously, you can simply specify a background image that lives behind the folder's icons.

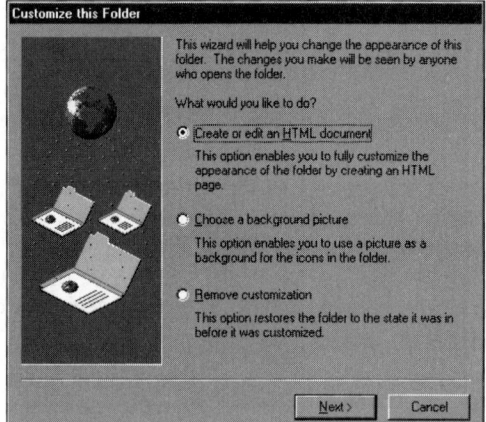

Figure 12-3:
Web
desktop or
not, you can
Web-ify
individual
folders.

Some of you may not have an instant liking for the Web view desktop, with its numerous settings and tweaks and distractions. However, before you give up on it, read through this chapter. The Registry gives you a bit more control over the desktop's look and feel than you might think. And you can always turn off the Web view if you tire of it, thank you very much; it'll be there later if you change your mind.

Internet Explorer

If you've ever installed Internet Explorer 4 onto a Windows 95 machine, you have a pretty good understanding of what Windows 98's Web browsing capability looks like. The Internet Explorer browser is a full-featured and highly regarded tool that supports most Internet Web standards and runs neck and neck with Netscape Communicator in speed, features, and ease of use.

In Windows 98, Internet Explorer and Windows Explorer look similar, share a few tools (the back and forward buttons and the address bar), and they're cross-functional, too — you can use Internet Explorer to browse the local desktop, and Windows Explorer to browse the Internet.

Other ways that Windows 98 adds to its Internet capabilities include the following:

- ✔ **Push publishing:** The ability to select Internet *channels* that provide you with regularly updated Web content.

- ✔ **Outlook Express:** Formerly Internet Mail and News, an improved Internet e-mail and newsgroup reader, although at this writing it doesn't integrate fully with America Online, Compuserve, Microsoft Mail, Microsoft Exchange Server 4 or earlier, Microsoft Network (MSN), or cc:Mail.

- ✔ **FrontPage Express:** An HTML editor, based on the capable editor in FrontPage 97.

- ✔ **HTML Help:** The new Web-based standard for Windows 98 help files, using the same basic organization of Windows 95 help files but in browser-friendly form.

- ✔ **The subscription folder:** A folder into which you can place Web addresses that you want to update whenever you go online.

Some of you may prefer Netscape Communicator to Internet Explorer. That's a different matter than merely switching desktop views between Web style and Classic style; Internet Explorer is a genuine Type A personality 100 percent of the time, and always wants to be king of the jungle. One of Internet Explorer's advantages, however, is that it makes extensive use of the Registry, which means you can fiddle around with it to your hearts' content. Again, look over the material here to see if you may be able to fix some of your pet peeves about Internet Explorer with a bit of REGEDIT hacking.

The Web Desktop and the Registry

Training our binoculars on the Web-view desktop now, we explore in this section where the relevant settings live in the Registry and how we can customize them for fun and profit.

Where the Web desktop lives in the Registry

Your Web-view desktop settings live almost entirely in *HKCR* and *HKCU*. Here's a little more info on each.

HKCR

HKEY_CLASSES_ROOT (*HKCR* for short) contains information about every sort of software object in Windows 98 (as we explain in Chapter 6). Given that the Web view of the Active Desktop (and of individual folders) means that many more kinds of objects can live in *HKCR,* you expect to see some new software classes, and you do. The *HKCR* branch has more than 200 new entries since Windows 95, covering file types relating to ActiveMovie for digital video, DirectX controls for video and animation, HTML controls handling browser functions, and a variety of other new, shareable ActiveX objects.

By way of illustration, we're using one of the niftier aspects of the Web view feature: thumbnails. You can hover-select a graphical object in My Computer or Windows Explorer and see a thumbnail view of that object in the folder title pane (see Figure 12-4). You can also choose a thumbnail view of any folder, although that's too slow and uses too much monitor space for regular use.

Figure 12-4:
The Web view shows data file thumbnails.

Associated with this thumbnail viewing capability is a whole set of software objects, each with its own unique Class ID in the Registry (see Figure 12-5).

Figure 12-5:
New software object classes provide thumbnail handling abilities.

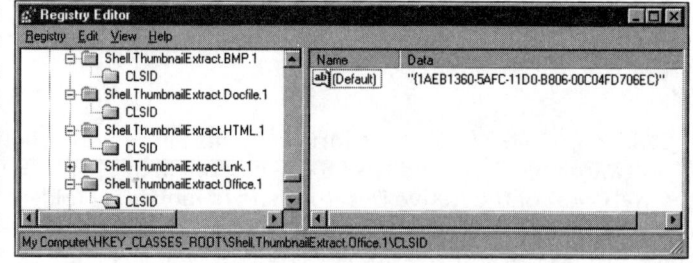

You can see from the key names that Windows 98 uses different software modules to display thumbnails for BMP files, HTML files, and files handled by Office 97 graphics filters. Tracking down the Class IDs with REGEDIT's Find command reveals that, for example, the Office graphics filters (class *Shell.ThumbnailExtract.Office.1*) handle graphics file types .CDR, .CGM, .DFX, .DRW, .EMF, .EPS, .PCD, .PCT, .PCX, .TGA, .TIF, and .WPG.

That's just one example; *HKCR* stores a lot more information that lets Active Desktop do its thing, including all the ActiveX software objects that handle toolbars, images, animations, and the like. These software objects perform the same functions for the Web view of the desktop (or specific folders) that they perform for the Internet Explorer browser window itself.

HKCU

The current user (that's you!) can set Web desktop options separately from other users that you may define on a PC set up for multiple user profiles (see Chapter 10). When you make changes to your Web view settings, for example using the command My Computer⇔View⇔Folder Options⇔Custom⇔Settings (see Figure 12-6), you're modifying the following keys and values in *HKCU\Software\Microsoft\Windows\CurrentVersion*:

✔ *\Explorer\ShellState*

✔ *\Explorer\IconUnderline*

✔ *\Explorer\CabinetState\Settings*

✔ *\Explorer\CabinetState\FullPath*

✔ *\Explorer\Streams\Settings*

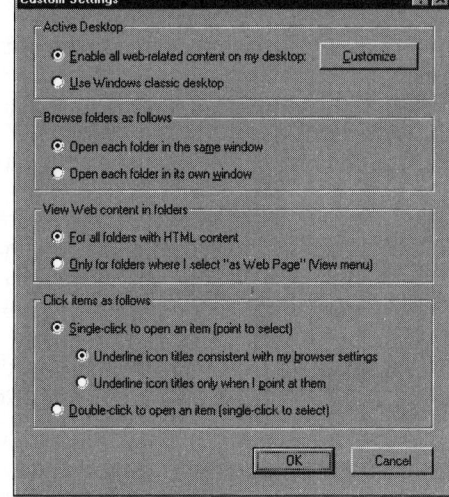

Figure 12-6:
Customizing the Windows 98 desktop behavior.

Some of the settings in the preceding list are complicated binary values that manage several settings in a single value. This makes defining a particular Web desktop "look and feel" fairly difficult to encapsulate in a REG file. If you want to set up a lot of PCs the same way, our suggestion is to set up a single PC the way you want it and then export all the above keys and values. (You'll have to manually combine them into a single REG file, using Notepad for example. See Chapter 13 for more on creating REG files.) Then, try importing that REG file onto a standard-issue Windows 98 PC and see if everything works the way you want, making sure to back up at least *HKCU\Software\Microsoft\Windows\CurrentVersion* first.

Customizing the Web desktop

Now that you know a little about where the Registry keeps Web view settings, what can you do with that knowledge? These three tweaking tips help you get started.

Grand Central Desktop

The Web-view desktop description file has the name DESKTOP.HTT and lives in a special folder on disk called *C:\Windows\Application Data\Microsoft\ Internet Explorer*. When you modify the Web view desktop, for example by adding a graphic to it via Start⇨Settings⇨Control Panel⇨Display⇨ Web⇨New (see Figure 12-7), Windows 98 handles modifications to this DESKTOP.HTT file. (The "HTT" stands for HyperText Template, but you can view the file in Notepad.)

All the other Web-view description files live in C:\WINDOWS\WEB. Why Microsoft had to put DESKTOP.HTT in its own weird subdirectory is beyond us.

If you're a network administrator, you may want to change the location of the file DESKTOP.HTT. For example, you may want this file to live on a server, where you could change the desktop on a periodic basis as a novel way of distributing information to employees. Well, you can store DESKTOP.HTT wherever you like, because the Registry specifies its location.

To change the location of DESKTOP.HTT, run REGEDIT, click the *HKCR* branch, and do a Find on the word **Desktop**. Chances are you'll find the CLSID key shown in Figure 12-8. Expand it as shown to discover the value *PersistMoniker*. This string value contains the path to the DESKTOP.HTT file. You can change the path to whatever makes sense in your situation (such as **file://F:\sharedwebpages\desktop.htt**). Just remember to begin the path with "file://". At the next reboot, the desktop will look to the new location for DESKTOP.HTT.

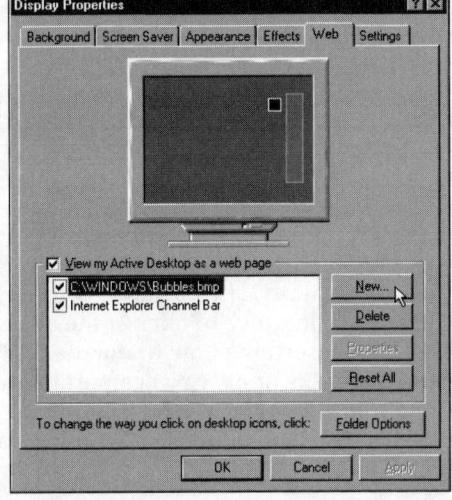

Figure 12-7:
Add Web-
view
desktop
items with
the New
button.

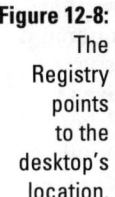

Figure 12-8:
The
Registry
points
to the
desktop's
location.

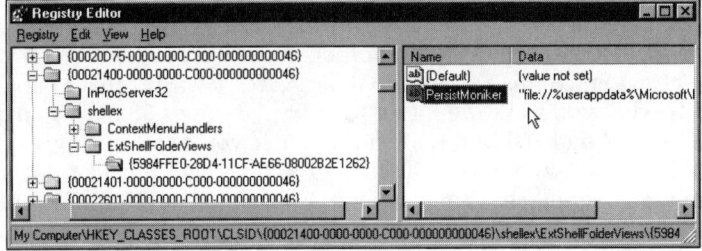

Grand Central Folders

You can perform the same wizardry as in the preceding trick with so-called *system folders,* like My Computer or Network Neighborhood. That is, you can tell the Registry to look for their Web file, which determines their Web view appearance (but not the folder contents), somewhere other than the usual location (C:\WINDOWS\WEB). The easy way is to simply hunt in the Registry's *HKCR\CLSID* key for the file names shown below in boldface, and modify the file location in the *PersistMoniker* subkey, just like in the preceding tip.

System folder	Web view file
My Computer	MYCOMP.HTT
Network Neighborhood	NETHOOD.HTT
Control Panel	CONTROLP.HTT

(continued)

(continued)

System folder	Web view file
Dial-Up Networking	DIALUP.HTT
Printers folder	PRINTERS.HTT
The Recycle Bin	RECYCLE.HTT
Scheduled Tasks folder	SCHEDULE.HTT

Of course, now that you know where these HTT files live, you can play around modifying them with Notepad in order to change the appearance as well as the location of the files, but describing how to rewrite HTT files using JavaScript is beyond our mandate in this book. (You can probably figure out a lot of it yourself by just looking at the different HTT files and seeing what the end results are on the desktop. You can also do some cutting and pasting between different HTT files.)

We're not really allowed to go into this as it doesn't involve the Registry directly, but we'll invoke artistic license. When you modify the Web view of a *regular* folder — that is, something other than the system folders we just listed, or of the special Desktop folder — with the My Computer command View⇨Customize this Folder, which activates a wizard that enables you specify what you want the folder to show, Windows 98 makes changes to DESKTOP.INI and FOLDER.HTT in the folder you're modifying. Just thought you'd like to know, in case you wanted to do something like, say, modify that annoying warning message when you browse to the WINDOWS folder (see Figure 12-9).

Figure 12-9:
A warning not to "monkey" around with the WINDOWS folder.

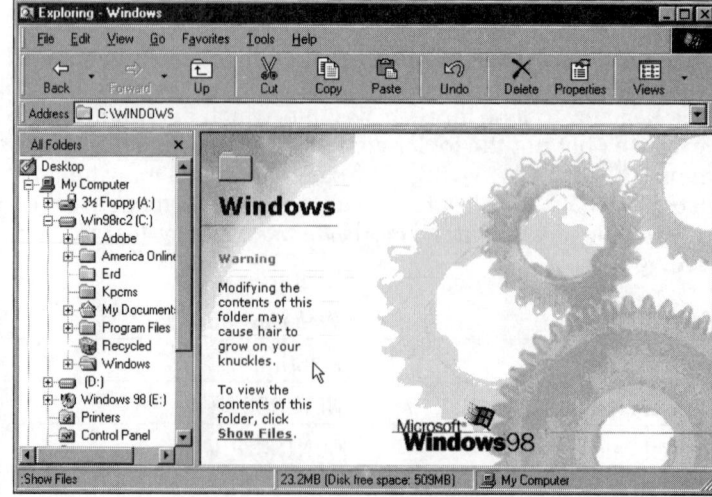

Losing "Find"

The Start menu's Find submenu has grown in Windows 98 to include two new commands:

- **Find⇨On the Internet:** This option takes you to a Web-based search engine (the default one being `home.microsoft.com/access/allinone.asp`).

- **Find⇨People:** This option fires up your address book and also lets you search various Internet-based address books.

Unlike some Start menu entries on the new Active Desktop, you can't right-click these options to delete them. Furthermore, although you can use the System Policy Editor to get rid of the Find menu entirely (the relevant policy is *Local User — Start Menu — Start Menu — Remove Find menu from Start menu*), you may prefer to leave the original Find commands (Files or Folders, and Computer) intact.

Removing either or both of the two new Find items from the Start menu requires a Registry edit. Start REGEDIT and navigate to *HKLM\Software\Microsoft\Windows\CurrentVersion\explorer\FindExtensions\Static*. Before going on, back up (export) this key for safekeeping (or in case you change your mind later). Then, delete the *InetFind* key to remove the Internet search option from the Find menu. Delete the *WabFind* key to remove the People search option. (FYI, the "Wab" is short for "Windows address book.")

If you want to keep the Find⇨On the Internet command while simply changing its default search page, modify the Registry string value *HKCU\Software\Microsoft\Internet Explorer\Main\Search Page*. This is a user-specific value that you can set separately for different users, if you've set the PC up for multiple user profiles (see Chapter 10). On a related note, you can change the default search page for Internet Explorer's toolbar Search button by modifying *HKCU\Software\Microsoft\Internet Explorer\Main\Search Bar*.

Internet Explorer and the Registry

You may hate the Web view of the desktop but still love Microsoft's Internet Explorer Web browser. In this section, you find out where IE takes up residence in the Registry, and pick up a few tips and tweaks to put more power in your browser.

Where Internet Explorer lives in the Registry

Most of the Internet Explorer Registry settings live in *HKLM* and *HKCU*. As usual for the Registry, *HKLM* typically contains global settings that apply for every user on the PC. *HKCU* contains settings that can vary from one user to the next, on a PC set up for multiple user profiles. Here are some details:

- ✔ *HKLM\Software\Microsoft\Internet Explorer* is the main folder for global Internet Explorer settings.

- ✔ *HKLM\Software\Microsoft\IE4* contains settings for the Internet Explorer installation.

- ✔ *HKLM\Software\Microsoft\Internet Mail and News* contains installation settings for Outlook Express. (The old name for this program was Internet Mail and News.)

- ✔ *HKLM\Software\Microsoft\Internet Explorer\Main* contains more Internet Explorer installation and current settings.

- ✔ *HKLM\Software\Microsoft\Java VM* contains settings pertaining to the Java Virtual Machine that handles Java applets in Internet Explorer.

- ✔ *HKLM\Software\Microsoft\Windows\CurrentVersion\Internet Settings* contains global settings that you can change through the Internet control panel.

- ✔ *HKCU\Software\Microsoft\Internet Explorer* contains the current user's Internet Explorer preferences.

- ✔ *HKCU\Software\Microsoft\Internet Account Manager* contains the current user's Internet accounts for accessing the Web.

- ✔ *HKCU\Software\Microsoft\Microsoft Comic Chat* contains the current user's Comic Chat settings.

- ✔ *HKCU\Software\Microsoft\Outlook Express* contains the current user's Outlook Express settings.

- ✔ *HKCU\Software\Microsoft\Windows\CurrentVersion\Internet Settings* contains user-specific preferences that can be changed through the Internet control panel.

Sometimes values in the preceding keys don't match up. If you have problems with the wrong search page settings, improper cache directories, and so on, make sure that *all* your directories are correct in all these Registry folders.

Customizing Internet Explorer

Now for a few tips on pinstriping your IE Web browser with the Registry and the Internet control panel.

Putting up new Window curtains

You can add title bar text to the Registry, in values named *Window Title,* to give Internet Explorer your own custom title bar (see Figure 12-10). The specific string value to add is *HKLM\Software\Microsoft\Internet Explorer\Main\Window Title.*

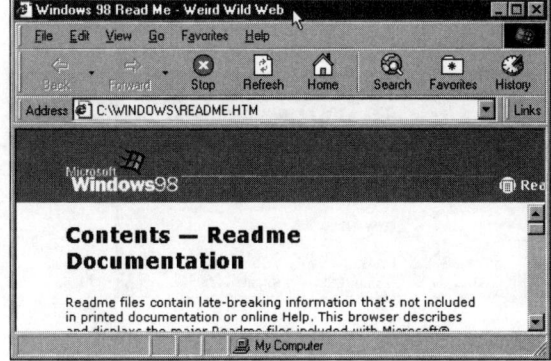

Figure 12-10: Your own title bar for Internet Explorer.

Incidentally, you can do the same thing with Outlook Express, but the value name must be *WindowTitle* (no space). The key is *HKCU\Software\Microsoft\ Outlook Express.*

Spreading your cache around

The Temporary Internet Files folder (also known as *browser cache*) normally lives in *C:\WINDOWS\Temporary Internet Files.* This folder can take up a lot of space on your primary hard drive, so you may prefer to place these files where you can more easily manage them — say, a second hard drive, or a data partition that you keep separate from program files. Or, your D: drive may be faster than your C: drive, and you want to improve performance by moving the browser cache.

The fastest way to move your browser cache is to choose the Internet control panel, click the Settings button in the Temporary Internet Files panel on the General tab, and click the Move Folder button. Choose the new location in the Browse For Folder window that appears. What happens under the hood is that the Registry value *HKCU\Software\Microsoft\ Windows\CurrentVersion\Explorer\Shell Folders\Cache* changes to reflect the new location (see Figure 12-11).

The ~*Windows**CurrentVersion**Explorer**Shell Folders* key is actually fairly important, because it specifies the location of various system folders. On a system with user profiles enabled (depending on the options set in the Users control panel — see Chapter 6), many of the string values in the *Shell Folders* key point to user-specific directories beneath C:\WINDOWS\PROFILES.

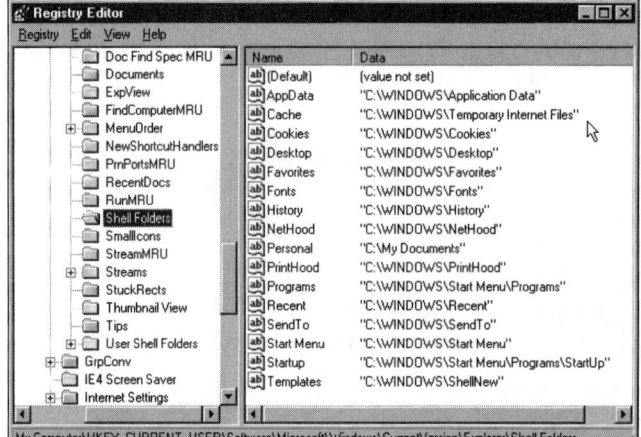

Figure 12-11:
A Registry key points to the browser cache folder and other system folders.

Making a refreshing change

When you're surfing the Web and you go back to pages you've seen already that session, you can tell Internet Explorer whether to check for updates (*refresh* the display) or just use the cached files it "remembers" from your previous visit. The latter usually works well and makes for snappier surfing, but it may mean that you don't see changes to a site that occurred during your online session. The safest setting, and the slowest, is "Every visit to the page." The riskiest setting, but the fastest, is "Never." Your choice depends on your surfing style and how often the Web pages you visit actually change.

Run the Internet control panel, click the General tab and the Settings button, and you see the screen in Figure 12-12. The three radio buttons under the heading Check for newer versions of stored pages define the refresh options. These are per-user settings, so if you have multiple user profiles set up, you need to change 'em for each logged-on user.

Naturally, the page refresh setting lives in the Registry, and you can change it for a large number of PCs using a REG file that contains the DWORD value *HKCU**Software**Microsoft**Windows**CurrentVersion**Internet Settings*\ *SyncMode*. (See Chapter 13 for details on creating REG files.) Here are the values that correspond to the control panel settings:

Figure 12-12:
Controlling
IE's
refreshment
rate.

Web Page Refresh Setting	DWORD Value
Every time you start Internet Explorer	00000002
Every visit to the page	00000003
Never	00000000

Mapping some bits

You can place a bitmap image behind the Internet Explorer toolbar and button bar. Doing so is fun and educational too, because it shows how the Internet Explorer and Windows Explorer programs use most of the same plumbing internally.

To place a bitmap behind the IE toolbar, just follow these steps:

1. **Start REGEDIT.**

2. **Add the string value** BackBitmap **to the**
   HKCU\Software\Microsoft\Internet Explorer\Toolbar **Registry key.
   (Chapter 4 provides details on adding Registry values.)**

3. **Give BackBitmap a data field that specifies an image location (try**
   C:\WINDOWS\WEB\WVLEFT.BMP **for fun).**

Your IE window now has some pizzazz (see Figure 12-13). Of course, if you're artistically inclined, you can experiment with different BMP files and sizes that you create.

Now for the educational part. Right-click My Computer and choose Explore. What do you see? Now just select My Computer. What do you see now? The same Registry change affects both My Computer and Explorer because they're really the same program.

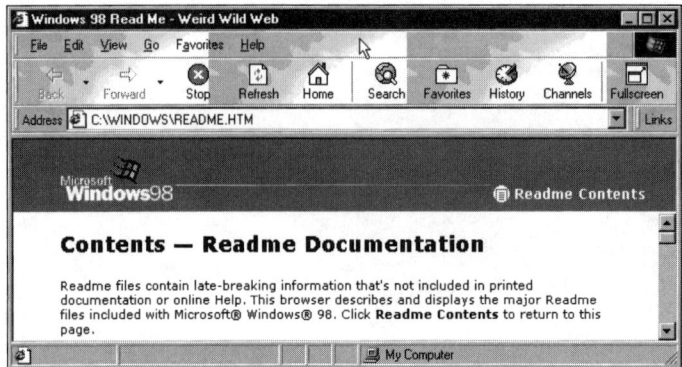

Figure 12-13:
Adding a backdrop to the Internet Explorer toolbars.

Editing the Edit button

Want to use your favorite HTML editing program when you click the Edit button in Internet Explorer? You can easily modify the file type association to use your program choice instead of the one Microsoft selects for you. Just follow the steps below.

1. **Choose My Computer and select View⇨Folder Options⇨File Types.**

2. **Maneuver down to** `Microsoft HTML Document 4.0` **and click the Edit button.**

3. **In the Actions list, highlight Edit by clicking it (as shown in Figure 12-14), and then click the dialog box's Edit button.**

4. **Use the Browse button to find your favorite HTML editor, click OK, and click the Close button twice to finish.**

You've just edited the (Default) value in the Registry key *HKCR\htmlfile\ shell\edit\command.*

Protecting your privacy

Updating Windows device drivers and programs has always been a big job. CyberMedia has done well with a product called *Oil Change,* which navigates the Internet and periodically updates Windows files automatically. In Windows 98 (and NT Workstation 5.0), Microsoft usurps this concept in the form of Windows Update, which runs Internet Explorer and links to `www.microsoft.com/windowsupdate`.

Corporate administrators, beware: The potential for *software fragmentation* (that is, different versions of system files on different PCs) has just increased dramatically! However, Windows Update does make it easier to obtain the latest device drivers for users of standalone PCs. And Microsoft provides a system policy (see Chapter 9) to turn Windows Update off for network users; it's *Local Computer — Windows 98 System — Windows Update — Disable Windows Update.*

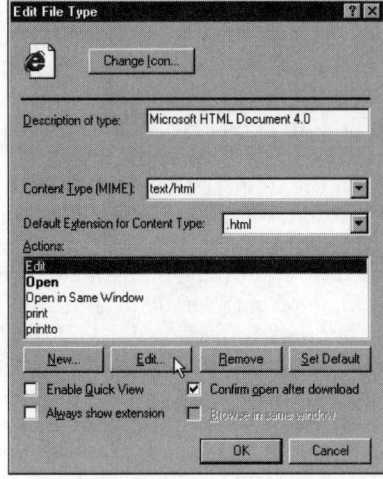

Figure 12-14:
Telling
Windows
which HTML
editor you
prefer.

One problem some users have with Windows Update is that it wants you to register with Microsoft before you can use it. For those of you who want the Windows Update feature, but would just as soon Microsoft not know any more about you than it already does, run REGEDIT and change the value *RegDone* to "1" in the key *HKLM\Software\Microsoft\Windows\ CurrentVersion*. Also, change the *(Default)* value to "1" in the key *HKLM\Software\Microsoft\Windows\CurrentVersion\Welcome\RegWiz*. Now you can use the update feature without registering.

Turbocharging dial-up Internet links

If you don't use TCP/IP for dial-up Internet access, hike right past this section.

One Windows 98 problem that has received surprisingly little press is the issue of *TCP/IP packet size* over dial-up connections. *TCP/IP*, or Transmission Control Protocol/Internet Protocol, is the network communication language of the Internet and (increasingly) of internal company networks. A *packet* is a unit of data transmission over a network.

The problem, in a nutshell, is that Windows 98 sets the maximum packet size at a fairly large value (1,500 bytes) for any connection other than dialup adapter. This size is fine for a company network but not so great for a dial-up Internet connection. Many Internet traffic devices can't handle a 1,500-byte packet, so they chop it up into smaller pieces and then reassemble it at the destination. That can slow down a dial-up link's performance by 50 percent or even more.

The relevant Registry entry for changing TCP/IP packet size is *HKLM\ System\CurrentControlSet\Services\Class\NetTrans\000n\MaxMTU* where *000n* is the number of the dial-up network adapter's TCP/IP link. Change this MaxMTU value to 576 (add the value if it doesn't exist) to reduce the likelihood of packets getting chopped up in transit.

To figure out what 000n should be in the Registry key path from the previous paragraph, first go to *HKLM\Enum\Root\Net\0000* and look for the *DeviceDesc* value, which may say something like AOL Adapter if, for example, your Internet dial-up link uses America Online. If you don't see such a description, look in *HKLM\Enum\Root\Net\0001,* and so on. When you find the right key, look at the *Bindings* subkey, which will read something like *MSTCP\0002.* Assuming that's the case for this example, jump to *HKLM\Enum\Network\MSTCP\0002* and look for the value named Driver. This points you to *NetTrans\000n,* which is the number you need. Yes, this is horribly convoluted, but you can let a shareware program run down the right number for you (see the "On the CD" icon two paragraphs down).

Other Registry entries have an effect on dial-up TCP/IP performance, too, but this subject gets very complicated very fast. Fortunately, some cool tools exist to handle the Registry modifications for you.

Rob Vonk's EasyMTU, Mike Sutherland's MTUSpeed, and Patterson Software Design's TweakDUN are all handy freeware or shareware utilities for modifying the TCP/IP packet settings. Our favorite is EasyMTU (see Figure 12-15) because it clearly shows you which of the possibly several TCP/IP connections your PC uses are dial-up connections, and which are local network connections (which you don't want to change). You can find the latest version of all these programs on the Internet at www.download.com.

Figure 12-15: EasyMTU's Bindings tab indicates that the program is about to modify an America Online (AOL) connection.

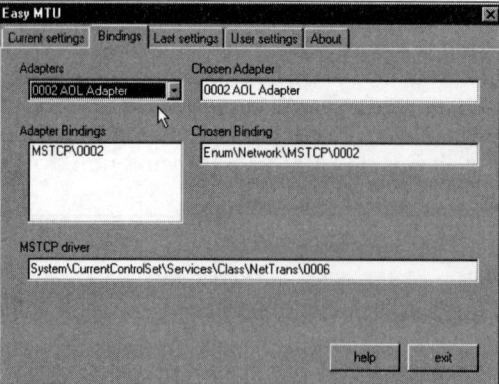

Adding the URL History folder to the Start menu

If you spend a fair amount of time on the Internet, you may find adding the Uniform Resource Locator (URL) History list to your Start menu a convenient customization. By doing so, you can quickly return to a site you visited recently without having to run Internet Explorer as a separate step. Here's the procedure:

1. **Right-click the Start button and choose Explore.**

   An Explorer window that displays the structure of the Start menu appears.

2. **Right-click any empty space in the right pane and choose New⇨Folder.**

3. **With the new folder name highlighted, type in the following:**

   ```
   URL History folder.{FF393560-C2A7-11CF-BFF4-
       444553540000}
   ```

   If you want to make sure that you avoid a typing error, you can use REGEDIT to pluck the URL history folder CLSID out of the Registry by searching for "URL history folder" in the value Data fields. When you locate the URL history folder, right-click the CLSID key, choose Rename, and press Ctrl+C to copy the CLSID key to the Clipboard. Press Ctrl+V to paste the key into the Explorer window, after typing the **URL History folder.** prefix (don't forget the trailing period). Press Esc to get out of the Rename operation, then close REGEDIT.

4. **Close the Explorer window and try out your new Start menu option.**

Click the Start button, then choose the URL History folder. All your most recently visited web sites magically appear. Select a site and Internet Explorer vaults into action, primed with the intended Web page.

Part IV

Expert Hunting: Registry Mastery

The 5th Wave   **By Rich Tennant**

"I wish someone would explain to Professor Jones that you don't need a whip and a leather jacket to edit the Registry."

In this part . . .

*O*ne morning on safari, George scratched his itching neck, discovering to his dismay an engorged tick the size of his thumb. Quickly his guide bundled him into the truck and headed for the pond where, yesterday, they'd seen egrets watering. The guide told George to lie still on the grass, tick side up, and then hid behind a nearby tree. Soon, an adult egret approached and neatly pecked the tick from George's neck. On the drive back, the guide explained: "Egrets are the 'debuggers' of the savanna. They pluck fleas and ticks out of the feet and hides of larger creatures." George, in awe of his guide's cleverness, could only say "Thanks for saving my neck."

Well, our editors *said* they wanted a book with lots of trips and ticks. But seriously, folks, for those of you who are bored with mere competence and want to become Registry experts, we happily present Part IV. Here, we explain how to track what happens to the Registry when you install or remove software or hardware, change a control panel setting, or do just about anything else affecting your system's configuration. After you use your newfound monitoring skills to unearth great new tips, we show you how you can share Registry changes with others, in the form of INF and REG files. Finally, this part offers tips on trimming Registry fat to reduce disk and memory waste and improve speed.

Chapter 13

Tracking and Hacking

*W*atching what happens to the Registry after you change a control panel setting or even install a new program is a great way to explore how the Registry works and to discover new Registry tricks. Being able to share your tricks with other users is even more rewarding. This chapter shows you how to do both.

You've heard the saying that if you give a man a fish, you feed him for a day, but if you teach a man to fish, you're pretty much wasting his time if he lives in the Kalahari Desert. This chapter is inspired by that time-honored cliche. Sure, we could give you a few dozen more pages on specific ways you can customize the Registry. But true Registry mastery, grasshopper, means discovering your *own* Registry tricks and distributing them to other PC users. Fortunately, some handy tools and techniques can ease your pioneering journey as you track and hack the Registry in search of the Next Great Registry Tip.

Tracking the Wild Registry: A Photo Safari

How can you find out exactly what happens to the Registry after you change a control panel setting, install a new program, or install an INF file? You have several options, including snapshotting and using REGMON.

Snapshotting

One method to track Registry changes is to take a snapshot of the Registry before you do something that you think will alter the Registry, take another snapshot afterwards, and compare the "before" and "after" pictures to see what changed. You can make this comparison without any fancy special-purpose software; just create an export REG file by using REGEDIT's Registry⇨Export Registry File command. Name your "before" snapshot BEFORE.REG and your "after" snapshot AFTER.REG.

If you have a pretty good idea of which key an action is likely to affect, export that key only. Comparing very long files, such as an entire export of *HKLM*, can take several minutes even on a fast PC.

Okay, now you need some way to compare the differences.

With a word processor

One way to compare your before and after snapshots is to use any top-of-the-line word processor. For example, in Word 97, load the first file by choosing File⇨Open. Then load the second file by choosing Tools⇨Track Changes⇨Compare Documents. Whatever the "after" snapshot includes that's missing from the "before" snapshot shows up as strikethrough text in a different color. Whatever entries were deleted show up as underlined text.

With a file comparison utility

Alternatively, you can use a special file comparison utility. Microsoft offers a freebie called *WinDiff,* which comes with programming toolkits such as Visual C++. Norton Utilities comes with Norton File Compare, which works in similar fashion to the word processor comparison method mentioned in the previous section. (See Figure 13-1.).

With a specialized Registry tracker

Programs such as First Aid 98 from CyberMedia or Norton Registry Tracker from Symantec (part of Norton Utilities, see Figure 13-2) are specially designed for taking and comparing Registry snapshots. Because these tools highlight Registry changes by using the hierarchical structure that you're used to seeing in the Registry Editor, they're more convenient to use than the word processor method or the file comparison method. However, Norton Registry Tracker doesn't let you track the *HKCU* branch and therefore is only really useful for tracking *HKLM*.

Watching in real time: REGMON

Snapshotting isn't the only way to track Registry changes. One of our favorite Registry utilities and one we include on the enclosed CD-ROM is a freebie: REGMON from Mark Russinovich and Bryce Cogswell. (See

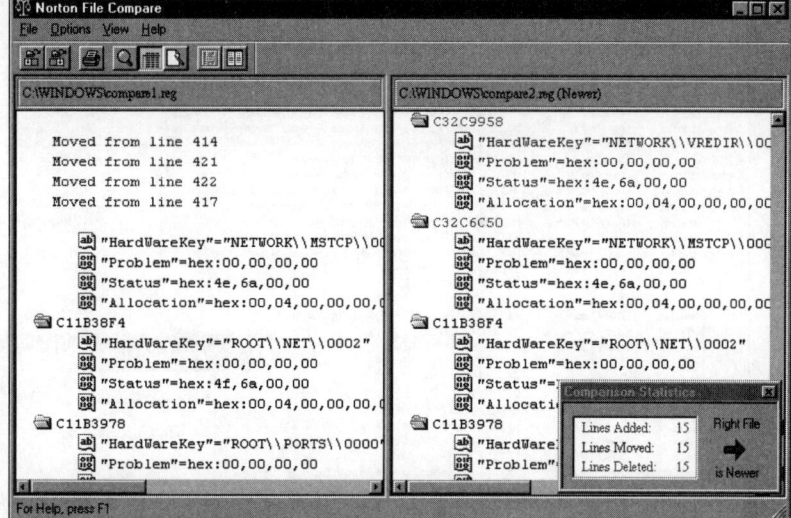

Figure 13-1:
Norton File
Compare
can
highlight
REG file
differences.

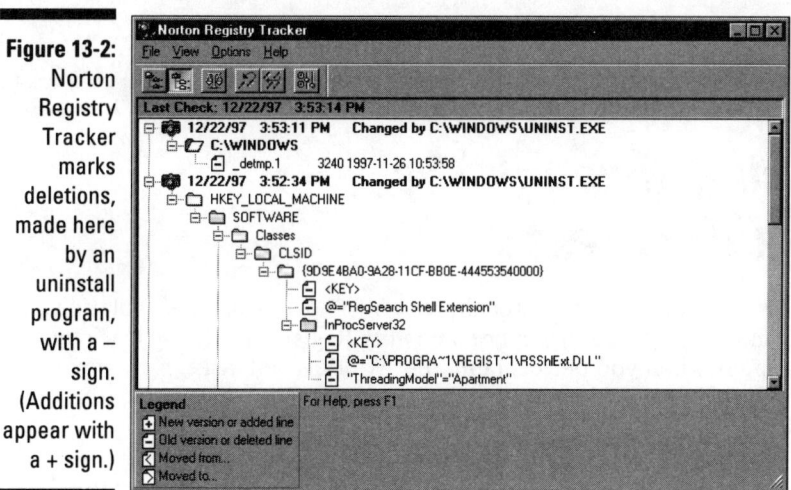

Figure 13-2:
Norton
Registry
Tracker
marks
deletions,
made here
by an
uninstall
program,
with a −
sign.
(Additions
appear with
a + sign.)

Figure 13-3.) REGMON tracks Registry accesses in *real time,* or as they occur.
The data can be overwhelming, but you get a complete picture of every
Registry access — reads as well as writes and edits. You'll be amazed by
how many Registry accesses even a seemingly simple act like opening
Network Neighborhood generates.

Keep up-to-date with the latest version of REGMON by checking the Internet
site www.sysinternals.com.

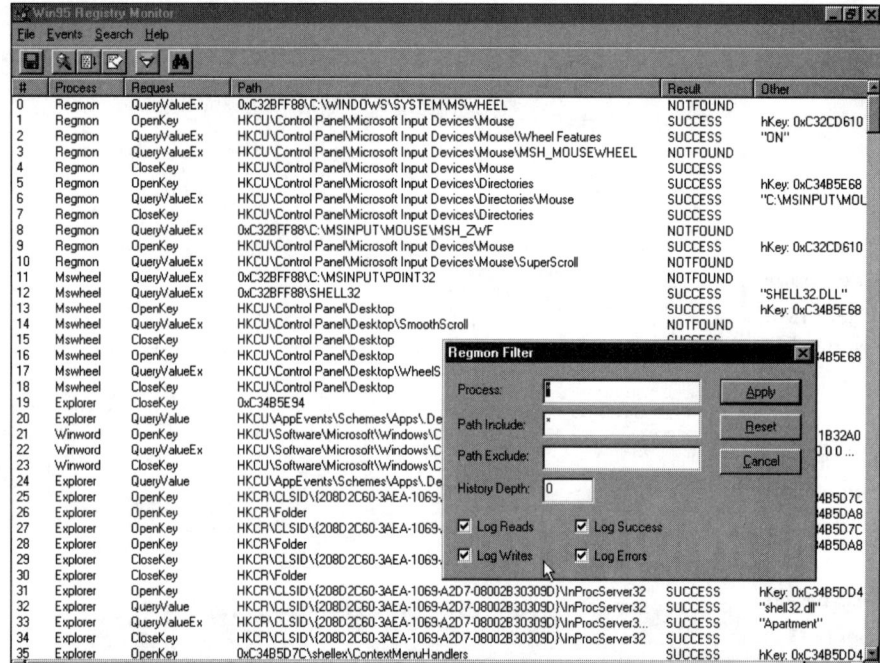

Figure 13-3:
REGMON
gives you a
complete
picture of
Registry
activity.

Hackpacking through the Registry Wilderness

After a bit of practice, you master the arts of snapshotting and real-time Registry monitoring. You discover some nifty Registry hacks by tracking what happens when you perform different Windows 98 tasks. Now, you want to share those hacks with other people — at the office, in your local computer users group, or even on the public Internet.

Or, maybe you're a network manager, and you see the convenience of grouping a bunch of control panel settings or other system settings together into a single file that you can run on each PC in one fell swoop. An example might be sharing Dial-Up Networking connections with other users. (These settings live in *HKCU\RemoteAccess*.)

Whatever the situation, a Registry master must know about the different ways available to distribute Registry modifications safely and effectively.

Shooting yourself in the foot with a Registry error is one thing, but walking down the hall and shooting 10 or 20 other people in the foot with a Registry error that you propagate is something else entirely. REG, INF, and BAT files are powerful tools. Be very careful with their design and test them yourself before distributing them to others.

REG and INF files: Registry road maps

The two types of files that you can use to distribute your Registry hacks to others are REG (for REGistry file) and INF (for INstallation File). The two file formats have several similarities:

✔ Both are plain text files that you can edit with Notepad.

✔ You can run both file types from a batch file (*.BAT), although with different commands.

✔ Both can add new Registry entries and modify existing ones.

✔ Both can mess up someone's PC in a big hurry if they're buggy.

Here's a quick summary of the differences between REG and INF files:

✔ REG files are simpler.

✔ REG files can only change existing Registry entries or add new ones. INF files, however, can delete existing Registry entries.

✔ INF files can do lots of things in addition to modifying the Registry, including file copying, renaming, and deleting, as well as modifying INI file settings. Because of the flexibility of INF files, hardware vendors use them to install device drivers via the Add New Hardware control panel wizard.

✔ INF files don't know the difference between binary and DWORD values; REG files do.

✔ Accidentally installing changes in a REG file is easier because double-clicking a REG file and blowing by the warning dialog box updates the Registry, while you have to right-click an INF file and choose Install to update the Registry.

It would be great if a single file format handled all the kinds of Registry modifications you'd ever want to do, but in reality, you need to find out about both REG and INF files to master the art of distributing Registry hacks.

Rules and REGs

REG files are easy if you don't have to create them yourself from scratch. Just run the Registry Editor, highlight the key in the key pane that you want to export, and choose <u>R</u>egistry⇨<u>E</u>xport Registry File. Give the thing a name and that's it!

You do need to guard against exporting Registry values that don't pertain to the change you want to distribute to others. Accidentally exporting too many values or keys is easy to do. You can always trim the REG file in Notepad after you create it, if you find that you exported a tad bit too much.

If you want to create your own REG file from scratch — and we can't think of too many cases where you'd prefer doing so versus just modifying the current Registry and performing an export — then you must pay close attention to the rules of REG file construction. Here they are, in brief:

- ✔ Begin your REG file with a single line that reads `REGEDIT4` in all capital letters.
- ✔ For every key in which you want to add or change a value, create a new REG file section with the key name in square brackets.
- ✔ To enter a Default value, use the format `@=valuedata` where valuedata is in double quotes.
- ✔ If a backslash appears in a Registry value, it appears as a double backslash in the REG file.

The best way to get familiar with these rules is to export a good-sized REG file from the current Registry and then open the REG file with Notepad or a word processor. Compare the lines in the REG file that identify specific keys and values with how the keys and values appear in REGEDIT.

A common problem with shared REG files occurs when your machine uses different folder or file names than the machine or machines to which you're distributing the REG file. Say you want to share a REG file that makes a change to a word processor that we'll call SuperWord, and you have the application installed in C:\PROGRAM FILES\SUPERWORD. Now you export a Registry key that references a file in that directory. A user who has the program installed in the C:\SUPERWORD folder may not be able to use your REG file successfully. This sort of situation is one more reason to use the application's default installation folder when adding programs to your PC. However, if you don't, you may want to advise whomever you're sending the REG file to that a little editing with Notepad may be necessary.

Instructions for INFs

You've probably seen INF files on the diskettes that come with new hardware devices, or on the CD-ROMs containing new applications. The hidden directory C:\WINDOWS\INF is normally where Windows 98 keeps copies of the INF files that it's used over time.

You can't automatically create an INF file like you can create a REG file, so the following section is a crash course in writing your own INF files for modifying the Registry. (We don't take the time to tell you how to copy, delete, or rename files from within an INF file; that's a skill that hardware manufacturers must master, not Registry editors. If you need that sort of information, check out the Microsoft Windows 98 Software Development Kit (SDK). Not even the *Microsoft Windows 98 Resource Kit* is much help on this subject.

The header

An INF file for Registry editing should begin with the following lines:

```
[Version]
Signature= $Chicago$
```

Chicago was the code name for Windows 95 during its development, and Windows 98 INF files use the same term even though Windows 98's code name was Memphis. (The dollar signs are self-explanatory.)

The main section

After the header, add the following lines:

```
[DefaultInstall]
AddReg=Add.Entries
DelReg=Del.Entries
```

You can make *Add.Entries* and *Del.Entries* whatever you want, but you must leave *DefaultInstall, AddReg,* and *DelReg* as shown. The values to the right of the = signs tell the INF file to be on the lookout for later sections called [Add.Entries] and [Del.Entries] that contain information to add to or remove from the Registry, respectively.

If you're only adding information to the Registry, you can omit the DelReg line, and vice versa.

Add entries

The part of the INF file that adds keys or values to the Registry looks something like this:

```
[Add.Entries]
HKLM,HARDWARE\Junk,JunkVal,, INFTest
```

Again, you can name the section something other than Add.Entries, but it needs to match the name on the AddReg line under [DefaultInstall]. The above example adds a new key, *HKLM\HARDWARE\Junk* and creates the new string value JunkVal with the value data "INFTest."

The generic format for a Registry entry in an INF file is as follows:

```
Branch, Key, ValueName, ValueDataType, ValueData
```

where Branch is the abbreviated main Registry branch (*HKLM, HKU, HKCU, HKCC,* or *HKCR*), and where ValueDataType is 0 for string (*ValueData* in quotes, like "INFTest"), 1 for binary (*ValueData* expressed as hexadecimal numbers separated by commas), 2 for string (but don't replace an existing value if one exists), and 3 for binary (but don't replace an existing value).

If you leave out the ValueDataType, as we do in the preceding JunkVal example, then the value is assumed to be a string type, rather than binary. You do, however, have to leave in the same number of commas (four) as when you specify the ValueDataType (note the two commas between JunkVal and "INFTest"). One old saying goes: There are three kinds of people in the world: those who can count, and those who can't. For successful INF files, count your commas.

Delete entries

If you want to delete a key or value, your INF file lines look like this:

```
[Del.Entries]
HKLM,HARDWARE\Junk,JunkVal
```

This example removes the JunkVal value from *HKLM\HARDWARE\Junk,* but leaves the *Junk* key intact. Omit the value name JunkVal if you want to delete the entire *Junk* key, but leave in the trailing comma.

Delete before add: Required, but bad

It doesn't matter whether the [Add.Entries] or [Del.Entries] section comes first in your INF file; Windows 98 always processes Registry deletions before additions. We discovered this fact playing around with a sample INF file that would create a bogus key and value, then delete it. After "installing" the INF file, we kept seeing the bogus data in the Registry, even though we'd followed the INF file syntax to the very last comma. After pulling out a certain amount of our remaining middle-aged hair, we eventually figured out that Windows 98 was deleting the value first — or at least trying to, because it didn't exist yet — and then adding it afterwards.

We haven't yet stumbled upon any way to tell an INF file to process Registry additions first. This isn't a huge problem as long as you're aware of it.

DWORD of the day is: "Unavailable"

The INF file format has a major Achilles' heel when it comes to updating the Registry: You can't create a value with the DWORD data type. (The ValueDataType qualifier we mention earlier in the "Add entries" section doesn't have an option to specify DWORD, just binary.)

Big deal? Well, it can be. You can't just assume that a binary value will work the same way in the Registry that a DWORD value does. Cases do exist where Windows 98 needs to see a DWORD value, and even if a binary value with the same numbers is present, it won't work. For example, we've discovered that if you replace a particular Registry binary value with a DWORD value, you can get rid of the Internet Explorer desktop icon; but just modifying the binary value's numbers and leaving it as binary doesn't do the trick.

For those of you who are interested in getting rid of the Internet Explorer desktop icon, change the binary value *HKCR\CLSID\{871C5380-42A0-1069-A2EA-08002B30309D}\ShellFolder\Attributes* to the DWORD value 00100022. You have to delete the binary value and then add the DWORD value, as REGEDIT doesn't have a command to change a value's data type. You can also get rid of the icon with the System Policy Editor if you load the SHELLM.ADM template file. (See Chapter 9 for procedural details.)

What's the solution? We'll tell you, but it isn't pretty. You have to use a REG file, perhaps in combination with an INF file, if you need the ability to add a DWORD value. At least you can make life easier for others by creating a batch file that automatically runs both a REG file and an INF file; see the section "Via batch files" later in this chapter.

Comments, please

You can put your own notes and comments in an INF file if you begin the line with a semicolon (;). Providing comments in your files is a good idea. Other people can understand your work more easily, and you can go back to a file that you created months earlier and understand it more quickly, too.

Putting it all together

Here's a sample INF file that changes the file type association for GIF and JPG graphics so selecting them no longer runs Internet Explorer, but rather the Kodak Imaging for Windows program that comes with Windows 98. You need an INF file for this operation, because you have to delete some existing keys.

```
[version]
signature=$Chicago$

[DefaultInstall]
DelReg=Del.Entries
AddReg=Add.Entries

[Del.Entries]
HKCR, giffile\shell\open\ddeexec ,
HKCR, jpegfile\shell\open\ddeexec ,

[Add.Entries]
HKCR, giffile\shell\open\command ,,, c:\windows\kodakimg.exe
          %1
HKCR, jpegfile\shell\open\command ,,, c:\windows\kodakimg.exe
          %1
```

Chapter 8 offers a taste of what INF files can do by looking at the special case of MSBATCH.INF, the file that controls the Windows 98 installation process. You can also look at some sample INF files by checking out C:\WINDOWS\INF*.INF. Most of these files are for installing hardware device drivers, but many of them modify the Registry.

Distributing INF and REG files

Okay, you've put in some quality time creating safe, accurate, reliable INF or REG files. You've tested them once, and then tested them again. You're ready to share them with other Windows 98 aficionados.

Via e-mail

E-mail can be a convenient way to distribute Registry changes. You can send INF and REG files as e-mail *attachments,* which is far preferable to sending the files' text as part of an e-mail message's main body. The chance always exists that your recipient may not copy the text accurately in creating his or her own INF or REG file.

We recommend, however, that you compress your INF or REG files into a ZIP format, using a tool such as WinZip (provided on this book's enclosed CD-ROM). A recipient can easily and accidentally double-click a REG file attachment. You may even want to change the file suffixes to something like IN_ or RE_, and include instructions in your e-mail for renaming the files just before installing them.

Via batch files

You can use the old standby batch file (*.BAT) to install REG or INF file changes. True, users can easily install REG file changes by just double-clicking the REG file, but you can't just double-click an INF file to apply its changes. Further, in either case, you may want to make the process completely automatic — for example, by including your batch file in a network logon script. Or, you may want to offer a polite caution to users and give them the option to cancel the program if they don't have a current Registry backup.

The commands that you use vary depending on whether your Registry changes use the REG or INF file type. The following is a batch file for a REG file called NEW.REG that lives on drive F:, which may be a network drive or a removable cartridge drive. (You would replace NEW.REG and F: in the following example with the name and location of your REG file. Also, this example assumes Windows 98 lives in the usual C:\WINDOWS directory.)

```
@ECHO OFF
REM Sample Batch File to Install a REG File
CLS
ECHO This program modifies your Registry.
ECHO If you don t have a current backup of
ECHO your Registry, press Ctrl-C now.
PAUSE
START C:\WINDOWS\REGEDIT.EXE F:\NEW.REG
CLS
ECHO Registry update complete!
```

If you want to change the batch file to accommodate an INF file, you can do so, but it takes a bit of wizardry. Replace the third to last line (START and so on) with the following (which must be all one line):

```
C:\WINDOWS\RUNDLL.EXE SETUPX.DLL,INSTALLHINFSECTION
               DEFAULTINSTALL 132 F:\NEW.INF
```

For the curious, a bit of explanation: The RUNDLL.EXE program calls the SETUPX.DLL program library, which actually processes the INF file's [DefaultInstall] section. We're not entirely sure what the "132" does, but we know you need it.

A Microsoft tech note stating that your REG file must be in the same directory as your BAT file to avoid an error message seems to be flat-out incorrect. Just remember to specify the full path name of your REG file on the line that runs REGEDIT, and you should be fine.

Via network logon scripts

If you want to update user Registries automatically and your users are on a network, you can use the batch file technique from the previous section and call your batch file from a system-wide network logon script.

Unlike some other kinds of automatic upgrades, you don't have to worry about the Registry changes being applied repeatedly by people who log on multiple times during the period when the batch file is part of the logon script. It doesn't hurt anything to update a user's Registry with the same change several times.

We suggest that you at least consider placing an informative message in the logon script that the user's Registry is about to be modified and provide an "escape clause" if the user is nervous about proceeding. Check the documentation for your particular network regarding the details for creating or modifying logon scripts.

Via REGEDIT in remote mode

If you're on a network that meets all the criteria for remote Registry editing — that is, it's a client/server type network, the PCs use 32-bit networking software, they all have the Remote Registry Service installed, and you're listed as an administrator in those PCs' Network control panel — then you can run the Registry Editor and connect to those other PCs. At that point, you can import your REG files into the remote user's Registry, much as you would import them into your own local Registry.

This method isn't automatic like the preceding one, but if you only need to modify a few users' Registries, you may prefer to do it this way.

For more on remote Registry editing, please see the Chapter 4 section, "Where's the remote?"

Via diskette

Using a diskette to distribute your new REG or INF file isn't wrong, but we suggest you place them in a subdirectory rather than at the diskette's root directory. Putting a REG or INF file out of sight a bit lessens the chance of someone accidentally activating it.

Using a REG file to run a program automatically

We end this chapter with a fun little trick that lets you use a REG file to specify that a particular program should run at the next Windows 98 restart. The program can be an EXE, COM, or BAT file, for example, that you provide on the same diskette (or network drive) as the REG or INF file.

The technique is to add an entry to the Registry's RunOnce key, which specifies a program to be run one time and one time only. You could add this entry using the System Policy Editor, but we'll add it using the Registry Editor so that we can easily create the REG file fragment.

1. **Fire up REGEDIT and navigate to** *HKLM\Software\Microsoft\ Windows\CurrentVersion\RunOnce.*

   The key should be empty; Windows 98 clears it after each reboot.

2. **Add a new value specifying the program you want to run.**

   The name can be whatever you want, but the data should be the full pathname to the program. Using long filenames is okay, but don't put the pathname in double quotes.

3. **Export the RunOnce key.**

Now you can either crank up Notepad and manually add the "meat" from the REG file you've just created to your master REG file, or simply distribute it on its own.

Chapter 14

Keeping the Registry Lean, Mean, and Efficient

• •

In This Chapter

▶ Finding out why you should periodically clean up the Registry

▶ Speeding up the Registry by defragmenting your hard disk

▶ Caring for orphans

▶ Compressing the Registry

• •

*T*he Registry is like the attic or basement in an old house: Over time, it collects all sorts of junk that you don't really need anymore. This chapter provides tips for cleaning and optimizing the Registry files for better performance — the tips appearing in order from the simplest to the most complex.

Some of the material in this chapter is a little on the advanced side. However, we're reminded of a bumper sticker that reads "I didn't fight my way to the top of the food chain to be a vegetarian." If you're reading this book front to back, you didn't fight your way this far without wanting to wring the absolute best performance possible from the Registry. If you're skipping around, however, we do suggest that you at least look over the stuff in Chapters 2, 4, 5, and 6 to sharpen your steak knife before slicing into the metaphorical meat of this chapter.

Why Lighten the Jeep?

We have yet to see the computer operating system that performs all housekeeping chores automatically. Macintosh users periodically have to rebuild the desktop and perform a chore known cryptically as "zapping the PRAM." DOS users have to run the SCANDISK hard drive utility from time to time. Windows 3.*x* users have to clean out their INI files and delete temporary files. Windows 98 users need to run SCANDISK, defragment their disks, and — ta-daa! — clean out and compress the Registry, the subject of this chapter. Windows 98 is a bit more capable than Windows 95 in terms of automatic Registry housekeeping. However, you'll still want to perform certain tasks that Windows 98 either omits from its routine, or doesn't do as well as it should (in our humble opinion).

The Microsoft-supplied Windows 98 documentation — even the *Windows 98 Resource Kit* — doesn't offer much advice on how to keep your Registry lean, mean, and efficient. However, doing so is a very good idea, from several standpoints.

Disk space

Much like the typical middle-aged waistline or the population of coat hangers in your clothes closet, the Registry's natural behavior is to grow over time, and never to shrink. But unlike the coat hanger population, the Registry doesn't even shrink if you remove entries from it. After a while, the Registry grows from its typical initial size of about 2MB to 3MB or even more. The Registry Checker automatically reduces the amount of disk space that the Registry needs, but only in certain circumstances, as we explain further in "Compressing the Entire Registry" later in this chapter.

An extra few hundred kilobytes may not sound like much space, but remember that the Registry Checker automatically keeps five compressed Registry backups on your hard disk, increasing the effect of Registry bloat. Also, on a network of 100 users, with all users backing up their Registries to a network drive, the size difference becomes magnified as well. (Those server disks tend to be expensive, too.) Finally, if you use a tool other than Registry Checker for backup purposes (as you may, for example, if you need to back up the Registry to diskette — see Chapter 2), keeping the Registry's size to a minimum can mean the difference between needing two diskettes and needing three or four. The quicker and easier it is to make backups, the more likely it is that we'll actually make them.

RAM

The bigger the Registry, the more Random Access Memory (RAM) Windows 98 and programs like REGEDIT need in order to load their contents. On a machine with 32MB of RAM, the need for additional RAM isn't a big problem. On a machine with 16MB or less, it can affect performance — especially given Windows 98's larger appetite for RAM compared to Windows 95.

Speed

Contrary to some comments you may see in computer magazines, a smaller Registry doesn't usually help Windows 98 and other application programs access specific Registry entries faster. The Registry's tree-like structure means that programs can get to particular keys fairly quickly, even if the Registry database is large; that's one of the Registry's big advantages over the old INI file system in Windows 3.*x*.

However, a smaller Registry is certainly faster to back up and restore — especially if you use the Registry Editor's export and import feature to do so. Those REG files can take a *long* time to process. And if you ever need to print a large chunk of the Registry, keeping it lean and mean reduces print time, too.

Easier troubleshooting

Navigating the Registry and hunting down potential problems is worlds easier if you don't have to wade through a bunch of flotsam and jetsam left over from old software you don't use anymore.

Defragmenting the Registry

We remember, not that many years ago, when a 5MB hard drive cost $3,000. (It was the Apple Profile, and it was about the size of a small briefcase.) Some older computer pros can remember when hard drives cost upwards of $20,000 per megabyte. In those days, operating system designers had to put a very high premium on squeezing the most space possible out of those expensive disks. So, these designers of yesteryear built in the ability to *fragment* files — chop 'em up into little pieces — just in case a hard drive only had a few separate pockets of free space left. The operating system could then break the file down into pieces and store those pieces in the pockets of free space.

What does that have to do with Windows 98? Everything. Much of Windows 98 traces its roots back to MS-DOS, CP/M (Control Program for Microprocessors), and older operating systems. Windows 98 still fragments files in the course of its daily activities. This fragmentation occurs behind the scenes, and it slows down your computer. The hard disk read/write head has to bounce around all over the disk in order to read a fragmented file.

Figure 14-1 shows a fragmentation report generated by Norton Utilities' Speed Disk utility. You can see that SYSTEM.DAT is pretty heavily chopped up, with 14 separate fragments. By an ironic twist, and we did *not* rig it this way, even Windows 98's DEFRAG.EXE program shows fragmentation!

Figure 14-1:
Norton
Speed Disk
lets you
inspect
fragmentation
at the file
level.

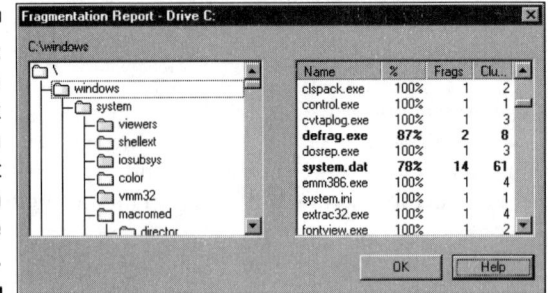

Windows 98 includes provisions to protect its *swap file* from fragmentation (the swap file is the disk file that Windows 95 uses as a slow substitute for RAM memory when RAM is in short supply). You can just set a minimum swap file size in the System control panel and guarantee that at least that part of the swap file remains *contiguous* (defragmented). However, Windows 98 has no such provision for protecting the Registry files USER.DAT and SYSTEM.DAT from becoming fragmented. When these files are fragmented, they slow down. It's not a huge problem, but it is noticeable, and a National Expert on Registry Details won't stand for it.

Windows 98 provides a program, DEFRAG.EXE, to defragment a hard drive. Just right-click a drive icon in My Computer or Explorer, choose Properties, click the Tools tab, and click the Defragment Now button. Defragment your hard drive once a month, and your system will work faster. If the C drive is more than 75 percent full, you should defragment it more often, say weekly.

The problem with this is that it doesn't let you change any of the defragmenter's settings, nor does it let you automatically defragment multiple drives with a single command. So, we prefer the command Start➪Programs➪Accessories➪System Tools➪Disk Defragmenter. With this method, you see the dialog box in Figure 14-2.

If you click the Settings button, you can click the top checkbox and tell DEFRAG to arrange the disk so that programs load faster. Without getting into all the details here — this is a book about the Registry, after all — this option uses a sophisticated technique to place bits and pieces of program files in the precise order that a program needs them when it starts. Ironically, DEFRAG therefore actually *fragments* program files to make them faster! DEFRAG operations take longer this way, but the performance optimization is a nice improvement over Windows 95, where you had to get Norton Utilities to achieve it.

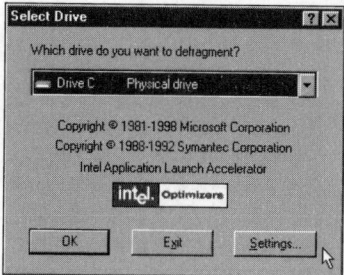

Figure 14-2:
You have
more
control
running
DEFRAG
from the
Start menu.

The best new feature of the Windows 98 DEFRAG command, though, is that it defragments the Registry! (The Windows 95 defragment command skips hidden files, and both USER.DAT and SYSTEM.DAT are hidden.) However, the Windows 98 DEFRAG still doesn't defragment the swap file.

You may want a different utility if you want to defragment the swap file as well as the Registry; the most popular one is the Speed Disk program in Symantec Norton Utilities. You can even tell Speed Disk to put the Registry files at the end of your disk, where they become fragmented less quickly (see Figure 14-3). At this writing, Speed Disk undoes the DEFRAG program speedup scheme; watch the Symantec Web site for a fix.

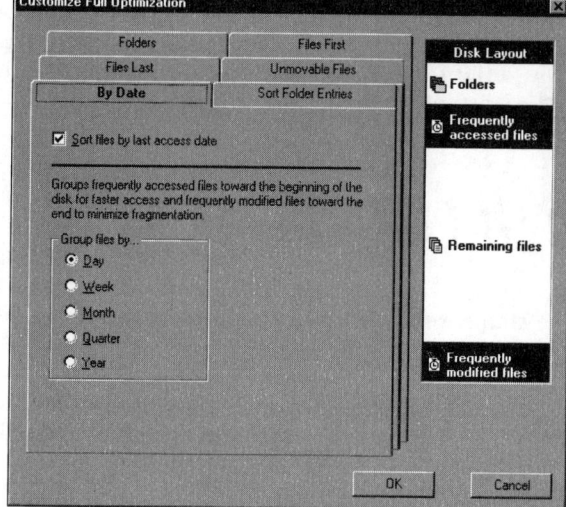

Figure 14-3:
Norton
Speed Disk
offers a
variety of
options to
fine-tune
disk defrag-
menting.

Defragmenting the Registry is great, but having Windows 98 do it for you automatically is even greater. You can set up this capability by running Start➪Programs➪Accessories➪System Tools➪Scheduled Tasks, and by stepping through the "Add New Task" wizard. You can always change the

schedule later by right-clicking the Disk Defragmenter icon in the Scheduled
Tasks window, and making different choices on the three property sheet
tabs (Task, Schedule, and Settings). We like to defrag our drives every night
(see Figure 14-4).

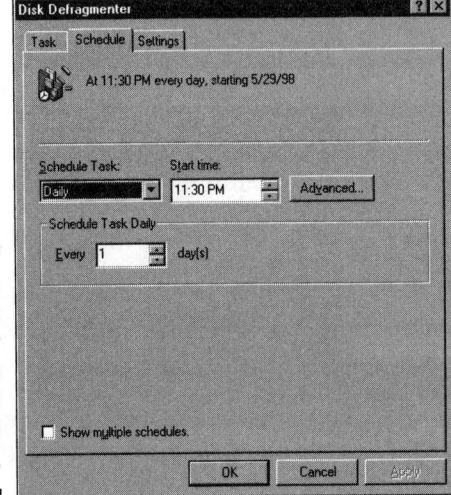

Figure 14-4:
This
computer
runs
DEFRAG
daily, in the
evening.

Defragmenters typically can't defragment open files, so close all other
programs before running the defragment command. Also, if you use the
Windows 98 DEFRAG utility, leave the details hidden; displaying them by
clicking the Show Details button slows the program way down.

Exterminating Old File Types

Now we move into the subject of ridding the Registry of stuff you don't need
anymore. A good example of this kind of junk is old *file type associations,*
which reside in the Registry.

Most application programs have their own file types — DOC for a word
processor, HTM for a Web browser, and so on. When you uninstall a program
using the Control Panel's Add/Remove Programs wizard, the uninstallation
procedure is supposed to delete these old file type associations, but in our
experience, the deletion doesn't always happen. Also, many programs aren't
considerate enough to put themselves on the list of uninstallable programs
in the Add/Remove Programs screen, leaving you with no convenient way to
even *try* removing old file type associations. Finally, you may have created
some file type associations of your own, using the suggestions in Chapter 11,
and you may now want to remove them.

Whatever your situation, you can manually strip out some junk from the Registry's *HKey_Classes_Root* (HKCR) branch by deleting old file type associations. Here's the procedure:

1. **Start Windows Explorer by right-clicking the My Computer icon and choosing Explore.**

2. **Click View⇨Folder Options to display the Folder Options dialog box.**

3. **Click the File Types tab to display the list of registered file types.**

   The list looks something like Figure 14-5.

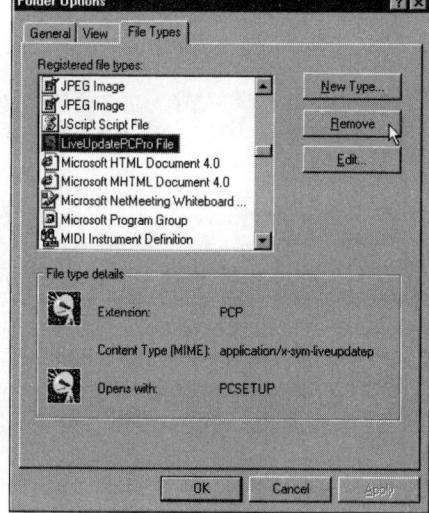

Figure 14-5:
Delete old file type associations using Explorer, without running REGEDIT.

4. **Scroll through the list, deleting file types that you know you no longer need by selecting the file types to be deleted and then clicking the Remove button.**

   The Opens With line in the File Type Details area helps you by identifying the program that the Registry associates with each type, as you highlight a type by clicking it in the Registered File Types list.

You can verify the Registry cleanup by running the Registry Editor and looking through *HKCR* at the list of file type extensions. The Registry doesn't become physically smaller, but the structure becomes simpler, and the list of file types becomes more manageable.

Removing a program's file type association doesn't necessarily remove all Registry entries relating to that program. Commercial utilities such as CyberMedia Uninstaller and Quarterdeck CleanSweep can do a more thorough job.

REGCLEAN: Free, Unsupported, and Mysterious

REGCLEAN is a little utility that can be a handy aid for stripping the choles-terol out of your Registry's arteries. Microsoft supplies REGCLEAN free on its Internet Web site. (The location of the program varies from month to month, but at this writing it's at `support.microsoft.com/support/ downloads/dp3049.asp`. You can go to Microsoft's home page, `www.microsoft.com`, and use the Search option to find REGCLEAN if Microsoft has moved the program.) You can also find REGCLEAN on the Office 97 Resource Kit's Tools and Utilities CD-ROM, but it's not the latest version, which at this writing is 4.1a.

Installing REGCLEAN is simply a matter of copying the file REGCLEAN.EXE to your hard drive; no fancy setup program exists. We suggest that you use Explorer or My Computer to create the directory C:\PROGRAM FILES\REGCLEAN and copy the file there.

If you plan to use REGCLEAN 4.1a (the current version as we write) on Windows 95 as well as Windows 98 PCs, then you may need to update some of the system files on your hard disk before REGCLEAN works reliably. At this time, the update file is named OADIST.EXE, and you can download it over the Internet from `www.microsoft.com/kb/articles/q164/5/29.htm` or `ftp://ftp.microsoft.com/Softlib/MSLFILES/oadist.exe`. After you have OADIST.EXE on your PC, just double-click it to update the neces-sary files automatically. (Specifically, you need the updated files in order to avoid the error messages `REGCLEAN.EXE is linked to missing export OLEAUT32.DLL:421` and `A device attached to the system is not correctly functioning`.) You do not need OADIST.EXE if you plan to use REGCLEAN only on Windows 98 PCs.

REGCLEAN doesn't fix messed-up Registries. Only run REGCLEAN on a Registry that seems to be working correctly. Don't run any version of REGCLEAN earlier than 4.1; earlier versions can create problems by remov-ing an important key (*HKCR\Interface\{00020400-0000-0000-C000-000000000046}*, if you're interested, and we hope you're not). Finally, as always, you're smart to back up your Registry before running REGCLEAN or any utility that modifies the Registry.

What REGCLEAN does

Microsoft hasn't documented REGCLEAN well, but here's what we've been able to determine by working with the program. REGCLEAN looks for Registry keys common to all Windows 98 and NT PCs and for keys that pertain to Microsoft Office programs; the program then scans those keys for errors. Specifically, REGCLEAN looks for references to files on disk that no longer exist or that no longer exist at the location specified in the Registry. (If you have Symantec Norton Utilities, you may prefer its Registry cleanup features to REGCLEAN's; see "Distinguishing Good Orphans from Bad" later in this chapter.)

Most of REGCLEAN's activity seems to focus on the keys *HKLM\Software\Classes* and *HKLM\Software\Classes\TypeLib*.

What REGCLEAN doesn't do

As is often the case with freebie software, REGCLEAN 4.1a has a number of limitations. Specifically, it doesn't

- ✔ Advise you when it finds no problems in your Registry. REGCLEAN behaves the same way whether it finds problems or not.

- ✔ Try to fix Registry references to files that don't exist where the Registry says they exist; REGCLEAN merely deletes the Registry references. If you move a Microsoft Office program to a different directory without rerunning that program's setup utility, REGCLEAN doesn't scan your hard drive to figure out where you moved the program.

- ✔ Do a complete job on the first run-through. Microsoft advises that you shouldn't have to run it more than four times in a row, though!

- ✔ Come with a help file to explain what sort of surgery it performs on your Registry.

- ✔ Try to remove Registry entries that pertain to software other than the base Windows 98 product and Microsoft Office.

Running REGCLEAN

Fortunately, running REGCLEAN is easier than describing it. Here's the process:

1. **Double-click the REGCLEAN.EXE icon in the folder where you installed the program.**

   REGCLEAN loads a copy of the part of the Registry it knows about and scans for errors (see Figure 14-6). Microsoft advises that the scanning process can take from 2 to 30 minutes, depending on your Registry's size and your computer's speed, so don't give up if the program seems stalled.

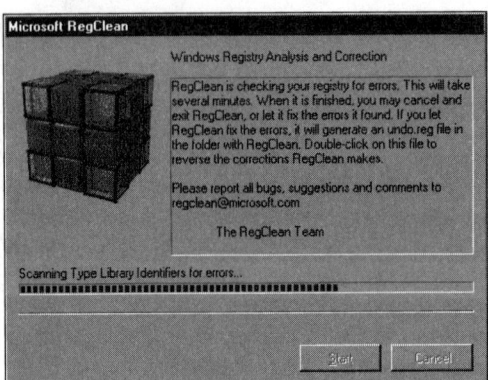

Figure 14-6:
The
Microsoft
REGCLEAN
utility
displays
progress
bars while
scanning
for errors.

2. **After the progress bars disappear, click the Fix Errors button to make the corrections REGCLEAN suggests, or click Cancel if you've had an attack of nerves.**

   No actual changes to your Registry have been made up to this point, but after you click the Fix Errors button, REGCLEAN makes the changes and creates an undo file (see "Recovering from a bad cleanup" later in this section).

3. **In My Computer or Explorer, right-click the most recent undo file created by REGCLEAN (located in the same directory as REGCLEAN.EXE) and choose Edit. If the undo file contains what appear to be Registry entries, repeat Steps 1 and 2. If it doesn't, you're done.**

If you notice that some of your Microsoft Office icons were changed, simply running the affected program or programs from the Start menu is usually enough to fix the icons.

After running REGCLEAN and restarting your PC, double-click one example of each different data file type (word processing, spreadsheet, and so on) you use on a regular basis to make sure REGCLEAN hasn't fouled something up for you.

Recovering from a bad cleanup

Although generally reliable, REGCLEAN can create certain kinds of problems as it fixes others. Most noticeably, REGCLEAN causes problems to users of the Microsoft Network online service.

The best feature of REGCLEAN from a safety standpoint is that you can easily undo the changes the program makes. After you run REGCLEAN and choose to save the changes it makes, REGCLEAN creates a file (in the same directory where REGCLEAN.EXE resides) with a name like *Undo MOOSE 19971203 120031.REG.* (The general format is *Undo **computername date time**.REG.*)

You can undo REGCLEAN's changes three ways:

✔ Double-click (or single-click, if you've enabled the desktop Web view) the undo file (assuming that you haven't changed the REG file association).

✔ Right-click the undo file, and choose Merge.

✔ Run REGEDIT, choose Registry➪Import Registry File, and choose the undo file.

Note that REGCLEAN 4.1a always produces an undo file, even if the program finds no errors in the Registry.

Distinguishing Good Orphans from Bad

A Registry *orphan* is an entry that points to a file or to another Registry entry that doesn't exist. The most common reason for your Registry to have orphans is that an application program doesn't remove itself completely from the Registry when you run its uninstall program or when you uninstall the application manually by deleting directories and files in My Computer or Explorer.

Microsoft is a prime violator of the rule that a program should remove its unique Registry entries when it is uninstalled. The list of Registry keys and values that Microsoft Office leaves in your Registry after you remove Office contains dozens of entries. The tech notes that Microsoft publishes on this subject merely state that "This behavior is by design." We suspect that this statement is a euphemism for "This product ships tomorrow and tidying up the Registry is task number 366 on our to-do list." When a user reinstalls a Microsoft Office program, the setup utility re-creates any Registry entries that are missing and required, so no good reason exists to leave the entries behind after an uninstall.

Most orphans don't do any harm other than cluttering up the attic. They're just Registry entries that don't do anything. However, you can improve your operating speed, conserve RAM, and simplify your Registry by removing orphans that point to files on your hard drive that don't exist anymore.

Some orphans are actually *good* to leave in the Registry. Specifically, string values that point to directories on a CD-ROM drive may be useful when you rerun a particular program's setup utility. If you delete these kinds of orphans, the setup program may no longer know where to look for the files it needs. You may have to tell the program where to find the files, which can be a bit of a pain, especially if the files lie several directories deep on the CD-ROM.

Other entries that you may as well leave in place are those that appear in keys having the name *Recent file list* or something similar. Many programs maintain a list of files that you've recently opened (you may see the acronym *MRU,* for *Most Recently Used*). Deleting such orphans doesn't free up any Registry space because these programs just rebuild the recent file list when you open more data files.

Finding orphans

REGCLEAN removes orphans that pertain to certain Windows 98, Windows NT, and Microsoft Office keys (see the previous section in this chapter, "REGCLEAN: Free, Unsupported, and Mysterious"), but it doesn't remove orphans that pertain to other software. So how do you go looking for these orphans?

REGEDIT doesn't include an orphan-hunting option, but Norton Registry Editor (NRE) does in Symantec Norton Utilities for Windows 95 Version 2.0 and newer — which is a good thing because finding orphans manually would take you days and wouldn't be worth the effort. We tested Norton Utilities for Windows 95 on Windows 98, and it seems to work fine, as do nearly all Windows 95 programs you need to run on a Windows 98 machine, but you're smart to use Symantec's LiveUpdate to stay current. Here's the procedure for finding orphans in NU version 2.0:

1. **Run Norton Registry Editor, usually by clicking Start⇨Programs⇨ Norton Utilities⇨Norton Registry Editor.**

2. **Choose Edit⇨Find to display the Find dialog box.**

3. **Click the Orphans radio button and click the Find Now button.**

   NRE begins its search. It may consult CD-ROM drives, diskette drives, and network drives in its hunt for files that the Registry points to. The status bar at the bottom of the NRE window gives you a progress report and says Done searching after it's done searching. The process usually takes no more than a couple of minutes, and the results appear in the Find Results window in the bottom third of the NRE window.

Version 3.0 of Norton Utilities takes the orphan search out of the Norton Registry Editor and makes it part of the new WinDoctor utility (see Figure 14-7). The procedure is as follows:

Figure 14-7:
The Norton
WinDoctor
program in
Norton
Utilities
Version 3.0
finds and
categorizes
Registry
orphans.

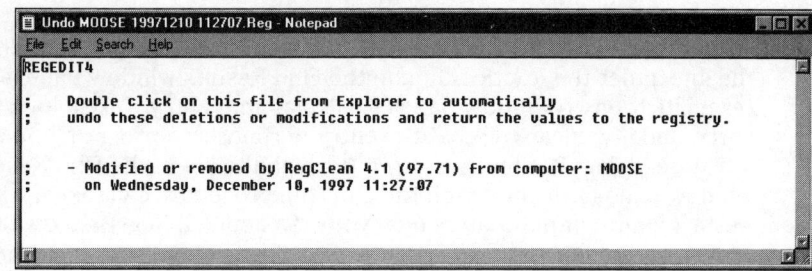

1. **Choose Start⇨Programs⇨Norton Utilities⇨WinDoctor.**

2. **In the Norton WinDoctor Wizard dialog box, select Perform All Norton WinDoctor Tests (Recommended), and click Next.**

3. **When you see the** Finished Scanning **message, click Next, read the message, and click Finish to see the list of Problems Found.**

4. **Double-click each problem category to review and repair the listed problems automatically.**

Deleting orphans

After you identify orphans using Norton Registry Editor or WinDoctor (see the preceding section), you're ready to do away with the little idlers. Remember, however, that you only want to get rid of the bad orphans (the ones that point to your hard drive); leave the good orphans (the ones that point to your CD-ROM drive) and the ones that just keep running back to the Registry (the recent file list orphans).

As you scroll through the list of orphans that NRE or WinDoctor found, you're likely to see a large number that point to your CD-ROM drive or network drives. You can detect these orphans by the drive letter that appears in the Data column of the Find Results window. If the drive letter is something other than C:, chances are that the value is pointing to a CD-ROM or network location. (Some PCs may have additional drive letters that point to the hard drive; when in doubt, open the My Computer window and look at the icons corresponding to the different drive letters.)

The entries that point to your hard drive are probably orphans that you can safely delete. Allow some time for this chore, as NRE or WinDoctor may find hundreds of such orphans.

Before you delete orphan values, back up your Registry, just in case! Chapter 2 provides all the gory details.

The procedure for deleting orphan values in NRE is simple. Just double-click the line under the Root column in the Find Results window pane, and NRE resets its top two window panes to display that entry. Take a look at the entry, and if you can tell that the entry pertains to a program you don't use anymore, delete it. Continue down through the list in the Find Results window pane until you reach the end (the procedure can take a while!). Restart your computer and enjoy your streamlined Registry. Test the programs you use to be sure that everything is copacetic, and you're done. If something has gone haywire, restore the Registry from the backup that you made prior to your orphan-deleting session.

Compressing the Entire Registry

Okay, here's where things get really fun. In this section, you're going to slim down your Registry so it's as skinny as it can possibly be. The preceding sections on finding and deleting Registry orphans is helpful for making the Registry easier to navigate and troubleshoot, but deleting orphans doesn't in itself make your Registry files physically smaller. Physical compression is the subject of this section, and it brings the benefits of lower disk space requirements, quicker boot times, and faster Registry backups.

It used to be that the only way to make your Registry super-lean was to export the Registry's contents, create a brand-new Registry database, and reload the contents. You can still use this method, but Windows 98 provides another option, and if you have Norton Utilities, you may want to try yet a third technique.

The percentage reduction you'll see in USER.DAT and SYSTEM.DAT varies depending on how long you've been using your PC and how many programs you've installed on it (and uninstalled from it).

We suggest that you do some experimenting of your own to see which of the following methods works best for you. In our experience, the tried-and-true REGEDIT method creates the smallest files, but it does involve more steps than using SCANREG.

Make sure you have a good, recent Registry backup before proceeding further in this section. For example, you may want to run the Registry Checker (by choosing Start⇨Programs⇨Accessories⇨System Tools⇨ System Information, then Tools⇨Registry Checker) to make sure that you have an up-to-the-minute backup in CAB file format (see Chapter 2 for more details). We haven't run into any problems with any of the three methods described here, but if you do, it's nice to know you can easily restore your previous Registry.

SCANREG method

You can choose to rely solely on Windows 98's automatic Registry compression. If the Registry contains over 500K in unused space, Registry Checker (SCANREG) automatically compresses the Registry when it runs, behind the scenes, during the first Windows 98 boot of the day. That's okay, but 500K is a fairly high threshold in our view.

You can force SCANREG to optimize your Registry at any time, without being subject to the 500K threshold, using the undocumented command-line qualifier **/OPT**. (We read about this qualifier in the Windows 98 beta program release notes, and it still works with the shipping version of Windows 98, but you won't see it listed if you type **SCANREG /?** at a command prompt!) However, you *must* restart your computer and boot to a command prompt for this method to work. So, follow these instructions exactly!

If you merely restart the computer in MS-DOS Mode and run SCANREG /OPT as described in the following procedure, Windows 98 will tell you that it's found problems with your Registry, and will make you restart the computer so it can run SCANREG /RESTORE. You probably won't hurt anything if this happens, but it's never a good idea to tempt fate.

We've found that this SCANREG method is a little quicker than the REGEDIT method described later, and produces results that are almost as good. Here's the procedure for forcing a SCANREG compression:

1. **Back up the Registry by using your favorite method (see Chapter 2).**

   We suggest you also make backup copies of SYSTEM.INI and WIN.INI (these files are in the C:\WINDOWS directory, or whatever you've named your main Windows 98 directory).

2. **Run REGCLEAN if you have it.**

   See previous section "REGCLEAN: Free, Unsupported, and Mysterious" in this chapter.

3. **Defragment your hard drive.**

   See the previous section "Defragmenting the Registry" in this chapter. This optional step makes everything go a little faster.

4. **Reboot your computer and hold down Ctrl during startup.**

5. **Choose the Command Prompt Only option.**

6. **After the command prompt appears, type the command:**

```
SCANREG /OPT
```

This command runs the real-mode Registry Checker and tells it to compress, or *optimize,* the files. You don't get any sort of confirmation message when the command finishes, but the C:> prompt returns as your cue that SCANREG has done its thing.

7. **Restart Windows 98 with the three-finger salute, Ctrl+Alt+Del. Let Windows 98 start normally.**

Norton Optimization method

Norton Utilities for Windows 95 offers an alternative method for compressing Registry files via the Norton Optimization Wizard. You can run this utility and select "Registry Files Optimization" without running the other optimization tools (swapfile optimization and SpeedStart). However, on a test system using version 3.0 of the program, we noted that while SYSTEM.DAT became 100K smaller, USER.DAT became 200K *larger.* We also noticed that the utility leaves behind some junk in AUTOEXEC.BAT — nothing serious, just some lines that cause you to see a couple of extra "C:>" prompts when you boot to command prompt mode.

It's possible that this utility performs some other speed optimization tricks that require the expansion of USER.DAT, but as of version 3.0 of this program, we don't recommend it as a method for compressing Registry files. We fully expect Symantec to refine this tool with time.

REGEDIT method

Here's the Registry compression procedure that we've been using for Windows 95, version OSR2 (that is, the "B" and "C" releases). It involves the most steps, but in our experience produces the smallest Registry files in Windows 98. It also has the virtue of working with Windows 95 OSR2, so if you have to manage systems running that version of Windows, you can use one technique that works with both operating systems.

To use the REGEDIT method:

1. **Back up the Registry by using your favorite method (see Chapter 2).**

We suggest you also make a backup copy of SYSTEM.INI and WIN.INI (these files are in the C:\WINDOWS directory, or whatever you've named your main Windows 98 directory).

2. **Run REGCLEAN if you have it.**

   See previous section "REGCLEAN: Free, Unsupported, and Mysterious" in this chapter.

3. **Defragment your hard drive.**

   See the previous section "Defragmenting the Registry" in this chapter. This optional step makes everything go a little faster.

4. **Reboot your computer and hold down Ctrl during startup.**

5. **Choose the Command Prompt Only option.**

6. **After the command prompt appears, type the command:**

   ```
   REGEDIT /E TOTAL.TXT
   ```

   This command exports your entire Registry to a text file.

7. **After the command prompt returns, type the command:**

   ```
   REGEDIT /C TOTAL.TXT
   ```

   This command recreates your Registry, compressing it in the process.

8. **Restart Windows 98 with the three-finger salute, Ctrl+Alt+Del. Let Windows 98 start normally.**

After you confirm that Windows 98 and your Windows 98 applications work fine following the compression procedure, delete C:\TOTAL.TXT from your hard drive. (It'll be pretty large, 3MB or more.)

Part V

Escaping from Quicksand: Registry Troubleshooting

"SOFTWARE SUPPORT SAYS WHATEVER WE DO, DON'T ANYONE START TO RUN."

In this part . . .

Quicksand bogs can sneak up on you. As George's ostrich-skin boots slid slowly beneath the deadly ooze, he called out to his faithful guide. "Stay back! Quicksand! Get a rope!" His guide replied, "It's back at the camp — we don't have time!" George's mind raced. "Pull the spare tire from the back of the truck and throw it to me!" Puzzled, the faithful guide obeyed. George leaned his elbows on the rim and hoisted himself onto his air-filled, makeshift chair. "Quicksand's thicker than in the movies, and this big spare tire has a high surface-to-weight ratio. Now you've got time to get that rope," he said from his perch. "But do toss me a sandwich first."

Even the most expert jungle guides occasionally find themselves in quicksand. Part V is your guide to getting safely back to camp when you find yourself suddenly faced with Registry trouble. From solutions for twenty common problems to methods of recovering your Registry from a backup, this part prepares you for most of the unpleasant Registry surprises that can "bog down" your PC.

Chapter 15

Twenty Tricky Registry Problems (And Solutions!)

● ●

In This Chapter

▶ Fixing problems at Windows 98 startup

▶ Dealing with Registry Editor error messages

▶ Discovering what to do when double-clicking and right-clicking don't work correctly

▶ Solving REG file problems

● ●

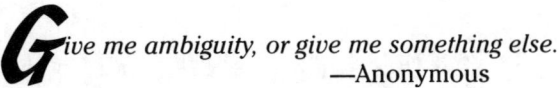*ive me ambiguity, or give me something else.*
— Anonymous

Problems are inevitable if you spend very much time working with PCs. When they occur, one of three things happens.

✔ You see no error message at all; something just doesn't work as it should (most common).

✔ You see an ambiguous error message that doesn't help you zero in on the problem (next most common).

✔ You see a detailed and accurate error message that tells you exactly what to do to fix the problem (least common).

This chapter presents some of the more common Registry-related problems and ways to get around them.

I Can't Upgrade My Windows 95 System

When you try to upgrade a Windows 95 system to Windows 98, you may see the following message:

```
Setup must be able to create short filenames with numeric
tails for files with names longer than 8 characters. Enable
this option and try running Setup again.
```

If you see the preceding message, someone has modified the Windows 95 Registry to disable the *numeric tails* that appear on the short version of long file names. (For example, the directory *Program Files* gets shortened to *Progra~1* in a DOS window, and *~1* is the numeric tail.)

We don't recommend disabling numeric tails, and not only for this reason; the practice can also wreak havoc on batch files that try to run programs in the *Progra~1* directory. Anyway, here's how to fix the problem: Use REGEDIT to delete the value *NameNumericTail* in the key *HKLM\System\ CurrentControlSet\Control\FileSystem*.

Windows 98 Displays a Registry Error at Startup, Part 1: MSDOS.SYS

When starting Windows 98, you may see the following error message:

```
Warning: Windows has detected a registry/configuration
error. Choose, Command prompt only, and run SCANREG.
```

Windows 98 then leaves you at a command prompt, starting at C:> and wondering where all your windows went.

Even though the Windows 98 error message suggests that something's wrong with the Registry, it ain't necessarily so. For example, something may be wrong with the startup file C:\MSDOS.SYS. The file may be missing, in which case you can restore it from an earlier backup (see Chapters 2 and 16). Or, the file may be damaged, in which case you can edit it according to the following steps.

1. **At the command prompt, type the command**

```
ATTRIB -R -H MSDOS.SYS
```

This command clears the startup file's Read-only attribute.

2. **Run the DOS text editor with the command**

```
EDIT C:\MSDOS.SYS
```

3. **Change the first few lines so that they read as follows (assuming your main Windows 98 drive and directory is C:\WINDOWS):**

```
[Paths]
WinDir=C:\WINDOWS
WinBootDir=C:\WINDOWS
HostWinBootDrv=C
```

In particular, if the *WinBootDir* value is incorrect, you'll see the error message mentioned at the start of this section.

4. **Save MSDOS.SYS, set the attributes back to read-only and hidden (same command as in Step 1 but use + instead of – both places), and restart.**

If the Registry error message goes away, you must be living right!

Windows 98 Displays a Registry Error at Startup, Part 2: Corrupt Registry

If MSDOS.SYS is okay, then you may truly have Registry problems. The most common Registry error message appears in Figure 15-1. After you click OK, Windows 98 reboots into MS-DOS Mode and runs SCANREG with the /FIX parameter. If you're lucky, the operation is successful, and your PC now works normally.

Figure 15-1:
This error
probably
means
Registry
corruption.

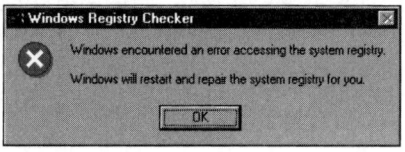

If the automatic operation doesn't work — or if you see a slightly different error message that reads as follows:

```
Windows was unable to process the registry. This may be
fixed by rebooting to Command Prompt Only and running
SCANREG/FIX. Otherwise there may not be enough conventional
memory to properly load the registry.
```

If you see the preceding error message, you can try manually rebooting to Safe Mode, Command Prompt Only and typing the command **SCANREG /FIX**.

If you still can't boot Windows 98 normally, you may have to manually restore the Registry using the **SCANREG /RESTORE** command, or by using whatever backup utility you use on a regular basis.

Finally, if you don't have a good backup, you can try rebuilding the Registry at the command prompt with the following three commands, in sequence:

```
CD C:\WINDOWS
REGEDIT /E TOTAL.REG
REGEDIT /C TOTAL.REG
```

The second command (/E) exports the Registry to the file TOTAL.REG, and the third command (/C) rebuilds the Registry by importing TOTAL.REG. If you're not at the command prompt, get there by restarting Windows 98, holding down the Ctrl key during startup, and choosing Safe mode command prompt only.

If all else fails, read "SCANREG Says It Can't Process the Registry" later in this chapter.

Registry Checker Says the Disk Is Full

And it's probably correct. The actual message, which may appear at startup (when Registry Checker makes an automatic backup) or when you attempt to make a manual Registry backup using Registry Checker, appears in Figure 15-2.

Figure 15-2:
Registry
Checker
complains
about
elbow
room.

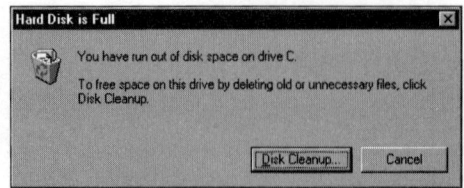

You may be more likely to bump into this problem with Windows 98 compared to Windows 95, because the newer operating system uses a lot more disk space. We've seen cases where Internet surfers let their disk caches build up to the point that even large disks run out of room. The problem is more likely to occur with:

✔ Notebook computers that have smaller drives to start with

✔ Drives that you've partitioned to use multiple drive letters

✔ Systems with lots of applications

✔ Systems with very large data files (such as digital video)

The Windows 98 Disk Cleanup wizard, which you can run from the dialog box in Figure 15-2, is a handy utility for freeing up space. You can also take some of the following steps:

✔ Reduce your Web browser cache size (see your browser's online help)

✔ Reduce your Recycle Bin size (modify its property page)

✔ Reduce the number of backups Registry Checker makes (see Chapter 2)

✔ Consider converting to the more efficient FAT32 disk format

If you're curious about how much space you could free up by converting to the FAT32 disk format, Microsoft provides an analysis tool, buried on the Windows 98 CD-ROM as \TOOLS\RESKIT\CONFIG\FAT32WIN.EXE. Running the analysis tool produces a report such as that shown in Figure 15-3. Just be careful you don't click the Convert button by accident! You can't easily undo the conversion!

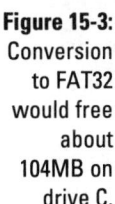

Figure 15-3: Conversion to FAT32 would free about 104MB on drive C.

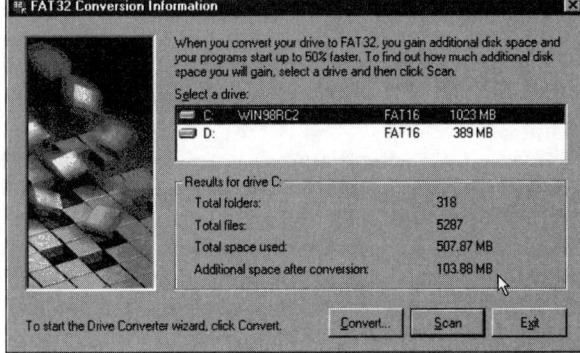

Windows 98 Says It Can't Load a Device It Needs

Windows 98 boots, warns that `Windows 98 cannot find a needed device file` and then gives you the file name. The reason for the problem is that the Registry (if the file ends in .VXD), or maybe even SYSTEM.INI (if the file ends with .386), contains a reference to a file that's no longer present on the hard drive. You can acknowledge the message and let Windows 98 continue to boot, and you may not even notice any problems with Windows 98 or with Windows applications after the system starts.

Most of the time, such an error appears after you've attempted to manually uninstall an application by just deleting the application's program directory. Removing that directory doesn't remove the Registry entries that refer to those files.

What you have to do is reinstall the program, then uninstall it with the vendor's supplied removal routine. You should be able to run the Control Panel's Add/Remove Programs utility and see the program listed on the Programs tab, at which point you can click it and then click the Add/Remove button. Some vendors provide a separate remove program that doesn't use the Add/Remove Programs wizard, however.

If reinstalling and uninstalling don't do the trick, or if the vendor provides no removal program, edit SYSTEM.INI with Windows Notepad and look for the line that contains the .386 file mentioned in the error message. You can place a semicolon at the front of that line to tell SYSTEM.INI to ignore it. If the error message refers to a .VXD file, then you can hunt it down with REGEDIT and delete the relevant key or value (back it up first!).

REGEDIT Displays Error Messages

Boot time isn't the only time when you may get a Registry-related error message; you may see one when starting REGEDIT. Here are a few of the more common error messages that the Registry Editor may display:

- **The specified file is not a registry script.** The only way REGEDIT can tell whether a file is a registry script or not is by looking at the very beginning of the file for the line `REGEDIT4`. If this line is missing, you get this error.

- **Unable to delete all specified values.** REGEDIT doesn't let you delete the (Default) value in the value pane (right window). If you want to get rid of a key, delete it in REGEDIT's key pane (left window).

✔ **Unable to rename (key name). The specified key name contains illegal characters.** You see this message if you try to use the backslash character in a key name; it's *verboten*.

✔ **The specified key name already exists.** Key names have to be unique, at least within a particular group.

SCANREG Says It Can't Process the Registry

If you get an error message when trying to run SCANREG.EXE from a command prompt — for example, by restarting in MS-DOS Mode — then it could be that you don't have enough *low memory* for SCANREG to carry out its business.

SCANREG is the Registry Checker's command prompt version, and it uses memory in the bottom 640K of the PC's memory space, or *low memory*. (The version of Registry Checker that you use from the Windows user interface is SCANREGW.EXE, which uses so-called *protected mode* memory above the 1024K boundary.) If you're loading device drivers or programs in CONFIG.SYS and AUTOEXEC.BAT, you may not have enough low memory left over for SCANREG.

In this case, you should free up low memory by commenting out (deactivating) any lines in CONFIG.SYS or AUTOEXEC.BAT that aren't absolutely essential. You can simply use the DOS EDIT command to place the letters REM at the beginning of a line to tell Windows to ignore that line; the *REM* is short for *remark*. Commands that load CD-ROM drivers or network software come to mind as good candidates. Then, restart the PC, and see if SCANREG is happier.

I Can't Boot to Safe Mode

Several times in this book, we advise you to restart Windows 98 in its so-called *safe mode,* which enables you to make changes to the Registry — such as a total restore — that you otherwise can't safely make. Working in safe mode is also a way of sidestepping problems with certain hardware device drivers that don't want to start properly in a normal boot.

The usual procedure for getting to safe mode is to restart the operating system, press Ctrl until you see the text menu, and choose *Safe mode command prompt only* from that menu. (You can use a graphical version that's just called *Safe mode,* which you may need in order to run the Registry Editor without errors — see the section later in this chapter titled "Importing Fails with Real-Mode REGEDIT.") The F8 key also displays the boot menu, if you happen to press it at just the right time; Microsoft has removed the "Starting Windows..." message that gave the cue to press F8 in Windows 95, in the interest of saving a nanosecond at boot time.

What if you can't get the system to display the menu of choices after you restart the operating system, either with the Ctrl key or F8? One possibility is that someone's tinkered with the MSDOS.SYS text file. Here's how to fix this problem:

1. **In Explorer, right-click C:\MSDOS.SYS and choose P̲roperties.**

   If you can't see MSDOS.SYS, choose V̲iew⇨Folder O̲ptions⇨View and choose the radio button labeled Show All Files.

2. **Clear the Read-only and Hidden check boxes and click OK.**

3. **Shift+right-click MSDOS.SYS and choose Op̲en With.**

4. **Clear the check box (if it's checked) that reads Always U̲se This Program to Open This Type of File, and select Notepad from the list of programs.**

5. **If you see the line** BootKeys=0 **in the [Options] section, change the line to read** BootKeys=1 **so that the F8 and Ctrl keys work at startup.**

   If BootKeys is zero, neither the Ctrl nor the F8 key work. If you want to give yourself more time to hit the F8 key, under the [Options] section, add or modify the line BootDelay=*n* where *n* is the number of seconds you want. If you don't want to worry about hitting F8 at all, and want the system to always present the boot menu choices, under the [Options] section, add the line BootMenu=1.

6. **After you're finished, close Notepad, and reverse the changes you made in Steps 1 and 2.**

For a detailed discussion of safe mode, please see Chapter 16, specifically the section "There's no mode like safe mode."

I Can't Reverse Restrictive Policies

The System Policy Editor, POLEDIT, allows you to set a policy for the current Registry that disables the Registry Editor (expand *Local User — Windows 98 System — Restrictions;* and select the Disable Registry Editing Tools check box). Later, you can use POLEDIT to reverse this setting if you want to run REGEDIT.

However, you may not be able to run POLEDIT if you've also added restrictions to what programs Windows 98 is allowed to run (expand *Local User — Windows 98 System — Restrictions;* select the Only Run Allowed Windows Applications check box). Figure 15-4 shows POLEDIT after the user has selected the Disable Registry Editing Tools and Only Run Allowed Windows Applications check boxes. If POLEDIT isn't on the list of allowed Windows applications, then you can't run the program to remove the restrictions on itself and on REGEDIT. Oh no! A vicious circle! And one with teeth, at that.

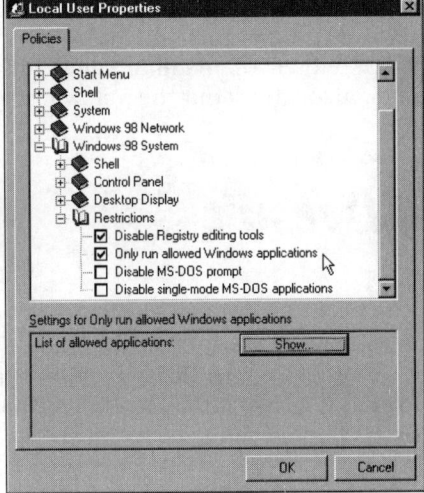

Figure 15-4: The System Policy Editor can disable REGEDIT and restrict allowed applications to a list that you create.

Happily, you're not really trapped. Various Microsoft technical documentation hints that you may have to reinstall Windows 98 in this scenario, but that's baloney. What you need to do is create a REG file that looks like the following:

```
REGEDIT4

[HKEY_CURRENT_USER\Software\Microsoft\Windows\CurrentVersion\Policies\Explorer]
  RestrictRun =dword:00000000
```

You can even create this text file on another computer and bring the file over on diskette, if you find that you can't run any programs at all. This REG file — call it UNLOCK.REG or something similar — resets the RestrictRun value to zero, effectively switching off the policy that restricts you to only running certain applications.

You can't run REGEDIT directly in order to import this REG file because you've disabled Registry editing tools with the Policy Editor. However, this situation is no sweat for those in the know. Use Windows Explorer to locate the REG file, right-click it, choose Merge, and presto chango — the program restrictions disappear. You can now run the Policy Editor and fine-tune the restrictions until they're the way you *really* want them.

After reading this section, you may think that setting restrictions by selecting the Disable Registry Editing Tools check box isn't very secure because you can still modify the Registry by simply right-clicking a REG file. Hey, this restriction is even less secure than that! You can also right-click an INF file and choose Install, which enables you to not only modify and add to Registry values but also to outright delete them. Remember, the security in Windows 98 is West Coast casual. Also, check out the following problem.

The REGEDIT Policy Doesn't Restrict Other Editors

The Disable Registry Editing Tools system policy that we discuss in the preceding problem is effective in restricting the Registry Editor REGEDIT, but it does nothing to restrict other Registry Editing tools you may use — such as Norton Registry Editor or CleanSweep Registry Genie.

If you want to limit access to such programs, either put 'em on a network server where you can make them available only to certain users or groups, or hide their application directories on the local disk so other users aren't tempted to find and run them.

The Wrong Program Runs When I Select a File

When you double-click a data file (or, in the Web view desktop, single-click it) and run an unexpected program, the usual culprit is a messed-up file type association list. Fortunately, you can probably fix the problem without using the Registry Editor, although you do modify the Registry (specifically the *HKCR* branch).

1. **Open My Computer or Explorer and choose View⊏>Folder Options.**

2. **Click the File Types tab, and then scroll down to the file type that's acting up and click it.**

3. **Click Edit and modify the Open action in the Edit File Type dialog box to specify the program that you want.**

   (*Open* is the same as *double-click* in the Classic desktop mode of Windows 98, and *single-click* in the Web view desktop mode.) You can also browse to the program's location.

The Properties Option Crashes Windows 98

If you can't see the property sheet for data files and desktop icons when you right-click them and choose the Properties option, you have to run REGEDIT to correct the problem (or, at least, to identify the problem). Many variations of this problem exist, but we offer up one example from our own experience to illustrate the troubleshooting technique. The example borrows several tricks and techniques from different chapters. If you can read through it once or twice and understand more than half of it, you're ready to graduate from Registry U with honors!

Recently, after Glenn removed the Novell NetWare Client32 software from his Network control panel, he found that accessing the property sheet for just about any kind of Windows 98 object — shortcut, data file, program, you name it — crashed the system with the error message shown in Figure 15-5.

Figure 15-5:
Property sheets have gone haywire on Glenn's PC, offering only this error message.

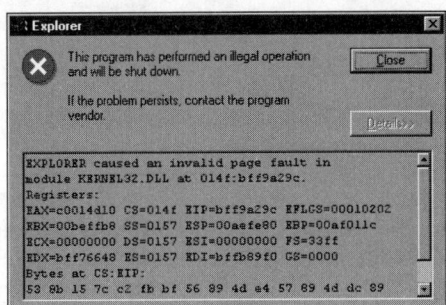

Because the problem seems to be nearly universal and affects almost all file types, we suspect the asterisk key (*) in the Registry's *HKCR* branch. Anything in the (*) key applies more or less universally to Windows 98 icons and files. Opening *HKCR*\shellex\PropertySheetHandlers* reveals the keys in Figure 15-6, which are unique tags — Class Identifiers (CLSIDs) — pointing to the programs that manage property sheets.

Figure 15-6:
REGEDIT
shows the
class IDs
for property
sheet
programs.

Those CLSIDs don't mean diddly to us. We know, however, that the Registry contains more information about each CLSID under *HKCR\CLSID*. (Chapter 6 explains this key in more detail.) We just have to find the right CLSID among the hundreds of CLSIDs on Glenn's PC. Fortunately, REGEDIT has a Find command.

Being essentially lazy and not wanting to retype the whole long CLSID, we highlight the CLSID key in the screen shown by Figure 15-7, right-click it, choose Rename, then hit Ctrl+C to copy the long ID to the Windows Clipboard. (A quick Esc deselects the key name, which we don't really want to change.) We then hit Ctrl+F to bring up the Find dialog box and press Ctrl+V to paste the suspicious CLSID into the Find What field. Our find operation brings up the entry that we need (see Figure 15-7).

Figure 15-7:
The
HKCR\CLSID
key holds
more clues.

Expanding the key, we see that a subkey called *InProcServer32* resides below it. This subkey indicates the program or program library that Windows 98 associates with the CLSID. Clicking *InProcServer32* reveals the file: NWSHELLX.DLL. Sure enough, a quick check using Windows Explorer shows NWSHELLX.DLL sitting innocently with most of the other program libraries in C:\WINDOWS\SYSTEM.

The NW at the start of the file name suggests that NWSHELLX.DLL is a NetWare related file. We can't check its property sheet (remember, the property sheets are broken), but it's a good working hypothesis. So, we go back to *HKCR*\shellex\PropertySheetHandlers* and delete the key that we've just discovered points to a NetWare file. We removed NetWare from the PC earlier, so we're not too worried that this key is something that we still need. Nevertheless, we export the key to a small REG file before deleting it, just in case we're wrong, so we can import it later. (See Chapter 4 for details on importing and exporting REG files.)

After closing REGEDIT, right-clicking NWSHELLX.DLL, and choosing Properties, the property sheet now appears — success! — and we see in the Novell Inc. copyright notice that this file is, in fact, a leftover from the NetWare Client32 software. The leftover file doesn't work right anymore because Glenn deactivated the Client32 software by using the Network control panel. Why is this file still hanging around and why does its property sheet handler still exist in the Registry? We may never know for sure, but a less-than-tidy deinstallation script seems a probable cause. The main thing is that the property sheets work again. We didn't have to reinstall Windows 98, and knowing about the Registry made the troubleshooting process a quick one.

Importing Fails with Real-Mode REGEDIT

You try to run REGEDIT in real mode (command prompt only, or safe mode command prompt only), for example, to import a tiny little REG file. Alas, every time you make the attempt, you see the following error message:

```
Unable to open Registry (14) — SYSTEM.DAT
```

Or, perhaps you're importing a rather large REG file, and you see the message:

```
Error accessing the registry: The file may not be complete.
```

Both of these errors stem from the same problem: REGEDIT's inability to deal with a really large Registry, or a really large REG file, in its command prompt mode of operation.

The best solution is to boot Windows 98 normally, if possible, and use REGEDIT in its graphical, protected mode — where it has access to more memory. Chances are that your import operation now proceeds smoothly. If you can't boot Windows 98 normally, however, you have a few options, none of them especially convenient:

✔ See whether you can boot Windows 98 into safe mode (the graphical version, not *Safe mode command prompt only*). See the section earlier in this chapter, "I Can't Boot to Safe Mode," for details.

✔ Boot your PC from the emergency startup diskette and try running REGEDIT. Your PC should have a little more available memory this way. (Make such a diskette via the Add/Remove Programs wizard.)

✔ Chop your large REG file into two or more smaller pieces, using a text editor such as the DOS Edit program. (REG files list each key as a complete path, so where you perform your surgery doesn't matter much.)

Importing a REG File Misses Some Keys

You perform an import (or merge) of a REG file, maybe a REG file that you wrote yourself, but some or all the keys in the REG file don't appear in the actual Registry.

Windows 98 is very nitpicky about the punctuation in REG files. The most common problems are as follows:

✔ The file doesn't start with a separate line containing the word *REGEDIT4*. (This word must be all capital letters.) In this case, REGEDIT displays the message in Figure 15-8.

Figure 15-8:
If you see this message, your REG file doesn't have the correct first line.

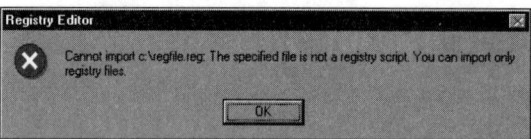

✔ The file includes keys or values that are missing a curly bracket ({ or }).

✔ The file includes string values that are missing the enclosing double quotes.

✔ The file includes path names that use single backslashes instead of the required double backslashes.

Rather than creating the REG file from scratch, it's much easier to export a REG file of the key you want to modify and then change the REG file to your liking by using Notepad.

We also need to mention that REGEDIT gives you absolutely no indication whether it finds invalid statements in a REG file after it finds the REGEDIT4 header at the beginning of the file. Because you don't see an error message, the only way you know your REG file works is to run REGEDIT and check the keys and values manually. To illustrate, take a look at Figure 15-9. We merged this utterly bogus REG file into the Registry (after making a backup first!), and the result was the cheery message that the information in JUNK.REG had been "successfully entered into the Registry." Yecch. (Incidentally, Windows 98 still ran perfectly normally.)

Figure 15-9:
This sham
REG file
imports
without
prompting
an error
message.

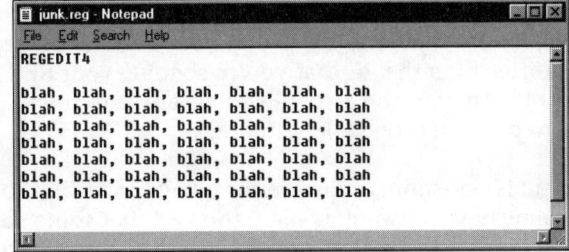

Importing a REG File Creates Unwanted Duplicates

This problem is a subtle variation on the preceding one. When Windows 98 processes a REG file, instead of changing the value of a particular key or value, REGEDIT seems to add a new key or value with the same name (see Figure 15-10).

Figure 15-10:
The strange
case of
duplicate
values,
which
supposedly
REGEDIT
doesn't
permit.

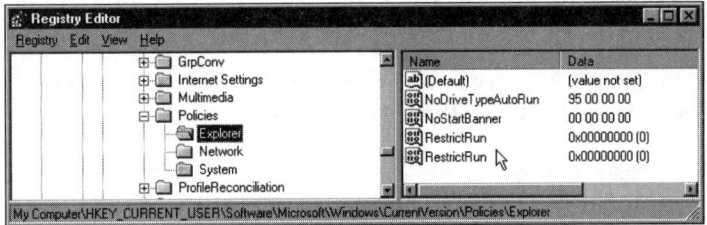

The most likely cause of this strange problem is a space at the end of the key name in your REG file. If such a *trailing space* exists, then REGEDIT interprets the key or value as new and different and adds it to the Registry, instead of changing the existing entry. Solution: If you write your REG files from scratch, make sure your key and value names have no trailing spaces.

REG and INF Files Aren't Working on Other PCs

The most likely reason for this problem is that your PC uses different folders for program directories than the PC that you're sending your REG or INF file to. Find out what folder names the target PCs use, and edit the REG or INF file with Notepad to point to those folder names.

This sort of problem is one more argument for using the default folder names when installing new software. It's just too bad that some software vendors still haven't cottoned on to the notion that all application files should go into subfolders beneath C:\Program Files. Consistency may be the hobgoblin of little minds, but it's a virtue for computers.

After Restoring the Registry the Fonts Are Gone

You've restored your Registry to fix a particular problem, using any of the various methods we describe in Chapter 16. Your problem goes away as a result of your efforts, but now you have a new one: All the TrueType fonts seem to be absent from the font list in your application programs. When you go to the Fonts control panel, it's empty. When you try to add a font, Windows 98 gives you an error message stating that the font is already installed! It's a catch-22.

Most likely, the Registry key *HKLM\Software\Microsoft\Windows\CurrentVersion\Fonts* is either missing or damaged.

> ✔ If the key is missing, run C:\WINDOWS\SYSTEM\FONTREG.EXE to create the key quickly; then go to the Fonts control panel and reinstall your fonts (they usually reside in C:\WINDOWS\FONTS) with the File➪Install New Font command.

✔ If the key is present, it's probably damaged. Use Windows Explorer to move all the TTF files from C:\WINDOWS\FONTS to a different folder, run REGEDIT, delete the key mentioned previously, and re-add it. Go to the Fonts control panel and reinstall your fonts (they reside in the new directory you created) with the File➪Install New Font command.

System Policy Editor Doesn't Save a File

You're working with the System Policy Editor (POLEDIT.EXE), creating a policy file to restrict or customize Windows 98 along the lines we mention in Chapter 9, and you want to save the POL file. When you do, you see the message in Figure 15-11.

Figure 15-11:
A crotchety POLEDIT decides not to save your file if the target directory uses a long filename.

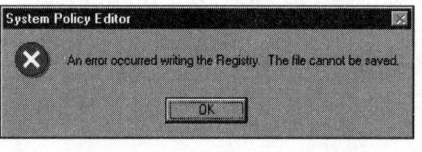

Why is the Policy Editor, as the error message states, trying to write the Registry? Maybe the message means that POLEDIT has encountered an error when *writing* to (saving) a file (your POL file) that will ultimately become part of the Registry. Or maybe the message is just screwy.

Fortunately, the correction is simple, but it's gonna make you mad. Turns out that POLEDIT can't handle directories with long filenames. (Wasn't that one of the reasons we all moved to Windows 98 in the first place? Grrr.) If you're trying to save TEST.POL in the directory C:\TEST DOCUMENTS, you have to type the short filename equivalent in the Save As dialog box's File Name field, like this:

```
C:\TESTDO~1\TEST.POL
```

Then POLEDIT saves your file properly. The short name equivalent is usually just the first six characters of the long directory name, followed by ~1. When in doubt, run Windows Explorer and check the directory's property sheet; the General tab shows the short name equivalent.

Oh, and by the way, you may see another error message (although different, for variety) if you browse to a file by choosing File⇨Open, clicking the Browse button, navigating to the file and highlighting it, and clicking the Open button. Here again, if you type the complete path with the short filename equivalent in the File Name field of the Open Policy File dialog box, POLEDIT opens your file without a problem.

Avoid this problem completely by keeping all your POL files in directories with eight or fewer characters.

Windows Reboots Are Slow

Windows 98 restarts somewhat more quickly than Windows 95, although to some extent the effect is misleading — for a few seconds after the desktop appears, you don't get quick response from the system, because it's still furiously loading software in the background. Anyway, when working with the Registry, you often need to restart the PC, and the faster you can make that process, the better. Here's a trick for speeding up reboots a smidgen.

1. **Right-click the desktop and choose New⇨Text Document.**

2. **Name the file REBOOT.BAT and answer Yes to the confirmation dialog box.**

3. **Right-click REBOOT.BAT and choose Edit. In Notepad, type the single command @EXIT and save the file when closing Notepad.**

4. **Right-click REBOOT.BAT in Windows Explorer and choose Properties.**

5. **On the Program tab, choose Close on Exit.**

6. **Click Advanced, choose MS-DOS Mode and clear the checkbox labeled Warn Before Entering MS-DOS Mode.**

Now, whenever you want to restart the PC, just choose your REBOOT.BAT file. Seconds saved are seconds earned.

I Can't Find Stuff in the Registry That I Know Is There

This problem breaks out into three common situations that we describe in the following sections. All three involve a Registry search that produces nothing more than the dialog box in Figure 15-12. It's bad enough when you can't find your car keys, but it's worse when you can't find your Registry keys.

Figure 15-12:
Coming up
empty in
REGEDIT.

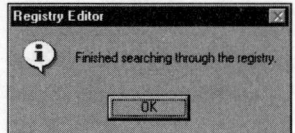

Context menu search strings

When you're using the Registry Editor's Find command, or a third-party Registry search tool, to locate text that you've seen in a context menu, you come up empty. (*Context menus* are menus that appear when you right-click a desktop object.) As we say throughout this book, the Registry defines how context menus look and act. So what gives?

One reason could be that the context menu command lives in a separate file that the Registry merely references, in which case your Registry search cannot succeed. However, it could also be that the context menu command that you're looking for contains an underlined character, which the Registry marks with a leading ampersand (&). For example, if the *t* in *Properties* appears underlined, then a search for *Properties* will fail, but a search for *Proper&ties* will succeed.

Find command follies

A very common reason that a Find operation fails in REGEDIT is that the My Computer icon isn't highlighted in the key pane (the one on the left). The Registry Editor's Find command starts with the highlighted key, works downward, and stops when it gets to the bottom. REGEDIT doesn't wrap around to the top of the file and search the area above the highlighted key, like most good word processors do. So, if you don't remember to click My Computer, it could be that the item you're searching for is located above the currently highlighted key.

The short and long of it

You may be hunting for a particular file reference in the Registry. The secret here is to remember to try both the *regular* long filename version, and the truncated short filename equivalent. If your search for **C:\Program Files\Internet Explorer\iexplore.exe** comes up empty, try **C:\Progra~1\Intern~1\iexplore.exe**.

Chapter 16

Restore and Restart as a Last Resort

*I*n Chapter 2, we advise you to make Registry backups for a rainy day. This chapter explains the reverse procedure: restoring your Registry from those backups.

Just as a photo safari guide hopes he'll never need to use his elephant gun, we hope that you never need this chapter. However, if the troubleshooting tips in Chapter 15 don't cure your beleaguered PC, don't start firing off rounds randomly and don't despair. You can probably fix whatever problem is threatening your machine by restoring your Registry from an earlier backup.

You may sacrifice some recent settings by doing so, which is why we say that a Registry restore is your last resort before you have to reinstall Windows 98 itself. (Okay, reinstalling Windows 98 is *really* your last resort, but we had to have something catchy for this chapter's title, and "penultimate resort" doesn't cut the mustard.)

Depending on how diligent you've been about making periodic backups, restoring the Registry may not turn out to be a big deal. (We had to do it a few times in the course of researching this book, and it never took more than ten minutes.) Even if you've been a delinquent backer-upper, we may at least be able to save you from having to wave the white flag and reinstall Windows 98 from scratch.

As Chapter 2 discussed, you can back up your Registry with several differ-ent tools and techniques. This chapter is a mirror image of Chapter 2 and provides the restore procedures that match up with the various backup procedures.

There's No Mode Like Safe Mode

You may need to start Windows 98 in *safe mode* to restore your Registry, so here's the least you need to know about this mode. Windows 98 can run in two modes. Its usual, graphical mode is called *protected mode* (or in some Microsoft documentation, *protect mode*). In this mode, Windows 98 is actively using the Registry. You can back up the Registry in protected mode, although you're better off doing so with no Windows programs running, as we advise in Chapter 2. Restoring the Registry, though, is a different matter.

If you only need to restore part of the Registry, you may be able to do so in protected mode. Importing a small REG file doesn't usually present a problem. However, if you need to restore the whole dadgum Registry, you generally don't want to be running in protected mode. Doing so is a little like changing a flat tire while your Land Rover's still moving. You need to restart Windows 98 in *real mode,* or what the Windows 98 startup menu calls *Safe mode command prompt only* (we abbreviate it SMCPO). This method brings up Windows 98 in a text-only command prompt screen that looks a lot like MS-DOS. (It also avoids Windows 98 creating new RB*.CAB backup files, which occurs in a "regular" safe-mode startup.)

The procedure for starting Windows 98 in real mode is simple. Start the computer and hold down Ctrl when booting. The following menu appears (it may not be identical on your PC):

```
Microsoft Windows 98 Startup Menu
=====================================
1. Normal
2. Logged (\BOOTLOG.TXT)
3. Safe mode
4. Step-by-step confirmation
5. Command prompt only
6. Safe mode command prompt only
7. Previous version of MS-DOS

Enter a choice:
```

Choose the *Safe mode command prompt only* option, either by typing the corresponding number (6 in the above example) or by scrolling with the up and down arrow keys.

When it starts in SMCPO, Windows 98 skips processing the startup files — CONFIG.SYS, AUTOEXEC.BAT, SYSTEM.INI, and the Registry. Therefore, even if your Registry is badly damaged, Windows 98 can start in SMCPO without hiccuping because it doesn't so much as glance sideways at the Registry in this mode.

If you're on a network, when you restart and hold down the Ctrl key, you won't notice the choice *Safe mode with network support* anymore. (It was present in Windows 95.) If you want network access in safe mode, for example to access Registry-editing tools that may be on the network but not on the local PC, you must create a separate batch file (such as NETSAFE.BAT) that loads your network's real-mode drivers. This batch file should contain the same commands that you'd use in AUTOEXEC.BAT to configure a DOS or Windows 3.*x* machine for network access. Alternatively, if you're able to run Windows 98 in protected mode and connect to the network that way, you can copy whatever utilities or Registry backups you need from the network down to your local hard drive, and then restart in SMCPO to perform the restore.

Specific Restore Procedures

Here are the restore procedures that go with the backup procedures we talked about in Chapter 2. Read this stuff carefully, sloooowly, twice, before you actually do anything.

Restoring from CAB files

As Chapter 2 explains, Windows 98 automatically backs up USER.DAT and SYSTEM.DAT to the cabinet files RB0*.CAB the first time the operating system starts on any given day without detecting any major problems. You can also create as-needed backups by running the Registry Checker manually, also as detailed in Chapter 2.

If you think you've made a mistake during a Registry editing session, you haven't made your own Registry backup, you've modified SCANREG.INI to only keep a single backup (as you may on a notebook PC with limited disk space), and you want to go back to the CAB file backup, *don't restart Windows 98 normally!* If Windows doesn't think that your mistake is any big deal, it views the restart as a successful one and overwrites the CAB file with a new one — burning your bridge behind you. The same warning applies if you've left SCANREG.INI alone so that it makes its normal number of five backups, but you don't discover your Registry error until five or more days later.

Restoring the entire Registry

Here's how to restore your entire Registry from the RB0*.CAB files:

1. **Restart Windows 98 in Safe mode command prompt only. (See "There's No Mode Like Safe Mode" earlier in this chapter.)**

Windows 98 doesn't make a new CAB file backup when it starts in Safe mode command prompt only. Also, note that Microsoft's documentation says it's okay to restart in MS-DOS Mode for a Registry restore, but we like to be a bit more cautious.

2. At the command prompt, type the following line:

```
SCANREG /RESTORE
```

The Registry Checker lists available backup archives, up to a total of five. (See Figure 16-1.)

3. Using the up and down arrow keys, choose which backup you want to restore from.

SCANREG politely displays which backups actually resulted in a successful Windows 98 startup, to help you choose the safest one.

4. Using the left and right arrow keys, highlight the Restore command and press Enter.

5. Restart Windows 98 normally.

We found a major flaw in the SCANREG /RESTORE command: If you've set up SCANREG.INI to make more than the typical five backups, you can't see them all when you go to restore! We discovered that you can work around this problem by renaming the RB0*.CAB files that do appear with a different suffix, like CAX. Then, SCANREG will show you up to five other archives. Rinse and repeat as needed. (You can also move the archives you know you don't need to a directory other than SYSBCKUP, where SCANREG won't be able to find them.) Not exactly convenient, we know, but at least it works.

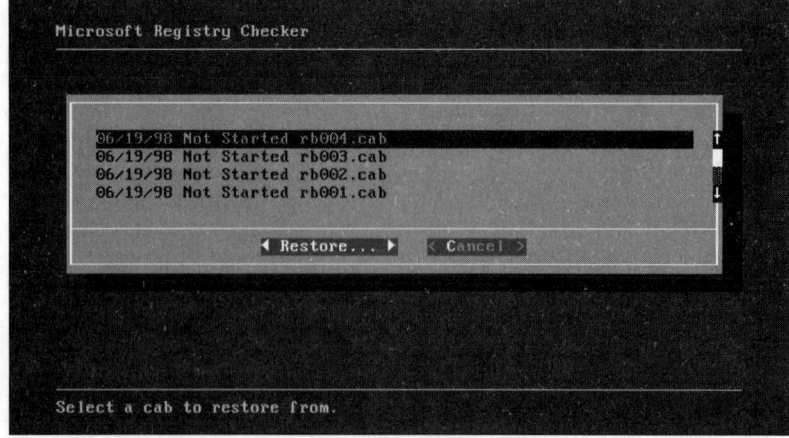

Figure 16-1:
Restoring
the Registry
with
SCANREG.

Restoring a single file

You may occasionally bump into a situation where you need to restore only one file from a Registry Checker archive rather than all the files in the archive. You can't accomplish this with SCANREG (another demerit for this utility), but you can use the command-line EXTRACT program.

First, you need to view the CAB file's contents to make sure you get the file name right. Do this by restarting to Safe mode command prompt only, and then typing a command like the following:

```
EXTRACT /D RB000.CAB *.*
```

(The *.* is required, strangely, to prevent EXTRACT from actually extracting anything.) After you view the CAB file's contents and verify the spelling of the file you need, use a command such as

```
EXTRACT /Y RB000.CAB filename.ext
```

where *filename.ext* is the name of your desired file. The /Y part of the command gives EXTRACT permission to overwrite an existing file with the same name. If you want to put the file somewhere special, use /L followed by the directory name.

The export/import bank

If you created a Registry backup by using the export technique, you can restore the Registry with the (you guessed it) import technique, described here. If you want to restore a partial Registry backup and you can boot to Windows 98 normally, follow these steps:

1. **Close all Windows programs and then run the Registry Editor, for example by clicking Start⇨Run⇨REGEDIT and OK.**

2. **Click Registry⇨Import Registry File to display the dialog box in Figure 16-2.**

3. **Specify the directory in the Look In field and name the file in the File Name field.**

   REGEDIT defaults to showing files with the suffix .REG.

4. **Click the Open button to restore the data.**

If you don't already have REGEDIT open and you know where your REG file is, you can save a few mouse clicks and import your REG file by right-clicking it in Explorer and choosing Merge. The results are identical.

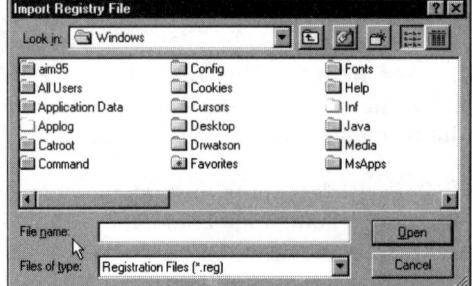

Figure 16-2:
Importing or
merging a
REG file into
the current
Registry
with
REGEDIT.

Be aware that an import operation isn't a complete replacement of an existing Registry key. Importing can only change or add keys — it can't delete keys. If you feel that you need an exact image of the earlier backup, you must first delete the particular key in REGEDIT (back it up first for safety) and then perform the import.

You can't restore a *full* Registry backup when Windows 98 is running in its graphical, protected mode, and be completely certain that the resulting Registry is identical to the one you backed up. To restore the entire Registry, follow these steps:

1. **Restart Windows 98 in Safe mode command prompt only. (See "There's No Mode Like Safe Mode" earlier in this chapter.)**

2. **At the command prompt, change to the Windows directory with a command like** CD C:\WINDOWS.

3. **Create a new Registry from your backup file with the command**

```
REGEDIT /C filename.REG
```

4. **Restart the computer normally.**

The REGEDIT /C command is *very dangerous!* It creates a whole new Registry based on the contents of *filename*.REG. If that REG file doesn't contain a full Registry backup, you're in a heap o' trouble. Make *very* sure that the REG file that you specify is the result of a complete Registry export operation.

Here's another *gotcha* if you're creating a new Registry in safe mode. If you have a very large Registry and REGEDIT gives you an error message because it doesn't have enough memory to handle the procedure, restore SYSTEM.1ST, by using the procedure in the section later in this chapter, "SYSTEM.1ST is really SYSTEM.LAST." After you can boot Windows 98 into its graphical protected mode, you can run REGEDIT and import the file that way. The import problem doesn't affect REGEDIT when it's running in protected mode, just command prompt mode. The basic reason is that REGEDIT can use a bunch more memory in protected mode.

If you need to restore a single Registry key but Windows 98 won't start into its graphical protected mode, you can use the real mode REGEDIT program. Follow the numbered steps listed previously, but in Step 3, leave out the /C qualifier, so you perform a merge instead of creating a new Registry.

Microsoft Backup 98

Restoring the Registry, or any other file set for that matter, is easy with Microsoft Backup 98, the backup utility included with Windows 98. Just run the program by choosing Start⇨Programs⇨Accessories⇨System Tools⇨Backup, click the Restore tab, and enter the appropriate settings and options. If you want to restore the Registry, make sure that you click the check box "Restore Windows Registry" under Job⇨Options⇨Advanced.

If you have to restore *all* your files from a Backup 98 backup set, not just the Registry files, you can follow a somewhat streamlined procedure that uses your Windows 98 emergency startup diskette, your Windows 98 CD-ROM, and your backup tape. This "system recovery" procedure uses a special batch file in the CD-ROM directory's \TOOLS\SYSREC folder. Check the Backup 98 help topic titled "Restoring all your files" for the details, then read RECOVER.TXT in \TOOLS\SYSREC for good measure. Just remember that you should only choose the option to restore Registry files if you haven't changed your hardware configuration (that is, for example, you haven't replaced an EIDE boot drive with a SCSI boot drive). The Registry contains hardware settings that will no longer be accurate if you change the disk type.

Batching it

If you took our advice in Chapter 2 and used a batch file and DOS commands to back up your Registry, you're sitting in the catbird seat (that is, sitting pretty). If you haven't read James Thurber's short story, *The Catbird Seat,* check it out at the library and treat yourself; it's hilarious. But we digress. Here's the modus operandi for a full Registry restore:

1. **Restart Windows 98 in Safe mode command prompt only. (See "There's No Mode Like Safe Mode" earlier in this chapter.)**

2. **At the command prompt, type the following lines (replace** E:\REG **with the drive letter and directory where your backup files reside):**

```
CD C:\WINDOWS
ATTRIB -H -R USER.DAT
ATTRIB -H -R SYSTEM.DAT
RENAME USER.DAT USER.BAD
```

```
RENAME SYSTEM.DAT SYSTEM.BAD
REM The next 2 lines may be necessary if you backed
REM up the files with the hidden attribute intact:
ATTRIB -H E:\REG\USER.DAT
ATTRIB -H E:\REG\SYSTEM.DAT
COPY E:\REG\USER.DAT /V /Y
COPY E:\REG\SYSTEM.DAT /V /Y
ATTRIB +H +R C:\WINDOWS\USER.DAT
ATTRIB +H +R C:\WINDOWS\SYSTEM.DAT
```

3. **Add lines such as the following if you've enabled user profiles on the PC (repeat for each user):**

```
CD C:\WINDOWS\PROFILES\MARK
ATTRIB -H -R USER.DAT
RENAME USER.DAT USER.BAD
REM The next line may be necessary if you backed
REM up the file with the hidden attribute intact:
ATTRIB -H E:\REG\PROFILES\MARK\USER.DAT
COPY E:\REG\PROFILES\MARK\USER.DAT /V /Y
ATTRIB +H +R USER.DAT
```

4. **Restart Windows 98 normally.**

Note that we rename the existing Registry files with the *.BAD suffix in the preceding procedure. You may find that these files are okay and that the problems that cause you to restore the Registry turn out to be non-Registry-related. If that happens, you can go back to the *.BAD files, which may be convenient if your most recent Registry backup — the one you restored — was a few weeks or months old. Otherwise, delete the *.BAD files after a week or two.

You may want to use Notepad to make a little batch file containing the commands in Steps 2 and 3. Just don't give the file a long name (over eight characters in the main part of the name); you'll be running it from a command prompt, where long file names are a hassle.

For those of you who read Chapter 2 with an eagle eye and are wondering why we don't just use the XCOPY command to save a lot of typing in Steps 2 and 3, here's the reason. XCOPY doesn't offer the /H, /K, and /R qualifiers when it runs in real mode (don't ask us why). (The /H switch copies system and hidden files, /K copies file attributes, and /R overwrites read-only files.) So we have to use ATTRIB to make the *.DAT files visible to the COPY and RENAME commands. We also use ATTRIB to put the active Registry file attributes back the way they were.

Norton to the rescue (disk)

If you've used Norton Utilities version 3.0 or newer to make a set of rescue diskettes, restoring the Registry is a snap. Here's the drill:

1. **Pop the first of your rescue diskettes into the diskette drive (it's a boot diskette).**

2. **Restart the computer.**

3. **When you see the command prompt, type** A:\RESCUE **and press Enter.**

4. **Select the items you want to restore.**

5. **Press Alt+R to begin the restore process and follow the instructions on screen.**

   Here's what happens behind the scenes. Norton Rescue restores the Registry from the file C:\WINDOWS\REGISTRY.RSC, unless you use the ZIP-plus-diskette combination and specified at the last backup that you wanted to copy the Registry files to the ZIP disk.

6. **When the rescue program is done, take the diskette out of the drive and hit** R **to reboot the PC to Windows 98.**

Restoring from general-purpose backup programs

If you've made a backup by using a general-purpose disk backup program, such as Cheyenne Backup, Seagate Backup Exec, or NovaBACKUP, then you can restore the Registry files from within your backup program. Each package works differently, but the general sequence is to run the backup software, insert your backup media (such as a tape cartridge), tell the program to read the catalog of files on the backup media, choose the files to restore, and then run the restore operation.

Booting to a diskette or in Safe mode command prompt only before running the restore program is a safer approach than restoring the Registry while running Windows 98 in its graphical protected mode — if, that is, your backup program can run from a command prompt.

Still using Windows 95 utilities?

We don't recommend using Windows 95 utilities to back up your Windows 98 Registry, but we know that some people are doing it, and you may just run into a situation one of these days in which someone used CFGBACK or ERU to save a Windows 98 Registry. This section addresses such situations.

If neither you nor anyone in your organization has access to Windows 95 Registry utilities, please skip this section!

CFGBACK to the future

We don't discuss how to use the Microsoft Configuration Backup program to make backups in Chapter 2 because even Microsoft admits that this program is unreliable (although the company still distributes it). However, if you have to work with a PC on which someone else used CFGBACK to save the Registry, here's the restore procedure:

1. **Buy the person who ran CFGBACK a copy of this book and dog-ear Chapter 2, so the user doesn't depend on CFGBACK in the future.**

2. **Start Windows 98 normally, but don't load any programs.**

   CFGBACK doesn't run in safe mode, either the graphical version or the command prompt version. If the Registry is so traumatized that Windows 98 insists on starting in safe mode automatically, then you can't restore with CFGBACK. To make things worse, CFGBACK's backup files use a unique compressed format that no other program can read. (You can begin to see why we don't recommend this program.)

3. **If the backup file or files that you want to restore aren't in C:\WINDOWS, copy them there now, using Windows Explorer.**

   The filename has the form REGBACK*n*.RBK, where *n* is a number from 1 to 9. CFGBACK looks for previous backups in C:\WINDOWS only.

4. **Run CFGBACK.EXE by locating it in Windows Explorer and double-clicking it.**

5. **Click the Continue button three times to get past all the information screens.**

   You see the Configuration Backup dialog box in Figure 16-3.

6. **Click the backup that you want to restore in the List of Previous Backups window.**

7. **Click the Restore button.**

8. **Click Yes in the Warning dialog box to completely replace the current Registry with your backed-up version.**

9. **If you see yet another confirmation dialog box, click Yes again.**

   CFGBACK displays a message about separating system and user information. (It combines SYSTEM.DAT and USER.DAT into a single file when it makes a backup.) After a ridiculously long time (five minutes is typical), CFGBACK displays a success message.

10. **Restart the computer normally, cross your fingers, kneel in the direction of Redmond, Washington, and hope everything went well.**

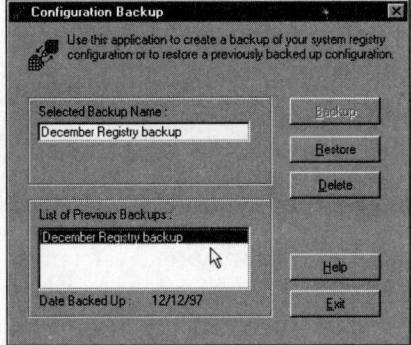

Figure 16-3:
Restoring
the Registry
with
CFGBACK.

A word about ERD

If you (or someone else) made a backup with the Windows 95 Emergency Recovery Utility (ERU), then restoring is a simple procedure. You use the ERD.EXE program that ERU created in your backup directory. (We'd like to think that ERD stands for End Registry Despair, but it probably just stands for boring old Emergency Recovery Disk.) Here are the details:

1. **Restart Windows 98 in Safe mode command prompt only. (See "There's No Mode Like Safe Mode" earlier in this chapter.)**

   Unlike CFGBACK, ERD runs in safe mode, and safe mode only. If you try running ERD in a regular DOS window in Windows 98 protected mode, ERD refuses to run. Restoring in safe mode avoids problems with any Windows programs that may be writing to the Registry during a restore operation. Being able to restore the Registry is also nice if Windows 98 can *only* start in safe mode, as may be the case with a seriously trashed Registry.

2. **At the command prompt, change to the disk and directory where your backup files reside, with a command such as** CD C:\REGBACK.

3. **Type** ERD **and press Enter to run the recovery program.**

4. **Use the up and down arrow keys and the Enter key to pick the files that you want to restore.**

   Normally, you include both SYSTEM.DAT and USER.DAT.

5. **Arrow down to the Start Recovery option and hit Enter.**

   ERD goes about its business much more quickly than CFGBACK, and in a minute or less, you see a success message.

6. **Restart the computer and let Windows 98 boot normally.**

SYSTEM.1ST is really SYSTEM.LAST

When you first install Windows 98, the setup program creates a file in the root directory called SYSTEM.1ST. Windows 98 doesn't touch this file again, so it remains a snapshot of your initial PC setup. But the file isn't there merely for nostalgia.

When all else fails and you can't seem to get your Registry back to working condition, you may consider restoring this primordial version of SYSTEM.DAT. You have to reinstall all your application software and drivers for any hardware that you've added since your initial Windows 98 setup. However, this situation may be preferable to reinstalling Windows 98 itself from scratch.

The easy way to activate SYSTEM.1ST is to rename SYSTEM.DAT to something else and then copy SYSTEM.1ST to SYSTEM.DAT. Here's the procedure:

1. **Restart Windows 98 in Safe mode command prompt only. (See "There's No Mode Like Safe Mode" earlier in this chapter.)**

2. **At the command prompt, type the following lines:**

```
CD C:\WINDOWS
ATTRIB -H -R SYSTEM.DAT
RENAME SYSTEM.DAT SYSTEM.BAD
ATTRIB -H C:\SYSTEM.1ST
COPY C:\SYSTEM.1ST C:\WINDOWS\SYSTEM.DAT
ATTRIB +H SYSTEM.DAT
```

3. **Restart Windows 98 normally.**

   You may have to go through the last few screens of the Windows 98 SETUP program because of the fact that SYSTEM.1ST contains SETUP-related entries in its "RunOnce" Registry key. You may need to supply the Windows 98 CD-ROM, also, so Windows 98 can copy over a few files. (We *told* you this procedure is a last resort!) After this rigmarole, you're able to run Windows 98 in its virginal state.

Windows 98 doesn't build a similar initial snapshot of USER.DAT, but maybe restoring the original SYSTEM.DAT is enough to get you out of the rough water. Reinstalling all your applications is easier than reinstalling Windows 98. Note that we rename the suspect Registry file with the suffix *.BAD in Step 2 so that you can go back to it if you eventually discover that the problem lies elsewhere.

The old Windows 95 method of simply moving or renaming SYSTEM.DAT and SYSTEM.DA0, and letting Windows 95 install SYSTEM.1ST automatically upon reboot, no longer works in Windows 98.

Part VI

Trekking Onward:
The Part of Tens

In this part . . .

"**O**kay, George," said his faithful guide around the evening campfire, "Let's see how smart you really are. Name ten famous safari-goers." George lit a cigar, leaned back in his canvas lounge chair, and thought for a minute. "Teddy Roosevelt, Isak Dinesen, Winston Churchill, Roy Rogers, George Eastman, Ernest Hemingway, David Livingstone, and Henry Morton Stanley." "Not bad, but that's only eight," replied the guide. "True," said George. "Well, Weadock and Wilkins tackled the jungle of the Windows 98 Registry, and lived to write about it." "Touché," the guide replied.

Every ...*For Dummies* book ends with a Part of Tens. First, we list ten Internet sites that contain Registry-related material. Visit these periodically to stay current with the most recent tips and tricks, especially as Windows 98 makes its way into the marketplace. Especially useful are ten slick Registry tricks that we couldn't figure out where else to include, but felt you'd want to know about. Finally, we wrap up our Registry odyssey on a humorous note by presenting ten Registries that have nothing in the world to do with Windows 98.

Chapter 17

Ten Registry-Related Internet Sites

● ●

In This Chapter

▶ Finding some of the Internet's best search services

▶ Discovering nine World Wide Web sites with Registry information

▶ Checking out one UseNet newsgroup

● ●

*I*n addition to allowing you to book an African safari online, the Internet offers several useful resources for you as you delve into the inner workings of the Registry. Because the Internet is more like the "information spaghetti bowl" than the "information superhighway," we thought you'd appreciate knowing about ten specific locations to start you on your Internet surfin' safari. (We really give you *more* than ten locations, but this chapter is in the Part of Tens, so we had to sneak in the extra ones. Keep your eyes peeled.)

Before running any program that you download from these or other Internet sites, scan the file or files with a good, up-to-date antivirus utility to make sure that you're not bringing a virus into your computer. Cheyenne, McAfee, and Symantec (among others) all make good antivirus programs (see Appendix B).

Internet *search services* (Web sites that help you find stuff using keywords) are great for finding Registry-related information. You may want to use *Windows 98 Registry* as a search phrase; if you just use *Registry,* you're likely to pull up hundreds of references to Windows 95 and Windows NT, too. Type in the name of the particular Registry branch you're interested in to narrow the search even further. Although most Internet documents use the standard Registry branch abbreviations that we use in this book (*HKLM, HKCR,* and so on), some use even shorter abbreviations (*HLM, HCR,* and so on). Here are some of the more popular search services:

- ✔ AltaVista (`altavista.digital.com`)
- ✔ Excite (`www.excite.com`)
- ✔ HotBot (`www.hotbot.com`)
- ✔ Lycos (`www.lycos.com`)
- ✔ Yahoo! (`www.yahoo.com`)

If you have a slow-speed Internet connection, consider turning off Web graphics in your browser for faster surfing. Here's how:

- ✔ In Internet Explorer 4, choose View⇨Internet Options⇨Advanced and uncheck the Show Pictures check box under the "Multimedia" heading.

- ✔ In Netscape Navigator 4, choose Edit⇨Preferences, click the Advanced category, and uncheck the Automatically Load Images check box.

- ✔ In Netscape Navigator 3, choose Options⇨Auto Load Images and then clear the check mark.

Also take a look at the section "Turbocharging Internet dial-up links" in Chapter 10, if you connect to the Internet via modem, for a speed tip.

www.imaginations.com

At this site, after filling out a long survey (you can cheat and skip most of the overly personal questions), you can obtain the latest version of the famous Windows Registry FAQ (Frequently Asked Questions) document in preview form. At this writing, the preview requires that you have Adobe Acrobat Reader 3.01 or newer; if you don't, you can download it from www.adobe.com. The Registry FAQ file is about 4 megabytes — Acrobat files are notoriously bulky — so plan for a fairly long download time. Check this site occasionally for updates to the Registry FAQ.

www.sysinternals.com

Mark Russinovich and Bryce Cogswell perform a great public service by posting useful Windows 9x and NT utilities on this site. In particular, REGMON and FILEMON are great to have (see Chapter 3). Another keen utility for dual-boot PC users (who run more than one operating system on the same PC) is a file system driver that lets Windows NT see Windows 98 FAT32 disk partitions in read-only mode.

www.winmag.com

Windows Magazine's online site is a wealth of information about the Registry. Just use the site search engine and type **Registry**. Most of the material you find is helpful and technically accurate. You can find a ton of non-Registry Windows 98 stuff here, too.

www.zdnet.com

The Ziff-Davis Web site is a great place to keep up with the PC and Windows worlds; we often go to the home page to see late-breaking news. This site is also your gateway to several online magazines, including

- ✔ PC Magazine (www.zdnet.com/pcmag)
- ✔ PC Computing (www.zdnet.com/pccomp)
- ✔ PC Week (www.pcweek.com)
- ✔ Windows Sources (www.zdnet.com/wsources)

Search the Ziff-Davis site by pointing your browser to www.zdnet.com and clicking the Search button on the site map.

One of the more famous Windows 98 Web sites is the "Windows 98 Annoyances" site, created and maintained by Creative Element in San Francisco. Here, you not only see what "bugs" other Windows 98 users (pardon the pun), but you can also pick up workarounds and helpful tips.

www.winfiles.com

Steve Jenkins' site (formerly www.windows95.com) is a good source for all kinds of tips, tricks, drivers, bug fixes, tutorials, and news. It's one of the better sites around.

support.microsoft.com/support

At Microsoft's Internet support site, you can gain access to the massive Microsoft knowledge base of common problems and solutions, as well as downloadable freebies.

www.microsoft.com/windows/windows98

Visit the main Microsoft Windows 98 site for news and product updates, straight from the horse's mouth.

www.download.com

This site, sponsored by CNET, is a great source of Windows 98 downloadable software. You can search the software library by using the keyword *Registry* to see only those freeware and shareware utilities that have to do with the Registry. We like to browse the top downloads occasionally, too.

comp.os.ms-windows.win95.misc

Not a Web site, but rather a *UseNet newsgroup* (a sort of Internet bulletin board) with lots of postings about the Windows 98 and 95 Registry, this location is a good place to post a question when you can't get an answer anywhere else or when you just want to read what other Windows 9*x* users are saying.

Here are a few other newsgroups of interest:

✔ `microsoft.public.win98.pre-release`

✔ `comp.os.ms-windows.misc`

✔ `alt.windows95`

You need newsreader software in order to read postings from these newsgroups. Windows 98 comes with Outlook Express, formerly Microsoft Internet Mail and News, which has a capable newsreader. If you use America Online to access the Internet, you can't use Outlook Express but you can use AOL's built-in newsreader. Just choose keyword *newsgroups,* click the Expert Add button, and type in the newsgroup name from this section's title.

Chapter 18

Ten Registry Tricks — Useful and Otherwise

In This Chapter

▶ Recovering a lost Internet Explorer password

▶ Restarting the Registry without a reboot

▶ Putting your own tech notes into the Registry

▶ Adding sounds to programs that don't provide sound schemes

This little chapter contains some miscellaneous Windows 98 Registry tricks that we couldn't figure out where else to put. Most are potentially very convenient and useful, and one is just for fun.

These tricks typically involve using the Registry Editor, so if you haven't looked over Chapter 4, you may want to do so. We assume in this chapter that you're familiar enough with REGEDIT to know how to add, delete, and change keys and values. Also, the standard grandmotherly caution applies here, as everywhere: Back up your Registry before making any of the changes in this section.

What's New on the Menu?

When you right-click any open space on the desktop and choose New, you open a submenu (see Figure 18-1) that lets you create a new file of that type on the desktop. After giving the new file a name, you can select it (with a single-click in Web view, or a double-click in Classic view) and run the program in which you normally create files of that type. For example, the bitmap image type opens Microsoft Paint.

After a few months' worth of using Windows 98, the New menu becomes cluttered with programs you're not likely to use to create desktop icons. The flip side of the coin is that there may be file types you'd like to add to the New menu.

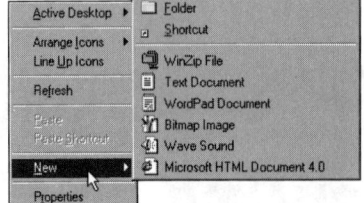

Figure 18-1:
Quickly
create a
new file by
right-
clicking the
desktop.

Removing a file type

If you have the TweakUI control panel (we tell you how to install it in
Chapter 11), run it, go to the New tab, and clear the check boxes for any
existing file types that you want to remove. (See Figure 18-2.)

If you don't have TweakUI on your PC, fire up the Registry Editor and go to
the file extension key under *HKCR* for the type you want to remove from the
New menu. (For example, if you want to remove "Bitmap Image," go to
HKCR\.bmp.) In case you change your mind, first export the *ShellNew* key
underneath the file extension key. Then, delete it. No more listing on the
New menu!

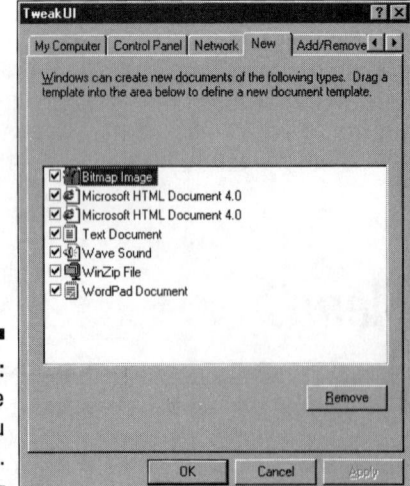

Figure 18-2:
Putting the
New menu
on a diet.

Adding a file type

To add a file type by using TweakUI, create a blank file as a template (this is what your new file will look like when you create it), and drag-and-drop it into the window containing the check boxes. There's often a slicker way to add a file type, however, using the Registry Editor.

Run REGEDIT, go to the file extension key under *HKCR,* and create the ShellNew key beneath it. Now, in the ShellNew key, add a string value named *NullFile* containing an empty string ( ). Many applications can open an empty file, and you don't have to create a separate template file with this method. If this method doesn't work with a particular program, use the TweakUI method.

Recover a Lost Internet Explorer Password

Our modern heads are full of passwords, e-mail addresses, personal identification numbers, clothing sizes, birthdays, and other codes that are hard to remember. As computer programs add more and more security capabilities, we're bound to forget a password at some point. If you forget the supervisor password for the content advisor ratings in Internet Explorer 4 (see Figure 18-3), which you may use to prevent little Jimmy from browsing www.wildjunglelove.com on your home PC, you're in luck: The Registry can help.

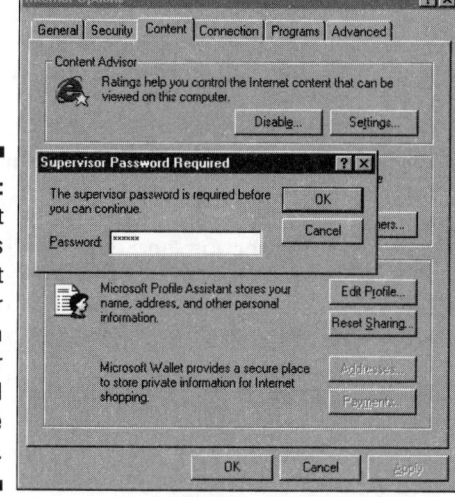

Figure 18-3: Internet Explorer's content advisor requires a supervisor password to make changes.

Run the Registry editor and sashay over to *HKLM\Software\Microsoft\ Windows\CurrentVersion\Policies*. Delete the Ratings subkey, and the password restriction goes away. You can now go to Internet Explorer and create a new supervisor password.

Lock Out File Type Changes

We talk in Chapter 11 about the file type settings that you can make from My Computer's View⇨Folder Options⇨File Types screen. What if you get these settings just the way you want, and you don't want anyone else to be able to change them? As usual, the Registry provides a way.

The secret lies in an obscure Registry setting called *EditFlags*. When you get a particular file type set up the way you want it via the File Types screen, you can lock out future changes by running the Registry Editor. The general procedure is to navigate to the relevant file type key in *HKCR's* lower half and add the EditFlags binary value, which you then set to 01 00 00 00. As an example, here's how to lock out changes to the REG file type.

1. **Run the Registry Editor, for example by choosing Start⇨Run⇨REGEDIT.**

2. **Navigate to *HKCR\regfile* in the key pane and click it.**

3. **Right-click the value pane and choose New⇨Binary Value.**

4. **Name the new value** EditFlags, **press Enter, and key in** 01 00 00 00 **for the value data.**

   Your screen should look like Figure 18-4.

5. **Close REGEDIT.**

   Now, when you choose View⇨Folder Options⇨File Types, you don't even see a listing for Registration Entries. You can't change what you can't see.

You can regain the ability to make file type changes by deleting the EditFlags key that you created.

Sometimes you want to go in the reverse direction, and enable file type editing for types that normally don't permit editing at all, or that Windows 98 has restricted your ability to edit to some degree. To do this, just replace the existing EditFlags value with 00 00 00 00. That value turns on all editing capabilities.

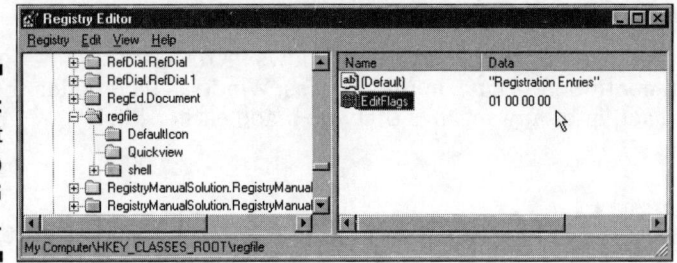

Figure 18-4:
Lock out
changes to
the REG
file type.

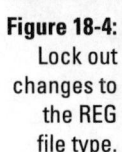

Lots of intermediate EditFlags values can turn specific buttons in the File Types screen on and off, but 99 percent of the time you either want all editing options on or all options off. You can perform those two actions without having to know the nuances of binary addition. That's good, because *we* haven't figured out the nuances of binary addition, nor do we want to.

Restart the Registry Faster

Lots of changes that you make to the Registry don't take effect immediately — Windows 98 activates them the next time the operating system starts. Rebooting, however, can be a time-consuming process, especially on slower computers where it can take upwards of a minute and a half. Here's a great undocumented tip to force Windows 98 to rebuild the Registry (at least, all of it except *HKDD,* the Plug and Play branch) without actually rebooting your computer.

1. **Save any data files in open programs and then close all programs.**

   This step isn't strictly necessary, but we like to walk on the safe side of the river.

2. **Give your PC the three-finger salute (Ctrl+Alt+Del) to display the Close Program dialog box.**

3. **Click Explorer and End Task.**

   The "Explorer" in question is the Windows 98 desktop shell, not the Windows Explorer file manager. The Shut Down Windows dialog box appears because Windows 98 figures that if you want to shut down the desktop, then you want to shut down the computer. Not this time!

4. **Count to ten. (Yes, we're serious.)**

   After a few seconds, you see the Explorer message box. Windows 98 notices that you haven't shut down and wants to know whether it can kill the shell.

5. **Click the End Task button.**

Explorer terminates, but then Windows 98 reloads it right away so you can continue working. In the process, Windows 98 rebuilds the Registry and activates any settings that you made earlier. Slick!

Automatically Log On to the Desktop

Here's a tip to save you time at startup if security isn't a big concern for you. Just be aware that anybody can log on to Windows 98 (and your network, if you're on one) if you make the following change. Also, know that you're storing a password in unencrypted format in the Registry, where anyone who's read this book can find it.

Run REGEDIT and hop on over to *HKLM\Software\Microsoft\Windows\CurrentVersion\Winlogon*. Change the values DefaultUserName and DefaultPassword to match the ones you normally enter manually. If you don't see the entries, add them — they're string values. Also, add the string value AutoAdminLogon and key in **1** as the value data. The Winlogon key looks like Figure 18-5. That's it! Remove these keys later if you want to disable the automatic logon.

If you have the TweakUI control panel installed (see Chapter 11), you can achieve automatic logon more easily by filling in the information on the Network screen. However, we know some network administrators who purposely don't install TweakUI for this very reason. Those same administrators will probably confiscate this book if they see you reading it, just because we include tips like this one. We suggest that you tape over this book's cover with a cover from a more innocent book, such as "How to Be a Model Employee."

You may still see the Windows logon dialog box at restart, but if you do, just wait a couple of seconds, and the dialog box disappears as Windows 98 logs you on automatically.

Remove Programs from the Install/Uninstall List

Sometimes, a user who isn't familiar with the Control Panel's Add/Remove Programs wizard tries to delete a program by simply running Explorer and deleting the program subdirectory. If that occurs, the program may still show up on the Install/Uninstall tab, even though the deinstall program doesn't work because the files aren't there anymore. If the deinstall program fails, the program doesn't remove itself from the list of installed programs.

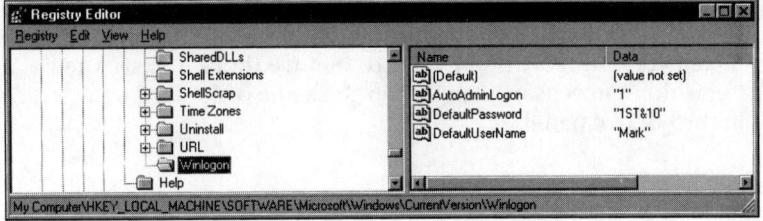

Figure 18-5:
Speedy
logons for
the non-
security
conscious.

Another possibility is that you update a program by installing a new version over an old one, but the deinstallation program for the old version is still hanging around on the Install/Uninstall tab. You can often avoid this problem by deinstalling the old version before installing the new version, but most programs don't require this step and you probably don't know which ones do. (They don't always tell you in their documentation.)

Fortunately, you can use the Registry Editor to remove those annoying holdovers from the Install/Uninstall list. Slide on over to *HKLM\Software\Microsoft\Windows\CurrentVersion\Uninstall*. A screen like Figure 18-6 appears. Scroll around the list until you find the key corresponding to the program entry that you want to delete and delete the key. Voilà — the program no longer appears when you run the Add/Remove Programs wizard from the Control Panel.

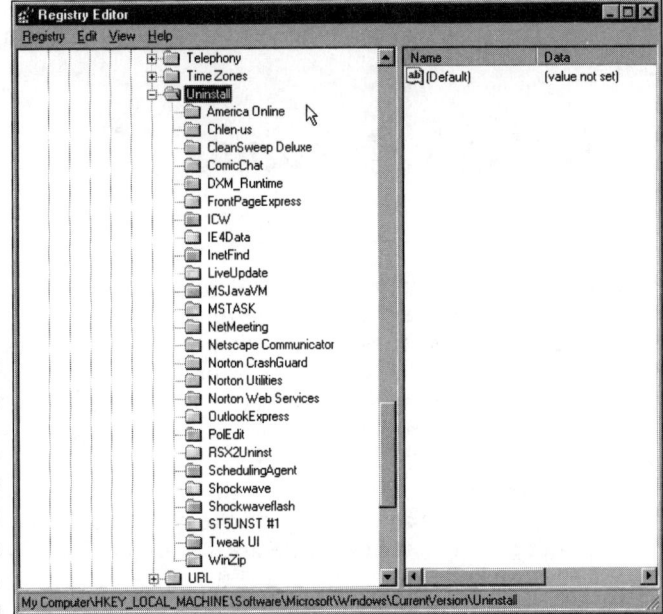

Figure 18-6:
The
Registry
location of
the installed
programs
list.

Be careful when deleting items from the Registry's uninstall list. Some of these items appear on the Windows Setup tab of the Add/Remove control panel; you probably don't want to remove those Registry keys. Also, the items don't necessarily appear in the same order in the Registry as they do in the control panel.

Change the Registered Organization and Owner Names

You decide that you no longer wish to be known as Mark Wilkins and legally change your name to Marcus Wilkinson. Or, your company changes its name from Acme Cognac to Bargain-Basement Spirits. However, Windows 98 maintains your old name and organization name internally and displays them on the System control panel's General tab. This bugs you. It can actually become slightly inconvenient, too: Often, when you install new software, the installation program consults these internal owner and organization names and pops them up by default.

Change these names with the Registry Editor by skipping over to *HKLM\Software\Microsoft\Windows\CurrentVersion*. Here, you can modify the RegisteredOrganization and RegisteredOwner values. (See Figure 18-7.) To change either value as recorded by specific applications, use the Registry Editor's Edit⇨Find command. Just be aware that you may need to explain the change or changes when you call the vendor for technical support.

Change the Default Windows 98 Setup Directory

Often, when you buy a new computer, the default setup directory points to an area on the hard disk where the computer manufacturer has copied the Windows 98 installation files. These files can take up dozens of megabytes, however, and they duplicate the files on the Windows 98 installation CD-ROM. So you delete them, saving all sorts of disk space. However, the next time you do something that makes Windows 98 look for the original files — such as adding new software via the Network control panel — Windows looks for the original files in the original location (such as C:\WINDOWS\ OPTIONS\CABS), doesn't find them, and asks you to locate them. Doing so isn't usually a big deal (the normal answer is X:\WIN98,

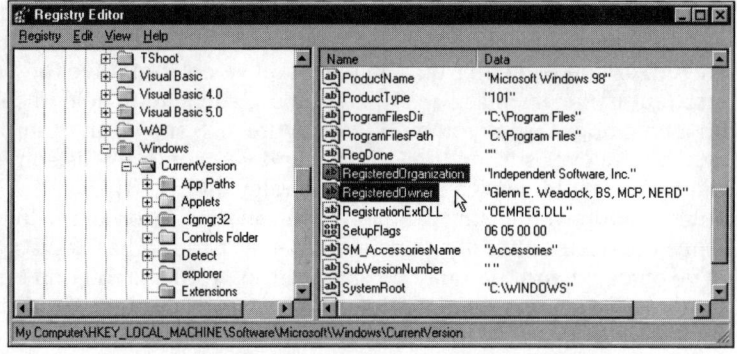

Figure 18-7:
The
Registry
location
of the
Windows
registered
organization
and owner
names.

where *X* is the drive letter that your computer assigns to the CD-ROM drive), but if you make a lot of changes to your system, retyping the correct location becomes a tad tedious. Fortunately, with the Registry Editor, you can tell Windows 98 to stop looking in the old location and automatically look in a new one.

Run REGEDIT and shuffle over to *HKLM\SOFTWARE\Microsoft\Windows\CurrentVersion\Setup*. Modify the SourcePath string value to point to your CD-ROM drive (or a network drive or wherever the Windows 98 setup files reside).

Of course, if you have tons of hard disk space (around 200MB) and you want to copy the files from the CD to a directory on your hard disk, you can do that, too, and use the same procedure to reset the location in the Registry. Putting the setup files on a hard disk makes a lot of sense for notebook computer users who don't have built-in CD-ROM drives.

Annotate the Registry

Documenting the changes that you make to your computer ranks right up there with flossing your teeth on the list of things you know you should do more often. (We know that we don't always record the changes that we make to our computers as often as we should.) You have two options open to you:

✔ Become more disciplined about documenting Registry changes in a text or word-processing file somewhere on the computer.

✔ Find an easier method.

We, being essentially lazy, prefer the second option. Happily, it exists. Just make your own special Registry values in the keys that you've added or changed, or one level up from the ones you've deleted. Give the values a consistent name, such as *TechTip,* and put a single data field in each value with a note about what you modified. Figure 18-8 shows an example. In this way, if you're ever surfing the Registry and you come across something that strikes you as odd, you can look for the relevant TechTip. Or, if you're troubleshooting a Registry problem, you can search for all the TechTips (hence the desirability of a consistent name) to see what Registry entries you've changed and that may be causing the problem. You don't have to hunt down a separate document — and because adding notes this way is so easy, you're more likely to do it.

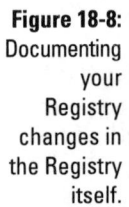

Figure 18-8:
Documenting
your
Registry
changes in
the Registry
itself.

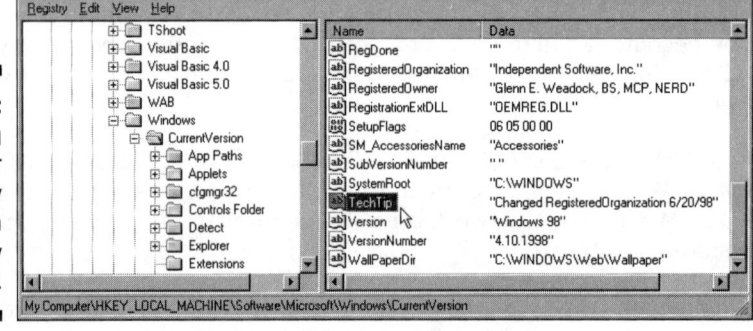

Create Application-Specific Sound Schemes

Here's a useless but fun tip. You probably already know that you can use the Windows 98 Sounds control panel to assign sounds to system events, such as the Windows 98 startup (Glenn likes the opening bars of Beethoven's Ninth) or a critical error message (Mark likes the sound of breaking glass).

Some application programs, such as CompuServe Information Manager, make Registry entries that enable you to assign sounds to those programs, too. However, most don't. If you want to assign sounds on a program-by-program basis to programs that don't already offer the capability in the Sounds control panel, you can do so with the Registry Editor and a little patience. Here's the procedure:

1. **Find out the name of the program.**

   The easy way to do this is to take a look at the property sheet for the shortcut on the desktop, or on the Start menu, that points to the program. What you want is the name of the main EXE file that the shortcut runs. You can also just use Windows Explorer to open the program's primary subdirectory and look for the EXE files. Sometimes, however, you see more than one EXE file, so you have to double-click each one until you get the right one. For example, the main EXE file for Ray Dream Designer is RDD.EXE, so the program name for our purpose here is RDD.

2. **Run the Registry Editor and navigate to** *HKCU\AppEvents\ Schemes\Apps.*

3. **Add a new key underneath the Apps key and give it the same name as the program to which you want to add sounds.**

   In our example, we name the new key RDD.

4. **Add keys underneath the key you added in Step 3 and name them according to the events that you'd like to associate with sounds.**

   The possibilities include Close, Open, RestoreUp, RestoreDown, Minimize, Maximize, MenuCommand, MenuPopup, SystemAsterisk, SystemExclamation, and SystemQuestion. Figure 18-9 shows the additions for our RDD example.

Figure 18-9: Adding sounds to applications that don't normally let you add sounds to them.

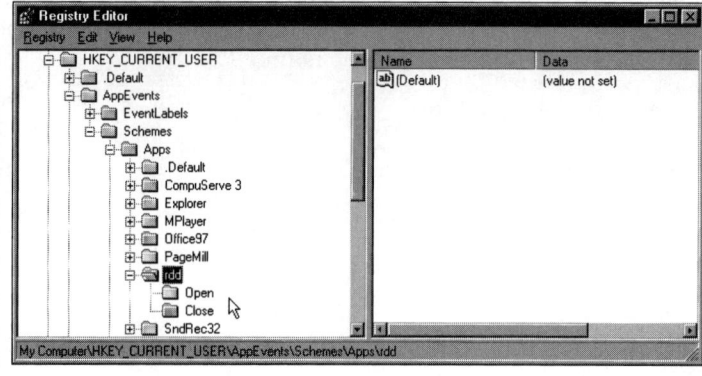

5. **Close REGEDIT and open the Sounds control panel.**

   Technically, we can continue using REGEDIT to finish the job, but we try to live by our rule to use control panels rather than REGEDIT wherever possible. Besides, the Sounds control panel enables you to browse for sound files and test them ahead of time.

6. **Scroll down the list until you see your newly added program, and assign sounds to events in the usual way.**

That's it! Your changes take effect immediately, so you can test them straightaway. You can find a bunch of fun sounds on the Windows 98 CD-ROM in the directory \CDSAMPLE\SOUNDS. The Office95 and Office97 CD-ROMs have additional fun sounds under \SOUNDS and \VALUPACK. You may want to copy the sounds you like to the C:\WINDOWS\MEDIA directory, which is a semi-standard place to store system sounds. One last hint: Your PC may suspend other processing duties while playing a sound clip, so keep the clips on the brief side.

Find a Lost CD Key

Okay, this is a part of Tens, and we're up to tip number 11. Hey, we're computer guys; we started counting at zero instead of one. Anyway, this one may come in *very* handy one day. Remember that little colored sticker on the back of your Windows 98 CD-ROM case? The one that says **Don't Lose This Number!** in bold lettering? The one you've lost?

No problem, as long as you never have to reinstall Windows 98. But if you ever do, you won't get past square uno if you don't have that CD key. Fortunately, even if your child wrote over the code with a laundry marker, you can probably find the CD key in the Registry. Look for the value *ProductKey* in *HKLM\Software\Microsoft\Windows\CurrentVersion.* (This is not the same as the *ProductID* number, which won't do you any good at all.) We suggest you write the CD key onto the top (labeled) part of your Windows 98 CD-ROM with the same laundry marker that your mischievous kid was playing with. Assuming you can find it.

Chapter 19
Ten Non-Windows Registries

During our research for this book, we ran across several Internet sites featuring Registries that have nothing to do with Windows 98. Sandwiched between the five million Web pages for engaged techno-yuppies who want you to know just which items at Crate and Barrel you should get them for a wedding present are a variety of Registry sites — some interesting, some useful, some hokey, some weird, and some that just tickled us. So, we end this book with the following reminders that there is life beyond Windows 98. Until we write *Windows 2001: A Registry Odyssey For Dummies,* we bid you *HKEY_Goodbye.*

International Star Registry

www.corporatestar.com

The International Star Registry is run by a company that "names" an actual star after someone you deem is deserving of such an astronomical honor. The lucky recipient gets a package with a star map and telescope coordinates so he or she can train the four-inch reflector to the precise point in the heavens where the newly titled "Bob Jones" distant sun twinkles in the firmament — a fitting reward for meeting his quarterly sales quota. (If "Bob" has any sense, he probably prefers a raise, a designated parking spot, some 12-year-old Scotch, or an expenses-paid date with Suzy in public relations, but a little piece of heaven is less stressful on the corporate coffers.)

Registry Hotels and Resorts

`www.registryhotels.com/registry/default.html`

The Registry Hotels and Resorts company has a lovely Web site that describes their various lodgings. We wonder if some Microsoft designers were kibbitzing in the lounge of one of these resorts, trying to figure out what to call the new Windows configuration database, when one of them happened to glance down at a cocktail napkin. "Wait a minute! Let's call it the Hotel!" "No, that's silly, let's call it the Resort!" "No . . ."

Bloomingdale's Bridal Registry

`www.bloomingdales.com`

Okay, we had to include a bridal registry, and Bloomies' site is the best-looking. Click the links to "Services" and "Bridal." We should also mention the Target bridal registry (`www.targetstores.com/TargetWWW/ClubWedd/fastend/index.htm`) because of its clever name. The surreal bridal registry award goes to `www.blackanddecker.com/bridal` in case you'd rather have power tools than place settings.

Early 911S Registry

`early911sregistry.org`

Porsche (and if you want to move in high society, you *must* pronounce the final "e") built the 911S from 1967 to 1973, and this site is brought to you by "enthusiasts who pay homage to this remarkable machine." (It is probably no coincidence that the mailing address is Newport Beach, California, where Porsches are outnumbered only by Rolls Royces, and driving a Honda is a class "A" misdemeanor.) This site is just one of several registries on the Web where car people like to track every little detail of a particular run of automobiles. We were unable to find a Geo Metro Registry, but you can bet that one exists.

Speedtrap Registry

www.speedtrap.com/speedtrap

Whether you've decided to buy an early Porsche after visiting the Early 911S Registry Web site, or just want to take that finely restored Mustang muscle car out for some exercise, you may want to know how to avoid those strategically located speed traps designated to fill county coffers by ticketing you for going 2 mph over the limit. This Web site presents speed trap locations all over the world.

National Pet Registry

www.nationalpetregistry.com

This worthy site combines commercialism and humanitarianism, which is better than pure commercialism alone, and it also happens to be nicely designed. It reports that over 12 million pets per year are lost in the U.S. and Canada. Twenty-five bucks registers your pet and gets you a brass ID tag with a toll-free number on it — just in case your pet wanders into the next county or is picked up by an unscrupulous petnapper and abandoned when the crook discovers he or she isn't house-trained.

Internet Social Registry

www2.aidg.com/isr

This service purports to match up people with common interests, and not just for the purpose of finding compatible dates (although the *Cupids Network* logo appears at the bottom of the site's home page). You fill out a questionnaire, and you get five matches per month for free (more and you have to pay something). If you're the type who isn't afraid to enter ads in the newspaper personals column, this site may be fun. If you find yourself out on a date with an ax murderer, don't blame us.

Official Registry of Persons Named Luke

`users.uniserve.com/~lukec/luke.htm`

Aside from the hilarious fact of this Web site's existence, we liked the Webmaster's sense of humor and overall world view. ("I am interested in meeting other people named Luke. . . . If you are a girl, then I'm interested in meeting you no matter what your name is.")

Registry of Educational Software Publishers

`www.microweb.com/pepsite/Software/publishers.html`

We thought this Web site, designed by Anne Bubnic and Warren Buckleitner for parents, educators, and publishers, was pretty cool. It includes a revue of children's software and links to hundreds of educational software vendors. Now that you've got your Windows 98 PC working properly with a little Registry knowledge, use it to teach your kids something other than how to rip an attacker's spinal cord out of his body.

American Beefalo World Registry

`www.virtualcities.com/trade/f/bf/8/tfbf8613.htm`

Proclaiming that "The breed of tomorrow is here today," the ABWR (as it's called by those in the know) actually maintains three registries: the Herdbook Registry, the Beefalo Ancestry Registry, and the Meat Registry. We had to include this site because the color picture (which is reminiscent of the famous Apple Macintosh "cowdog") is such a hoot for those of us city slickers who had never seen a beefalo before. (Yes, it's a real animal, and approved for consumer consumption by the U.S. Department of Agriculture. And you know what? Beefalo beef ain't bad at all.)

Part VII
Appendixes

The 5th Wave

In this part . . .

Shaking his guide's hand at the conclusion of their safari, George said, "You've been a marvelous companion and saved my life half a dozen times with your quick wit and brave heart. But before we part, I must know: Why do you wear a turban on your head at all times? I've never seen it off." The faithful guide smiled slyly and unrolled the turban, to reveal a cascade of flowing hair as delicate as an orchid bouquet and as black as the African night. "Good Lord - you're a woman!" George blurted out in amazement, realizing that his adventure was, after all, far from over.

Your Registry adventure isn't over, either. In the final part of this book, the Appendixes, you find definitions, sources for more information, and descriptions of the software on the included CD. Where you go with all this information is up to you, but there will surely be many surprises along the way.

Appendix A

Glossary

● ●

*T*his glossary defines most, if not all, of the technical terms in this book. We list definitions under acronyms rather than the expanded terms. Cross-referenced terms are in ***bold italics.*** You may see some cross-referenced terms that appear to be one term but are really two adjacent single terms, such as ***Registry branch,*** where ***Registry*** and ***branch*** each have their own entry.

ACPI (Advanced Configuration and Power Interface). A new standard for power management that gives Windows 98 more control over power-saving hardware features.

Active Desktop. A set of Windows 98 user interface features formerly called "Windows Desktop Update" and shipped with Internet Explorer 4. The desktop becomes a layered Web page that can include ***Java*** and ***ActiveX*** programs as well as text-plus-graphics ***HTML*** files. Active Desktop includes miscellaneous other enhancements, such as Taskbar customizability and data file previews.

ActiveX. An evolution of the Object Linking and Embedding (OLE) technology in Windows, ActiveX enables programmers to create programs that run "inside" other programs and that share program modules across disks and even across networks. ActiveX also includes the file type associations in the Registry's ***HKCR*** branch.

AGP (Accelerated Graphics Port). An Intel-developed display interface standard that promises high-speed 3D graphics. Supported by Windows 98, AGP typically requires a Pentium II computer to work and can't be retrofitted to older PCs.

Alias. A top-level ***Registry*** branch that points to a commonly used key somewhere else for more convenient access (that is, shorter key location paths) by programmers and users. For example, *HKey_Classes_Root* is an alias that points to *HKey_Local_Machine\Software\Classes*.

Application program. Often called simply **application.** Software that enables you to actually do stuff with your computer. Word processors and spreadsheets are examples of application programs. See also ***data file.***

Association. See *file association.*

Attribute. See *file attribute.*

AUTOEXEC.BAT. A PC startup file, essential on *DOS* PCs, that stands for AUTOmatically EXECuting BATch file, and whose functions — loading startup programs and *device drivers* — the Windows 98 *Registry* mostly replaces. Some older devices may still require AUTOEXEC.BAT.

Back up. To create a copy of your computer files, either for long-term storage or to provide a way to recover from a failure, like one that may result from an incorrect or damaging *Registry* entry.

Backup. The tapes or disks created when a computer is backed up, also called a *backup set.*

Basic Input/Output System. See *BIOS.*

Batch file. A file with the suffix .BAT that contains a sequence of DOS commands that run one after the other. Batch files are handy for making Registry backups.

Batch Setup. A Microsoft program (BATCH.EXE) that enables you to create an *INF* file to control what happens when you install Windows 98 from a *network server,* including how you make various *Registry* settings.

Binary file. A *data file* that you can't read or modify without a particular software *application program,* in contrast to a *text file.* If you open a binary file in a text editor like Notepad, all you see is gibberish. The *Registry* files are binary files.

Binary value. A *Registry* value whose *data field* consists of a sequence of two-digit *hexadecimal* numbers separated by single spaces. Modifying binary values is rarely necessary or advisable.

BIOS (Basic Input/Output System). Firmware (that is, software-on-a-chip) that loads before the *operating system* and handles low-level data transfer among disk drives, printers, keyboards, monitors and memory. The BIOS is an integral part of the *Plug and Play* specification.

Bit. Short for *binary digit,* the smallest unit of computer data, consisting of a one or a zero. Eight bits are usually needed to make a *byte,* which represents one alphanumeric character, though sometimes a byte may contain seven or nine bits.

Boot. 1) The process a computer goes through when it starts and loads the *operating system* into memory. 2) What you use to kick a *crashed* computer.

Branch. Any one of the six primary *keys* of the *Registry*. See also *HKCC, HKCR, HKCU, HKDD, HKLM,* and *HKU.*

Broadcast receiver card. A circuit board that plugs into your PC and can receive broadcast TV signals; required to use the Windows 98 TV-in-a-window capability.

Browser. The software tool that you run to view or "browse" Web servers and pages. Browsers present Web documents in a *GUI.* Browsers provide some navigation controls and may offer security and performance features. The Internet Explorer 4 browser comes with Windows 98.

Bus. A data highway inside a computer. Electronic traffic flows on buses between all the computer's component parts.

Byte. A chunk of computerized data corresponding to one alphanumeric character; composed usually of eight *bits.*

CAB file. Short for "CABinet." Files with the .CAB extension use a special Microsoft format for storing multiple files in a single, compressed file. The Windows 98 *Registry Checker* uses the CAB file format.

CardBus. A *PCMCIA* card with a 32-bit interface for faster data transfer.

CD-ROM (Compact Disc-Read Only Memory). An optical disc, similar in appearance to an audio CD, that stores about 650 *megabytes* of digital computer data. You can read, but not modify or erase, data on CD-ROMs, unlike CD-R (CD-Recordable) discs.

CFGBACK (Configuration Backup). One of the *Registry backup* tools that came with Windows 95 but not with Windows 98.

Channel. A link to an information service that lets *Internet Explorer* users subscribe to a Web site. Subscriptions let you download content automatically, browse it without being connected to the *Internet,* and get notified when the site changes. Windows 98 channels aren't compatible with Netscape channels.

Client/server network. A *network* (such as IntranetWare or *Windows NT Server*) in which a *server* computer running a network operating system handles resource-sharing responsibilities, such as file- and printer-sharing, for *client* computers (user workstations).

CLSID (Class ID). A unique number, such as {25336920-03f9-11cf-8fd0-00aa00686f13}, that identifies an object in Windows 98. An object can include data file types (such as a PowerPoint slide show) and program modules (such as the code that displays and processes dialog box radio buttons). Class IDs take the form of a 16-byte number enclosed in curly braces, each *byte* expressed by a two-digit *hexadecimal* number, arranged in a 4-2-2-2-6 grouping.

Command prompt. The famous MS-DOS prompt, usually C:>,which you can use to start a Windows 98 machine. You can reach the command prompt by choosing Start⇨MS-DOS Prompt or by rebooting to a command prompt-only mode (by holding down Ctrl).

CONFIG.POL. A *policy file* residing on a *network server* that becomes a mandatory part of every network user's *Registry.*

CONFIG.SYS. A PC startup file, essential on *DOS* PCs. The *Registry* mostly replaces the functions — loading memory managers and device drivers — of CONFIG.SYS.

Context menu. The menu of choices that appears when you right-click something in Windows 98. The *Registry* contains information about what should appear on the context menu depending on what the user clicks, and about what each menu option should do.

Control Panel. A special Windows 98 program that enables you to change various system settings. Start⇨Settings⇨Control Panel displays all the available control panels in a single window. Control panels typically modify the *Registry* and are safer to use and more user-friendly than the *Registry Editor.*

Crash. 1) The event that causes a computer system or *application program* to stop working suddenly, immediately, and irreversibly. 2) What you can do to your Jeep if you forget to steer while photographing Jackalopes.

Data field. The part of a *Registry value* that contains an actual setting, as opposed to the *name field,* which contains the setting's name or identifier.

Data file. A computer file that contains information you create. A word processing document and a *REG file* are data files. See also *application program.*

Database. A collection of related information stored in a computer, such as a sales history or customer list, that you can search, edit, add to, delete from, and print. The *Registry* is a database.

DDE (Dynamic Data Exchange). A technique that Windows programs may use to exchange data and/or commands between two running programs.

Decimal notation. A way of expressing a number in base 10, with digits ranging from 0 to 9.

Defragment. To disassemble, move, and reassemble files on a disk so that all the files' data are on physically adjacent sectors, rather than scattered around your hard disk. Defragmentation improves performance of disk files, including *Registry* files.

Deinstall. To remove a program from a computer. (Yeah, we think *remove* is a better term, too, but *deinstall* is what the industry uses.) Synonymous with *uninstall.*

Device driver. Software that enables a computer to communicate with a particular input or output device, such as a mouse. Device drivers interpret computer data and provide the commands or signals needed by the device.

Device ID. A unique *Registry* identifier for a hardware device.

Dial-Up Networking (DUN). Microsoft's remote access software for *Windows 98, Windows 95, Windows NT Workstation,* and *Windows NT Server,* which enables remote PCs to connect to a *network* over phone lines.

Digital signature. A code attached to a computer file that guarantees the file's authenticity. Windows 98 uses digital signatures for *device drivers.*

Directory. An organizational structure that permits the grouping of individual files in a single area, much like a manila folder permits the grouping of individual paper documents. Windows 98 typically includes most of its files under the C:\WINDOWS directory.

DirectX. A Microsoft technology that lets programs work quickly and efficiently with multimedia devices; used by many game programs. Windows 98 supports DirectX 5.

Diskless workstation. A computer without diskette drives or *hard drives.* Such a computer reduces security risks both outbound (confidential data) and inbound (virus-infected files).

DLL (Dynamic Link Library). A file containing program code (and sometimes icons). Much of the Windows 98 *operating system* consists of DLLs, which Windows 98 and *application programs* can load into memory to use as needed.

Domain name. A user-friendly name for an *Internet* site, such as www.dummies.com.

DOS (Disk Operating System). The most popular *operating system* for IBM-compatible PCs until *Windows 95* became popular (earlier versions of Windows still use DOS extensively, while Windows 95 and 98 contain relatively little DOS code).

Download. To copy a file from another computer to your computer, over a network connection, modem link, or direct cable connection. See also *upload.*

Driver. See *device driver*.

DVD (Digital Versatile Disc or **Digital Video Disc,** depending on whom you talk to**).** An optical disc storage medium that can hold computer data, audio data, and video data on the same disc.

DWORD (double-word) value. A *Registry* value whose *data field* consists of a sequence of four two-digit *hexadecimal* numbers, not separated by spaces, introduced by "0x" and usually followed by the equivalent *decimal* number in parentheses. For example, 0x0000027d (637).

Edit flag. (Sometimes referred to as *editflag*.) A *Registry* value that specifies restrictions. For example, an edit flag may cause certain buttons to appear grayed-out and inactive in a dialog box. Edit flags are *binary values* having four *bytes*.

Enumerate. What Windows 98 does when it *boots* and assigns unique *device IDs* to *Plug and Play* hardware components. The *Registry* has several *keys* named "Enum" which is short for this term.

ERD (Emergency Recovery Disk). The *Registry restore* program that comes with Windows 95, but not Windows 98, as the counterpart to *ERU*.

ERU (Emergency Recovery Utility). One of the better *Registry backup* utilities that comes with Windows 95, but not Windows 98.

Explorer. 1) The Windows 98 file management utility. 2) The Windows 98 desktop (or *shell*). The terminology is confusing, we know — this is the sort of thing that happens when hundreds of programmers work on the same project!

Export. To create a full or partial *Registry backup* by using the *Registry Editor's* Registry⇨Export Registry File command. The result is a *REG file*. See also *import*.

FAQ (Frequently Asked Questions). A document featuring a list of common questions and their answers.

File association. In *ActiveX* (what we used to call *OLE*), a connection between a file suffix (such as .TXT) and an *application program* (such as Notepad), so that double-clicking the file runs the associated application program. The *Registry* maintains all file association information in Windows 98.

File attribute. Information stored with a computer file that determines under what conditions the file can be viewed, modified, copied, or deleted. For example, the attribute of "Read-only" means that you cannot modify or delete the file. Windows 98 file attributes also include System, Hidden, and Archive.

File server. A *network server* that shares files among users, as opposed to a print server (which shares printers), and an application server (which shares programs).

File type. A category of all files having a particular *file association*.

FILEMON. A free utility that tracks file accesses and changes as they occur.

Folder. See *directory*.

Full backup. A *backup* of all the files on your computer's *hard drive* or drives.

GIF (Graphics Interchange Format). A compact computer graphics file format that appears frequently on the *Internet*.

Gigabyte (abbreviated GB). A measure of data storage capacity equaling 1,024 *megabytes*, or roughly a billion *bytes*, a byte being equivalent to one letter or number.

Group. A collection of *network* users who have the same rights and restrictions to shared resources. With the *Registry*, you can assign access restrictions by group, using the *System Policy Editor*.

GUI (Graphical User Interface, pronounced "gooey"). A software interface, such as that of Microsoft Windows, that presents a graphical "face" to the user — as opposed to a text-mode interface like the *DOS* command line or a simple text mainframe terminal.

Happy. What you'll be if you *back up* the *Registry* religiously before making any changes to it.

Hard drive (also called "hard disk"). A computer storage device in which a stack of magnetic disks spin at high speed in a sealed enclosure. Hard drives retain information even when no power is supplied to them. Hard drives can be written to, erased, and rewritten a large number of times. Capacity is measured in *megabytes* or *gigabytes*.

Hardware configuration. A feature of Windows 98 that lets you define multiple hardware setups; for example, a docked *notebook* and an undocked notebook. The Registry stores hardware configurations in *HKey_Local_Machine\Config*, and it stores the current hardware configuration in *HKey_Current_Config*.

Hardware tree. The tree-structured representation of your PC's hardware setup, used by *Plug and Play* and viewable from the System *control panel's* Device Manager tab. The *Registry* stores hardware tree information in the *HKDD branch*.

Headache. What you get from working with the Registry too long.

Hexadecimal (hex) notation. A way of expressing a number in base 16, with digits ranging from 0 to F, where A corresponds to decimal number 10, B to 11, and so on. The *Registry* uses hexadecimal notation to express *binary values* and *DWORD values.* Hex numbers appear in the Registry grouped by two-digit *bytes,* for example, C8 06 00 00.

HKCC (HKey_Current_Config). The *Registry branch* containing information about the current *hardware configuration.* HKCC is an *alias* to one of the keys below *HKLM\Config.*

HKCR (HKey_Classes_Root). The *Registry branch* containing information about *file associations* and drag-and-drop behavior. HKCR is an *alias* to *HKLM\SOFTWARE\Classes.*

HKCU (HKey_Current_User). The *Registry branch* containing information about the current user logged on to Windows 98, including individual preferences and settings. *HKCU* is an *alias* to a subkey of *HKU.*

HKDD (HKey_Dyn_Data). The *Registry branch* containing information about the *hardware tree* and *Plug and Play.* This branch resides completely in *RAM,* and Windows 98 rebuilds it at each restart.

HKLM (HKey_Local_Machine). The *Registry branch* containing information about the computer that doesn't vary from user to user or reflect individual user preferences. This branch includes the contents of *HKCC* and *HKCR.*

HKU (HKey_Users). The *Registry branch* containing information about all persons who can use the computer. This branch includes the contents of *HKCU.*

Home page. The starting location of an *Internet* site; for example, Microsoft's home page is www.microsoft.com.

HTML (HyperText Markup Language). A specification for *text files* that describes the layout and content of a World Wide Web page, including links to other pages. You can use HTML documents to customize the display of the Windows 98 desktop and of individual *directories.*

Import. To *merge* a full or partial *Registry backup* in the form of a *REG file* into the current *Registry* by using the *Registry Editor's* Registry⇨Import Registry File command. See also *export.*

INF file. A *text file* having a specific, predefined format that can be installed onto the computer. *Application program* software vendors and hardware vendors typically provide an INF file to modify the *Registry* as necessary and to copy required files into the proper *directories* on your *hard drive.*

INI file. A configuration *text file,* such as *WIN.INI* or *SYSTEM.INI,* that contains *operating system* or *application program* settings. Windows 3.*x* and Windows 3.*x* programs make heavy use of INI files, but Windows 98 depends on them to a much lesser extent, having moved most (but not all) of their responsibilities to the *Registry.*

Internet. The world's largest computer *network,* hosting all manner of private, public, and commercial uses. Physically, the Internet is a collection of millions of computers, each with its own unique network address to identify itself to other computers. Each computer on the Internet speaks the same basic communications language — *TCP/IP.*

Internet Explorer. The Web *browser* that comes with Windows 98, and enables users to view *Internet* and *intranet* documents.

Interrupt. A signal to the computer's main processor from a device that needs attention, usually to service an input or output demand (such as a keystroke or a file save request).

Intranet. A network based on *Internet* technologies such as *TCP/IP* and *HTML,* but run within a private organization, for example to publish company information that employees can view with a Web *browser.*

IRQ (Interrupt ReQuest). See *interrupt.*

Java. A programming language supported by Internet Explorer and Active Desktop. Java (developed by Sun Microsystems) is derived from the C++ programming language and is known for its portability (that is, it works on lots of different types of computers).

JPEG (Joint Photographic Experts Group). A computer graphic file format in wide use on the *Internet* for its ability to compress photographic images and still make them appear lifelike.

Key. A location for storing data in the *Registry.* Keys look like folders in the *Registry Editor* window's left-hand pane.

Key pane. The left-hand pane of the *Registry Editor* window, where *keys* appear.

Kilobit. 1,024 bits, where a *bit* is a zero or one.

Kilobyte (abbreviated K). 1,024 bytes, where a *byte* is a character equivalent to one letter or number.

Logical structure. The way the *Registry* looks when viewed by the *Registry Editor,* that is, as a single *database* with a tree-like organization consisting of *branches, keys, subkeys,* and *values.* See also *physical structure.*

Megabit (abbreviated Mb). About one million *bits,* a bit being a one or a zero. See also *bit.*

Megabyte (abbreviated MB). A measure of data storage capacity equaling 1,024 *kilobytes,* or roughly a million *bytes,* a byte being equivalent to one letter or number.

Merge. To combine the contents of a *REG file* with the current *Registry* contents. Merging can overwrite existing Registry entries and create new ones, but cannot delete existing entries.

MIME (Multipurpose Internet Mail Extensions). A set of extensions to the original *Internet* e-mail standards that enable you to send and receive data types other than text.

MRU (Most Recently Used) list. A list of documents, programs, or *Internet* locations, maintained in the *Registry* or on disk for your convenience.

MS-DOS Mode. A special mode of Windows 98 in which Windows effectively removes itself from memory and makes the PC look like a *DOS* machine; when you type EXIT at the *command prompt,* Windows 98 reloads into memory. An option on the Start⇨Shut Down dialog box. Also called *Single MS-DOS Mode.*

Name field. The part of a *Registry value* that contains a setting's identifying name, as opposed to the *data field,* which contains the actual setting.

Network. Two or more computer systems connected to enable communication or resource sharing.

Notebook. A portable computer, the size of a large and unusually heavy paper notebook.

Object. Anything that a user or programmer can manipulate in Windows 98. For example, objects include data files (such as a PowerPoint slide show) that users can click, programs (such as PowerPoint) that users can run, and program modules (such as the code that displays and processes dialog box radio buttons) that software developers can call upon in their programs. See also *ActiveX, CLSID,* and *OLE.*

OLE (Object Linking and Embedding, pronounced "oh-LAY"). A Windows technology that enables you to create compound documents with data coming from more than one program. OLE also allows in-place editing, or the ability to edit cut-and-pasted data without having to leave the *application program* that you pasted the data into. A big part of OLE is *file associations.* See also *ActiveX.*

Operating system. The basic software that enables a computer to interact with users, manage files and devices, and communicate over a *network*. *Windows 98,* UNIX, MacOS, and OS/2 Warp are all operating systems. Operating systems designed for network *servers,* such as NetWare and *Windows NT Server,* are called NOSs (Network Operating Systems).

Orphan. A *Registry* entry that points to a file that doesn't exist on disk anymore. Many *application programs* leave orphans in the Registry after you uninstall them.

OSR2 (OEM Service Release 2). A version of Windows 95 sold only on new PCs. An OSR2 machine displays the version number 4.00.950B or 4.00.950C on the System *Control Panel.* OSR2 contains a slightly different version of the *Registry Editor* than that which accompanied the original Windows 95 release.

Packet. A unit of information on a *network,* containing data and address information. You can modify the *Registry* to improve the performance of *TCP/IP* by changing the maximum packet size.

PC Card. See *PCMCIA.*

PCMCIA (Personal Computer Memory Card Industry Association). The group that standardized what are now called "PC Cards," which plug into *notebook* computers. The *Plug and Play* specification views PC Card as a separate *bus.* See also *CardBus.*

Physical structure. The way the *Registry* looks as viewed by a file management program such as Windows *Explorer,* that is, as a collection of files, consisting of *SYSTEM.DAT, USER.DAT,* and an optional *policy* file. See also *logical structure.*

Plug and Play (often abbreviated PnP). A set of standards developed by Microsoft, Intel, Compaq, and Phoenix (among others) to ease the configuration of hardware devices by automatically detecting and setting device characteristics. A full implementation of PnP requires compatibility at all levels, from the *BIOS* to the *operating system* to the *device driver.* The *Registry* contains Plug and Play information in the *HKLM* and *HKDD branches.*

POL file. See *policy file.*

POLEDIT. See *System Policy Editor.*

Policy file. An optional *Registry* component with the suffix .POL that applies restrictions and customizations to the information in *USER.DAT* and *SYSTEM.DAT.* For example, you can create a policy that prevents users from running the Registry Editor. You create policy files with the *System Policy Editor.*

Property sheet. A window (usually, a dialog box) that displays information about a file or *control panel.* The window usually permits you to change some or all the information it contains in predefined ways, for example via text fields, radio buttons, and check boxes. You typically get to a property sheet by right-clicking an icon and choosing Properties from the *context menu.*

Protected mode. The usual mode of running Windows 98, in which programs and data use *RAM* above the 1MB boundary and enjoy some protection from each other to help ensure reliability. If Windows 98 can't start in protected mode, for example due to a severely damaged *Registry,* you may have to troubleshoot the problem in *real mode.*

RAM (Random Access Memory). Chip-based memory in a computer, which is both faster and more expensive than disk-based memory *(hard drives).* A computer's RAM contains the currently active programs and data files, and its contents start empty every time the computer restarts.

RB0xx.CAB. The backup files created by Windows 98's *Registry Checker* utility. The *xx* sequence number starts at 00 and has a maximum value of 99.

Real mode. A mode of running Windows 98 in which only the DOS components of the *operating system* are activated, usually accomplished by restarting the computer and booting to a *command prompt.* The *Registry Editor* and *Registry Checker* can run in a limited way in real mode for troubleshooting purposes. See also *protected mode.*

Refresh. To update a display. For example, refreshing the *Registry Editor* window with the F5 key updates it to show any changes that Windows 98 or a Windows 98 program has made since the window first opened.

REG file. A *text file* having a specific predefined format that can be *imported,* or *merged,* into the *Registry. Exporting* a file from the *Registry Editor* creates a REG file, and *application program* software vendors sometimes provide a REG file to modify the Registry as necessary to accommodate their particular needs.

REGCLEAN. A software utility, provided by Microsoft at its Web site, that automatically removes certain inaccurate or obsolete *values* and *keys* from the *Registry.*

REGEDIT. See *Registry Editor.*

Registry. The central store of information that Windows 98 and Windows 98 programs use to track all the software and hardware on the machine, including details about how that software and hardware are configured.

Registry Checker. The Windows 98 utility that creates automatic *Registry backups,* fixes some forms of Registry damage, and compresses Registry files. SCANREGW.EXE is the Windows version, SCANREG.EXE is the *DOS* version.

Registry Editor. The tool (REGEDIT.EXE) that comes with Windows 98 and enables you to view, edit, print, *export,* and *import* the *Registry.* The Symantec Norton Registry Editor is a better version of REGEDIT.

REGMON. A free utility that tracks *Registry* accesses and changes as they occur.

Remote Registry Service. Software that comes with Windows 98 that enables a user on one computer to view and edit the *Registry* on another computer on the same network. This service only works in a *client/server network.*

Rescue disk. A diskette (or, more likely, a set of diskettes) created by a utility such as Norton Utilities that enables you to start your computer from the diskette drive and *restore* critical system files. Most rescue disk programs can't handle *Registry* files that don't fit on a single diskette; the Norton Utilities 3.0 Rescue Disk program can, if you use the ZIP disk option, but you have to add the Registry files to the list manually.

Restore. To copy files to your computer's *hard disk* that you previously *backed up.* You can restore the *Registry* using a variety of techniques and utilities, including *CFGBACK* and *ERD.*

Root directory. The top-level *directory* on a disk, under which all other directories reside.

Sad. What you will be if you don't *back up* the *Registry* religiously before making changes to it.

Safari. A Swahili word with Arabic origins. "Safara" in Arabic means "to unveil, discover, or to enter upon a journey."

Safe mode. A Windows 98 startup option that you activate by holding down Ctrl at startup and choosing either "Safe Mode" (which loads the *GUI*) or "Safe Mode, Command Prompt Only" (which takes you to a *command prompt*). You may need to restart in safe mode to perform certain *Registry* troubleshooting and *restore* operations.

SCANREG. See *Registry Checker.*

SCANREG.INI. The *text file* that lets you customize the *Registry Checker.*

Server. 1) A computer that provides *network* services, such as file and printer sharing. 2) The combination of server hardware and programs. 3) The person who ignores you in a French restaurant.

Shell. The part of an *operating system* that presents computer resources to you and enables you to work with the machine, as opposed to the part of the operating system that talks to devices or software. In Windows 98, the usual shell is *Explorer.*

Shortcut. A file (with the suffix .LNK) that points to a local or *network* file, *directory,* program, *control panel, disk drive,* or printer in order to increase user convenience by making resources more easily accessible (for example, via a desktop icon).

Startup disk. A diskette you create with the *Control Panel's* Add/Remove Programs option to enable you to start your computer from the diskette drive. Windows 98 does not copy the *Registry* to the startup disk, so making your own startup disk is useful for starting a computer that won't boot at all, but is not useful for restoring a damaged Registry.

String value. A *Registry* value whose *data field* consists of a sequence of alphanumeric characters. String values almost always appear in the *Registry Editor* surrounded by double quotes.

Subkey. A *Registry key* that resides underneath another key.

Swap file. An area of *hard drive* space that your *operating system* (for example, *Windows*) uses as a low-speed supplement to your main memory, *RAM.* Windows 98 swap file settings reside in *SYSTEM.INI.*

Switch. A command modifier. In the command SCANREG /RESTORE, which restores an earlier version of the *Registry,* the switch is the "/RESTORE" part. Also called *qualifier.*

System Information. The Windows 98 program that acts as both a configuration reporting tool and as a gateway to several other Windows 98 utilities, such as the *Registry Checker,* which appear on the Tools menu.

System Policy Editor. The tool (POLEDIT.EXE) provided with Windows 98 that enables you to apply restrictions and customizations to the current *Registry,* or create a *policy file* that applies those changes every time your PC starts.

SYSTEM.1ST. The very first *SYSTEM.DAT* file created when you install Windows 98. This file resides in the *root directory.*

SYSTEM.DA0. A *backup* of *SYSTEM.DAT* that Windows 95 creates at each successful startup. Windows 98 no longer uses DA0 files, but instead uses files named *RB0xx.CAB.*

SYSTEM.DAT. A primary component of the *Registry's physical structure,* SYSTEM.DAT is a file that contains all machine-specific settings for both hardware and software. It resides in the C:\WINDOWS *directory.*

SYSTEM.INI. A Windows configuration *text file* that exists in Windows 98 primarily for compatibility with Windows 3.*x* programs, but which still contains some important information that the *Registry* does not contain.

TCP/IP (Transmission Control Protocol/Internet Protocol). A set of *network* standards for file transfer, network management, and messaging — the public *Internet* uses TCP/IP.

Template. A file with the extension .ADM that tells the *System Policy Editor* how to modify particular *Registry* entries.

Text file. A *data file* consisting of nothing but standard alphanumeric characters that you can read with a wide variety of *application programs.*

TweakUI. A *control panel* that comes on the Windows 98 CD-ROM. TweakUI enables you to change the Windows 98 desktop in ways that normally require the *Registry Editor.*

Uninstall. See *deinstall.*

Upload. To copy a file from your computer to another computer, over a network connection, modem link, or direct cable connection. See also *download.*

URL (Uniform Resource Locator). The address that points you to a specific *Internet* or *intranet* location (a Web page or a file to *download*).

USB (Universal Serial Bus). A *bus* for connecting computer devices, such as mice and keyboards, in a daisy-chain of cables that plugs into a single computer port. Windows 98 supports USB devices, which you can connect and disconnect without rebooting the PC.

User profiles. A Windows 98 feature that permits multiple users to share a single PC and still see their own individual preferences and settings. User profiles also permit *network* users to log on to any networked PC and still see their preferences and settings, by maintaining multiple copies of *USER.DAT.* The *Registry* maintains user profile information in *HKey_Users* and the current user's profile information in *HKey_Current_User.*

USER.DA0. A *backup* of *USER.DAT* that Windows 95 creates at each successful startup. Windows 98 no longer uses DA0 files, but instead uses files named *RB0xx.CAB.*

USER.DAT. A primary component of the *Registry's physical structure,* USER.DAT is a file that contains all user-specific settings. If *user profiles* are not enabled, only one USER.DAT file exists, and it resides in the C:\WINDOWS *directory.* If user profiles are enabled, multiple and different USER.DAT files reside in the C:\WINDOWS\PROFILES directory.

USER.MAN. A mandatory *user profile* that resides on a *network server* and overrides any information in the network user's *USER.DAT* file.

Value. A chunk of information contained in a *Registry key.* Values have a *name field* and a *data field,* and have three types: *binary value, DWORD value,* and *string value.* A single Registry key can contain multiple values.

Value data. See *data field.*

Value name. See *name field.*

Value pane. The right-hand pane of the *Registry Editor* window, where *values* appear.

Verb. Some action you can perform on a Windows 98 object. For example, if you open a program, *open* is the verb and *program* is the object. *Edit* and *print* are other examples of verbs.

VRML (Virtual Reality Modeling Language). A language specification, supported by Windows 98, for presenting 3-D information using *HTML.*

Windows. A family of *operating systems* from Microsoft that put a graphical face onto your computer, enabling you to run multiple programs at once and easing the copying and pasting of data among programs. Versions in current use include Windows 3.1, Windows for Workgroups 3.11, *Windows 95, Windows 98, Windows NT Workstation,* and *Windows NT Server.*

Windows 95. A very popular PC *operating system* from Microsoft that succeeds Windows 3.*x* and makes much heavier use of the *Registry.*

Windows 98. An evolutionary upgrade to the Windows 95 *operating system* that includes lots of bug fixes, new utilities, and an enhanced user interface that dovetails with the included Internet Explorer 4.

Windows NT Server. A *network operating system* from Microsoft featuring relatively easy installation and management and strong security. Windows NT Server 4.0 uses the same *GUI* as Windows 95, and Windows NT Server 5.0 uses the same GUI as Windows 98.

Windows NT Workstation. A workstation *operating system* from Microsoft for PCs requiring high performance, high security, or high reliability; more expensive than *Windows 98,* both in purchase price and in hardware requirements.

Windows Update. A Windows 98 Start menu command that connects to the *Internet* and downloads an *ActiveX* program that scans your PC for outdated system *DLLs* and *device drivers* and then lets you choose which ones you want to install. You can disable Windows Update with the *System Policy Editor*.

WIN.INI. A Windows configuration *text file* that exists in Windows 98 primarily for compatibility with Windows 3.*x* programs. Most of the information that Windows 3.*x* placed in WIN.INI now exists in the Windows 98 *Registry*.

WWW (World Wide Web). The multimedia face of the *Internet*. Web pages can include color graphics and even sound and video. They can also include convenient and automatic links to other Web pages. Much *Registry*-related software is available on the Web.

Appendix B
References and Resources

• •

*T*his book mentions several companies that offer Registry-related products, and in case you want to explore their products further, this appendix provides contact information. We also direct you to a few good books and magazines that can add to your knowledge of the Registry.

Companies Mentioned in This Book

This section provides Internet addresses (Web where available, e-mail otherwise), phone numbers (both the free-in-the-USA "800" and "888" variety, where available, and toll numbers for the convenience of international readers), and physical addresses for the companies we mention in this book.

Cheyenne (Division of Computer Associates International, Inc.)

www.cheyenne.com

800-243-9462; 516-465-5000

3 Expressway Plaza, Roslyn Heights, NY 11577

CyberMedia, Inc.

www.cybermedia.com

800-721-7824; 310-581-4700

3000 Ocean Park Boulevard, Suite 2001, Santa Monica, CA 90405

Exabyte Corp.

www.exabyte.com

800-EXABYTE; 303-442-4333

1685 Thirty-eighth Street, Boulder, CO 80301

Helix Software Company

www.helixsoftware.com

800-451-0551; 718-392-3100

47-09 Thirtieth Street, Long Island City, NY 11101

imagine LAN, Inc.

www.imagine-lan.com

800-372-9776; 603-889-5889

76 Northeastern Boulevard, Suite 34B, Nashua, NH 03062

Innovative Software Ltd.

www.ghostsoft.com

800-817-5119; 414-964-2200

5225 N. Ironwood Road, Milwaukee, WI 53217

Intrasoft, Inc.

www.keyvision.com

888-539-8474; 919-419-9427

6320 Quadrangle Drive, Suite 370, Chapel Hill, NC 27514

Inso Corp.

www.inso.com

800-733-5799; 617-753-6500

31 St. James Avenue, Boston, MA 02116

Iomega Corp.

www.iomega.com

800-697-8833; 801-778-1000

1821 W. Iomega Way, Roy, UT 84067

ISES Incorporated

ises@ix.netcom.com

800-447-ISES; 908-766-1109

102 Sunrise Drive, Gillette, NJ 07933

McAfee Associates, Inc.

www.mcafee.com

800-332-9966; 408-988-3832

2085 Bowers Avenue, Santa Clara, CA 95051-0963

Microsoft Corp.

www.microsoft.com

800-426-9400; 206-882-8080

One Microsoft Way, Redmond, WA 98052

Mijenix Corp.

www.mijenix.com

800-MIJENIX; 608-277-1981

6666 Odana Road, Suite 122, Madison, WI 53719

Netscape Communications Corp.

home.netscape.com

800-638-7483; 415-254-1900

501 E. Middlefield Road, Mountain View, CA 94043

Novastor Corp.

www.novastor.com

800-668-2786; 805-579-6700

80-B W. Cochran Street, Simi Valley, CA 93065-6219

Novell, Inc.

www.novell.com

800-453-1267; 801-222-6000

1555 N. Technology Way, Orem, UT 84757

PKWare, Inc.

www.pkware.com

414-354-8699

9025 N. Deerwood Drive, Brown Deer, WI 53223-2437

PowerQuest Corporation

www.powerquest.com

800-965-7576; 801-437-8900

1083 N. State Street, Orem, UT 84057

Quarterdeck Corp.

www.quarterdeck.com

800-354-3222; 310-309-3700

13160 Mindanao Way, Marina del Rey, CA 90292-9705

Seagate Software (Information Management Group)

www.seagatesoftware.com

800-877-2340; 800-663-1244 (Canada); 604-681-3435

1095 W. Pender Street, 4th Floor, Vancouver, BC, Canada V6E 2M6

Seagate Technology, Inc.

www.seagate.com

800-SEAGATE; 408-438-6550

920 Disc Drive, Scotts Valley, CA 95066-4544

Steven J. Hoek Software Development

shoek@ix.netcom.com

6173 Sunningdale Drive, Hudsonville, MI 49426

Symantec Corp.

www.symantec.com

800-441-7234; 408-253-9600

10201 Torre Avenue, Cupertino, CA 95014-2132

SyQuest Technology, Inc.

www.syquest.com

800-245-CART; 510-226-4000

47071 Bayside Parkway, Fremont, CA 94538

Wedge Software

www.wedgesoftware.com

P.O. Box 431, Davisburg, MI 48350-1223

Books

These titles are worth a look next time you find yourself lost among the rows of computer books at your local bookstore-slash-coffee house — or wandering cyberspace bookstores such as www.amazon.com. Few Windows 98 books are out as we write this, and the ones that are have lots of inaccuracies because they're based on beta releases (unlike *this* book, which we based on the final shipping version, or "golden code" as it's known in the biz). However, some of the Windows 95 books listed here are being updated to Windows 98 versions, so keep your eye out.

Bulletproofing Windows 95

Glenn E. Weadock

McGraw-Hill

350 pages, $34.95

Inside the Registry for Microsoft Windows 95

Gunther Born

Microsoft Press

346 pages, $24.99

Inside the Windows 95 Registry

Ron Petrusha

O'Reilly & Associates

575 pages, $32.95

Microsoft Windows 98 Resource Kit

Microsoft Press

1,576 pages, $69.99

The Mother of All Windows 95 Books

Woody Leonhard and Barry Simon

Addison-Wesley

922 pages, $39.95

Troubleshooting and Configuring the Windows NT/95 Registry

Clayton Johnson

Sams Publishing

612 pages, $49.99

The Windows 95 Bug Collection

Bruce Brown

Addison-Wesley $14.95

Windows 95 Registry For Dummies

Glenn Weadock and Mark Wilkins

IDG Books Worldwide, Inc.

384 pages, $29.99

Windows 95 For Dummies, **2nd Edition**

Andy Rathbone

IDG Books Worldwide, Inc.

386 pages, $19.99

The Windows 95 Registry: A Survival Guide for Users

John Woram

MIS:Press

350 pages, $24.95

Magazines

Here are a few magazines that cover Windows technology. A quick skim of these publications can keep you up on current trends.

Computerworld

www.computerworld.com

508-879-0700

500 Old Connecticut Path, Framingham, MA 01701

Information Week

techweb.cmp.com/iw

516-562-5051

600 Community Drive, Manhasset, NY 11030

Infoworld

www.infoworld.com

800-457-7866; 847-647-7925

P.O. Box 1172, Skokie, IL 60076

PC Computing

www.pccomputing.com

800-676-4722; 303-665-8930

P.O. Box 58229, Boulder, CO 80322-8229

PC Magazine: The Independent Guide to Personal Computing

www.pcmag.com

212-503-5255

One Park Avenue, New York, NY 10016-5802

PC Week

www.pcweek.com

617-393-3700

10 Presidents' Landing, Medford, MA 02155

Windows Magazine

www.winmag.com

516-733-8300

One Jericho Plaza, Jericho, NY 11753

Windows NT Magazine

www.winntmag.com

800-621-1544; 970-663-4700

P.O. Box 447, Loveland, CO 80539-0447

Appendix C

About the CD

• •

*H*ere's some of what you can find on the *Windows 98 Registry For Dummies* CD-ROM:

- ✔ Norton Utilities 3.0 from Symantec, featuring the Norton Registry Editor, Norton Registry Tracker, and WinDoctor
- ✔ NovaBACKUP 6.0 from NovaStor software, a full-featured backup program
- ✔ Registry Monitor, which tracks Registry activity as it occurs

System Requirements

Make sure that your computer meets the minimum system requirements listed below. If your computer doesn't match up to most of these requirements, you may have problems using the contents of the CD.

- ✔ A PC with a 486 or faster processor (a Pentium processor is recommended).
- ✔ Microsoft Windows 95 or later.
- ✔ At least 16MB of total RAM installed on your computer. For best performance with Windows 98, at least 24MB of RAM is recommended.
- ✔ At least 150MB of hard drive space available to install all the software from this CD. (You need less space if you don't install every program.)
- ✔ A CD-ROM drive — double-speed (2*x*) or faster.

If you need more information on the basics, check out *PCs For Dummies,* 5th Edition, by Dan Gookin or *Windows 95 For Dummies,* 2nd Edition, by Andy Rathbone (both published by IDG Books Worldwide, Inc.).

How to Use the CD

To install the items from the CD to your hard drive, follow these steps.

1. **Insert the CD into your computer's CD-ROM drive.**

2. **Click the Start button and click Run.**

3. **In the dialog box that appears, type** D:\SETUP.EXE.

   Most of you probably have your CD-ROM drive listed as drive D under My Computer in Windows 98. Type in the proper drive letter if your CD-ROM drive uses a different letter.

4. **Click OK.**

   A License Agreement window appears.

5. **Since we're sure you'll want to use the CD, read through the license agreement, nod your head, and then click the Accept button. After you click Accept, you'll never be bothered by the License Agreement window again.**

   From here, the CD interface appears. The CD interface is a little program that shows you what is on the CD and coordinates installing the programs and running the demos. The interface basically enables you to click a button or two to make things happen.

6. **The first screen you see is the Welcome screen. Click anywhere on this screen to enter the interface.**

   Now you're getting to the action. This next screen lists categories for the software on the CD.

7. **To view the items within a category, just click the category's name.**

   A list of programs in the category appears.

8. **For more information about a program, click the program's name.**

   Be sure to read the information that appears. Sometimes a program may require you to do a few tricks on your computer first, and this screen tells you where to go for that information, if necessary.

9. **To install the program, click the appropriate Install button. If you don't want to install the program, click the Go Back button to return to the previous screen.**

   You can always return to the previous screen by clicking the Go Back button. Doing so allows you to browse the different categories and products and decide what you want to install.

   After you click an install button, the CD interface drops to the background while the CD begins installation of the program you chose.

Important Note: Some installations may seem to freeze after the progress bar reaches 100 percent (particularly on machines with less than 32MB of RAM). Please be patient. The installation may continue for 2 minutes or more without informing you that progress is being made.

10. **To install other items, repeat Steps 7, 8, and 9.**

Important note: If you find that installations are unacceptably slow (usually due to running Windows 98 on a PC with limited resources — a sub-200 MHz processor and/or less than 32MB RAM) you may want to use Explorer to navigate to the individual directories on the CD-ROM and install the programs you want one at a time without using the IDG Books Worldwide CD interface. Doing so may speed up your installation time. Look for a program named either INSTALL.EXE or SETUP.EXE in each program directory to install that program.

11. **When you're done installing programs, click the Quit button to close the interface.**

You can eject the CD now. Carefully place it back in the plastic jacket of the book for safekeeping.

What You'll Find

Here's a summary of the programs on this CD and the categories in which you can find them.

Registry Managers and Editors

The CD contains a number of programs that are useful for both managing and editing the Windows 98 Registry. Check out the following menu.

KeyVision

You get a trial version of KeyVision 1.5, a very interesting Registry management tool for networks from Intrasoft Inc. KeyVision's server component runs on a Windows NT Server machine and its client component runs on Windows 98, 95, and NT workstations. You can schedule and deploy Registry changes to any and all network clients, or to clients grouped by department. You can also centrally restrict users from making Registry changes.

Important Note: This software requires Windows NT Server 4.0 or later, 32MB RAM (64MB RAM recommended), and Internet Explorer 4.0, or Netscape Navigator 4.0 or later. Be sure to read the installation instructions, D:\UTILITY\KEYVISN\DOCUMENT\INSTALL.TXT, before installing this software.

MTUSpeed

MTUSpeed 3.08 is freeware from Mike Sutherland that enables you to change the Registry's TCP/IP settings for more efficient Internet access. Normally, Windows 98 sets its maximum transmission unit size to a value that's appropriate for local area networks, but not efficient over a dial-up link. This utility helps you correct the problem by reducing the maximum packet size for your dial-up connections.

Norton Utilities

Norton Utilities 3.0 from Symantec Corp. contains the Norton Registry Editor, Norton Registry Tracker, and WinDoctor. The software on the CD-ROM is a trialware version.

- ✔ Norton Registry Editor is a better version of the Windows 98 REGEDIT program, offering an "undo" feature as well as a read-only mode.

- ✔ Norton Registry Tracker lets you take before-and-after "snapshots" of the Registry and compares them, automatically highlighting additions, deletions, and changes.

- ✔ WinDoctor performs a raft of analytical tests, but its most common function is to help you locate Registry orphans — entries pointing to files that no longer exist on your system.

Important Note: This software has a "time-out" feature so that it expires within thirty (30) days after you load the software onto your system. The time-out feature may install hidden files on your system which, if not deleted, might remain on your computer after the software has been removed. The purpose of the time-out feature is to ensure that the software is not used beyond its intended evaluation period.

To be sure that all files, hidden or otherwise, are removed when you uninstall this program, you can install one of the uninstaller utilities first, and then allow the utility to monitor the installation of Norton Utilities. This guarantees the clean removal of the program if you decide not to keep it.

Registry Search and Replace

Registry Search and Replace 2.10 is a shareware utility from Steven J. Hoek Software Development that enables you to find and replace specific text strings in the Registry. It's a handy tool that you might use, for example, when you manually relocate an application's files to a different directory. Registry Search and Replace can log your search or search-and-replace session to a file. It works with remote Registries as well as the local one.

Regmon

Regmon 3.0 is a freeware utility from Mark Russinovich and Bryce Cogswell. The program monitors Registry activity as it occurs. You get a listing of every Registry access — read, write, or modify — and after a monitoring session you can save the log to a plain text file. Regmon is a useful utility if you want to see exactly what happens when you change a control panel setting, install or uninstall an application, or perform some other Windows 98 task, such as logging on to a network.

TweakDUN

TweakDUN 1.2.82 is a limited demo version of a shareware program from Patterson Software Design that enables you to change the Registry's TCP/IP settings for more efficient Internet access using Dial-Up Networking. Normally, Windows 98 sets its maximum transmission unit size to a value that's appropriate for local area networks, but not efficient over a dial-up link. As a result, your TCP/IP packets get chopped up and reassembled in transmission, reducing your actual data throughput. This utility helps you correct the problem by reducing the maximum packet size for your dial-up connections. It also modifies other, related TCP/IP settings for better performance.

Registry Monitors

For those times when you want to get a look at what's going on with your Registry, we offer a couple of useful utilities from Mark Russinovich and Bryce Cogswell.

Filemon

Filemon 3.0.4 is a freeware utility from Mark Russinovich and Bryce Cogswell that monitors file activity as it occurs. It tracks reads as well as writes, and after a monitoring session you can save a Filemon log to disk as a plain text file. You can also set filters to control which types of events Filemon logs. Filemon is especially useful if you're performing an application install or uninstall and you want to see exactly what happens at the file system level. It doesn't show you Registry activity in terms of specific keys and values, though; that's the province of Regmon (described later in this section).

Regmon

Regmon 3.0 is a freeware utility from Mark Russinovich and Bryce Cogswell. The program monitors Registry activity as it occurs. You get a listing of every Registry access — read, write, or modify — and after a monitoring session you can save the log to a plain text file. Regmon is a useful utility if you want to see exactly what happens when you change a control panel setting, install or uninstall an application, or perform some other Windows 98 task, such as logging on to a network.

Utilities

The remaining programs on the CD are utilities that have some usefulness regarding the Windows 98 Registry.

CleanSweep Deluxe

CleanSweep Deluxe removes unnecessary files and Registry entries from your PC. It looks for Registry orphans (the "Registry Sweep" command), duplicate files on disk, and rarely-used files. Its Registry Genie is a viable alternative to REGEDIT. CleanSweep "knows" about hundreds of application programs and can deinstall them even when they can't deinstall themselves. CleanSweep also includes the ability to move entire applications from one directory to another. This is a trialware version of a commercial utility from Quarterdeck Corporation.

DU Meter

This shareware Download/Upload Meter utility (version 2.0) from Hagel Technologies tells you how much of your communications channel's capability you're using, and whether that channel is a local area network link or a dial-up connection. You can use DU Meter in combination with TweakDUN (see later in this section) to see the effect of changing TCP/IP Registry settings on communications efficiency.

EZDesk

Melissa Nguyen's shareware program EZDesk 1.8 is a Windows desktop manager that, among other things, fixes a Registry problem that leads Windows 98 to rearrange your desktop icons periodically against your will. It can also clear some of your "most recently used" history lists and perform other tricks that usually require Registry manhandling.

First Aid 98

This trial version of Cybermedia Inc.'s commercial utilities package resembles a Swiss Army Knife in that it comes with several different and handy tools in a user-friendly package. First Aid looks for software conflicts and Windows configuration problems, including Registry problems. It also comes with a Registry change-tracking tool. Hardware diagnostics and tune-up tools add to the mix.

GHOST

GHOST is a disk and/or partition copying program from Ghost Software. It is designed to minimize installation times for operating systems by "cloning" a drive and to create complete backups of disks. Using GHOST is a good solution if you want to clone an operating system over a network in which the clients are composed of the same hardware components.

Important note: This software has a "time-out" feature so that it expires thirty (30) days after you load the software on your system. Moreover, the expiration that the splash screen shows when you install the software is unreliable, often reading **February 1, 1998.** Please ignore whatever time-out date is given and try using the software anyway. The date should be correct after the first time you use the software (unless you have previously installed a trial of the program, in which case you still can't use it a second time).

NovaBACKUP

NovaBACKUP is a trial version of a full-featured commercial backup utility from NovaStor Corp. that supports full and partial backups, including the Registry. This versatile program features virus protection, automatic backup scheduling, multiplatform and multilanguage support, automatic log files, and more. NovaStor's Web site is http://www.novastor.com.

If you back up to a tape drive, you need to install NovaBACK 6.0 for QIC, SCSI, or IDE, depending on which kind of tape drive you use. (If you are using an IDE tape drive, be sure to read the file D:\UTILITY\ NOVABACK\ IDEWARNI.TXT before you attempt to install this software). If you back up to another hard drive or to a removable medium like ZIP or JAZ disks, you need to install NovaDISK 6.0.

Important Note: This software has a "time-out" feature so that it expires within thirty (30) days after you load the software on your system. The time-out feature may install hidden files on your system which, if not deleted, might remain on your computer after the software has been removed. The purpose of the time-out feature is to ensure that the software is not used beyond its intended evaluation period.

To be sure that all files, hidden or otherwise, are removed when you uninstall this program, you can install one of the uninstaller utilities first, and then allow the utility to monitor the installation of NovaBACKUP. This guarantees the clean removal of the program if you decide not to keep it.

Oil Change

Oil Change is a trial version of a commercial software update utility from Cybermedia Inc. Oil Change connects you to a Web or FTP site from which it can download software updates to your system. It includes "undo" capability and automatic update notification. If you use any of the other software on this CD, you may want to use Oil Change to keep it updated, although some vendors (such as Symantec) maintain their own update sites.

PowerDesk Utilities 98

The trial version of PowerDesk Utilities 98 version 3.02, from Mijenix Corp., introduces you to a program that started enhancing the Windows Explorer back in Windows 95 days and continues the tradition with Windows 98. PowerDesk's file management abilities still beat out the Windows 98 Explorer tool; use them (for example) to keep track of all the REG files you'll create with the help of this book.

Uninstaller

This trialware version of Cybermedia's commercial software uninstaller is one of the more popular entries for this utility category. Many applications leave behind Registry junk when you remove them with the vendor-supplied uninstall routines. Uninstaller is good at clearing out all traces of applications you no longer want, including leftover Registry entries.

WinZip 95

WinZip 6.3 is a shareware file compression and decompression utility from Nico Mak Computing, Inc. that's handy for moving files over modem links. It's also very useful for saving disk space by archiving little-used files, and you can put it to use making compressed Registry backups, too. Some of the files on this CD are compressed using the ZIP format, and you can use WinZip to decompress them. WinZip offers a step-by-step wizard mode for those who want to fiddle with the program as little as possible, or a "classic" mode for users who want access to all the program's features. The program also supports long filenames, and the creation of self-extracting EXE archives (which you could use, for example, to distribute a bunch of REG files containing Registry hacks you want to share with others).

If You've Got Problems (Of the CD Kind)

We tried our best to compile programs that work on most computers with the minimum system requirements. Alas, your computer may differ, and some programs may not work properly for some reason.

If you get messages like `Not enough memory` or `Setup cannot continue`, you can try the following fixes:

- ✔ **Turn off any anti virus software that you have on your computer.** Installers sometimes mimic virus activity and may make your computer incorrectly believe that it is being infected by a virus.

- ✔ **Close all running programs.** The more programs you're running, including those that run automatically at boot time, the less memory is available to other programs. Installers also typically update files and programs; if you keep other programs running, installation may not work properly. Many of the programs on this CD run in the background and start up as soon as you start your computer. Make sure to turn off things like Norton Utilities and DUMeter and to have only one uninstaller program monitoring the new installations.

✔ **Close the CD interface and run demos or installations directly from Windows Explorer.** The interface itself can tie up system memory or even conflict with certain kinds of interactive demos. Use Windows Explorer to browse the files on the CD and launch installers or demos.

✔ **Have your local computer store add more RAM to your computer.** This is, admittedly, a drastic and somewhat expensive step. However, adding more memory can really help the speed of your computer and enable more programs to run at the same time.

✔ **Download a newer version of the software from the vendor's Web site.** Could be there's a compatibility problem with your hardware or software that a newer version fixes.

If you still have trouble with installing the items from the CD, please call the IDG Books Worldwide Customer Service Center phone number: 800-762-2974 (outside the U.S.: 317-596-5430).

Index

Expert Registry knowledge is as
close as your keyboard with:

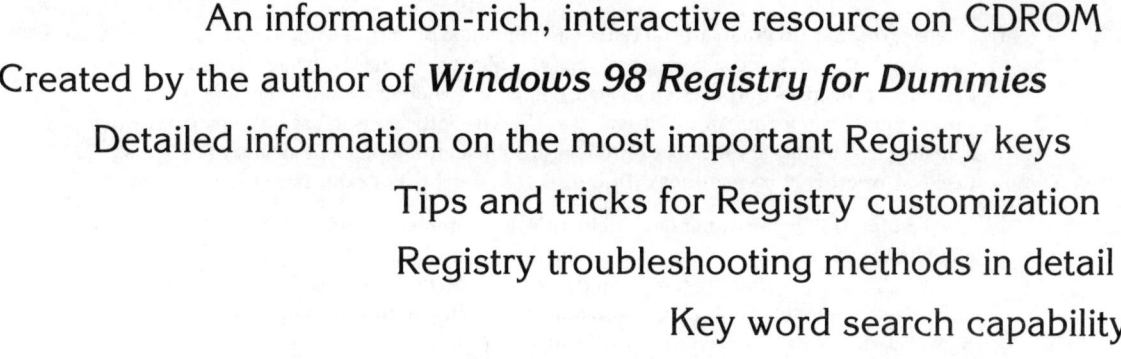

Windows® 98 Registry Reference

NEW

An information-rich, interactive resource on CDROM

Created by the author of *Windows 98 Registry for Dummies*

Detailed information on the most important Registry keys

Tips and tricks for Registry customization

Registry troubleshooting methods in detail

Key word search capability

Requires 486/66 or better PC with CDROM drive

Coupon price: $49.95 (US)   Regular price: $69.95

IDG Books Worldwide, Inc., End-User License Agreement

READ THIS. You should carefully read these terms and conditions before opening the software packet(s) included with this book ("Book"). This is a license agreement ("Agreement") between you and IDG Books Worldwide, Inc. ("IDGB"). By opening the accompanying software packet(s), you acknowledge that you have read and accept the following terms and conditions. If you do not agree and do not want to be bound by such terms and conditions, promptly return the Book and the unopened software packet(s) to the place you obtained them for a full refund.

1. **License Grant.** IDGB grants to you (either an individual or entity) a nonexclusive license to use one copy of the enclosed software program(s) (collectively, the "Software") solely for your own personal or business purposes on a single computer (whether a standard computer or a workstation component of a multiuser network). The Software is in use on a computer when it is loaded into temporary memory (RAM) or installed into permanent memory (hard disk, CD-ROM, or other storage device). IDGB reserves all rights not expressly granted herein.

2. **Ownership.** IDGB is the owner of all right, title, and interest, including copyright, in and to the compilation of the Software recorded on the disk(s) or CD-ROM ("Software Media"). Copyright to the individual programs recorded on the Software Media is owned by the author or other authorized copyright owner of each program. Ownership of the Software and all proprietary rights relating thereto remain with IDGB and its licensers.

3. **Restrictions on Use and Transfer.**

   (a) You may only (i) make one copy of the Software for backup or archival purposes, or (ii) transfer the Software to a single hard disk, provided that you keep the original for backup or archival purposes. You may not (i) rent or lease the Software, (ii) copy or reproduce the Software through a LAN or other network system or through any computer subscriber system or bulletin-board system, or (iii) modify, adapt, or create derivative works based on the Software.

   (b) You may not reverse engineer, decompile, or disassemble the Software. You may transfer the Software and user documentation on a permanent basis, provided that the transferee agrees to accept the terms and conditions of this Agreement and you retain no copies. If the Software is an update or has been updated, any transfer must include the most recent update and all prior versions.

4. **Restrictions on Use of Individual Programs.** You must follow the individual requirements and restrictions detailed for each individual program in Appendix C of this Book. These limitations are also contained in the individual license agreements recorded on the Software Media. These limitations may include a requirement that after using the program for a specified period of time, the user must pay a registration fee or discontinue use. By opening the Software packet(s), you will be agreeing to abide by the licenses and restrictions for these individual programs that are detailed in Appendix C and on the Software Media. None of the material on this Software Media or listed in this Book may ever be redistributed, in original or modified form, for commercial purposes.

5. **Limited Warranty.**

   (a) IDGB warrants that the Software and Software Media are free from defects in materials and workmanship under normal use for a period of sixty (60) days from the date of purchase of this Book. If IDGB receives notification within the warranty period of defects in materials or workmanship, IDGB will replace the defective Software Media.

   (b) **IDGB AND THE AUTHOR OF THE BOOK DISCLAIM ALL OTHER WARRANTIES, EXPRESS OR IMPLIED, INCLUDING WITHOUT LIMITATION IMPLIED WARRANTIES OF MERCHANTABILITY AND FITNESS FOR A PARTICULAR PURPOSE, WITH RESPECT TO THE SOFTWARE, THE PROGRAMS, THE SOURCE CODE CONTAINED THEREIN, AND/OR THE TECHNIQUES DESCRIBED IN THIS BOOK. IDGB DOES NOT WARRANT THAT THE FUNCTIONS CONTAINED IN THE SOFTWARE WILL MEET YOUR REQUIREMENTS OR THAT THE OPERATION OF THE SOFTWARE WILL BE ERROR FREE.**

   (c) This limited warranty gives you specific legal rights, and you may have other rights that vary from jurisdiction to jurisdiction.

6. **Remedies.**

   (a) IDGB's entire liability and your exclusive remedy for defects in materials and workmanship shall be limited to replacement of the Software Media, which may be returned to IDGB with a copy of your receipt at the following address: Software Media Fulfillment Department, Attn.: *Windows 98 Registry For Dummies,* IDG Books Worldwide, Inc., 7260 Shadeland Station, Ste. 100, Indianapolis, IN 46256, or call 800-762-2974. Please allow three to four weeks for delivery. This Limited Warranty is void if failure of the Software Media has resulted from accident, abuse, or misapplication. Any replacement Software Media will be warranted for the remainder of the original warranty period or thirty (30) days, whichever is longer.

   (b) In no event shall IDGB or the author be liable for any damages whatsoever (including without limitation damages for loss of business profits, business interruption, loss of business information, or any other pecuniary loss) arising from the use of or inability to use the Book or the Software, even if IDGB has been advised of the possibility of such damages.

   (c) Because some jurisdictions do not allow the exclusion or limitation of liability for consequential or incidental damages, the above limitation or exclusion may not apply to you.

7. **U.S. Government Restricted Rights.** Use, duplication, or disclosure of the Software by the U.S. Government is subject to restrictions stated in paragraph (c)(1)(ii) of the Rights in Technical Data and Computer Software clause of DFARS 252.227-7013, and in subparagraphs (a) through (d) of the Commercial Computer–Restricted Rights clause at FAR 52.227-19, and in similar clauses in the NASA FAR supplement, when applicable.

8. **General.** This Agreement constitutes the entire understanding of the parties and revokes and supersedes all prior agreements, oral or written, between them and may not be modified or amended except in a writing signed by both parties hereto that specifically refers to this Agreement. This Agreement shall take precedence over any other documents that may be in conflict herewith. If any one or more provisions contained in this Agreement are held by any court or tribunal to be invalid, illegal, or otherwise unenforceable, each and every other provision shall remain in full force and effect.

Installation Instructions

To install the items from the CD to your hard drive, follow these steps.

1. **Insert the CD into your computer's CD-ROM drive.**

2. **Click the Start button and click Run.**

3. **In the dialog box that appears, type** D:\SETUP.EXE.

   Most of you probably have your CD-ROM drive listed as drive D under My Computer in Windows 98. Type in the proper drive letter if your CD-ROM drive uses a different letter.

4. **Click OK.**

   A License Agreement window appears.

5. **Since we're sure you'll want to use the CD, read through the license agreement, nod your head, and then click the Accept button. After you click Accept, you'll never be bothered by the License Agreement window again.**

   From here, the CD interface appears. The CD interface is a little program that shows you what is on the CD, and coordinates installing the programs and running the demos.

For more information on the CD, check out Appendix C, "About the CD."

IDG BOOKS WORLDWIDE BOOK REGISTRATION